SYNERGIZING MANAGEMENT, TECHNOLOGY AND INNOVATION IN GENERATING SUSTAINABLE AND COMPETITIVE BUSINESS GROWTH

PROCEEDINGS OF THE 11TH INTERNATIONAL CONFERENCE ON SUSTAINABLE COLLABORATION IN BUSINESS, TECHNOLOGY, INFORMATION AND INNOVATION (SCBTII 2020), BANDUNG, INDONESIA. 10 JULY 2020

Synergizing Management, Technology and Innovation in Generating Sustainable and Competitive Business Growth

Edited by

Ratih Hendayani, Indira Rachmawati, Hani Gita Ayuningtias, Cahyaningsih & Dania Syanetta Dennyra
Telkom University, Indonesia

Routledge
Taylor & Francis Group

CRC Press/Balkema is an imprint of the Taylor & Francis Group, an informa business

Typeset by MPS Limited, Chennai, India

Library of Congress Cataloging-in-Publication Data

Applied for

Published by: CRC Press/Balkema
Schipholweg 107C, 2316 XC Leiden, The Netherlands
e-mail: Pub.NL@taylorandfrancis.com
www.routledge.com – www.taylorandfrancis.com

ISBN: 978-0-367-68756-4 (Hbk)
ISBN: 978-1-003-13891-4 (eBook)
ISBN: 978-0-367-68758-8 (Pbk)
DOI: 10.1201/9781003138914

Synergizing Management, Technology and Innovation in Generating Sustainable and Competitive Business Growth – Hendayani et al (eds)
© 2021 Taylor & Francis Group, London, ISBN 978-0-367-68756-4

Table of contents

Synergizing Management, Technology and Innovation in Generating Sustainable and Competitive Business Growth – Hendayani et al (eds)
© 2021 Taylor & Francis Group, London, ISBN 978-0-367-68756-4

Preface

The 11th Conference on Sustainable Collaboration in Business, Information and Innovation (11th SCBTII) is an international virtual conference that brings together academics, professionals, entrepreneurs, researchers, learners, and other related groups from around the world who have special interest in theories, as well as practices in the field of management, science and technology for global competitiveness.

This international conference is held by the School of Economics and Business, Telkom University. This year's event is different from the previous events in that it is held as virtual event due to the Covid19 pandemic. However, the committee has kept the commitment to maintain quality and benefits of this event. We are proud to mention that 86 (eighty six) papers submitted to this conference were coming from various universities and higher educational institutions from Indonesia, Malaysia, India, the United States of America, the United Kingdom and Spain, and 60 (sixty) of them have been reviewed by our respected reviewer team from various universities in Indonesia, Malaysia, and also Thailand. The presenters came from various backgrounds, such as: practitioners, academicians, and also government agents.

This event was taking place in one day with two main sessions of plenary sessions and parallel sessions which were attended by around 250 participants. The first plenary session was entitled: "Synergizing Management, Technology and Innovation in Generating Sustainable and Competitive Business Growth". The plenary session featured some experts as the invited speakers, i.e. Mr. Hartono, VP Enterprise Planning and Strategy of PT. Telkom Indonesia, Dr. Muhammad Haseeb from Taylor's Business School (TBS), Taylors University Lakeside Campus Subang Jaya Selangor Malaysia, Dr. Dadan Rahadian, Vice Rector for Academic Affairs of Telkom University; and Mr. Herry Irawan, M.M, M.T from Telkom University as the moderator of discussion. For the parallel sessions, call-for-paper participants were divided into six sessions with 4 major areas: Entrepreneurship and Economy, Digital Based Management, Finance and Corporate Governance and Accounting. This annual event is supported by Telkom University, Indonesia and also privileged to engage in partnership with Universitas Garut.

On behalf of the committee, I would like to express our gratitude to all distinguished speakers, authors, presenters, participants and sponsors for the successful event of 11th SCBTII 2020.

Bandung, July 10th, 2020
Dr. Irni Yunita

Synergizing Management, Technology and Innovation in Generating Sustainable and Competitive Business Growth – Hendayani et al (eds)
© 2021 Taylor & Francis Group, London, ISBN 978-0-367-68756-4

Acknowledgment

In accordance with the publication of the Proceedings of 11th SCBTII, we would like to take this opportunity to thank Telkom University, PT. Telkom as sponsor and also Universitas Garut as university partnership.

Synergizing Management, Technology and Innovation in Generating Sustainable and Competitive Business Growth – Hendayani et al (eds)
© 2021 Taylor & Francis Group, London, ISBN 978-0-367-68756-4

Scientific committee

Synergizing Management, Technology and Innovation in Generating Sustainable and Competitive Business Growth – Hendayani et al (eds)
© 2021 Taylor & Francis Group, London, ISBN 978-0-367-68756-4

Organizing committee

Steering Committee

Dean of School of Economics and Business Telkom University
Vice Dean I of School of Economics and Business Telkom University
Vice Dean II of School of Economics and Business Telkom University

Chairperson

Dr. Irni Yunita, S.T., M.M.

Secretary

Nike Mandasari, S.Si.
Wulandari Ayuningtyas, S.Ikom., M.M.

Treasurer & Funding

Sari Rahmawati, S.M.B., M.M.
Kharisma Ellyana, S.M.B.

Programme Division

Tri Widarmanti, S.M.B., M.M.
Muhammad Azhari, S.E., M.B.A.
Elvira Azis, S.E., M.T.

Call for Paper Division

Vaya Juliana Dillak, S.E., M.M.
Ardan Gani Asalam, S.E., M.Ak.
Dr. Fajra Oktrina, SE., MM

Paper Publication Division

Ratih Hendayani, ST., MM., Ph.D.
Indira Rachmawati, ST., MSM., Ph.D.
Dr. Cahyaningsih, SE, Ak., M.Si.
Hani Gita Ayuningtias, S.Psi., M.M.
Dewa Putra Khrisna S.E., M.Si.

Sponsorship Division

Tieka Trikartika Gustyana, S.E., M.M.
Ir. Tri Djatmiko., M.M.
Erni Martini, S.Sos., M.M.
Dr. Maria Apsari Sugiat, SE., MM., Ak.
Khairunnisa, SE., M.M.

Publication, Accomodation, and Logistic Division

Andrieta Shintia Dewi, S.Pd., M.M.
Mochammad Yudha Febrianta, S.T., M.M.
Husna Rahmi, S.Sos.
Indra Gunawan, S.Kom.
Asep Sudrajat, S.Kom.

Synergizing Management, Technology and Innovation in Generating Sustainable and Competitive Business Growth – Hendayani et al (eds)
 ISBN 978-0-367-68756-4

Predictive analytics games diamond buyer through portal games

L.M. Pranedya, A. Alamsyah & H. Irawan
Magister Management, Faculty of Economics and Business, Telkom University, Bandung, West Java, Indonesia

ABSTRACT: This study is to analyze Garena Free Fire game users, and what significant variables influence a person to purchase diamonds through a telecom games portal, by using machine learning predictive analytics. Four models build in python with optimized hyper-parameter to get optimum recall value; these are logistic regression, random forest, extra gradient boost and neural network. Results of those models are evaluated by confusion matrix and one model chosen as the selected model to predict potential buyers compared to customers who actually do not buy. Analysis of feature importance will give marketing insight into what variables must be followed up to increase customer awareness of diamond purchases through a games portal. Analytics were based on customer behaviors with 117 unique variables per customer within 390,908 customers. This research method can be used by cellular operators to know their customers so that they can determine the right promotion and marketing strategy based on the customer's behavior.

1 INTRODUCTION

The development of the global mobile game market has shown promising growth. Based on Global Games Market (Newzoo 2019), the growth of the mobile game market is higher than the increase in the global cellular telecommunications market. When playing online games, a player develops their social relationships in the virtual world (Hsiao & Chiou 2012). In a massively multiplayer online role-playing game (MMORPG), from the perspective of social interaction, Yee (2006) found that players play with different goals to fulfill each other's motivational desires.

The mobile games market grows by +10.2% year on year to $68.5 billion with a 45% share of the global games market of 2019. Of that number, $54.9 billion came from smartphone games. Global growth of the telecommunications market reached $1,662 billion USD in 2017, growing by 1.4% when compared to the previous year (IDC Forecast 2017). The high data usage is apparently not enough to meet the demands of the development of cellular business in Indonesia. Cellular operators in Indonesia must continue to innovate by carrying out digital transformation to maintain business dominance going forward. One of the programs is to develop digital service products related to games, Portal Games, a game payments portal. This research examines data based on the existing gaming customer profiles to provide insight to cellular operators to predict customers who will buy diamonds through their digital product, portal games, using predictive analytics by machine learning.

2 RELATED WORK

There is much research for big data, consumer behavior, and targeting marketing. In the case of cellular operators, customer segmentation and behavioral targeting use logistic regression to predict purchase behavior using cellular operator official portals (Umar Fudin 2018). This study is similar with this case, using predictive analytics to identify potential buyers. Another case also describes how consumer behavior should seize the opportunities to use big data for generating insights, theories, and hypotheses, and the social, online, and mobile environments to execute rigorous field tests (Charles F. Hofacker Edward Carl Malthouse Fareena Sultan 2016).

In addition, on marketing part, Mihaela DIACONU (2000) has researched a conceptual framework of the importance that integrated marketing communication of the main communication tools used in social media. Also, recent research has said that managers consider marketing big data analytics to be a series of tools and capabilities used to inform product innovation and marketing strategy-making processes (Debra Zahay, Debika Sihi, Laurent Muzellec, Devon S. Johnson 2019).

3 APPROACH

3.1 *Research step*

In general, in this study the technical steps can be translated as follows, starting from the data preparation to the prediction deployment. Data is combined from a total of 121 attributes (columns) consisting of:

a. User behavior data, consisting of 117 columns related to customer mobile phone activity in using data service in the cellular network. This consists of 39 applications and each application host consists of three data elements, the amount of payload consumed, the number of sessions performed, and the length of time in accessing the application host.
b. Customer ID, which in this case is the customer's MSISDN (mobile subscriber integrated services digital network number).
c. Registration data, which consists of two data: age and gender.
d. Transaction data, a purchase data of digital game products, which is the target of this classification model that will be built.

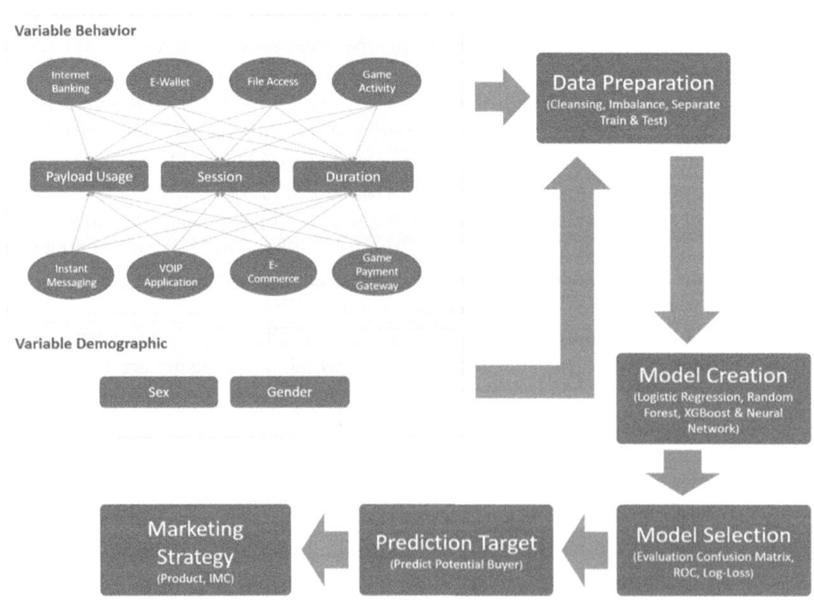

Figure 1. Technical step research.

Table 1. Training and testing dataset.

Status	Training Data Set (70%)	Testing Data Set (30%)	Total	Total (%)
Not-Buy	35.258	15.149	50.407	50%
Buy	35.311	15.096	50.407	50%
Total	70.569	30.245	100.814	100%

Table 2. Confusion matrix testing dataset.

Status	Accuracy	Sensitivity	Specificity	Precision
Logistic Regressions	77.0%	78.5%	75.6%	76.2%
Random Forest	83.1%	88.2%	78.0%	80.0%
XGBoost	82.4%	88.9%	75.9%	78.6%
Neural Network	80.7%	78.8%	82.7%	81.9%

3.2 *Dataset description*

This study uses cellular operator data customers in one island, which amounted to 4,927,980 customers. Then it is pursed to data customers who actively play the Garena Free Fire game, with data from December 2018 to April 2019, with a total of 390,908 customers. Total customers of Free Fire players who bought diamonds amounted to 50,407. Data down sampling has been done to avoid data imbalance, which may impact to the model result and continue to divide the population of the data into two datasets, data train and data test:

3.3 *Modeling*

Modeling has been done with several models, and each model will be evaluated based on the results of each confusion matrix. Optimization hyper-parameters are performed to get the optimum results of recall or sensitivity on the confusion matrix. Best results will be chosen to be discussed in more detail related to user behavior and then used in formulating marketing strategies. The four model are Logistic regression, Random forest, Extra gradient boost (Xgboost), and Neural network. Model evaluation is done based on the value of the confusion matrix given in the test data and on this case XGBoost model selected with 88.9% of the recall or sensitivity.

3.4 *Feature importance*

The most important parameter analysis, commonly referred to as Feature Importance, is carried out to see the main factors of customer profiles that make a customer to buy a diamond. "What is the significant variable that affects customers making purchases of diamonds in a game based on the results of predictive analytics?" The answer to this research question refers to feature importance (Figure 2).

3.5 *Model operationalization*

In accordance with the technical stages of the research, the next stage is the operationalization of the model by predicting a dataset. The dataset used to predict is the same dataset as previously used but filtered by only customers who actually did not buy or in other words the dataset is

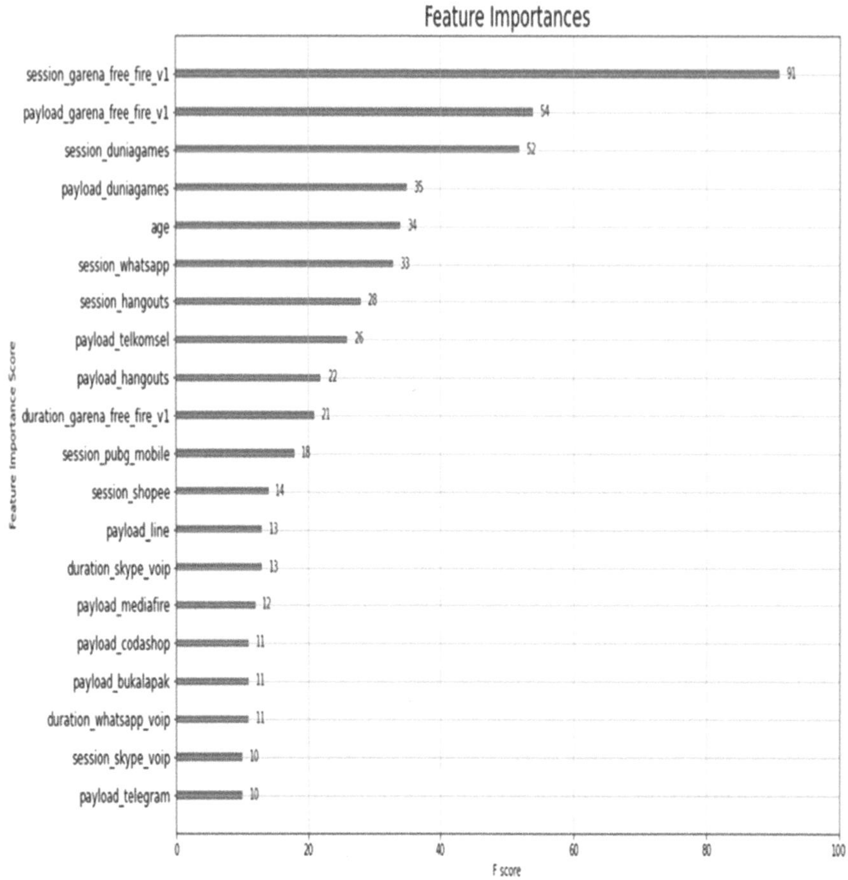

Figure 2. Feature importance.

"active customers playing Free-Fire but not Portal Games buyers." The prediction is done using the selected model XGBoost. The purpose of this prediction is to predict potential buyers from the same dataset and understand what marketing strategies need to be built or improved so that customers can start buying. The number of non-buyers in the dataset is 340,501 customers. Researchers then use XGBoost model to predict what potential customers would buy diamonds; with the result that from 340,501 customers who actively played Free-Fire but did not buy diamonds there were 3,131 potential customers to buy diamonds.

4 STRATEGY MARKETING DIGITAL

To be able to reach the target market effectively, a comprehensive marketer will use creatively all forms of communication (Kotler 2016). Digital marketing strategy is defined as an approach which implements digital technology platforms in support of marketing and business goals (Chaffey 2016). Treatment of existing customers is done through a customer lifecycle management approach, which is the stage of each customer that will be passed in a long-term relationship; they are acquisition (retain), retention (extend), and extend (expansion), as shown in Figure 3.

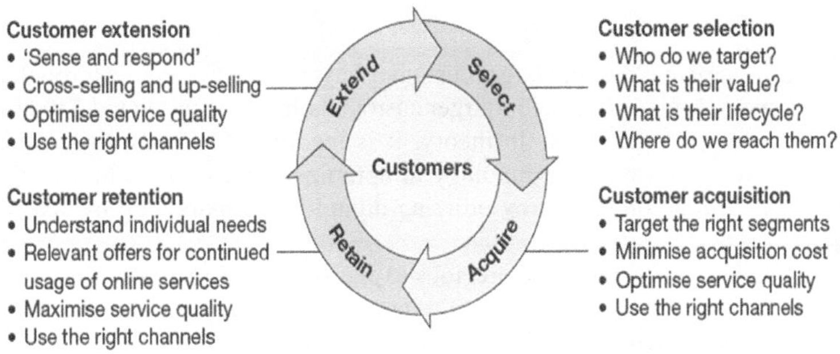

Figure 3. Marketing activity on customer relationship management.

Table 3. Training and testing dataset.

No	Feature	Application	Avg. Value Potential Buyer	Avg. Value Actual Buyer
1	Session	Free Fire	394,12	1183,34
2	Payload	Free Fire	26,53 (MB)	71,35 (MB)
3	Session	Portal Games	0,13	18,43
4	Payload	Portal Games	0,02 (MB)	0,86 (MB)
5	N/A	Age	28,0	28,61

4.1 *Retention customer*

Based on the customer behavior model in the preceding table and if it is adjusted to marketing activities in customer relationship management (CRM) as shown in the CRM image in Figure 3, to retain existing customers the following need to be considered:

a. Understand customer needs. This refers to the importance of features, what things matter for them according their behavior.
b. Relevant offers in order to continue using the service. It is clear that these actual buyers are also actively using other applications. Bundling product offerings between Games + Diamond + Instant Messaging + E-Commerce can be one of the superior product options to target this group or segment.
c. Maximizing service quality. The quality of service in the gaming experience can be improved by providing special products such as game accelerators or turbo games.
d. Use the right channel. Channel to reach buyers can be done by analyzing user behavior by also considering existing digital channels such as social media (Facebook fan page Portal Games, Twitter Portal Games, and Instagram Portal Games).

4.2 *Acquisition customer*

Potential buyers refer to actual non-buyers who have been predicted using the best algorithmic model in this study, resulting in a total of 3,131 customers as potential prospect buyers. Before conducting a marketing analysis, researchers first analyze based on the following importance features.

Significant difference between a potential and actual buyer can be seen in the Portal Games feature where the difference reached 43 times from the payload even 141 times from the session.

Adjusted for marketing activities in CRM, to make the acquisition of these customers the following need to be considered:

a. Target the right segment. Potential target customer buyers have been done through the selection made by the model. It identified 3,131 target customers from the predicted 340,501 customers.
b. Optimization of acquisition costs. In theory, it is mentioned to minimize acquisition costs, but researchers want to use the terminology to optimize acquisition costs. In online business, acquisition costs can be optimized by utilizing digital-based marketing by accurate customer targeting.
c. Optimizing service quality. As in the previous explanation, optimizing service quality needs to be done more thoroughly in each customer touch point, such as how is the performance of the Portal Games website itself?
d. Use the right channel. Channel to reach buyers can be done by analyzing user behavior by also considering existing digital channels such as social media (Facebook fan page Portal Games, Twitter Portal Games, and Instagram Portal Games).

REFERENCES

Alamsyah, A. & Johannes, R. 2015. *Sales Prediction Model Using Classification Decision Tree Approach for Small Medium Enterprise Based on Indonesian E – Commerce Data*. The 6th Seminar & Conference on Business & Technology in ICT Industry (SCBTII 2015).

Chaffey, D. 2016. *Digital Marketing: Strategy, Implementation, and Practice (6th)*. Pearson Education.

Fudin, U. 2016. *Increase Number of Data Package Purchaser in Mytelkomsel Apps by Leveraging Predictive Analytics*.

Indrawati & Alamsyah, A. 2017. *Social Network Data Analytics for Market Segmentation in Indonesian Telecommunications Industry*. 2017 Fifth International Conference on Information and Communication Technology (ICoICT).

Lee, M. 2009. Understanding the behavioral intention to play online games. *Online Information Review*, Vol. 33 Iss 5 pp. 849–872. Retrieved from Emerald Insight.

Mozny, L. 2017. Key Elements of Strategy in the Telecommunication Industry Overview of Discussion. *Business Trends*, vol.7, no.3 p 60–71.

Persaud, A., & Azhar, I. 2011. *Innovative mobile marketing via smartphones Are consumers ready?* Retrieved from Emerald Insight.

Schultz, D. E. 1993. Integrated Marketing Communications. *Marketing News*, January 18, vol. 27, no. 2, p. 17.

Yee, N. 2006. Motivations for Play in Online Games. *Cyber Psychology & Behavior*, 9(6), 772–775. Retrieved from Emerald Insight.

Zahay, D., Sihi, D., Muzellec, L. & Johnson, D. 2019. *The marketing organization's journey to become data-driven*. Retrieved from Emerald Insight.

Synergizing Management, Technology and Innovation in Generating Sustainable and Competitive Business Growth – Hendayani et al (eds)
© 2021 Taylor & Francis Group, London, ISBN 978-0-367-68756-4

Corporate social responsibility disclosure based on Shariah enterprise theory

A.A. Basit, M.D. Ungkari & E. Kusmiati
Faculty of Economics, Garut University, Garut, West Java, Indonesia

ABSTRACT: This study aims to determine the information disclosed by Islamic banks in their corporate social responsibility reports and identify the suitability of information regarding corporate social responsibility (CSR) with the concepts and characteristics of CSR disclosure based on Shariah enterprise theory (SET). This research is qualitative research with a phenomenological approach. The object of this research is PT Bank Muamalat Indonesia. The results showed that the disclosure of CSR conducted by Bank Muamalat included SET disclosure items. The level of disclosure of CSR obtains an average of 81%. This shows that Bank Muamalat Indonesia has revealed its social responsibility as very informative.

1 INTRODUCTION

Until now, there are no standard reporting and measurement standards for corporate social responsibility (CSR) intended for Sharia business institutions (Ridwan & Mayapada 2020). This is why CSR reporting on sharia companies still uses conventional corporate CSR reporting standards (Trianaputri et al. 2017). An example conducted by PT. Bank Muamalat Indonesia, in reporting and measuring CSR, still uses the Global Reporting Initiative (GRI) index G4, where the GRI index is an index used by conventional banking (Alamer et al. 2015).

Research conducted by Ridwan and Mayapada (2020) shows that disclosure of social responsibility undertaken by Islamic commercial banks in Indonesia is still voluntary and several items do not adequately meet the Islamic index, which refers to SET (Sharia enterprise theory). The most appropriate theory to express corporate social responsibility (in this case, Islamic banks) is SET because it has dimensions that include vertical accountability and horizontal accountability (Devirahtiasari et al. 2018; Masud & Kabir 2016).

Disclosure of Sharia corporate social responsibility that does not meet Sharia rules/indices ultimately results in an inconsistency between the disclosure of Islamic/Sharia-based corporate social responsibility with something that becomes the reference, in this case, the Sharia-based social responsibility disclosure index (Farag et al. 2014; Nor & Hashim 2015).

Based on this description, this paper intends to analyze the disclosure of corporate social responsibility based on Shariah enterprise theory.

2 LITERATURE REVIEW

2.1 *Corporate social responsibility report*

CSR reporting is the process of communicating the social and environmental impacts of an organization's economic actions on certain community groups and society as a whole (El-halaby & Hussainey 2015; Jusoh & Ibrahim 2017; Trianaputri et al. 2017). The expansion of an organization's accountability becomes the scope of CSR reporting, not just presenting financial accounts for shareholders. This expansion is based on the assumption that corporate responsibility is not limited to generating profits for shareholders, but is broader than that (Khan & Usman, 2016; Muhamat et al. 2017).

2.2 *Sharia Enterprise Theory (SET)*

In SET, the important concept is God as the creator and sole owner of all the resources in this world, then God as the ultimate trustee. The resources owned by stakeholders in principle are mandated from God, which is inherent in a responsibility to use in the manner and purpose set by the provider of trustees (Meldona et al. 2020; Saleh et al. 2018;. Thus, SET has a broader vision, which appears in the broad scope of the company's stakeholders. According to this theory, stakeholders include direct participants and indirect participants, which are different from direct and indirect participants of enterprise theory (Aryani & Zuchroh 2018; Devirahtiasari et al. 2018).

2.3 *CSR disclosures based on sharia enterprise theory*

There are several dimensions offered by SET in the disclosure of CSR, especially by Islamic banking. These dimensions are vertical accountability and horizontal accountability (Aryani & Zuchroh 2018). This vertical accountability is aimed only at God. Some examples of items aimed at showing vertical accountability to God according to SET are the Sharia Supervisory Board's opinion and the disclosure of fatwas and operational aspects that are obeyed and not obeyed along with their reasons (Hussein 2018; Jusoh & Ibrahim 2018). Horizontal accountability is aimed at three parties, namely direct stakeholders, indirect stakeholders, and nature. The parties referred to as direct stakeholders according to SET are customers and employees, and those who are indirect stakeholders according to SET are the community (Aryani & Zuchroh 2018; Meldona et al. 2020).

3 METHODS

3.1 *Characteristics and research stages*

This research is qualitative research with a case study approach. The object of this research is PT Bank Muamalat Indonesia. Interviewees were part of the Human Resources Bank Muamalat Branch Office in Garut. Secondary data was obtained in the form of data that has been documented on the official website of Bank Muamalat Indonesia, such as annual reports and sustainability reports of Bank Muamalat from 2014 to 2018.

The specific description in this analysis is as follows: (1) Determine SET disclosure items. SET disclosure items were adopted from Aryani and Zuchroh (2018) and Meldona et al. (2020) developed from two dimensions of accountability, namely vertical accountability and horizontal accountability; (2) Scoring. If there are items that are disclosed, then they are given a score of 1 (one) and if there are no items, then a score of 0 (zero) is given. CSR disclosure items based on SET in this study amounted to 46, so the total score that can be obtained if all items are disclosed is 46; (3) Carry out analysis and assessment; and (4) Provide conclusions, where disclosure scores are classified into four categories (Table 1).

4 RESULTS AND DISCUSSION

4.1 *Scoring results for CSR disclosures sub-item based on SET index*

Following are the results of the 2014–2018 Bank Muamalat SET index score based on SET disclosure dimensions or sub-items, which consist of vertical accountability to DSN (National Sharia Board) and DPS (Sharia Supervisory Board) and horizontal accountability to direct stakeholders, namely customers and employees, and indirect stakeholders, namely community and nature/environment.

Table 1. Predicate level of lharia bank CSR disclosure.

Predicate	Index Value
Very informative	81–100
Informative	66–80
Slightly informative	51–65
Not at all informative	0–50

Table 2. Scoring results for CSR risclosures sub-item based on SET index.

No.	Disclosure Sub-Item	2014	2015	2016	2017	2018	Average
1	National Sharia Board & Sharia Supervisory Board	100%	100%	100%	100%	100%	100%
2	Customer	70,59%	88,24%	88,24%	88,24%	82,35%	83,53%
3	Employee	100%	100%	100%	100%	100%	100%
4	Community	100%	88,89%	88,89%	66,67%	66,67%	82,22%
5	Environment	37,5%	50%	62,5%	37,5%	37,5%	45%

Table 2 shows the acquisition of the highest number with a maximum score by vertical accountability for DSN and DPS and horizontal accountability for employees, which is 100%. The lowest score with a score of 45% is obtained on horizontal accountability to nature. The results of the scoring of vertical accountability are in line with the results of the interview, which stated that DPS has an effect mainly on products in Muamalat Bank, which are determined through a discussion process between the board of directors and the Sharia Supervisory Board.

The results of the scoring of the horizontal accountability of employee dimensions are in line with the results of interviews that stated that Bank Muamalat Indonesia already has a very effective system, namely Muamalat Human Power, which is very useful for all employees to check benefits, salary slips, leave permits, and others using employee identification number (NIK) of each employee to facilitate employees in using existing facilities provided by the company. BMI also ensures that each employee has sufficient competence with the demands of his work through the implementation of various training and education to improve knowledge and skills and improve the spiritual quality of each employee. The scoring results for the horizontal dimension of accountability show very low results. It is recognized that previously there was a specific internal policy regarding saving energy and electricity and minimizing the use of paper. However, in 2013, the policy regarding similar matters was no longer disclosed.

4.2 *CSR disclosure level based on SET index*

Based on the results of the SET scoring at Bank Muamalat Indonesia (BMI) in 2014–2018, the scores and percentage values obtained are shown in Table 3.

From the calculation of Bank Muamalat Indonesia's CSR disclosure level based on the SET index in 2014–2018, in terms of the level of CSR disclosure Bank Muamalat Indonesia gets the title for each year as follows in Table 4.

From the predicate table of CSR disclosure based on the SET above, it can be concluded that Bank Muamalat Indonesia during the 2013 period has expressed its social responsibility in an informative manner. Furthermore, an increase in 2014–2018 became very informative.

If the average is calculated from 2014–2018, a disclosure rate percentage of 81% is obtained. This value is between 81% s.d. 100% with the title very informative, so it can be concluded that Bank Muamalat Indonesia has revealed its social responsibility very informative.

Table 3. Level of CSR disclosures based on SET.

No.	Year	Number of items disclosed	Level of disclosure
1	2014	36	78%
2	2015	39	85%
3	2016	40	87%
4	2017	36	78%
5	2018	35	76%
		Average	81%

Table 4. Predicate CSR disclosures based on SET.

No	**Year**	**Level of Disclosure**	**Predicate**
1	2014	78%	Informative
2	2015	85%	Very informative
3	2016	87%	Very informative
4	2017	78%	Informative
5	2018	76%	Informative
	Average	81%	Very informative

5 DISCUSSION

CSR activities not only affect the surrounding community but have a positive impact on the company's reputation (Platonova et al. 2016; Platonova et al. 2018). The results of this study enrich the literature on CSR disclosure with the SET approach. Another similar study was conducted by Aryani and Zuchroh (2018), who examined the implementation of CSR in Islamic banks based on SET conducted on 10 Islamic banks in Indonesia. The results of the study revealed that a large, high-profit Islamic bank as well as implementing good corporate governance will affect how its CSR is implemented by paying more attention to horizontal and vertical relationships that are following SET.

6 CONCLUSION

Based on the results of research conducted on Bank Muamalat Indonesia's Annual Report, it can be concluded that the disclosure of CSR conducted by Bank Muamalat has included SET disclosure items, namely vertical and horizontal accountability consisting of direct stakeholders (customers and employees) and indirect stakeholders (community and nature). In the period 2018–2018, disclosure items that received a maximum score of 100% were vertical accountability and horizontal accountability to employees. Meanwhile, the lowest score is obtained on horizontal accountability to nature, which is an average of 45%. The level of disclosure of CSR for 2014–2018 obtained an average percentage of 81%. This shows that Bank Muamalat Indonesia has revealed its social responsibility as very informative.

REFERENCES

Alamer, A. R. A. *et al.* 2015. 'CSR's Measuring Corporate Social Responsibility Practice in Islamic Banking: A Review', *International Journal of Economics and Financial Issues*, 5, pp. 198–206.

Aryani, D. N. & Zuchroh, I. 2018. 'GCG , ROE and Size on CSR Based on Sharia Enterprises Theory', *Tazkia Islamic Finance and Business Review*, 12(1), pp. 61–80.

Devirahtiasari, Fitrarahmasari, R. & Fadah, I. 2018. 'CSR In Islamic Perspective', *International Journal Of Scientific & Technology Research*, 7(12), pp. 50–53.

El-halaby, S. & Hussainey, K. 2015. 'The Determinants of Social Accountability Disclosure: Evidence from Islamic Banks around the World', *International Journal of Business*, pp. 1–29.

Farag, H., Mallin, C. & Ow-yong, K. 2014 'Corporate Social Responsibility and Financial Performance in Islamic Banks', *Journal of Economic Behavior and Organization*. Elsevier B.V., pp. 1–42. doi: 10.1016/j.jebo.2014.03.001.

Hussein, N. H. A. El. 2018. 'The Sharia Supervisory Board: Does it Influence Corporate Social Responsibility Disclosure by Islamic Banks? A Review', *Journal of Islamic Studies and Culture*, 6(1), pp. 121–132. doi: 10.15640/jisc.v6n1a13.

Jusoh, W. N. H. W. & Ibrahim, U. 2017. 'Corporate Social Responsibility of Islamic Banks: Arising Issues', *Islamic Economic Studies*, 25, pp. 155–172. doi: 10.12816/0036188.

Jusoh, W. N. H. W. & Ibrahim, U. 2018. 'The Significance of Corporate Social Responsibility Disclosure to Islamic Banks in Malaysia: An Islamic View', *Journal of Islamic Finance*, 7(1), pp. 1–8.

Khan, M. M. & Usman, M. 2016. 'Corporate Social Responsibility in Islamic Banks in Pakistan', *Journal of Islamic Business and Management*, 6(2), pp. 179–190.

Masud, M. A. K. & Kabir, M. H. 2016. 'Corporate social responsibility evaluation by different levels of management of Islamic banks and traditional banks: evidence from banking sector of Bangladesh', *Problems and Perspectives in Management*, 14(3), pp. 194–202. doi: 10.21511/ppm.14(3-1).2016.06.

Meldona *et al.* 2020. 'Corporate Social Responsibility Disclosure Through Sharia Enterprise Theory', in *3rd Asia Pacific International Conference of Management and Business Science (AICMBS 2019)*, pp. 171–179.

Muhamat, A. A., Jaafar, M. N. & Basri, M. F. 2017. 'Corporate Social Performance (CSP) Influences on Islamic Bank's Financial Performance', *Journal of International Business, Economics and Entrepreneurship*, 2(1), pp. 11–16.

Nor, S. M. and Hashim, N. A. 2015. 'CSR and Sustainability of Islamic Banking: The Bankers View', *Jurnal Pengurusan*, 45, pp. 1–16. doi: 10.17576/pengurusan-2015-45-07.

Platonova, E. *et al.* 2016. 'The Impact of Corporate Social Responsibility Disclosure on Financial Performance: Evidence from the GCC Islamic Banking Sector', *Journal of Business Ethics*. Springer Netherlands, pp. 1–21. doi: 10.1007/s10551-016-3229-0.

Platonova, E. *et al.* 2018. 'The Impact of Corporate Social Responsibility Disclosure on Financial Performance: Evidence from the GCC Islamic Banking Sector', *Journal of Business Ethics*. Springer Netherlands, 151(2), pp. 451–471. doi: 10.1007/s10551-016-3229-0.

Ridwan, R. & Mayapada, A. G. 2020. 'Does sharia governance influence corporate social responsibility disclosure in Indonesia Islamic banks?', *Journal of Sustainable Finance & Investment*. Taylor & Francis, 0(0), pp. 1–20. doi: 10.1080/20430795.2020.1749819.

Saleh, M. *et al.* 2018. 'Profit And Loss Sharing System and Profitability of Islamic Rural Bank in East Jawa Indonesia', *The International Journal of Social Sciences and Humanities Invention*, 5(09), pp. 4986–4991. doi: 10.18535/ijsshi/v5i9.06.

Trianaputri, A. R., Siswantoro, D. & Dewi, M. K. 2017. 'CSR in Islamic Financial Institution: A Literature Review', *Tazkia Islamic Finance and Business Review*, 11(2), pp. 107–126.

Synergizing Management, Technology and Innovation in Generating Sustainable and Competitive Business Growth – Hendayani et al (eds)
© 2021 Taylor & Francis Group, London, ISBN 978-0-367-68756-4

Factors affecting tourist visits to Mount Talaga Bodas Garut

D.T. Alamanda, W. Susilawati, T. Mulyana & F. Rakhmawati
Faculty of Economics, Garut University, Garut, West Java, Indonesia

ABSTRACT: The development of mountain tourism in the Garut District still needs to be considered by tourism managers and local governments. This study aims to analyze factors affecting tourist visits to Mount Talaga Bodas. This study applied a survey method by distributing questionnaires to 135 tourists who had visited Mount Talaga Bodas. Then, the collected data were analyzed using exploratory factor analysis and software. The result shows that 4 new factors out of 14 factors tested are produced including factors of attraction, factors of knowledge and memory, factors of experience, and factors of the environment. This research is expected to provide input for the future development of tourism objects, especially Mount Talaga Bodas.

1 INTRODUCTION

The development of tourism as a key to the national economy depends on natural and cultural potential as well as the life of the local community (Dangi & Jamal 2016). Hence, it is expected to result in a reciprocal relationship between nature, culture, and life of the local community. This reciprocal relationship has to be mutually beneficial, meaning that tourism should be able to improve culture and nature, and then both culture and nature can improve tourism in a certain location (Ursache 2015).

Mount Talaga Bodas tourism is one of the leading tourism objects in the Garut District. It has many natural attractions to offer. The number of tourist visits to this district increases every year, and it significantly influences tourist visits to Mount Talaga Bodas. The District Tourism and Culture Office (2018) stated that a total of 182,443 tourists visited this tourism object in 2018, in which it passed the target of 100,000 visits.

Besides Talaga Bodas, Garut has some other potential natural attractions, but they are not managed well. The success of Mount Talaga Bodas tourism can be a positive input for other natural tourism objects in this district. Although some tourists posted negative opinions on an online review such as Google Review (Alamanda et al. 2019), this tourist attraction can attract more visitors each year. Based on the above phenomenon, this study aims to identify factors affecting tourists to visit Mount Talaga Bodas. This research is expected to provide input for the planning of natural tourism development in Garut District.

2 LITERATURE REVIEW

Innovations in research on tourism cover products, processes, managerial, marketing, and institutional (Hjalager 2010). Tourism is a composite product involving a wide variety of products and services offered by varied sectors of travel agents, tourist attractions, retail, transportation, accommodation, and so forth. (Ursache 2015). Currently, tourism marketing can be enhanced by more emphasis on the research on strategy and conceptual thinking (Li & Petrick 2008). Tsiotsou and Ratten (2010) added that consumer behavior, branding, electronic marketing, and marketing strategies are crucial research related to tourism marketing. Morrison (2013) states that tourism marketing includes how target marketing is planned, implemented, and evaluated; how management and target marketing are operated and organized; and how to do the business including the opportunities and challenges to compete in the global market.

Tourism destinations help to understand the complexity of multicultural and global markets in some fields that could potentially challenge the competitive behavior model in the tourism industry (Saraniemi & Kylänen 2011). Research on tourism destinations is crucial because the image of a tourism destination affects the process and decisions of tourism destinations (Anuwichanont & Mechinda 2014). Saraniemi and Kylänen (2011) identified four approaches to tourism destinations, including: (1) a geographically oriented economy; (2) marketing-oriented management; (3) customer oriented, and (4) culture. Moreover, Saraniemi and Kylänen (2011) consider tourism destinations as one of the key concepts of institutionalized tourism, which consists of a set of institutions and actors located in virtual space where transactions and marketing-related activities occur.

3 METHODS

This research is quantitative with exploratory design. It used a survey method with three stages. The first stage is the observation of Mount Talaga Bodas to identify the attractions, facilities, and infrastructure that exist in tourist attractions. The second stage is interviews with three informants of the Head of District Tourism Office (G), tourism manager (T), and tourist (RM). The interview was to identify factors affecting tourist visits to Mount Talaga Bodas. The third stage is the distribution of questionnaires to 135 tourists who had visited Mount Talaga Bodas. The questionnaire was distributed to test the findings of the interview.

Based on the observations and interviews, a total of 14 factors were tested using the questionnaire. Besides, there is preliminary research involving 30 respondents in which all factors to be tested get very good responses with scores between 338 to 580 with an average of 516 using the value range method. It indicates that respondents understand and agree that the factor of relaxing in the new atmosphere (X_1), getting pleasure (X_2), having memories with family (X_3), taking pictures to be posted on social media (X_4), educational tourism (X_5), having hoped to do tourism activities (X_6), free time (X_7), typical weather or climate (X_8), travel expense (X_9), popular myths (X_{10}), trekking (X_{11}), infrastructure (X_{12}), management of attraction (X_{13}), and artificial area that support special interests (X_{14}) are factors that can be tested in this research.

4 RESULTS AND DISCUSSION

4.1 *Validity test*

Based on the validity test using the KMO & Bartlett's Test, all factors tested have met the requirements to be analyzed with a KMO score of 0.725 and a significance level of 0.000. Then, based on the Anti-Image Correlation test, all factors tested correlate with >0.500, meaning that the test can proceed to the next stage.

4.2 *Factor analysis*

After the extraction (factoring) of the result of KMO & Bartlett's Test on a set of variables, it resulted in some new factors. The process of determining variables to be included in one of the formed factors was through comparing the correlations of each variable. This research managed to form 4 new factors out of the 14 variables tested, namely component 1, component 2, component 3, and component 4. It is because the eigenvalue for components 1 to 4 is higher than 1 (Table 3). The cumulative (%) column in initial eigenvalue shows the sum of the variances of each variable, which becomes a factor. The sum of the 4 factors is 44.30% + 14.95% + 12.72% + 10.68% = 82.65%, and the total variance of the 14 factors is 82.65%.

Table 1. Formed factors.

Formed Factors	Factors	Name of Formed Factor	Eigenvalue	New Loading Factor
Factor 1	Myths	Factor of Attraction	4,330	0,714
	Travel expense			0,712
	Trekking			0,691
	Typical weather or climate			0,673
	Management of attraction			0,600
Factor 2	Educational Tourism	Factor of Knowledge and Memory	1,495	0,921
	Having memories with family			0,799
	Taking pictures to be posted on social media			0,618
Factor 3	Relaxing in the new atmosphere	Factor of Experience	1,272	0,756
	Free time			0,633
	Getting pleasure			0,562
Factor 4	Artificial areas that support special interests	Factor of Environment	1,068	0,870
	Infrastructure			0,563

The Component Matrix of the rotation process shows a clearer variable distribution, considering that the loading factor that was initially small will be reduced and the larger will be enlarged. The results of the Rotated Component Matrix show the consistency of the factor position with changes in the loading factor values presented in Table 1. The table also shows the grouping of factors, which is tested based on the factor loading value, in which the first factor consisted of five forming factors, namely myths, travel expense, trekking, typical weather or climate, and management of attraction. Then, this first factor is called the factor of attraction.

The second factor consists of three forming factors, namely educational tourism, having memories with the family, and taking pictures to be posted on social media. Then, this factor is called the factor of knowledge and memory. The third factor also consists of three forming factors, namely relaxing in the new atmosphere, free time, and getting pleasure. Then, this factor is called the factor of experience. The last factor is the factor of the environment consisting of two forming factors, the artificial area that supports special interests' factor and infrastructure factors. The eigenvalue score shows that the dominant factor affecting tourists visiting Talaga Bodas is the factor of attraction with a value of 43.33%.

The attraction of tourist destinations is the perceived ability of a tourist destination to meet the needs of tourists (Vengesayi et al. 2009). This statement is supported by the findings of Anuwichanont and Mechinda (2014), in which the image of a tourist destination influences tourist intention to visit. The image of a tourist destination is influenced by the available attractions at the tourist destination (Vengesayi et al. 2009). Further, Satyarini et al. (2017) distinguish the influence of tourist attractions on tourists' interests and decisions to visit tourist attractions. The attractions available in Mount Talaga Bodas are not as varied as in Mount Papandayan, but this tourist destination has unique attractions that cannot be found in other mountain tourism in this district. The unique attractions are wide and beautiful sulfur lakes and the existence of famous mythic tours that raise the curiosity of the tourists every time any tourist passes through this attraction, as all the torches in the area will suddenly go off.

In addition to its beautiful view, this sulfur lake is often used as learning media about geotechnology. Many researchers have studied the potential of geothermal energy in Talaga Bodas (Sutopo et al. 2019). It makes Talaga Bodas attraction worthy of being an educational tourist attraction. The sulfur provides a beautiful and unique photo background as there are around 17,000 posts on Instagram with the hashtag of #talagabodas. It is not just a spot for taking photos, but it is often used for family tourism as stated by Durko and Petrick (2013), in which modern families make tourism a place to strengthen family ties, improve communication between family members, and reduce the potential for divorce.

The third factor is called the factor of experience. It is relevant to the definition of tourism experience according to Kang (2011), which consists of searching for knowledge, pleasure, and pleasant surprises. The environmental factors around the tourist attraction area attracts tourists to visit. The environmental factor consists of infrastructure and artificial tourism. Infrastructure refers to facilities, both physical and non-physical, that are built by the government and individuals to meet the basic needs of the community in the social and economic context. In tourism destinations, the involvement of the public sector both locally and regionally is needed to support the development of sustainable tourism (Mandic et al. 2018), which includes infrastructure development. Jafari and Xiao (2016) distinguish the definition of infrastructure and tourism infrastructure. The first consists of recreational facilities, spas and restaurants, hotels, and other accommodations. Talaga Bodas still have limited tourism infrastructure, and it should be a concern of tourism managers. The involvement of the local government in the development of new infrastructure is limited to improving road access to tourism destinations. It is because Talaga Bodas is managed by not only the local government but also a third party. Better road access has a significant impact on increasing the number of visits. Besides, Talaga Bodas also provides artificial attractions. Man-made attractions are classified as special tourist attractions that are artificially created and other human activities outside the natural and cultural tourism context. The artificial attractions in this tourism destination are interesting photo spots and towers that allow visitors to see tourist attractions from above.

5 CONCLUSION

Based on the results of the discussion, it can be concluded that the analysis of factors affecting tourists to visit Talaga Bodas covers the factors of attraction, knowledge and memory, experience, and environment. The most dominant factor is the factor of attraction, as it has the highest eigenvalue. Although the factor of the environment is in the fourth rank, the improvement of road access significantly influences the visits to Talaga Bodas.

REFERENCES

Alamanda, D. T., Ramdhani, A., Kania, I., Susilawati, W., & Hadi, E. S. 2019. Sentiment Analysis Using Text Mining of Indonesia Tourism Reviews via Social Media. *International Journal of Humanities, Arts and Social Sciences, 5*(3), 72–82. https://doi.org/10.20469/ijhss.5.10004-2.

Anuwichanont, J., & Mechinda, P. 2014. Examining the Impact of Brand Equity and Value Proposition of Ecological Destionation on Eco-touris Loyalty. *Universal Journal of Industrial and Business Management, 2*(7), 173–181. https://doi.org/10.13189/ujibm.2014.020705.

Dangi, T. B., & Jamal, T. 2016. An integrated approach to "sustainable community-based tourism." *Sustainability (Switzerland), 8*(6). https://doi.org/10.3390/su8050475.

Durko, A. M., & Petrick, J. F. 2013. Family and Relationship Benefits of Travel Experiences: A Literature Review. *Journal of Travel Research, 52*(6), 720–730. https://doi.org/10.1177/0047287513496478.

Hjalager, A. M. 2010. A review of innovation research in tourism. *Tourism Management, 3*(1), 1–12. https://doi.org/10.1016/j.tourman.2009.08.012.

Jafari, J., & Xiao, H. 2016. *Encyclopedia of Tourism* (1st ed.). Springer International Publishing.

Kang, S.-J. 2011. Identifying meaningful travel experiences for mature educational tourists. In *ProQuest Dissertations and Theses*.

Li, X., & Petrick, J. F. 2008). Tourism marketing in an Era of Paradigm Shift. *Journal of Travel Research, 46*(3), 235–244. https://doi.org/10.1177/0047287507303976.

Mandic, A., Mrnjavac, Ž., & Kordic, L. 2018. Tourism infrastructure, recreational facilities and tourism development. *Tourism and Hospitality Management, 24*(1), 41–62. https://doi.org/10.20867/thm.24.1.12.

Morrison, A. M. 2013. Marketing and managing tourism destinations. In *Marketing and Managing Tourism Destinations*. https://doi.org/10.4324/9780203081976.

Saraniemi, S., & Kylänen, M. 2011. Problematizing the concept of tourism destination: An analysis of different theoretical approaches. *Journal of Travel Research, 50*(2), 133–143. https://doi.org/10.1177/0047287510362775.

Satyarini, N. W. M., Rahmanita, M., & Setarnawat, S. 2017. The Influence of Destination Image on Tourist Intention and Decision to Visit Tourist Destination (A Case Study of Pemuteran Village in Buleleng, Bali, Indonesia). *TRJ Tourism Research Journal, 1*(1), 81. https://doi.org/10.30647/trj.v1i1.10.
Sutopo, Prabata, W., & Pratama, H. B. 2019. The development study of Karaha–Talaga Bodas geothermal field using numerical simulation. In *Geothermal Energy*. https://doi.org/10.1186/s40517-019-0139-2.
Tsiotsou, R., & Ratten, V. 2010. Future research directions in tourism marketing. *Marketing Intelligence and Planning, 28*(4), 533–544. https://doi.org/10.1108/02634501011053702.
Ursache, M. 2015. Tourism – Significant Driver Shaping a Destinations Heritage. *Procedia – Social and Behavioral Sciences, 188*, 130–137. https://doi.org/10.1016/j.sbspro.2015.03.348.
Vengesayi, S., Mavondo, F. T., & Reisinger, Y. 2009. Tourism destination attractiveness: Attractions, facilities, and people as predictors. *Tourism Analysis, 14*(5), 621–636. https://doi.org/10.3727/108354209X12597959359211.

Synergizing Management, Technology and Innovation in Generating Sustainable and Competitive Business Growth – Hendayani et al (eds)
© 2021 Taylor & Francis Group, London, ISBN 978-0-367-68756-4

Measuring customer relationship management using network analysis

A.P. Rabbani, A. Alamsyah & S. Widiyanesti
School of Economic and Business, Telkom University, Bandung, West Java, Indonesia

ABSTRACT: This study aims to explore the customer relationship management (CRM) performance of Indonesia's Fintech on social media. Social network analysis is performed by calculating its network properties to understand the conversation network characteristic effectively. In discovering the market majority thought, sentiment analysis is conducted. As case studies, we investigate Twitter conversation about GoPay, OVO, Dana, and LinkAja during the observation period from 1st October until 1st November 2019. The overall result shows that LinkAja perform CRM better by winning 4 out of 9 network properties and succeeded in gaining 72.57% positive sentiments. Besides, each company has its own competitive advantage; GoPay has strong relationship between users, OVO has a lot of audience among others, and LinkAja has the most engaged audience which make the information spread faster. These are insightful for companies to evaluate their CRM performance.

1 INTRODUCTION

Companies from various sectors use social media for their marketing activities. Social media allows companies to manage online conversation networks with both customers and the market. Moreover, social media also leads the companies to a new approach for engaging more customers by seeing them as a community instead of an individual. This undertaking is known as social customer relationship management (SCRM).

As one of the most popular social media, Twitter is powerful in conversation network for-mation. Besides, Twitter is capable of capturing users' emotions in a short-post. By providing some simple features such as tweet, reply, share, and like, Twitter succeeded in obtaining the large-scale database having more than 313 million active users with 1 billion unique monthly visits (Twitter 2019).

Fintech, an innovative technology-enabled financial service, is fast becoming a global phenomenon. In Indonesia, fintech companies are increasingly emerging as more people familiar with it. Social media play a role in this rapid growth. GoPay, OVO, Dana, and LinkAja are the leading on fintech in Indonesia (Jayani 2019). All these companies take favor of social media to enlighten customers about their services, respond to complaints, interact, and engage with their customers.

However, every business action should be measured to recognize if any improvement needed and to find out if the work is worth doing. Social network analysis (SNA) could be considered as an approach to measure SCRM effort since it gives businesses a way to administer and measure their performance in engaging audiences. This approach enables SCRM to develops and enhance the capabilities to engage customers and maintain conversations with a new methodological way (Alamsyah & Utami 2018).

In this exploration, we aim to measure and compare SCRM performance of Indonesia's fintech on Twitter. We perform social network analysis (SNA) method by counting its network properties and analyzing each fintech, i.e., GoPay, OVO, Dana, and LinkAja. Likewise, we utilize sentiment analysis to recognize which fintech has the most positive thoughts. Several earlier studies have been used to assist this exploration, such as the use of SNA and sentiment analysis to measure

SCRM performance and the empirical links between network characteristics and social engagement (Alamsyah & Indraswari 2017; Alamsyah & Utami 2018;). The results are beneficial for each company to understand both of their customers and competitors deeper and better. Moreover, this insight will help companies evaluate and make the decision for their future SCRM strategies.

2 THEORETICAL BACKGROUND

2.1 *Social customer relationship management*

Customer relationship management (CRM) is a comprehensive strategy to build superior value for the company and the customer through some processes such as acquiring, retaining, and partnering with customers that we choose as the target. Social media availability makes companies perform CRM much more accessible; this is called social customer relationship management (SCRM).

2.2 *Social network analysis*

Social network analysis (SNA) is a methodology that suitable as an approach for analyzing the connections between individuals and their behavior within social groups. Represented by a network that consists of nodes and edges which refer to actor and relations between actors, these models provide several metrics based on theory graph characteristic. SNA can be made to discover a wide range of business problems like strategy, sales and marketing, human resource, team-building, knowledge management and collaboration (Manzira & Bankole 2018). In this research, we calculate network properties with the SNA approach to measure social customer performance. Some previous studies use these network properties to understand the SCRM network (Alamsyah & Indraswari 2017; Alamsyah & Utami 2018;). Table 1 shows the description of each network properties.

2.3 *Sentiment analysis*

Sentiment analysis means a process to identify and classifies people's opinions, sentiments, appraisals, evaluations, attitudes, and emotions towards items such as products, services, individuals, organizations, events, issues, topics, and their attributes (Nasr et al. 2017). Automated sentiment analysis is a must because human reader on average has difficulty in determining relevant sites, extracting and summarizing the opinions in them. In this research, we use the Naïve Bayes classification method for its efficiency and high-level accuracy to support significant data processing (Normah 2019).

Table 1. Network properties description (Alamsyah & Indraswari 2017).

No.	Network Properties	Description
1.	Size	The quantities of nodes in the network
2.	Density	The fraction between number edges in-network and the maximum edges possible
3.	Modularity	The fraction of edges within communities minus the expected value of that fraction of the position of the edges is randomized
4.	Diameter	The shortest path between any pair of nodes with the largest distance
5.	Average Path Length	The average distance between every pair of nodes in the network
6.	Average Degree	The average quantity of links a node has to the other node in the network
7.	Reachability	The fraction of any pair of nodes that are connected
8.	Connected Component	The measure of nodes' maximal subset that reachable by some paths from each other

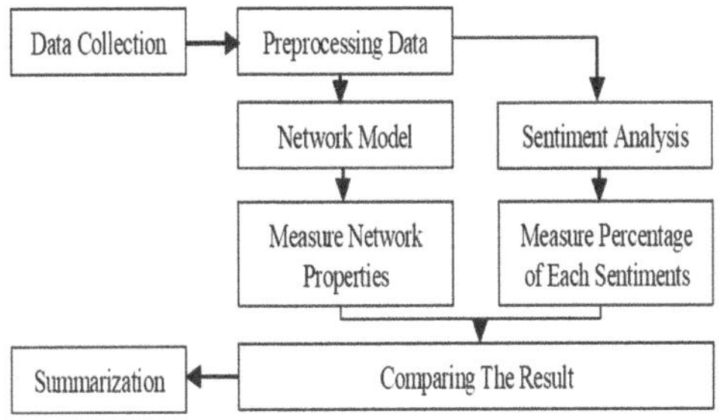

Figure 1. Research workflow.

Table 2. Network properties comparison.

No.	Network Properties	GoPay	OVO	Dana	LinkAja
1.	Size	3,478	6,495	5,682	4,531
2.	Edges	3,160	5,749	5,711	4,772
3.	Density	0.00049	0.00025	0.00033	0.00044
4.	Modularity	0.612	0.385	0.503	0.381
5.	Diameter	15	12	13	11
6.	Average Path Length	3.451	2.717	3.264	3.079
7.	Average Degree	1.817	1.770	2.01	2.106
8.	Reachability	0.0005	0.0002	0.0003	0.0005
9.	Connected Component	586	1.324	933	370

3 METHODOLOGY

There are four stages of methodology research involved in this study. The research workflow is shown in Figure 1.

First, we collect tweets data using Twitter Application Programming Interface (Twitter API). Then we determine the keyword related to this study's topics before collecting tweets; there are @gopayindonesia, @ovo_id, @danawallet, and @linkaja. The period of data collection is from 1st October 2019 until 1st November 2019. We then complete data preprocessing to support the methods applied in this research and get relevant data to the research objectives. After that, we construct the network models for each company to see the pattern of interactions between users with related topic; GoPay, OVO, Dana, and LinkAja. After that we calculate the network properties with Python. We also perform sentiment analysis with the Naïve Bayes classification method. This method includes separating tweets data into the data train and data test, labeling every tweet with positive and negative. After all the data train labeled, we use machine learning tools for labeling data tests automatically. This process also discovers classification performance with performance evaluation parameters such as precision, recall, F-measure, accuracy, and kappa score.

4 RESULTS AND ANALYSIS

Table 2 shows the results of network properties measurement. The visualization of GoPay, OVO, Dana, and LinkAja networks is in Figure 2. The result of sentiment analysis is in Table 3. The result of Naïve Bayes text classification performance is in Table 4.

Based on the network properties comparison results in Table 2, OVO performs best in size for both nodes and edges. The higher the number of nodes and edges means more users and more

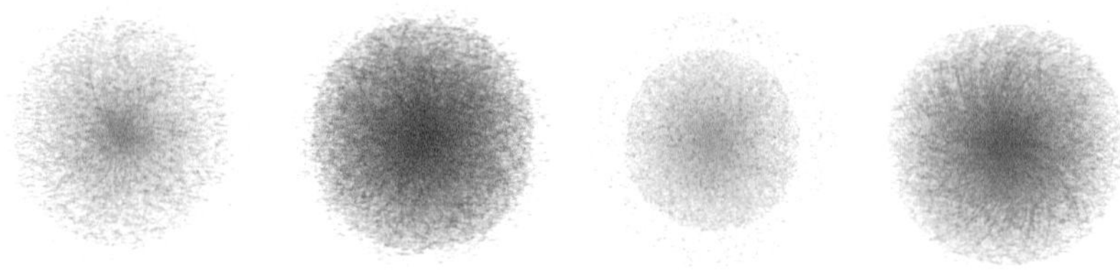

Figure 2. Network visualization of 2a. GoPay, 2b. OVO, 2c. Dana, and 2d. LinkAja.

Table 3. Sentiment percentage comparison.

No.	Sentiment	GoPay	OVO	Dana	LinkAja
1.	Positive	36.00% 509 tweets	47.37% 720 tweets	53.82% 818 tweets	72.57% 1,119 tweets
2.	Negative	64.00% 905 tweets	52.63% 801 tweets	46.18% 702 tweets	27.43% 423 tweets

Table 4. Naïve Bayes text classification performance.

No.	Parameter	GoPay	OVO	Dana	LinkAja
1.	*Precision*	83.48%	78.62%	77.29%	81.57%
2.	*Recall*	84.79%	80.91%	77.74%	76.51%
3.	*F-Measure*	81.43%	79.75%	77.51%	78.96%
4.	*Accuracy*	84.55%	79.03%	76.06%	83.56%
5.	*Kappa*	0.678	0.577	0.529	0.566

interaction between users in the conversation network, hence generate new connections and new possibilities. OVO also performs best in average path length. It has a lower value among others which means the chance to precipitate the information dissemination process is increases.

GoPay has the highest value of density and modularity. The higher the density value defines the more connections perform in every user in the network. The high number of modularity values mean more support in the formation group.

LinkAja conversation network performs best in diameter, average degree, and connected component. The lower diameter the better, it means the information dissemination process between two users with the longest distance only need fewer paths. The higher average degree value means more users get information directly. The lower connected component value, the better because it means that the users do not divide too much into small groups (Alamsyah & Indraswari 2017).

Based on reachability values, both GoPay and LinkAja have higher numbers, which means their networks manage the information dissemination simpler. The comparison results above point out that the LinkAja conversation network performs better by winning 4 out of 9 network properties.

Moreover, we construct the network model of each fintech. The colors of each fintech represent the edge of the relationship between nodes. The nodes illustrate the users involved in the conversation network. The network models are shown in Figure 2.

Table 3 shows the comparison results of sentiment analysis. As we can see, LinkAja has the highest numbers of positive sentiment opinion. And then followed by Dana with more than a half positive sentiment from total tweets data. OVO and GoPay have low positive sentiment results compare to the negative ones.

These results discover that both LinkAja and Dana have been succeeded in creating a positive image for their customers. Otherwise, based on the low results of positive sentiment both OVO and GoPay must pay attention more to their representation in the online conversation network.

Table 4 describes Naïve Bayes text classification performances. The performance evaluation parameter, such as precision, recall, F-measure, accuracy, and kappa, shows good results. The kappa value of each fintech varies between 0.5 until 0.7, which predicated a moderate agreement and substantial agreement of its classification model, while precision and recall value reach between 75–85%. F-measure value reach between 75–85% as harmonization of precision and recall value indicating the classification process is going well. Therefore, the Naïve Bayes classification method is suitable for sentiment analysis for the four fintech data tweets.

5 CONCLUSION

In this study, we explore the use of social network analysis to identify customer relationship management performance on social media. By calculating its network properties, we could measure and compare the conversation network characteristic of each company effectively. Sentiment analysis is conducted in this study as well to identify the major emotion in the conversation network. There are some different works from previous similar studies (Alamsyah & Indraswari 2017; Alamsyah & Utami 2018); calculate more network properties to understand the network characteristic deeper, and perform automated sentiment analysis using Naïve Bayes classifier with machine learning to gain more accurate result.

The overall result shows that LinkAja performs CRM better by winning 4 out of 9 network properties and succeeded in gaining 72.57% positive sentiments. Furthermore, each company has its competitive advantage; GoPay has a strong relationship between users, OVO has a lot of audiences, and LinkAja has the most engaged audience that makes the information spread faster. Based on sentiment analysis results, LinkAja and Dana have a quite high positive sentiment while GoPay and OVO have a low positive sentiment. These are insightful for companies to evaluate their CRM performance.

Several suggestions are given based on network properties, e.g., companies with low value on modularity and density are essential to produce more campaigns or competition associated with specific topics to entice more audiences joining the conversation network. Moreover, companies with a low average degree value can collaborate with influential people to create more brand awareness in the conversation network. Companies can also evaluate their performance based on the sentiment analysis result, e.g., being more responsive and friendly to customers, etc.

For the future research: Extend the data collection period to enrich the data so that the information generated is more accurate, identifying SNA metrics such as centrality, betweenness, closeness, and others for exploring further community detection, using text classification methods other than Naïve Bayes in sentiment analysis to explore, conduct more in-depth research to determine what topics are most discussed using an appropriate method such as topic modeling.

REFERENCES

Alamsyah, A. & Indraswari, A. 2017. Social network and Sentiment Analysis for Social Customer Relationship Management in Indonesia Banking Sector. *Advanced Science Letters* 23:3808–3812.

Alamsyah, A. & Utami, A. 2018. Social Network Performance Analysis and Content Engagement on Indonesia's E-Commerce. *2018 6th International Conference on Information and Communication Technology (ICOICT)*: 464–469.

Jayani D.H. 2019. The largest digital wallets in Indonesia, Q4 2017-Q2 2019. *Databoks*. Retrieved from https://databoks.katadata.co.id/datapublish/2019/08/23/inilah-daftar-dompet-digital-terbesar-di-indonesia.

Manzira, F.M. & Bankole, F.O. 2018. Application of Social Media Analytics in the Banking Sector to Drive Growth and Sustainability: A Proposed Integrated Framework. 2018 *Open Innovation Conference (OI)*: 223–233.

Nasr, M. M. et al. 2017. Enhancing Social Customer Relationship Management by Using Sentiment Analysis. *International Journal of Science and Research* 6: 803–807.

Normah. 2019. Naïve Bayes Algorithm for Sentiment Analysis Windows Phone Store Application Reviews. *Journal Publications & Informatics Engineering Research* 3: 1–19.

Twitter. 2019. Retrieved from https://about.twitter.com/en_us.html.

Synergizing Management, Technology and Innovation in Generating Sustainable and Competitive Business Growth – Hendayani et al (eds)
© 2021 Taylor & Francis Group, London, ISBN 978-0-367-68756-4

Factors influencing purchase intention for halal products

B.R. Arlisa, M. Ariyanti & R. Hendayani
Telkom University, Bandung, West Java, Indonesia

ABSTRACT: Halal has become a main discussed issue in the business world. Indonesia is ranked first as the country which has the largest Muslim population compared with other countries. However, one of the studies has shown that Indonesia is less concerned about halal food. There are many studies discussing halal food around the world, but meanwhile in Indonesia the research needs further development. This study's purpose is to test a new modified research model on whether it is possible to use them as a further option or not. In addition, this study wanted to test the model based on halal awareness, halal certification, product quality, marketing promotion, brand, halal knowledge, halal quality, and attitude toward halal food to purchase intention on halal food in Indonesia. The result of validity shows that there are two invalid question. It is also concluded that all variables used are reliable and that the model can be used for further research.

1 INTRODUCTION

The number of Indonesian populations increases every year. According to Indonesian statistic data center (BPS) in 2015, there were 238,518,000 people, and it is estimated that in 2020 there will be an additional number for a total of approximately 271,066,000 people. Moreover, about 88% of the total citizens are Muslim, making Indonesia to become ranked first as a country with Muslim population (Mon 2017). Alongside with the escalation of the population, demand for their primary needs are also increasing from one year to another. Therefore, producers are competing to dominate the market by producing various types of foods and beverages (Burhanuddin 2011).

Halal has become one of the main issues in every industry, especially in the food industry. In 2016, the amount of money spent by the people to buy halal foods was $1.245 billion, and it is predicted that in 2022 the number will continue to go up to $1.930 billion. However, despite the fact that Indonesia is a country with the biggest Muslim population, Indonesia does not correspond to the reports and the research done by Thomson Reuteurs (2018), where it was said that in "Top 10 Halal Food countries GIE Indicator Score," Indonesia is not included in the top 10 countries who pay attention to halal food. Several countries whose citizens are mostly not Muslim beat Indonesia as the country with the biggest Muslim population (Reuteurs 2018).

Ena Lubis, a member of the small and medium business union member from Culinary Center, stated that both producer and consumer have poor awareness in halal food. She also stated that the circumstances in Indonesia fall behind other countries such as Singapore where the citizens have more awareness in halal food (Damayanti 2019). One of the main cases in Indonesia about halal meat is the condition in which beef is mixed with pork, which has already happened several times (Adhey 2020). As consequences, buying interest and the income of butchers are declined. In the end, most buyers only asked the question about the authenticity of the meat without buying (Verawati 2020).

2 THEORITICAL BASIC AND LITERATURE REVIEW

2.1 *Theoritical*

Consumer behavior: Schiffman and Kanuk (2014:4) describe consumer behavior as an act shown by consumers in searching, purchasing, using, evaluating, and spending goods and services they expect will satisfy their needs. Meanwhile, Arnould, Price, and Zinkhan (2002:5) in Sumarwan (2015) define consumer behavior as individuals or groups acquiring, using, and disposing of products, services, ideas, or experiences. Also included are acquisition and use of information.

Purchase intention: Purchase intention is part of the behavioral component of the consumer attitude. Consumer buying interest is the stage where consumers form their choice among several incorporated brands, then make a purchase of an alternative they like best or the process where consumers purchase an item or service based on various considerations (Sukmawati and Suyono in Pramono 2012).

2.2 *Previous research*

Literature review was conducted to build the thinking framework in this study. In addition, two papers are also used as reference: one is written by Maichum et al. (2018) and the others is written by Aziz and Chok (2014). In a study conducted by Maichum et al., there were two independent variables, halal knowledge and halal quality; one mediating variable, attitude toward halal food; and one dependent variable, purchase intention. The object of his research is halal food in Thailand. In the research conducted by Aziz and Chok, there are five independent variables: halal awareness, halal certification, product quality, marketing promotion, and brand. There is one dependent variable, which is the purchase intention. The object of his research is halal food in Malaysia.

These variables are supported based on research conducted by Yunus et al. (2014), "Halal awareness has a positive influence on halal food purchase intention." Another study conducted by Awan et al. (2014) found that one of the factors that influence one's purchase intention on halal food in Pakistan is halal certification. According to the research of Faradiba and Astuti (2013), the quality of the product influences consumer purchase intentions in Semarang. According to the research conducted by Awan et al. (2014), marketing on halal food can increase consumer buying interest. Another study done by Yunus et al. (2014) shows that a brand has a positive effect on the customer purchase intention. Elias et al (2016) revealed that there is a significant relationship between halal knowledge and the intention to produce halal products. Above all, halal quality is one of the most important factors in the food industry (Soong 2007).

This research was made by adopting two paper frameworks using a different number. This thesis analyzes the object of Indonesian society because there are problems, as mentioned in the introduction. This study has different respondents from the paper made by Aziz and Chok and Maichum et al. because people in every country have a different frame of mind. Research by Maichum et al. was conducted in Thailand using Thai citizens as respondents; meanwhile, Aziz and Chok's research was conducted in Malaysia by targeting Malaysian citizens in the Kling Valley as respondents who were non-Muslim.

3 METHODOLOGY

This research uses validity and reliability to test the feasibility of each variable indicator. Before calculating the validity test, the content was previously done. Content validity is the extent of which items are used to measure whether research variables are logical in accordance with what will be measured. As a reference for this research, researchers discussed with three lecturers who are experts in business management studies. Next, the significance test is carried out using the criteria of r tables and r statistic comparisons. After conducting content validity, the questionnaire

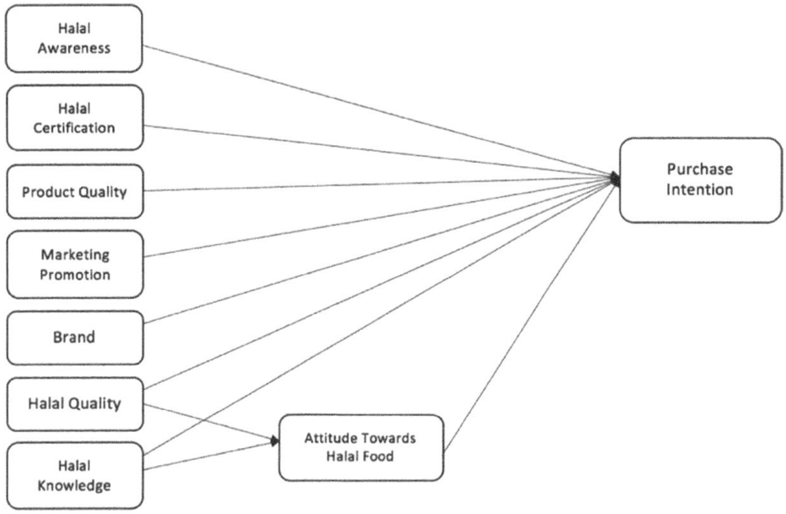

Figure 1. Modified theoretical framework.

is then distributed to 30 Indonesian respondents, who are familiar with and used to consume halal food in Indonesia, using online Google forms to distribute the questionnaire.

4 RESULTS AND DISCUSS

The questionnaire came from the question written by Maichum et al. (2018) and Aziz and Chok (2014). However, several questions were changed to adjust to the target respondents in Indonesia. The following validity results are processed using the IBM SPSS Statistics Version 24 for Windows 64 bit.

Based on the data validity test in the table above, two statements are invalid, the statements where Pearson correlation value is <0.361, which are statements HC1 and PI2. After conducting the validity of variable items, the variable reliability test is then performed. According to Sekaran (2016: 290), reliability indicates the extent to which the data is error free or reliable and therefore ensures the consistency of measurements over time and across various items in the instrument when the Cronbach alpha value is >0.60. Based on the data, it is found that all indicated variables are reliable because the Cronbach's alpha value surpasses the reference value above 0.6.

5 CONCLUSION

From this research, it can be concluded that the modification model used for this test is possible to become a measurement tool for further research. However, there are two question that must be removed from the study because they did not pass the validity test. If this research is carried further to examine Indonesian people's buying intention on halal food in Indonesia, we can find out which variables are the most effective on consumer purchase intention. With the results obtained, it is hoped that food entrepreneurs in Indonesia can better understand and focus on what influences the most purchase intentions of Indonesian consumers. Thus, they can increase their sales with these results. Because all of the variables are reliable, the authors suggest that in the future, entrepreneurs in Indonesia can sell more halal products. From the data, it is found that the highest reliable value

Table 1. Construct validity and reliability test result.

No	Item	Cronbach's alpha	r stat	r table	Validity	Reliability
1	HA1	0.742	0.699	0.361	VALID	RELIABEL
2	HA2		0.635	0.361	VALID	
3	HA3		0.634	0.361	VALID	
4	HC1	0.744	0.037	0.361	INVALID	RELIABEL
5	HC2		0.438	0.361	VALID	
6	HC3		0.671	0.361	VALID	
7	HC4		0.750	0.361	VALID	
8	PQ1	0.757	0.749	0.361	VALID	RELIABEL
9	PQ2		0.677	0.361	VALID	
10	MP1	0.672	0.631	0.361	VALID	RELIABEL
11	MP2		0.656	0.361	VALID	
12	BR1	0.780	0.616	0.361	VALID	RELIABEL
13	BR2		0.582	0.361	VALID	
14	BR3		0.330	0.361	INVALID	
15	HK2	0.685	0.454	0.361	VALID	RELIABEL
16	HK3		0.521	0.361	VALID	
17	HK4		0.701	0.361	VALID	
18	HQ1	0.713	0.512	0.361	VALID	RELIABEL
19	HQ2		0.686	0.361	VALID	
20	HQ3		0.666	0.361	VALID	
21	AT1	0.762	0.750	0.361	VALID	RELIABEL
22	AT2		0.607	0.361	VALID	
23	AT3		0.553	0.361	VALID	
24	AT1		0.552	0.361	VALID	
25	PI1	0.693	0.665	0.361	VALID	RELIABEL
26	PI2		0.603	0.361	VALID	
27	PI3		0.368	0.361	VALID	
28	PI4		0.390	0.361	VALID	
29	PI5		0.364	0.361	VALID	
30	PI6		0.531	0.361	VALID	
31	PI7		0.434	0.361	VALID	
32	PI8		0.433	0.361	VALID	
33	PI9		0.428	0.361	VALID	

is on the brand, so it is recommended for entrepreneurs who want to sell halal products, that they can focus more on the brand of the product.

REFERENCES

Adhey 2020. Waspada, Marak Penjualan Daging Sapi Dicampur Babi di Tangerang. https://pojoksatu.id/news/berita-nasional/2020/05/18/waspada-marak-penjualan-daging-babi-di-tangerang/. (Accessed 18 May 2020).

Aziz, Y.A. & Chok, N.V. 2014. The role of Halal awareness, Halal certification, and marketing components in determining Halal purchase intention among non-Muslims in Malaysia: a structural equation modeling approach. Journal of International Food & Agribusiness Marketing, 25(1), 1–23.

Awan, H.M. & Nabeel, A. 2015. Factors affecting Halal purchase intention – evidence from Pakistan's Halal food sector. Management Research Review, Vol. 38 Iss 6 pp. 640–660.

Burhanuddin. 2011. Pemikiran Hukum Perlindungan Konsumen dan Sertifikasi halal. Malang (ID): UIN-MALIKI Press.

Damayanti, I. 2019. Kesadaran Halal Konsumen-Produsen UKM Masih Rendah. https://republika.co.id/berita/ptsonl370/kesadaran-halal-konsumenprodusen-ukm-masih-rendah. (Accessed 15 May 2020).

Elias, M., Saifudin, A.M. & Othman, S.N. 2016. Halal awareness and knowledge among Muslim's student entrepreneurship program: A preliminary study. Paper presented at the In: 2nd International Conference on Global Social Entrepreneurship (2nd ICoGBSE2016), 13–14 March 2016, Koh Samui, Thailand.

Faradiba, F. & Astuti, S.R.T. 2013. Analisis Pengaruh Kualitas Produk, Harga, Lokasi dan Kualitas Pelayanan terhadap Minat Beli Ulang Konsumen (Studi pada Warung Makan "Bebek Gendut" Semarang). Diponegoro Journal of Management, 59–69.

Kotler, P. & Armstrong, G. 2018. Principles of Marketing. Edisi 15 Global Edition. Pearson.

Maichum, K., Parichatnon, S. & Peng, K.C. 2017. Factors affecting on purchase intention towards green products: A case study of young consumers in Thailand. Young, 16, 17.

Mon 2017. Islam Agama dengan Pertumbuhan Paling Cepat di Dunia. https://jogja.tribunnews.com/2017/06/02/penelitian-islam-agama-dengan-pertumbuhan-paling-cepat-di-dunia. (Accessed 7 April 2020).

Pramono, A.G. & Sri, S. 2012. Pertimbangan dalam Membeli Produk Barang Maupun Jasa. Jakarta: Intidayu Press.

Reuters, T. 2018. Outpacing The Mainstream State of Global Islamic Economy Global Report 2017/18 United State: Thomson Reuters.

Schiffman, L. & Wisenblit, J 2014 Consumer Behaviour. Pearson Education inc, New Jersey.

Sekaran, U & Bougie, R. 2016. Research Methods for Bussiness. United Kingdom: John Wiley & Sons Ltd.

Soong, S.F.V. 2007. Managing halal quality in food service industry.

Sumarwan, U. 2015 Perilaku Konsumen Teori dan Penerapannya dalam Pemasaran (kedua ed.) Bogor: Ghalia Indonesia.

Verawati 2020. Dampak Kasus Penjualan Daging Babi, Penjualan Daging Sapi di Pasar Banjaran Merosot. https://www.dara.co.id/dampak-kasus-penjualan-daging-babi-penjualan-daging-sapi-di-pasar-banjaran-merosot.html. (Accessed 18 Mei 2020).

Synergizing Management, Technology and Innovation in Generating Sustainable and Competitive Business Growth – Hendayani et al (eds)
© 2021 Taylor & Francis Group, London, ISBN 978-0-367-68756-4

Design of integrated inventory management system for food sector SMES

A. Fathurrachman, W. Puspitasari & M. Saputra
School of Industrial and System Engineering, Telkom University, Bandung, West Java, Indonesia

ABSTRACT: In the recent decades, most enterprises are moving toward a new age. With the recent growth in technology for the past decades, many enterprises saw the opportunity of improvement. In an enterprise who moves in the food industry, inventory is one of the most crucial parts of the business by the means of how to keep their inventory's overall quality as raw material's expiration is imminent. The purpose of this research is to identify enterprise resource planning (ERP) as the solution to the crucial inventory handling problem in small medium enterprises. ERP is an integrated large-scale system that allows organizations to integrate processes and information throughout the organization to boost its performance. The selected ERP software for this research is Odoo based on its open-source nature, flexibility, and ease of use. Lastly, a design of how the Odoo software, as the solution to the current quality management, is created

1 INTRODUCTION

A restaurant is a place or building that is organized commercially, which provides good service to all guests, whether in the form of food or drinks (Marsum 2018) It can then be concluded that restaurants can be small or large scale. At this time, many restaurants are competing to innovate and become the best in their respective trends. Due to Indonesia's diverse and unique culinary background, business in the culinary field is one of the business lines that is very closely related to the life of the Indonesian people. In data reported by Euromonitor International, it is estimated that in the last decade, the value of the culinary business rose by 9% by the analysis as told by Table 1.

One restaurant that moves in the spicy food trend is PT. XYZ. Although this restaurant is still new, based on sales data since it was first opened, PT. XYZ has become one of the restaurants favored by the residents of local patrons in searching for spicy dishes.

Table 1. Growth of indonesia's foodservice by subsector in US$ million (Marketeers 2019).

Subsector	2013	2014	2015	2016	2019	%CAGR 2010–14	%CAGR 2015–19
Restaurants	27,486.2	30,022.8	32,465.4	35,152.5	45,423.5	8.5	8.8
Cafes/Bar	3,298.6	3,634.9	3,969.0	4,338.8	5,756.0	9.4	9.7
Fast Food	1,442.8	1,651.3	1,861.1	2,092.8	2,941.5	12.7	12.1
Street Stalls	1,203.6	1,291.9	1,376.4	1,468.7	1,821.1	6.3	7.2
Home Delivery	14.9	17.1	22.8	29.8	59.8	57.2	27.3
Cafeterias	3,298.6	3,634.9	3,969.0	4,338.8	5,756.0	9.4	9.7
Total	33,625.9	36,814.8	39,906.4	43,310.8	43,310.8	8.7	9.0

In managing business in the culinary industry, inventory management is one of the most crucial tasks to handle. One of the biggest obstacles is to ensure the quality of raw goods in the warehouse, that they are still fresh. Each batch of items in the warehouse has a different expiration date. So, if a product is stored too long in the warehouse it becomes expired or is not suitable for consumption. Failing to do so will result in a huge loss in material.

PT. XYZ intends to use information technology as a solution in increasing the efficiency of its performance and reducing risk to ongoing business threats. One technology that can be used as a solution of the problems at PT. XYZ is enterprise resource planning (ERP). ERP is a system of effective planning and control of all resources used as material to make, produce, ship, and record for customer orders in manufacturing, distribution, and service organizations. The solution is offered in the form of software that is able to integrate parts of a company, such as inventory, finance, human resources, supply chains, etc. (Madanhire & Charles 2016).

To be able to implement ERP, ERP software is needed. Until now, there have been many ERP software developed, one of which is Odoo software. This research uses Odoo software because Odoo is an open-source ERP software, making it easier to design because of its availability. In addition, Odoo can be used as an integrated system, so that various relevant stakeholders can access and obtain accurate information about the business situation, which enables more appropriate decision making. In designing and implementing Odoo software, it is necessary to use one of the appropriate methods so that the implementation can run according to the planned business process. One method that will be used in this study is the Odoo QuickStart method. Odoo QuickStart has several stages, including Kick-off call, Analysis, Configuration, and Production (Odoo 2018). Based on the background above, Odoo as an ERP-based system is chosen to be the solution designed accordingly to PT. XYZ's problems as it is compatible to the needs of PT. XYZ.

2 PRODUCTION PLANNING

In the culinary industry, inventory is one of the key aspects of a business stability, as culinary inventory stock is often perishable. A wrong step in managing the inventory could lead to massive disruption to the business, which is why many businesses need to rethink the way they manage their inventory. Furthermore, the food industry is also a very regulated industry, as standards are regulated to make sure that food safety is ensured (Chan 2018).

As technology progresses, there are new ways to implement technology as a solution to current issues in the industry with the hopes of solving current problems. ERP systems are designed to support operational and functional processes of an organization's value chain, which usually comprises sales, inventory, finance, human capital, customer relationship management, and so on. ERP systems are purposed to bring similar information technology architecture across businesses in order to make sure of data consistencies and integration from other modular applications, in order to support business processes (Tian & Sean 2015).

Businesses in the culinary industry could benefit in a better management system, whether it's for the sales department, inventory department, or even the finance department by customizing the system based on the requirement and solution needed. A specific implementation of ERP solution in the inventory department is to make sure of the quality of current available items. By implementing an expiration timer on each lot of items, staff could predict and have a better idea of managing current inventory state. This reduces the possibility of spoiling items before used, which thus reduces unnecessary costs in wasted items.

3 RESEARCH METHODOLOGIES

The development of ERP design in PT. XYZ consists of many phases and activities. The methodology used for this development is Odoo QuickStart with system design artifacts as the product. QuickStart is a methodology by Odoo, formerly known as Odoo Implementation Method and made

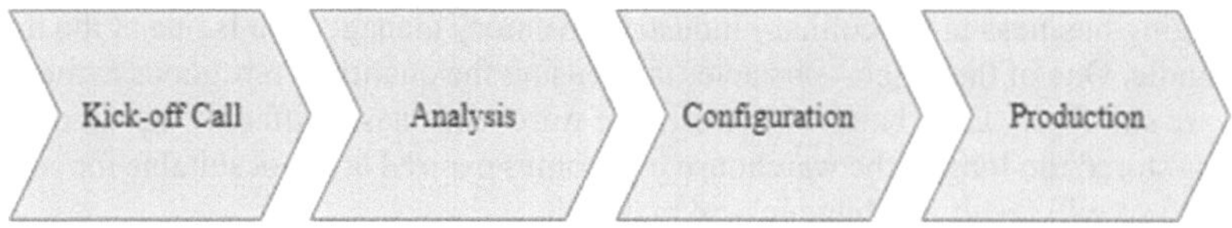

Figure 1. Odoo quickstart.

Table 2. PT XYZ business needs.

System	Application	Data	Products and Services
Software with integrated system and enables automated management and information availability	Software that able to be used as a tool to integrate management	Information and report to minimize human error and enable efficient management	Deliver high-quality service and products to costumers

specifically for Odoo implementation. Figure 1 shows the phases of the QuickStart methodology (Nafianto 2019).

According to Figure 1, the first phase of QuickStart methodology is the kick-off call, continuing with analysis, then configuration, and finally production.

4 ANALYSIS, CONFIGURATION, AND PRODUCTION

4.1 *Analysis*

Research is done to determine and to define the end-goal of current research based on the needs of PT. XYZ. The analysis is carried out by interview, analyzing the current business process to the proposed business process with the Odoo system (to be). The business needs of PT XYZ are explained by Table 2.

At this moment, the inventory management in PT XYZ is done every day after business hours, when the employee in charge will recap every existing item, which every item is clustered based on its type and expiration due. After being recapped. the employee recapitulates what items must be bought back for the next day. After the recap is complete, the employee will contact each vendor for each item that needs to be recapitulated. The main idea of current business process is drawn in Figure 2.

4.1.1 *Configuration*

The use case diagram of the designed application is as drawn in Figure 3. Based on the use case ciagram in the picture, there are two actors, namely Manager and Staff, as for now PT. XYZ hasn't placed a specific job desk on staff so that all staff are still considered to have the same privilege. Staff can log in, add products, view products, and scrap product. Meanwhile, admin has access to all staff capabilities and can create new users, change privileges, generate an inventory valuation, generate warehouse status reporting, and do modules level configuration to the Odoo application.

The system block diagram of the designed application is drawn as in Figure 4. The diagram illustrates how modules interact and communicate. Every module is connected by the Odoo central

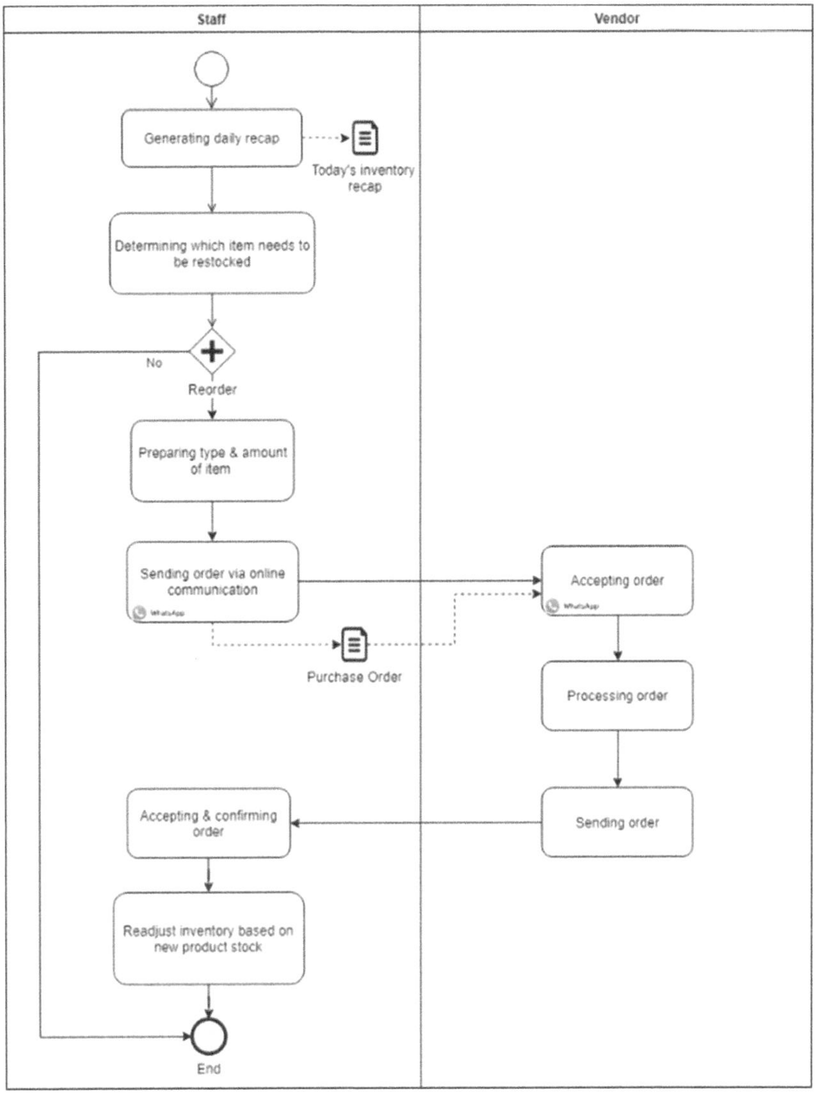

Figure 2. Existing business process.

database software and interacts based on its data needs. For example, in restocking current products, the inventory module communicates with the purchasing and invoicing module for product procurements.

4.2 *Production*

In the proposed business process in inventory replenishment, the recap will be done by the system. Each item will be recorded when used for production, which automatically reduces the number of items on the shelf. Then when the item will be expired, the system reports to the user as a reminder that the item will expire. After recap, the user is also able to contact the vendor directly. After an item is processed, delivered, and received, it is admitted into the warehouse and the inventory status will be readjusted by the system. Figure 5 draws the general idea of the business process.

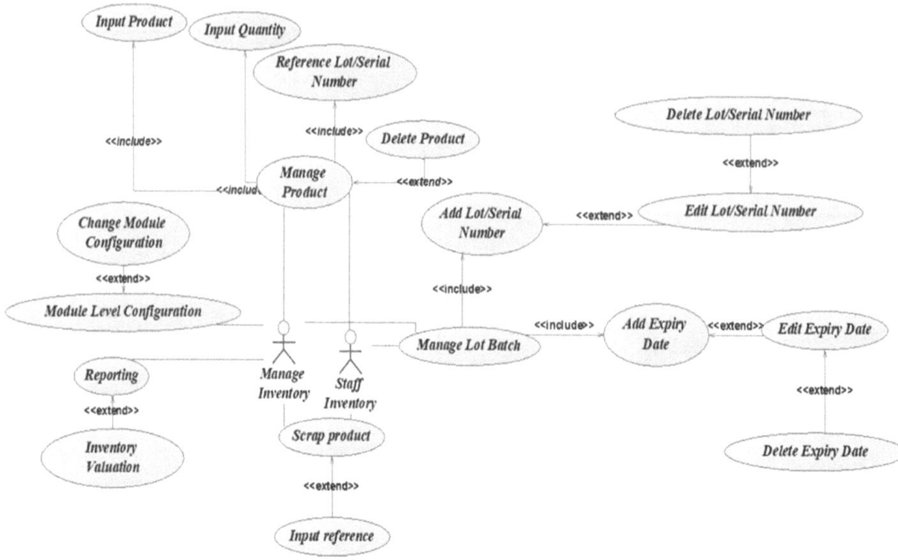

Figure 3. Use case diagram.

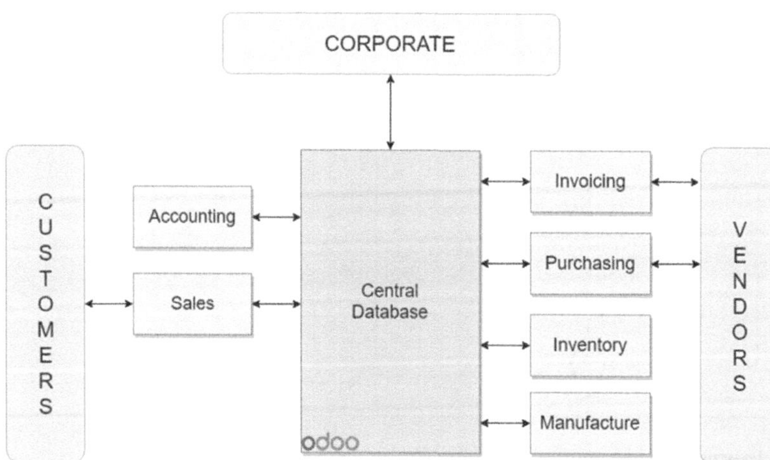

Figure 4. System block diagram.

5 CONCLUSION

The conclusion of this research is the development of ERP system design as a solution for PT. XYZ, using Odoo as the software and QuickStart methodology as the methodology. As an enterprise in the culinary business, raw materials are one of the most important elements in running a daily business due to its perishable nature. Applying the inventory module and customizing it by enabling an item expiration tracker will improve efficiency and reduce risks in inventory handling. By utilizing technology such as ERP, PT. XYZ could benefit in a better managing system with integration, which is why implementing ERP is a viable solution for the current existing problem in PT. XYZ.

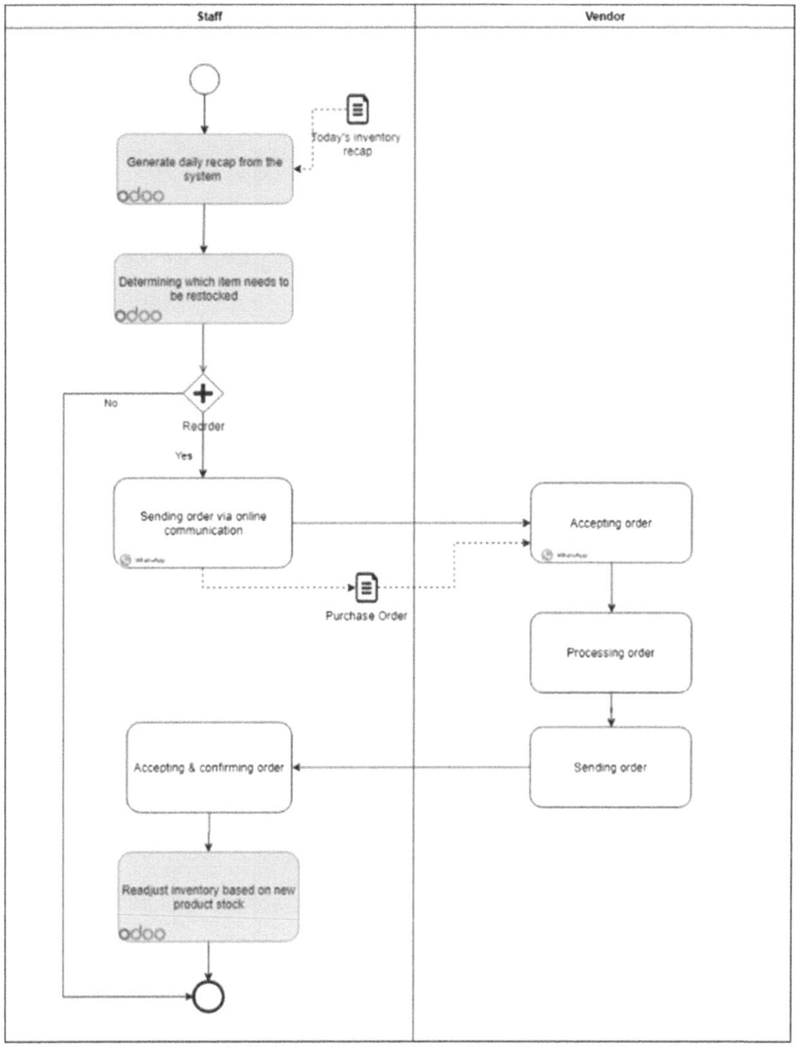

Figure 5. Proposed business process.

REFERENCES

Chan, M. 2018. The Role of Inventory Management in the Food Industry. unleashedsoftware.com,. https://www.unleashedsoftware.com/blog/role-inventory-management-food-industry.

Madanhire, I, & Charles M. Enterprise Resource Planning (ERP) in Improving Operational Efficiency: Case Study. *Procedia CIRP* 40, no. 2001 (2016): 225–29. https://doi.org/10.1016/j.procir.2016.01.108.

Marketeers. 2019. Mencicip Bisnis Restoran Indonesia di 2019, Marketeers.com/mencicip-bisnis-restoran-indonesia-di-2019/.

Marsum, A.W. 2018. Restoran Dan Segala Permasalahannya. *Restoran Dan Segala Permasalahannya*,

Nafianto, C. 2019. Pengembangan Flexible Production Scheduling Debgan Menerapkan Gantt Chart Pada Modul Manufacturing Open Source ERP, 2019, 6–19.

Odoo. 2018. Basics of the QuickStart Methodology, https://www.odoo.com/documentation/user/11.0/getting_started/documentation.html.

Tian, F. & Sean X.X. 2015. How Do Enterprise Resource Planning Systems Affect Firm Risk? Post-Implementation Impact, no. 1 (2015): 1–29.

Synergizing Management, Technology and Innovation in Generating Sustainable and Competitive Business Growth – Hendayani et al (eds)
© 2021 Taylor & Francis Group, London, ISBN 978-0-367-68756-4

User behavior in telemedicine during the pandemic: A text mining analysis

P.K. Sari
Telkom University, Bandung, West Java, Indonesia; Universitas Indonesia, Depok, Indonesia

A. Prasetio
Telkom University, Bandung, West Java, Indonesia

ABSTRACT: The pandemic situation of COVID-19 has been increasing the use of information technology services, including telemedicine. People conduct online consultations with physicians through websites or mobile health applications. One of the popular telemedicine service providers in Indonesia is Alodokter. This paper aims to investigate people's activities to do the online consultation through telemedicine during this condition. We use big-data analytics methods, especially text mining, to analyze health consultation data in the Alodokter website from January to April 2020. The results show there is an increasing trend of online consultation activities related to Corona or COVID-19 topics during March 2020 when the Indonesia government started to limit people's activities outside the home. Unfortunately, this trend did not last the following month, where the number of consultations also declined overall. This research has a practical contribution to telemedicine providers for improving their services and a theoretical contribution to user behavior studies.

1 INTRODUCTION

The World Health Organization (WHO) set COVID-19 as a global pandemic in mid-March 2020. Indonesia confirmed the first case in early March 2020. In the mid-March 2020, the Indonesia government established policies for people to work from home and reduce activities outside the home. They also reduced services to the community, including selective health services. People must postpone their plan to visit health care facilities if it is not an emergency. Therefore, some people utilized telemedicine services to have health care services from physicians. Telemedicine has become essential to help people to continue to get health services without having to meet directly with doctors in the hospital.

Telemedicine refers to provision clinical service like consultation, diagnosis, treatment, and transfer of medical data from one site to another using information and communication technology (Chang 2015; Leung et al. 2018). There are some variances of telemedicine services, like teleconsultation, tele-ECG, tele-USG, tele-dentistry, tele-dermatology, and many more. As other technologies develop, it is important to consider user behavior in using telemedicine. A previous study by Chang (2015) revealed some barriers to telemedicine implementation that can be divided into five categories: behavioral, organizational, technical, economical, and legal. Behavioral barriers included factors such as user's empowerment, acceptance, and fear of being replaced by technology. By understanding user behavior, the telemedicine provider could improve their services and gain more profit.

The existence of a pandemic can trigger changes in behavior in everyday life because people are required to stay at home and only go out of the house for things that are very important. This is indicated to trigger changes in the use of health services, which initially came directly to the servicc place to be more motivated to use telemedicine. The unified theory of acceptance and use of technology (UTAUT) proposed by Venkatesh et al. (Venkatesh et al. 2003) explains that the interest and behavior of using information systems such as telemedicine is influenced by (1) performance expectancy; (2) effort expectancy; (3) social influence; and (4) facilitating conditions. Facilitating conditions are the level of one's perception that the organization and infrastructure are sufficiently available to support the use of the system. The number of Indonesian Internet users that are more than 50% of the population (APJII 2018) make it easier for users to access telemedicine services. It is expected to affect telemedicine use as the need to be at home makes patients search for other things that can be done.

This behavior change can also be influenced by the incessant information about telemedicine carried out by the telemedicine platform and the government. The use of telemedicine, especially by new users, is influenced by public awareness about telemedicine. In the consumer behavior model, the increase in awarenessness in society in general is an impact of the incessant promotion carried out which will ultimately have an impact on the interests and behavior of the use of telemedicine. This promotion is increasingly being carried out by the government to support programs to limit community activities outside the home by collaborating with various telemedicine platforms by the end of March 2020.

In Indonesia, the first pilot project in telemedicine was established in 2012 to implement teleradiology and teleECG (Wiwekoet al. 2016). In the beginning, health care facilities that do not have adequate medical equipment or doctors used telemedicine to have a consultation with more qualified health care facilities in remote locations. Recently, telemedicine not only supports consultation between health care professionals but also directly from patients to doctors. Based on the Alexa site, the most popular telemedicine website in Indonesia is Alodokter.com. Alodokter has been established since 2014 with more than 18 million active users every month. It produces medical information that is accessible to anyone and is compiled by a team of doctors in the Indonesian language. As a telemedicine provider, Alodokter offer some services such as general health articles, online consultation with doctors, ability to make an appointment for medical examination, scheduling medical treatments at the hospital, and health protection.

In the earlier development of telemedicine, studies related to user behavior were mostly seen from the physician's perspective since they are the main actors to acquire expected outcome from telemedicine adoption. Studies were conducted in Korea (Kim & Chang 2007; Rho et al. 2014) and Malaysia (Maarop & Win 2012; Maarop et al. 2011; Zailani et al. 2014). Currently, studies of telemedicine adoption also involved patients' perspective, such as studies in China (Leung et al. 2018) and Indonesia (Mangkunegara et al. 2018). Most of those studies adopted Technology Acceptance Model (TAM) theory to investigate user's intention to use with some additional factors. Research method that is commonly used is to survey users, both physicians and patients.

This paper aims to investigate user behavior of telemedicine service, especially in online consultation activity. Therefore, this paper has the following research question: "How have people utilized telemedicine service during the pandemic season?" From the best of our knowledge, there are still rare previous studies about user behavior of telemedicine from the patient perspective in Indonesia. The previous study by Mangkunegara et al. (Mangkunegara et al. 2018) has different objects and methods than this current study. Therefore, this study is expected to give theoretical and practical contributions.

2 RESEARCH METHODS

To answer research questions, this study uses the text mining method. Text mining process flow (Chakraborty et al. 2013) includes five steps, namely, collect data, text parsing, text filtering, transformation, and text mining. We took the data from the Alodokter website during the COVID-19 period from January to April 2020. The first and second steps, data collection and text parsing processes, are done automatically using the Robotic Process Automation program from UIPath. The program scraps the Alodokter website to get text question data from each user for each topic

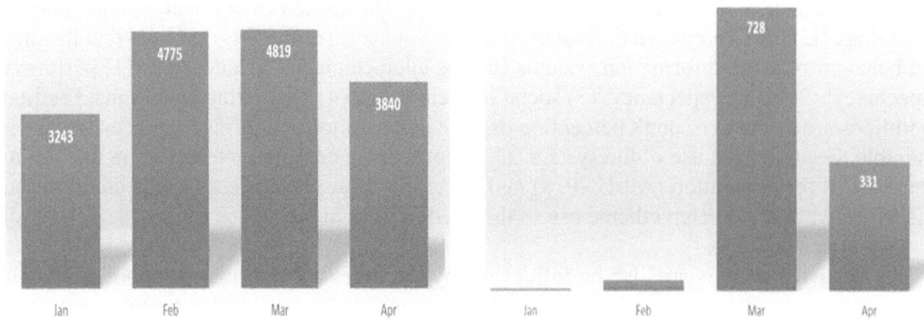

(1a) (1b)

Figure 1. Monthly trends for overall topic (1a) and corona-related topic (1b).

category. It looped until retrieving all questions from each topic category in 2020. Alodokter provides 1,208 topic categories in the list. The data is then processed further with text parsing to retrieve only the needed data and input it to an Excel file. This program's output is a sheet in Excel that consists of 16,677 unique questions with the following columns: Topic URL, Question Title, Name, Date, Time, Question, and Doctor. Text filtering data related to COVID-19 is carried out by filtering using Microsoft Excel to take items containing the words "covid" and "corona," as well as some variations, namely "copid," "corna," "crona," and "korona." From the first text filtering process, we obtained 1,088 unique questions data throughout the data collection period. The text filtering process is then carried out iteratively along with the transformation and text mining processes to extracted words to identify entities and removing stop words. This iterative process uses word cloud maker online tools, namely wordart.com, to convert existing words into algebraic representations of words that appear and turn them into a word cloud. In this process, we delete the words that are not needed to bring up only keywords related to COVID-19. To describe the trend of user activities in Alodokter, we create monthly trend graphic from January to April 2020 based on the number of questions from the initial text filtering of 1,088 unique questions. In addition, the daily trend was explicitly made for March 2020 to see the pattern of the number of questions posted by users during the COVID-19 socialization period.

3 RESULTS

3.1 *Consultation activities trend*

Figure (1a) describes the trend of consultation activities per month for overall topic. It shows increasing activities in February and March with 4,775 and 4,819 questions sequentially. In the following month, the number of questions is increased but not significantly different. Figure (1b) depicts a drastically increasing number of consultations related to COVID-19 in March, where the number of infected patients in Indonesia also increased. Within this time, the Indonesian government announced the first case of COVID-19 and WHO also set it as a global pandemic. It shows that people asked more frequently in this month where they became more aware about COVID-19 issue. However, in April, the activities were decreased even though the number of patients were still increased. It might be caused by more information being available on the Internet, and therefore people did not ask a doctor individually through telemedicine. Comparing to overall data in March, COVID-19 related topics take about 15% from total consultations.

To further analysis, we describe the activity trends per day in March 2020. Figure 2 shows an increase in the number of consultation activities starting from mid-March. This could be due to coinciding with the designation of COVID-19 as a global pandemic by WHO. At that time, the

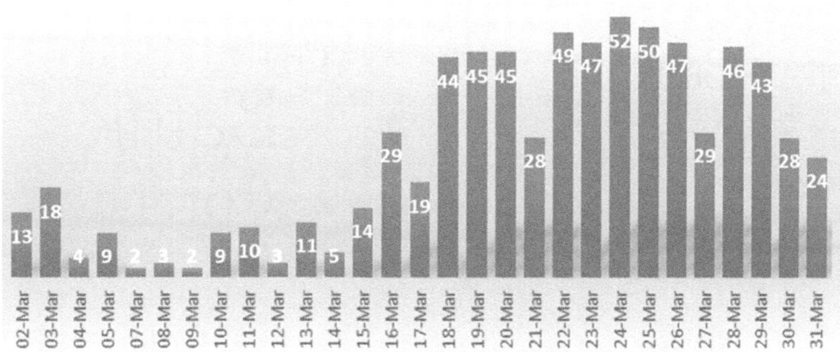

Figure 2. Daily activity trends with corona-related topic in March 2020.

Figure 3. Dominant topics in overall consultations.

government also began implementing work from home policies. It can be a driver for people to do consultation through telemedicine to look for more information related to COVID-19.

3.2 *Dominant topics*

To complement our analysis about consultation activities in telemedicine during pandemic season, we also extract the words and topic categories that are mostly asked by patients. Alodokter provides service in Indonesian language, including online consultation between patient and doctor in its website. Therefore, we present the data of dominant topics and words in the consultation also in the Indonesian language. For this service, patients should register themselves before asking for consultation. After that, the patient will fill a form consisting of title and text fields to save their consultation. In further process, the Alodokter team will tag the question in one or more topics related to the questions and distribute the question to the doctor who already cooperates with them.

For this purpose, we process non-distinct questions to get dominant topics and distinct questions for dominant words. Since one question can be categorized into more than one topic, we consider all topics tagged in as equally important (Figure 3). Describe dominant topics in overall consultations. From a total of 16,677 questions items that had been processed, the highest rank topic for overall questions is Sarscov2, which appears 924 times, followed by medicine (*obat*) with 886 times, children (*anak*) with 723 times, fever (*demam*) with 649 times, and baby (*bayi*) with 611 times. It means that topics related to COVID-19 have dominated online consultation in Alodokter for January to April 2020. The other topics in pediatrics like children and baby also appear frequently in this period. It is relevant with Figure 1a which shows a high number of consultation activities that are dominated by pediatric topics.

In Figure 4, we can see the dominant topics and words in the questions related to COVID-19. There are 1,088 questions obtained from the filter using the COVID-19 keyword. Figure (4a) shows that it is dominated by Sarscov2 topic with a frequency of 770 times appearing in consultations. The other topics are Virus infection (*infeksivirus*) with 248 times, Cough (*batuk*) with 140 times,

(5a) (5b)

Figure 4. Dominant Topics (4a) and words (4b) in consultations with COVID-19 keywords.

Fever (*demam*) with 113 times, Sore throat (*sakittenggorokan*) with 89 times, and Flu with 73 times appearance. It means that most people wanted to know about the symptoms of COVID-19 like cough, sore throat, fever, and flu, that they might have felt. Meanwhile, Figure (4b) shows top-rank words for questions that contain the keyword of "corona" and its variances as explained in the previous section. Those words are Cough (*batuk*) with 768 times of appearance, Corona with 756 times, Sick (*sakit*) with 601 times, Covid with 558 times, and Virus with 538 times. It means that questions related to corona might be asked by people because they felt the main symptom, which is cough, and curious whether it was COVID-19 or not.

4 DISCUSSIONS

The results of the trend in the number of questions indicate an increase in the use of Alodokter during the observation period, especially in March 2020. However, in April there was a decrease in the total number of questions asked by users to the Alodokter website. The increase in the number of user behaviors in asking questions can be influenced by two factors, namely awareness generated by promotions and changes in daily behavior in using technology that is supported by the existence of adequate facilitating conditions. Our data shows that there has been an increase starting mid-March, which is the impact of government policy to limit activities outside. This changing situation has made health service users switch from conventional health services to online services such as Alodokter's telemedicine platform. The cause is triggered if there is availability of facilities for an increasing Internet connection and the necessity to be at home throughout the pandemic.

On the other hand, data in April showed a significant decline in the number of consultation activities. These findings indicate that the increased public awareness generated by the promotion process both from the government and platform owners has less influence on the use of the telemedicine platform. This finding also indicates that the performance expectancy of telemedicine services still needs to be improved because the decline that occurred in April indicates that user loyalty still needs to be improved. This is supported by the finding that the average user only asks one to two questions.

Overall, the questions from patients are dominated by the topic of SarsCov. This is interesting because the number of questions filtered using the Corona or COVID-19 keywords is a much smaller number compared to the total number of questions (around 6.5%). This indicates the existence of real questions related to the SarsCov topic, which is part of the COVID-19 topic but does not contain specific words referring to COVID-19. An example of such a case is about mask availability. Cases like this make the questions not filtered during pre-processing. This is a limitation of the text mining analysis, which was carried out manually in this study.

5 CONCLUSIONS

This study shows there are increment activities in online consultation through the Alodokter website in the beginning of pandemic season. However, it started to decrease in the following months even though the number of cases is still high and health services in hospital are still limited. Questions that were related to COVID-19 have dominated online consultation for these four months. People mostly asked about the symptoms of the disease that might be what they felt or as early detection when they feel it. This research has a theoretical contribution in telemedicine user behavior that shows usage promotion from the government is not really impacting users to use this technology. User loyalty in telemedicine is still low where users are less likely to return to the website and do online consultation again. This study also proposed a new method in telemedicine user behavior inquiry by using text analysis. In a practical contribution, results of this study can give insight for telemedicine providers to improve their service and in considering user loyalty. For further study, it needs to consider the meaning of consultation itself not only from the keywords, since we found some missing item in the text pre-processing.

REFERENCES

APJII. 2018. Penetrasi & Profil Perilaku Pengguna Internet Indonesia 2018. Retrieved from https://www.apjii.or.id/survei.

Chakraborty, G., Pagolu, M., & Garla, S. 2013. *Text Mining and Analysis: Practical Methods, Examples, and Case Studies Using SAS*. USA: SAS Institute Inc.

Chang, H. 2015. Evaluation Framework for Telemedicine Using the Logical Framework Approach and a Fishbone Diagram. *Health Information Research, 21*(4), 230–238.

Kim, J., & Chang, H. 2007. The Model Predicting Telemedicine Adoption by Physicians: Comparison of Theory of Planned Behavior and Technological Acceptance Model. *Health Service Management Review, 1*(1), 1–12.

Leung, R., Guo, H., & Pan, X. 2018. Social Media Users ' Perception of Telemedicine and mHealth in China: Exploratory Study. *JMR MHEALTH AND UHEALTH, 6*(9), 1–8. https://doi.org/10.2196/mhealth.7623

Maarop, N., & Win, K. T. 2012. Understanding the Need of Health Care Providers for Teleconsultation and Technological Attributes in Relation to The Acceptance of Teleconsultation in Malaysia: A Mixed Methods Study. *J Med Syst, 36*, 2881–2892. https://doi.org/10.1007/s10916-011-9766-2

Maarop, N., Win, K. T., Masrom, M., & Singh, S. S. H. 2011. Exploring factors that affect teleconsultation adoption: In the case of Malaysia. In *15th Pacific Asia Conference on Informatioin Systems: Quality Research in Pacific* (pp. 1–12).

Mangkunegara, C. N., Azzahro, F., & Handayani, P. W. 2018. Analysis of Factors Affecting User's Intention in Using Mobile Health Application: A Case Study of Halodoc. In *ICACSIS* (pp. 87–92).

Rho, M. J., Choi, I., & Lee, J. 2014. Predictive factors of telemedicine service acceptance and behavioral intention of physicians. *International Journal of Medical Informatics, 83*(8), 559–571. https://doi.org/10.1016/j.ijmedinf.2014.05.005

Venkatesh, V., Morris, M. G., Davis, G. B., & Davis, F. D. 2003. User Acceptance of Information Technology: Toward a Unified View. *MIS Quarterly, 27*(3), 425–478.

Wiweko, B., Zesario, A., & Agung, P. G. 2016. Overview The Development of Tele Health and Mobile Health Application in Indonesia. In *ICACSIS* (pp. 9–14).

Zailani, S., Gilani, M. S., & Nikbin, D. 2014. Determinants of Telemedicine Acceptance in Selected Public Hospitals in Malaysia: Clinical Perspective. *J Med Syst, 38*(111), 1–12. https://doi.org/10.1007/s10916-014-0111-4

Synergizing Management, Technology and Innovation in Generating Sustainable and Competitive Business Growth – Hendayani et al (eds)
© 2021 Taylor & Francis Group, London, ISBN 978-0-367-68756-4

Brand experience and consumer engagement in MyXL: A consumer's perspective

E. Martini, K. Kusumahadi & A. Permanik
School of Economic and Business, Telkom University, Bandung, West Java, Indonesia

ABSTRACT: Social media are useful for escalating brand experience and engagement to the brand. This study aims to examine the impact of brand experience in MyXL Facebook brandpage toward consumer engagement. The variables that were used in this study include brand experience dimensions, which are perseptual, epistemic, social, and embodied experience. The data were collected from 100 respondent who followed XL Axiata on Facebook, using convenience sampling techniques. Descriptive analysis and multiple regression analysis were used as analytical tools to discuss the result. Results from this research show that respondents have a good perception on brand experience in the MyXL brand page. The study reveals that perceptual and epistemic experiences did not influence consumer engagement, while social and embodied experience influenced consumer engagement. The novelty of this study was using data from a consumer perspective that differed from previous study.

1 INTRODUCTION

The massive quantity of Facebook users was beneficial for the industry to enhance their marketing communication activity. XL Axiata, a telecommunications provider company in Indonesia, is one of the companies that uses social media as a medium for communication between companies and their customers. XL Axiata uses Facebook to inform and interact with its customers for their product promotions and brand events. Also, they use Facebook to convey the latest product information. Companies use the Internet to communicate with customers and business partners (Aaty & Koshy, 2015; Jayasingh & Venkatesh, 2015). Users in Indonesia use the Internet for social media. Data from We Are Social, a data analytic provider, shows that 59% of the Internet users in Indonesia spent their time accessing social media. They spent 3 hours and 26 minutes on daily average to consume social media. Facebook has become a popular social media used by internet users (Schivinski & Dabrowski, 2014).

Consumer engagement on social media on Facebook is the main proposition in this research. Previous research conducted by Tafesse in 2015 and 2016 suggested that consumer engagement can be used by companies to find out the extent of sensory forms, emotional ties, and interactions between companies and consumers on Facebook brand pages. Companies can expect and develop marketing communication strategies by involving consumers. It's also stated that social media can be a means to build consumer engagement. It is hoped that the creation of consumer engagement can generate individual customer motivation to be able to recommend, create word of mouth, exchange and interact with other consumers and companies, and even write a review of information and information-provided company on Facebook social media. Consumer engagement can also capture psychological tendencies and consumer behavior to interact such as giving likes or comments with brands and other consumers on social media (Hutter et al., 2013).

Company efforts to emerge consumer engagement through social media are formed through brand experience on the MyXL Facebook brand page. Brand experience enables consumers to get perceptual experiences such as viewing photos of links from MyXL, audio listening from videos of XL Axiata product promotion forms, or sensory touches on Facebook page links "MyXL." A form of social experience in MyXl brand page also allows consumers to feel the interaction between companies and consumers in the community features. Another experience that can be created though brand page is epistemic experience that allows consumers to get product education and new product notifications on Facebook "MyXL."

1.1 *Social Media and Brand Experience*

Social media Facebook has become very important in the development of business in the current technological era, according to Ashley, Kim, and Tuten (2015). Facebook is a very rich medium with the support of many media such as photos, videos, texts, links, and strategic messages in the form of emotional, functional, experimental, and brand image of a company. Social media give emotional bonds that exist between the company and the customer, and this becomes a big opportunity to fulfill the core goals of the relationship marketing by convincing the customer to purchase companies' products or services (Bowden, 2009; Barhemmati 2015). Social media also encourages consumers to interact with admin and other customers. Better customer participation is beneficial for the firms in encouraging customers to make decisions (Vivek, 2012). Brand experience can be felt directly or indirectly when consumers see advertisements or also when marketers communicate products through online media (Brakus et al., 2009). The brand is very influential on the selection of consumers of a product (Wasesa, 2011). Therefore, the experience of consumers with the brand becomes very important in adding value to the brand itself. According to Brakus et al., brand experience can influence consumer decisions when purchasing products.

1.2 *Consumer Engagement*

Customer management is behavior that allows consumers to make voluntary contributions to the brand of a company, where the contribution is not limited to the transaction (purchase) process (Jaakkola & Alexander, 2015). Contributions given by consumers are feedback, suggestions, or ideas. These contributions can be in the form of WOM (word of mouth), referrals, and others that can increase the company's acquisition, storage, and wallet share (Kajarluoto, 2015). Customer engagements have become an interesting issue for managers and consultants in a variety of different industries and companies. This is evidenced by the large number of posts, blogs, discussion forums, reviews or comments, seminars, and meetings held based on the large number of general searches about the word engagement itself (Sashi, 2012).

According to Tafesse (2016), there are four dimensions of brand experience that affect the consumer engagement model to engage consumers with a company or brand. First, perceptual experience: according to Ashley, Kim, and Tuten (2015), perceptual experience involves a person's sensory components such as vision, audio hearing, and touch that trigger consumer sensory interest. A good company brand page can facilitate great visual and auditory effects with dynamic brand image and sound. Second, social experience: Nysveen et al. (2013) and Schmitt et al. (2014) proposed that social experiences can capture consumer involvement and participation in creating interactive and meaningful experiences. Third, epistemic experience: Lin (2015) and Schmitt et al. (2014) proposed that epistemic experiences involve consumers' cognitive levels as well as the elaboration of new and relevant brand information. Forth, embodied experience: according to Joy and Sherry (2003) and Tafesse (2016), the experience that is realized involves the active physical interaction of consumers with company products.

2 METHOD

This study uses a correlational research method to find the relationship between the independent variable and the dependent variable. The population to be taken is all Facebook account users who follow the PT.XL Axiata page of 100 people with an error tolerance limit of 10%. The research

Table 1. Respondent profile.

Profile	Frequency	Percentage (%)	Profile	Frequency	Percentage (%)
Gender			**Occupation**		
Female	41	41	Student	34	34
Male	59	59	Private employee	27	27
Age			Goverment employee	5	5
<18 year	4	4	Entrepreneur	33	33
18–25 year	41	41	Housewife	1	1
26–30 year	21	21	**Income per month**		
			<2 million	22	22
			2–3,9 million	52	52
			4–5,9 million	21	20
			6–7,9 million	3	3
			>8 million	2	2

instrument used 23 research questions related to brand experience and customer engagement and 5 Likerts scales. The results of processing the validity and reliability of the data used Pearson product moment and Cronbachs Alpha. Data were analyzed using descriptive analysis to see respondents' responses regarding the variables studied, and correlation analysis with multiple linear regression to answer the research questions and hypotheses. The hypothesis proposed in this study is as follows:

H1: Perceptual experience influences consumer engagement.
H2: Social experience influences consumer engagement.
H3: Epistemic experience influences consumer engagement.
H4: Embodied experience influences consumer engagement.

3 RESULT

The results of data processing with SPSS 21 from a total of 100 research respondents showed the profile of research respondents and the responses of Facebook account followers MyXL for the brand experience and customer engagement dimensions that they felt when interacting in the old Facebook MyXL. Profile of respondents is illustrated in Table 1.

Based on Table 1, respondents in this research were dominated by age between 18–25 years old, their main job is as student and self-employed, with monthly earnings between 2–3,9 million per month.

3.1 *Hypotheses Testing*

Table 2 shows the results of data processing using the t-test based on decision making if T-count > T-table then H0 is rejected. The T-table value as a reference is 1.661, and the conclusions from the results of the hypothesis test can be explained in Table 3.

Based on data processing, the dimensions of social experience and embodied experience influence consumer engagement on Facebook MyXL, while the dimensions of perceptual and epistemic experience do not affect consumer engagement on Facebook MyXL. This shows that the content posted on the MyXL Facebook page that has content based on groups or communities as well as content that contains interactive games is more able to foster follower engagement with XL Axiata. Conversely, content that contains photos or videos, as well as content that contains XL product information, does not foster follower engagement.

The results of data processing showed an F-count value of 42,237 with a significance of 0,000. Thus, simultaneously or together F-count (42,237) > F-table (3,090) with Sig. (0,000) < 0.005. This

Table 2. T-test hypothesis.

Hypothesis	T-count	T-table	Decision	Summary
X1 → Y	0.813	1.661	H0 accepted	Perceptual experience did not influence consumer engagement
X2 → Y	3.375	1.661	H0 rejected	Social experience influences consumer engagement
X3 → Y	0.546	1.661	H0 accepted	Epistemic experience did not influence consumer engagement
X4 → Y	7.547	1.661	H0 rejected	Embodied experience influences consumer engagement

shows that there is a significant influence between brand experiences on consumer engagement. The coefficient of determination is 0.593 if presented at 59.3%. This means that consumer engagement on Facebook MyXL is influenced by 59.3% of brand experience dimension, while the effect of another 40.7% is influenced by other variables that have not been examined in this study. Based on the ß value of ANOVA, the equation of the research model is:

$$Y = 0{,}266 + 0{,}078\ X_1 + 0{,}247\ X_2 - 0{,}034\ X_3 + 0{,}361\ X_4 \quad (1)$$

This study has a different result from the previous study that had been conducted by Tafesse (2016). This different result can be caused by the differences of the methods that were used in this study. The characteristics from followers on social media in Indonesia also can result in this differentiation.

4 CONCLUSION

Consumer engagement in MyXL is influenced by social and embodied experience. This means that posts that contain content with social experiences and embodied experiences were likely to increase the willingness from consumers to like and share the posts. The magnitude of the influence of the brand experience dimension to customer engagement on Facebook MyXL was 59.3%. This result is beneficial for companies to consider managing their Facebook social media with more brand posts that contain social and embodied content on Facebook.

REFERENCES

Aaty, A., dan Koshy, S. 2015. The Use of Facebook as a Consumer Engagement Tool by Newspapers in the UAE: An Exploratory Study. *Journal of Media and Mass Communication*, 1(2), 90–96.

Alexander, M., & Jaakkola, E. 2015. Customer engagement and value co-creation. *Book chapter Customer Engagement*. Routledge Taylor & Francis Group, Abingdon, pp. 3–20. ISBN 9781138847385.

Ashley, K. & Tuten, T. 2015. Creative Strategies in Social Media Marketing: An Exploratory Study of Branded Social Content and Consumer Engagement. *Psychology and Marketing*, 32(1), 15–27.

Barhemmati, N., & Ahmad, A. 2015. Effects of social network marketing (SNM) on consumer purchase behavior through customer engagement. *Journal of Advanced Management Science* Vol, 3(4).

Bowden, J. L. H. 2009. The Process of Customer Engagement: A Conceptual Framework. *Journal of Marketing Theory and Practice*, 17(1), 63–74.

Brakus, J.J., et al. 2009. Brand Experience: What Is It? How Is It Measured? Does It Affect Loyalty? *Journal of Marketing*. 73(3), 52–68.

Hutter, K., Hautz, J., Dennhardt, S., & Füller, J. 2013. The Impact of User Interactions in Social Media on Brand Awareness and Purchase Intention: The Case of MINI on Facebook. *Journal of Product & Brand Management*, 22(5): 342–351.

Jayasingh, S., & Venkantesh, R. 2015. Consumer Engagement Factors in Facebook Brand Pages. *Asian Social Science*, 11(26), 19–29.

Joy, A. and Sherry, J.F. 2003. Speaking of Art as Embodied Imagination: A Multisensory Approach to Understanding Aesthetic Experience. *Journal of Consumer Research*, Vol. 30 No. 2, pp. 259–282.

Karjaluoto, H., Munnukka, J., & Tiensuu, S. 201). The Effects of Brand Engagement in Social Media on Share of Wallet. *Proceedings of the 28th Bled eConference*: e-WellBeing.

Lin, Y.H. 2015. Innovative Brand Experience's Influence on Brand Equity and Brand Satisfaction. *Journal of Business Research*, Vol. 68 No. 11, pp. 2254–2259.

Nysveen, H., Pedersen, P.E. and Skard, S. 2013. Brand Experience in Service Organizations: Exploring the Individual Effects of Brand Experience Dimensions. *Journal of Brand Management*, Vol. 20 No. 5, pp. 404–425.

Sashi, C.M. 2012. Customer Engagement, Buyer-seller Relationships, and Social Media. *Management Decision*, Vol. 50 No. 2, pp. 253–272. https://doi.org/10.1108/00251741211203551.

Schmitt, B.H., Brakus, J.J. and Zarantonello, L. 2014. The Current State and Future of Brand Experience. *Journal of Brand Management*, Vol. 21 No. 9, pp. 727–733.

Tafesse, W. 2015. Content Strategies and Audience Response on Facebook Brand Pages. *Marketing Intelligence and Planning*, 33(6), 927–943.

Tafesse, W. 2016. An Experiental Model of Consumer Engagement in Social Media. *Journal of Product and Brand Management*. 25(5), 424–434.

Vivek, S. D., Beatty, S. E., & Morgan, R. M. 2012. Customer Engagement: Exploring Customer Relationships beyond Purchase. *Journal of Marketing Theory and Practice*, 20(2), 122–146.

Wasesa, S. A. 2011. Political Branding & Public Relations. Jakarta: Gramedia Pustaka Utama.

Synergizing Management, Technology and Innovation in Generating Sustainable and Competitive Business Growth – Hendayani et al (eds)
 ISBN 978-0-367-68756-4

The effect of liquidity risk on banking performance

T.T. Gustyana
Universitas Pendidikan Indonesia, Bandung, Jawa Barat, Indonesia
Telkom University, Bandung, West Java, Indonesia

A. Jumran
Telkom University, Bandung, West Java, Indonesia

ABSTRACT: The banks' role in promoting the country's economy is important. The assessments of financial performance and liquidity risk are the internal factors in measuring banking performance. The liquidity risk measure by several factors, which are liquidity gap, cash, deposits, NPLs, and Bank Indonesia reference interest rates. Meanwhile, bank performances measure by earnings before tax. This research used a quantitative approach. The research objects are foreign banks registered in Indonesia during the 2014–2018 period. The sampling technique used purposive sampling following the criteria specified in this study. The data analysis technique used the multiple linear regression method. This research methodology used the F test, the determination coefficient, and partial testing done by the t-test. Based on the partial test results, NPL and deposits affect the EBT, while cash, liquidity gap, and interest rates did not affect the EBT. The simultaneous test results show all variables simultaneously influenced EBT.

1 INTRODUCTION

Kansil et al. (2017) stated that the banking sector is a strict sector regulated by Bank Indonesia because it had operational activities that involved many parties in the community. Therefore, a good understanding and bank management encourage a good financial system, and the banking process assessment can be done by looking at its financial performance.

According to Ramadanti and Meiranto (2015), measuring bank performance could be done from various sides, one of them is bank profitability. The bank profitability level influenced by external or internal factors, and one of the internal factors is liquidity. If the bank cannot fulfill its obligations, such as when the bank is unable to meet the funds used by depositors, it will result in bank liquidity in the form of liquidity risk. According to the Indonesian Bankers Association (2016), liquidity risk is the ability of banks to meet their obligations from cash flow funding sources, liquid repo assets without disrupting the financial activities of a bank.

The research purposes are to find out and analyze how much influence the liquidity risk has on the performance of a bank. According to previous research, this research will use liquidity gap, cash, deposits, NPL, and the Bank Indonesia reference interest rate as measurement of liquidity risk and earnings before tax (EBT) as a benchmark for bank performance.

2 LITERATURE REVIEW

Table 1. Variable in the study.

Variable	Definition
Liquidity Gap	According to Arif and Anees (2012), one of the main factors of liquidity risk is the maturity mismatch between assets and liabilities. In this study, the liquidity gap data obtained the difference between the value of the matured assets and the due obligations at the time studied.
Cash	According to Utami (2015), banks must be able to predict cash inflow and cash outflow every day. Cash is needed to maintain company liquidity. In this study, the cash data obtained from the amount of cash in the financial position statement on the asset side.
Deposit	According to Arif and Anees (2012), most banking operations are performed through deposits. In this study, the deposit data obtained from the amount of deposit without classification.
NPL	Ramadanti and Meiranto (2015) stated that if the NPL rate of a bank is high, the payment of credit received will be hampered, which could lead to liquidity risk. In this study, the NPL value was obtained based on the NPL formula, which are $NPL = (bad\ credit)/(total\ credit) \times 100\%$
Bank Indonesia reference interest rate	Based on research conducted by Tiara and Mayasari (2017) in measuring the effect of liquidity risk, the reference interest rate is a benchmark to measure how much influence it has in influencing bank performance. In this study the data used comes from the official website of Bank Indonesia with the BI Rate method and seven days repo rate.

3 DATA AND METHODOLOGY

The data used in this study were from 8 foreign banks in Indonesia in accordance with predetermined sample criteria using the purposive sampling method and using multiple linear analysis to determine how much influence the research variables had.

4 RESULTS

4.1 *Multicollinearity test*

Table 2. Multicollinearity test.

	Collinearity Statistics	
Model	Tolerance	VIF
Constant		
Cash	0.351	2.849
Deposit	0.483	2.068
Liquidity Gap	0.880	1.136
NPL	0.559	1.789
Reference Interest Rate	0.897	1.115

Source: Research data

Based on the results of the classical assumption test, there were no independent variables that correlate. These results are shown by the results of the tolerance calculation which shows the number that there was no value less than 0.10 and there were no independent variables that produce a number of more than 10.

4.1.1 *Autocorrelation test*

Table 3. Autocorrelation test (Lagrange Multiplier).

Model	Sig
(constant)	0.675
Ln cash	0.264
Ln deposit	0.598
Ln liquidity gap	0.369
Ln NPL	0.381
Ln BI reference rate	0.043
Unstandardized Residual	0.339

Source: Research data

Based on the autocorrelation test results using the Lagrange multiplier method the significance value of unstandardized residuals was equal to 0.339 smaller than the probability value of 0.05. It can be concluded that there was no autocorrelation in this study.

4.1.2 *Heteroscedasticity test*

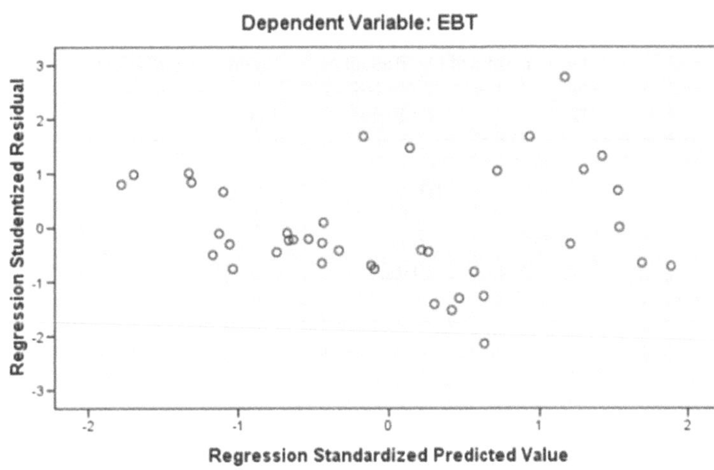

Figure 1. Heteroscedasticity test.

Based on the results of the analysis using scatterplots, the points spread above and below the 0 axis Y line randomly. Therefore, there was no heteroscedasticity in the regression model.

4.2 *Normality test*

Based on the analysis using the normal probability plot, the points coincide around the lines or diagonals. Therefore, the data in this study were normal distribution.

4.2.1 *Multiple linear analysis*

Based on the results of the tests conducted, the regression equation in this study was formulated as:

$$\begin{aligned}\text{EBT} = {} & 1.859\ \text{cash} + 0.022\ \text{deposit} - 0.006\ \text{liquidity gap} - 3.737^{13}\ \text{NPL} \\ & - 2.125^{13}\ \text{BI reference interest rate}\end{aligned}$$

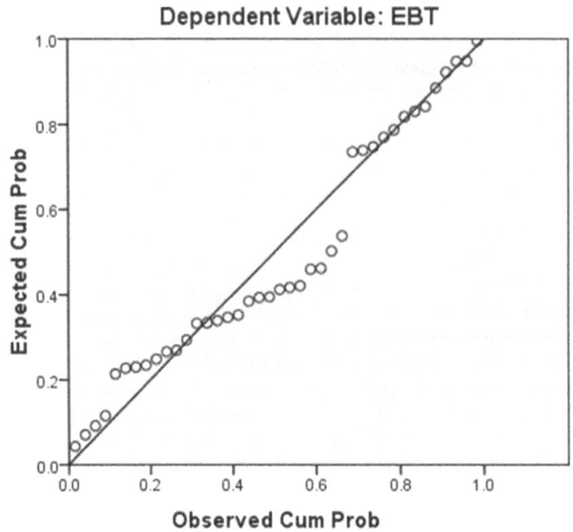

Figure 2. Normality test.

Table 4. Multiple linear analysis.

	Unstandardized Coefficient		Standard Coefficients		
Model	B	Std Error	Beta	T	Sig
1 (Constant)	2.489E12	9.666E11		2.575	0.015
Cash	−0.006	0.021	−0.039	−0.274	0.786
Deposito	1.859	1.647	0.253	1.129	0.267
Liquidity Gap	0.022	0.009	0.442	2.311	0.027
NPL	−3.737E13	1.036E13	−0.641	−3.608	0.001
Reference Interest Rate	−2.125E13	1.485E13	−0.201	−1.431	0.161

Source: Research data

4.2.2 *T test*

Table 5. Hypothesis results.

No	Hypothesis	Result
H1	There is an effect of liquidity gap on EBT in foreign banks registered with OJK in the 2014–2018 period.	Rejected
H2	There is an effect of cash on EBT in foreign banks registered with OJK in the 2014–2018 period.	Rejected
H3	There is an effect of deposit on EBT in foreign banks registered with OJK in the 2014–2018 period.	Approved
H4	There is an effect of NPL on EBT in foreign banks registered with OJK in the 2014–2018 period.	Approved
H5	There is an effect of Bank Indonesia reference interest rate on EBT in foreign banks registered with OJK in the 2014–2018 period.	Rejected

Based on the results of the study, the independent variables that significantly influence EBT were deposits and NPLs. Meanwhile, the three independent variables that have no partial effect on EBT were liquidity gap, cash, and the reference interest rate.

4.2.3 *F test*

Table 6. F test.

Model	Sum of Squares	df	Mean Square	F	Sig
Regression	2.757E25	5	5.514E24	4.526	0.003a
Residual	4.142E25	34	1.218E24		
Total	6.899E25	39			

Source: Research data

The F test results showed a value of 4,526 with a significance value of 0.003. The calculated F value of 4,526 is greater than the F table of 2.64 which means that the alternative hypothesis is accepted.

4.2.4 *Coefficient of determination*

Table 7. Coefficient of determination.

Model	R	R Square	Adjusted R Square	Std Error of the Estimate
1	0.632a	0.400	0.311	1.104E12

Source: Research data

Based on the results of the coefficient of determination, 31% of EBT as a dependent variable on foreign banks in Indonesia explained by independent variations, namely cash, liquidity gap, deposits, NPLs, and interest rates. Meanwhile, 69% of EBT explained by other factors.

5 CONCLUSION

Based on the test results, in this study, it can be concluded that partially, the independent variables that affect the performance of banks proxied by EBT are deposit and NPL variables. Deposits significantly affect EBT. Meanwhile, NPL significantly affects EBT. Furthermore, based on the simultaneous test, it was concluded that in this study, the independent variables simultaneously influence EBT.

REFERENCES

Arif, A. & Anees, A. N., 2012. Liquidity Risk and Performance of Banking System. *Journal of Financial Regulation and Compliance,* 20(2), pp. 182–195.

Ikatan Bankir Indonesia, 2016. *Manajemen Risiko 2.* Jakarta Pusat: PT Gramedia Pustaka Utama.

Kansil, D., Murni, S. & Tulung, J. E., 2017. Pengaruh Risiko Perbankan terhadap Kinerja Keuangan tahun 2013–2015 (Bank Pembangunan Daerah se-Indonesia). *Jurnal Riset Eknomi, Manajemen, Bisnis, dan Akuntansi,* pp. 3508–3517.

Ramadanti, F. & Meianto, W., 2014. Analisis Pengaruh Risiko Likuiditas terhadap Profitabilitas Perusahaan Perbankan di Indonesia. *Dipenegoro Journal of Accounting,* 4(2), pp. 1–10.

Tiara & Mayasari, M., 2017. Pengaruh Risiko Likuiditas dan Suku Bunga Bank Indonesia terhadap Proditabilitas Perbankan. *Jurnal Ilmiah Akuntansi dan Keuangan,* 3(2), pp. 86–97.

Utami, N., 2018. Pengaruh Risiko Likuditias dan Leverage terhadap Kinerja Bank yang terdaftar di Bursa Efek Indonesia Periode 2010–2015. *Jurnal Akuntasnsi, Auditing, dan Keuangan: BALANCE,* 15(2), pp. 189–209.

Synergizing Management, Technology and Innovation in Generating Sustainable and Competitive Business Growth – Hendayani et al (eds)
© 2021 Taylor & Francis Group, London, ISBN 978-0-367-68756-4

Factors influencing personal financial management behavior on students

A.S. Dewi, I. Yunita & C.M. Natasya
Faculty of Economics and Bussiness, Telkom University, Bandung, West Java, Indonesia

ABSTRACT: This research is focused on the students in the city of Jakarta to analyze the effect of financial literacy, financial attitudes, and parental income on personal financial management behavior in students both partially and simultaneously. The technique carried out to collect the data was using a questionnaire distributed to 400 students in the city of Jakarta. The statistical method used is the t test and F test. This study also used multiple linear regression analysis. The results of the study stated that there is a significant influence among financial literacy, financial attitudes, and parental income to personal financial management behavior. Individually, financial literacy and financial attitudes have a significant influence on personal financial management behavior. However, parental income does not have a significant influence on personal financial management behavior of students in the city of Jakarta.

1 INTRODUCTION

Students are a population with an age group of 15–29 years old, which is the largest age composition in Indonesia, amounting to 67.7% (Databoks 2018). Many students behave consumptively to meet their needs to be able to look attractive (Ainunnisa 2016). Consumptive behavior in these students is in accordance with the statement of the Financial Services Authority (OJK) that Indonesian people are increasingly consumptive and are starting to abandon their habit of saving. This is potrayed on the decline in Marginal Propensity to Save (MPS) and the increase in Marginal Prosperity to Consume (MPC) (Jatmiko 2015). This consumptive behavior can be triggered by students' finances. A member of the Board of Commissioners of the Financial Services Authority for Consumer Education and Protection, Tirta Segara said that understanding of finance and financial literacy in the younger generation is still low (Rahayu 2018). So it can be said that the importance of financial management is still not considered by students (Thionita 2019).

Mien and Thao (2015) explained the importance of responsibility related to personal financial management behavior in young people. Some previous studies have produced several factors that can influence personal financial management behavior. Mien and Thao (2015), Herdijono and Damanik (2016), Syafitri and Santi (2017), Yushita (2017), and Amilia et al. (2018) stated that financial literacy, financial attitudes, and parental income can significantly influence personal financial management behavior

According to Dwiastanti (2017), financial literacy has a very important role because financial literacy can affect the use of money such as income and financial management and in terms of decision making that can help us to manage our finances, such as decisions investment, saving money for the future, and others. Humaira and Sagoro (2018) explained that the financial attitude can be intrepreted as an income and an assessment of personal finance that is applied to the attitude. The Financial Services Authority said that a wise financial attitude and behavior can create better financial security in a variety of financial conditions (Financial Services Authority 2017). Putri and Rahmi (2019) stated that parental income is the entire income received by parents either in the form of money or goods that come from work or businesses to meet family needs. Students with

Table 1. Research characteristics.

No.	Research Characteristics	Type
1.	Research methods	Quantitative method
2.	Research purposes	Causal research
3.	Investigation type	Verificative
4.	Execution time	Cross sectional
5.	Author involvement	Not intervening data
6.	Unit of analysis	Individual

low-income parents rarely leave their monthly allowance, so to shape personal financial behavior, parental income is needed.

In the midst of a low level of financial literacy, financial attitudes that are not accompanied by sufficient knowledge, as well as allowance that still relies on parental income, can make personal financial management behavior owned by students quite alarming. This needs attention, especially as some previous studies related to financial literacy, financial attitudes and parental income did not make the city of Jakarta as the object of their studies. Because of differences in geographic and demographic factors, the case study of the problem in the city of Jakarta needs to be examined. According to these problems, the authors set the title of this research as "Analysis Factors Influencing Personal Financial Management Behavior on Students"

2 OBJECTIVES

The objectives of this study are as follows: (1) to understand the significant influence among financial literacy, financial attitudes, and parental income to personal financial management behavior, (2) to find out the significant influence among financial literacy and personal financial management behavior, (3) to find out the significant influence among financial attitudes and personal financial management behavior, (4) to determine the significant influence among parental income and personal financial management behavior.

3 RESEARCH METHODOLOGY

This research used a questionnaire as a data collection technique in a form of an ordinal scale, while the measurement scale used a Likert scale. This study drew respondents by the population of students in the city of Jakarta, which totaled 493,809 people (The Ministry of Research, Technology, and Higher Education 2020). By using the *Slovin* formula, a sample of 400 students was obtained.

4 RESULTS AND RESEARCH ANALYSIS

4.1 *Classic assumption test*

4.1.1 *Normality test*

The normality test uses the Kolmogorov-Smirnov test. The result is the Asymp value. Sig. (2-tailed) or a significance value >0.05, which is 0.176. So the conclusion can be drawn that the normality test is met because 0.176 >0.05.

4.1.2 *Multicollinearity test*

Based on these test results, it can be seen that the tolerance value for the three independent variables, namely financial literacy, financial attitudes, and parental income >0.1 and the VIF value for the

Table 2. Characteristics of respondents.

Criteria	Subcriteria	Number of respondents	Percentage
Age	12–16 years	2	0.5%
	17–25 years	389	97.2%
	26–35 years	9	2.3%
Gender	Male	143	35.75%
	Female	257	64.25%
Last education	SMA/Equal	55	13.75%
	D1	53	13.25%
	D2	55	13.75%
	D3	54	13.5%
	D4	60	15%
	S1	71	16.25%
	S2	52	14.5%
Job status	Working	74	18.5%
	Not working	326	81.5%

Source: Data processed, 2020

Table 3. Multicollinearity test.

Coefficients[a]

Model		Unstandardized coefficients		Standardized coefficients			Collinearity statistics	
		B	Std. Error	Beta	t	Sig.	Tolerance	VIF
1	(Constant)	3.060	1.746		1.753	.080		
	Financial literacy	.594	.041	.633	14.349	.000	.659	1.518
	Financial attitudes	.122	.050	.110	2.447	.015	.640	1.563
	Parental income	.114	.142	.029	.805	.421	.960	1.042

a. Dependent variable: Personal financial management behavior
Source: Data processed, 2020

three independent variables <10. So it can be concluded that the multicollinearity test is fulfilled because the tolerance value of all three variables >0.1 and the VIF value of all three variables <10.

4.2 *Multiple linear regression analysis*

Table 4 shows the results that the constants (a) get results of 3.060 and the regression coefficient (b) for financial literacy (X1) is 0.594, financial attitude (X2) is 0.122, and parental income (X3) is 0.114. So we get the multiple linear regression equation as follows.

$$Y = a + b1X1 + b2X2 + b3X3 \tag{1}$$

$$Y = 3.060 + 0.594X1 + 0.122X2 + 0.114X3 \tag{2}$$

All three variables have positive regression coefficient values. This shows a direct relationship among financial literacy, financial attitudes, parental income, and personal financial management behavior.

Table 4. Multiple linear regression analysis test results.

Coefficients[a]						
		Unstandardized coefficients		Standardized coefficients		
Model		B	Std. Error	Beta	t	Sig.
1	(Constant)	3.060	1.746		1.753	.080
	Financial literacy	.594	.114	.633	14.349	.000
	Financial attitudes	.122	.041	.110	2.447	.015
	Parental income	.050	.142	.029	.805	.421

a. Dependent variable: Personal financial management behavior
Source: Data processed, 2020

Table 5. Significant simultaneous test results (F test).

ANOVA[a]						
Model		Sum of squares	df	Mean square	F	Sig.
1	Regression	6403.982	3	2134.661	127.965	.000[b]
	Residual	6605.915	396	16.682		
	Total	13009.898	399			

a. Dependent variable: Personal financial management behavior
b. Predictors: (Constant), Parental income, financial literacy, financial attitudes
Source: Data processed, 2020

Table 6. Significant partial test results (t test).

Coefficients[a]						
		Unstandardized coefficients		Standardized coefficients		
Model		B	Std. Error	Beta	t	Sig.
1	(Constant)	3.060	1.746		1.753	.080
	Financial literacy	.594	.041	.633	14.349	.000
	Financial attitudes	.122	.050	.110	2.447	.015
	Parental income	.114	.142	.029	.805	.421

a. Dependent variable: Personal financial management behavior
Source: Data processed, 2020

4.3 *F test*

Table 5 shows that the calculated F value obtained is 127.965. Thus, the value of F calculated > F table (127.965 > 2.627), so H0 is rejected and H1 is accepted. It can be concluded that there is a significant influence among financial literacy, financial attitudes, and parental income to personal financial management behavior on students in the city of Jakarta.

Table 7. Determination coefficient test results.

Model Summary				
Model	R	R square	Adjusted R square	Std. error of the estimate
1	.702[a]	.492	.488	4.08431

a. Predictors: (Constant), Parental income, financial literacy, financial attitudes
Source: Data processed, 2020

4.4 *T test*

According to Table 6, it can be concluded as follows.

1. Financial literacy variable has a value of t calculated > t table (14.349 > 1.966) and a significant value < 0.05 (0,000 < 0.05), so H0 is rejected and H1 is accepted. That means, there is a significant influence among financial literacy and personal financial management behavior on students in the city of Jakarta
2. Variable financial attitude has a value of t calculated > t table (2.447 > 1.966) and a significant value < 0.05 (0.015 < 0.05), so H0 is rejected and H1 is accepted. That means there is a significant influence among financial attitudes and personal financial management behavior on students in the city of Jakarta
3. Parental income variable has a value of t calculated < t table (0.805 < 1.966) and a significant value > 0.05 (0.421 > 0.05), so H0 is accepted and H1 is rejected. That means there is no significant influence among parental income and personal financial management behavior on students in the city of Jakarta.

4.5 *Determination coefficient test*

Table 7 shows that the value of the correlation coefficient or R obtained is equal to 0.702 and the value of the coefficient of determination or R square is equal to 0.492. Furthermore, the value of R square (R2) will be used to calculate the coefficient of determination as follows.

$$\mathrm{Kd} = \mathrm{R2} \times 100\%$$

$$\mathrm{Kd} = 0.492 \times 100\%$$

$$\mathrm{KD} = 49.2\%$$

From the calculation above, the coefficient of determination obtained by 49.2%. So it means that the variables of financial literacy, financial attitudes, and parental income provide an effect of 49.2% on the behavior of personal financial management of students in the city of Jakarta.

5 CONCLUSION

This study was conducted to determine the effect of financial literacy, financial attitudes, and parental income on personal financial management behavior. Based on the test results, conclusions can be drawn as follows.

1. There is a significant influence among financial literacy, financial attitudes, and parental income to personal financial management behavior on students in the city of Jakarta.
2. There is a significant influence among financial literacy and personal financial management behavior on students in the city of Jakarta.

3. There is a significant influence among financial attitudes and personal financial management behavior on students in the city of Jakarta.
4. There is no significant influence among parental income and personal financial management behavior on students in the city of Jakarta.

REFERENCES

Ainunnisa, L. 2016. Perilaku Konsumtif Mahasiswa. *Kompasiana.com* [online]. Tersedia: https://www.kompasiana.com/lanainunnisa/58496b97149373f2100be561/perilaku-konsumtif-mahasiswa?page=all [Accessed 22 Desember 2019]

Amilia, S., Bulan, T. P. L., & Rizal, M. 2018. Pengaruh Melek Finansial, Sosialisasi Orang Tua, dan Teman Sebaya Terhadap Perilaku Menabung Mahasiswa Bidik Misi Fakultas Ekonomi Universitas Samudra. *Jurnal Samudra Ekonomika,* Vol. 2 No. 2, pp. 97–107. Diambil dari: https://www.researchgate.net/

Databoks. 2018. 2020, Penduduk Indonesia Diproyeksi Mencapai 271 Juta Jiwa. *Databoks.katadata.co.id* [online]. Tersedia: https://databoks.katadata.co.id/datapublish/2018/03/06/2020-penduduk-indonesia-diproyeksi-mencapai-271-juta-jiwa [Accessed 20 Desember 2019]

Dwiastanti, A. 2017. Analysis of financial knowledge and financial attitude on locus of control and financial management behavior. *Management and Business Review*, Vol. 1 No. 1, pp. 1–8. Doi: 10.1287/mksc.2017.1032

Financial Services Authority. 2017. Strategi Nasional Literasi Keuangan Indonesia (Revisit 2017). Jakarta: OJK.

Herdijono, I., & Damanik, L. A. 2016. Pengaruh Financial Attitude, Financial Knowledge, Parental Income Terhadap Financial Management Behavior. *Jurnal Manajemen Teori dan Terapan,* Vol. 9 No. 3, pp. 226–241. Diambil dari: https://e-journal.unair.ac.id/

Humaira, I., & Sagoro, E. M. 2018. Pengaruh Pengetahuan Keuangan, Sikap Keuangan, dan Kepribadian Terhadap Perilaku Manajemen Keuangan pada Pelaku UMKM Sentra Kerajinan Batik Kabupaten Bantul. *Jurnal Nominal, Barometer Riset Akuntansi dan Manajemen,* Vol.7 No.1, pp. 96–110. Diambil dari: https://journal.uny.ac.id/

Jatmiko, B. P. 2015. OJK: Orang Indonesia Makin Konsumtif. *Kompas.com* [online]. Tersedia: https://money.kompas.com/read/2015/08/08/110746226/OJK.Orang.Indonesia.Makin.Konsumtif [Accessed 22 Desember 2019]

Mien, N. T. N., & Thao, T, P. 2015. Factors Affecting Personal Financial Management Behaviors: Evidence from Vietnam. *Proceeding of the Second Asia-Pacific Conference on Global Business, Economics, Finance, and Social Sciences (AP15Vietnam Conference),* 10–12. Diambil dari: http://globalbizresearch.org/

Ministry of Research, Technology, and Higher Education. 2020. Grafik Jumlah Mahasiswa Aktif Berdasarkan Jenis Kelamin. *PDDIKTI* [online]. Tersedia: https://forlap.ristekdikti.go.id/ [Accessed 13 Februari 2020]

Putri, H. N., & Rahmi, E. 2019. Pengaruh Pendapatan Orang Tua Terhadap Perilaku Keuangan Mahasiswa Pendidikan Ekonomi FE UNP. *Jurnal Ecogen* Vol. 2 No.3, pp. 315–326. Doi: 103.216.87.80

Rahayu, Y. A. 2018. OJK Sebut Generasi Milenial Rentan Terkena Masalah Keuangan. *Merdeka.com* [online] Tersedia: https://www.merdeka.com/uang/ojk-sebut-generasi-milenial-rentan-terkena-masalah-keuangan.html [Accessed 8 Januari 2020]

Syafitri, T. M., & Santi, F. 2017. Dampak Sikap Terhadap Uang pada Perilaku Pengelolaan Keungan Pribadi dengan Pengendalian Diri Sebagai Variabel Pemoderasian. *Personal Financial Management Journal.* Diambil dari: https://www.academia.edu/

Thionita, V. 2019. Kesalahan Mengelola Keuangan Mahasiswa. *Finansialku.com* [online]. Tersedia: https://www.finansialku.com/kesalahan-mengelola-keuangan-mahasiswa/ [Accessed 20 Desember 2019]

Yushita, A. N. 2017. Pentingnya Literasi Keuangan Bagi Pengelolaan Keuangan Pribadi. *Jurnal Nominal, Barometer Riset Akuntasi dan Manajemen*, Vol.6 No.1, pp 11–26. Diambil dari: https://journal.uny.ac.id/

Synergizing Management, Technology and Innovation in Generating Sustainable and Competitive Business Growth – Hendayani et al (eds)
 ISBN 978-0-367-68756-4

Valuation of animal feed company in Indonesia using the FCFF and relative valuation method

B. Susanto & D. Rahadian
Faculty of Economics and Business, Telkom University, Bandung, West Java, Indonesia

ABSTRACT: This study aims to determine intrinsic value of stock in companies listed on the Indonesia Stock Exchange in animal feed subsector in 2018 with the approach of free cash flow to firm (FCFF) and relative valuation based on price earnings ratio (PER) and price book value (PBV). The discounted cash flow (DCF)-FCFF valuation results show that the Charoen Phokpand Indonesia (CPIN) in pessimistic and moderate scenarios is overvalued, while in optimistic scenarios it is undervalued. Japfa Comfeed Indonesia (JPFA) shares are undervalued in all scenarios, and Malindo Feedmill (MAIN) shares are in overvalued condition in all scenarios. The PER valuation results show that CPIN shares in pessimistic and moderate scenarios are undervalued, while in optimistic scenarios, they are overvalued. JPFA and MAIN stocks in all scenarios are overvalued. The PBV valuation results show that CPIN's stock in the pessimistic scenario is undervalued, while in the moderate and optimistic scenarios are overvalued condition. JPFA and MAIN stocks in all scenarios are overvalued.

1 INTRODUCTION

Stock exchange is a market group where long-term credits (long-term banking letters) are traded. There were previously two stock exchanges in Indonesia, the Jakarta Stock Exchange (JSX) and the Surabaya Stock Exchange (BES), which were established in June 1984. However, on December 1, 2007, the two stock exchanges were merged into the Indonesia Stock Exchange (IDX).

One of the subsectors in the Jakarta Stock Exchange is the animal feed subsector. Animal feed subsector is one of the subsectors that is expected to continue to develop along with the increasing demand for chicken meat in Indonesia. There are four companies listed in the animal feed subsector, which are still flat on the IDX. The four companies are PT. Charoen Phokpand Indonesia (CPIN), PT. Japfa Comfeed Indonesia (JPFA), PT. Malindo Feedmill (MAIN), and PT. Sierad Produce (SIPD). In terms of the animal feed market segment, CPIN reached 36%, followed by JPFA at 20%. CPIN also leads the 36% day-old chick market (DOC), followed by JPFA 28%. In the processed food market share CPIN also dominates with a market share above 50%. The contribution to the income of CPIN mostly comes from animal feed, about 80%, DOC 15%, and processed chicken 5% (*https://investasi.kontan.co.id/news/memanen-laba-emiten-pakan-ternak*).

Based on Table 1, it can be concluded that the growth of shares of animal feed subsector companies in Indonesia from 2013 to 2017 experienced fluctuating movements. The average share price growth of Indonesian feed companies listed on the Indonesia Stock Exchange from 2013 to 2018, CPIN of −1.18%, JPFA of 20.45%, MAIN of −11.12%, and SIPD is 12.42%. With the company's share price growth in the fluctuating animal feed subsector, it is necessary to calculate the intrinsic value of the stock price that can provide information to investors.

This study aims to determine whether the stock price in the feed subsector is undervalued, overvalued, or reasonable by estimating the intrinsic value of the stock and then comparing it with the stock price in the market.

Table 1. Stock return of animal feed subsector (2013–2018).

	Opening Price				Growth Rate (%)			
Date	CPIN	JPFA	MAIN	SIPD	CPIN	JPFA	MAIN	SIPD
2-Jan-13	3,600	1,230	2,500	500	−2.0%	1.63%	32.00%	0.00%
2-Jan-14	3,525	1,250	3,300	500	7.80%	−24.00%	−35.61%	2.00%
2-Jan-15	3,800	950	2,125	510	−31.18%	−36.32%	−35.06%	68.63%
2-Jan-16	2,615	605	1,380	860	18.16%	140.50%	−5.80%	−20.93%
2-Jan-17	3,090	1,455	1,300	680				

2 LITERATURE REVIEW

2.1 *Company value*

Company value is the investor's perception of the level of success of a company that is often associated with stock prices. High stock prices make the value of the company also high and increase market confidence not only in the company's current performance but also in the company's future prospects. Sartono (2010: 487) revealed that the value of a company is the sale value of a company as a business that is operating. The existence of excess selling value above the value of liquidation is the value of the management organization that runs the company.

2.2 *Valuation theory*

According to Damodaran (2006), knowing the value of an asset that will be the object of investment and what gives value to an asset is a prerequisite for making the right decision in choosing an investment for the portfolio. To be able to get a logical profit, investors will buy goods when the price is below its fair value.

2.3 *Discounted cash flow (DCF)*

Discounted cash flow (DCF) valuation method is a stock valuation method using the concept of time value of money (Wira 2014). The theory on which this method is based is the fair value of shares (present value) which is all the money that flows in the company in the future (future value) when discounted.

2.4 *Free cash flow to firm (FCFF)*

According to Wira (2014), FCFF is cash available to corporate funders or funders, namely shareholders and bonds after the company has carried out operational and investment activities.

$$FCFF = (EBIT \times (1 - Tax)) + Depreciation - Capex - \Delta NWC \tag{1}$$

2.5 *Price earnings ratio (PER)*

Another alternative in valuing to calculate the intrinsic value of shares or fundamental values is to use the value of earnings from the company (earnings) (Jogiyanto 2013). Estimates of the intrinsic value of shares in a company's analysis can be done using two important components of information from the company, namely earnings per share and earnings multipliers (Tandelilin 2007). Or in other words, the expected function of earnings per share and the amount of PER of a company's stock is the intrinsic value of a stock.

2.6 *Price book ratio (PBV)*

One alternative approach to determine the value of a stock with the relative valuation method is to use the relationship between the stock market price and book value per share (Tandelilin 2010). Theoretically, the market value of a stock must reflect the book's value.

3 RESEARCH METHOD

3.1 *Type of research*

The method used in this research is a descriptive verification method. Understanding descriptive methods is according to Sugiyono (2013: 53), which is a problem statement regarding the question of the existence of an independent variable, either only on one variable or more (an independent variable is a standalone variable, not an independent variable, because the independent variable is always paired with a dependent variable).

3.2 *Variable operations*

The research variable used in this study is the intrinsic value of shares based on the company's fundamental value (the value of the company). Then the variables will be calculated using the DCF method with the FCFF approach and using the relative valuation method with PER and PBV approaches.

3.3 *Population and sample*

The population that will be taken in this study are all publicly listed companies' shares in the animal feed subsector that are listed on the IDX.

The criteria of the purposive sampling technique in this study are as follows:

1. Shares on the IDX included in the Composite Stock Price Index, in the animal feed subsector industry.
2. Animal feed subsector shares that have a market capitalization value >1.5 trillion in the last two years.
3. Shares that until 2018 have active transaction volumes on the IDX and are not suspended.

Based on the process of selecting the sample criteria, a sample of three animal feed subsector companies were selected on the IDX to be examined in this study, namely CPIN 60.34 trillion market capitalization, JPFA 18.31 trillion, and MAIN 1.53 trillion.

3.4 *Data collection*

The availability of data sources is important in choosing research problems. Research data sources are subject sources from which data can be obtained. The data to be obtained and processed is secondary data from other sources such as the company's financial statements, the IDX, Yahoo Finance, Investment World, and so on. Secondary data used in this research sample are financial reports and annual reports of several animal feed subsector companies in the last five years (2013–2017).

3.5 *DCF-FCFF share value approach*

Estimating the share's intrinsic value stages using the DCF-FCFF approach is as follows (Damodaran 2006):

a. Classify the historical data as the basis for projection

In this stage, data classification from financial statements and company annual reports is in the form of sales data (revenue), the percentage of operating expenses (EB), depreciation and amortization costs (DA), EBIT, tax costs, capital expenditure, and net working capital. The data was taken in the range from 2013 to 2017. Based on the historical data, we can get the average data percentage (%) on revenue. That leads us to its cost behavior. The cost behavior is used as a reference for projecting over the next five years, namely 2018–2022.

b. Conduct projections and analysis of financial statement ratios
The basis of future financial statement projections is taken from financial statement data in the past. So that conducting company valuation involves elements of forecasts, estimates, and assumptions.

c. Calculating the free cash flow
After projecting the financial components that form the EBIT, such as sales, costs, and depreciation/amortization, then calculate FCFF using formula 1.

d. Calculating the estimated cost of capital
The next is determining the discount. In this approach, the discount rate used is WACC. WACC is calculated based on the proportion of the company's financing sources (equity and debt).

e. Figuring value terminals
In this research, the authors assume that growth is constant.

f. Calculating cash flows from FCFF and terminal value
The next step is to calculate the projection of free cash flows until 2021 and the cash flow of the terminal value assuming the company has a constant growth in 2022.

g. Calculating the enterprise value
Furthermore, the enterprise value is obtained from the sum between the number of FCFF present values from 2018 to 2021 plus the present value of the terminal value.

h. Calculating the company's equity value
The value of equity is obtained using the value of the company or enterprise value reduced by the amount of debt held, minus the ownership of the minority company, and summed by the amount of cash carried.

i. Calculating the intrinsic value of the stock
We need to divide the equity value with the number of shares outstanding to get the intrinsic value of the stocks. The intrinsic value per share will be different depending on the three scenarios of predetermined conditions (optimistic, moderate, and pessimistic).

j. Assessing and providing recommendations
After getting the intrinsic value, the value of the stock needs to be compared with the stock price in the evaluation period. The results of this comparison will conclude that the value of shares is in an undervalued, fair-valued, or overvalued condition.

3.6 *PER approach*

This method uses the value of earnings to estimate intrinsic value. The PER method is also called the multiplier method because investors will count the multiplier value of earnings reflected in the stock price. Thus, the PER method describes the ratio or comparison between stock prices and earnings per share of the company (Damodaran 2006). The higher the PER value, the smaller the profit for each share, because market prices are considered to be increasingly expensive. Conversely, the lower the PER value indicates the higher the benefit gained for each share since the price is considered cheaper (Damodaran 2006).

3.7 *PBV approach*

The steps that must be taken to determine the position of the stock are in an undervalued, fair valued, or overvalued position on the PBV method is quite simple. Ideally, the stock market price compared to the book value of its assets will approach one. Stocks that have a low price/book value ratio should be purchased to obtain a higher level of return at a certain level of risk (Damodaran 2006). PBVs that have a value below or close to one are considered good by investors, but a PBV

Table 2. Stock valuation based on PER value.

Stock PER	Valuation
PER > Average PER of Industry	Overvalued
PER < Average PER of Industry	Undervalued
PER = Average PER of Industry	Fair valued

that has a value above one means it is classified as expensive (overvalued). However, PBVs that have high value still can rise if the company has excellent performance and business processes. Business prospects can be seen from how high are the profits that can be produced by the company. Investors can see the amount of return on equity to know the company's ability to generate profits based on owned capital (Damodaran 2006). Further, since the native of relative valuation, we need to also consider the average PBV of industry to determine the position of evaluated shares in the market. Therefore, following is the guideline for the investors to determine the share position based on PBV (Neaxie & Hendrawan 2017).

a. If PBV > industrial PBV, then the stock is in an overvalued position
b. If PBV = industrial PBV, then the stock is in a fair-valued position
c. If PBV < industrial PBV, then the stock is undervalued

4 ANALYSIS AND RESULT

The historical data were derived from the company's financial reports from 2013–2017 and further taken as the reference for the free cash flow calculation. The projection of free cash flow to the firm is based on the cost behavior of the historical data from 2013–2017 for the projections of 2018–2022. In this research, we generated three scenarios of projected corporate revenue growth based on industry analysis, namely the pessimistic, moderate, and optimistic scenarios. A pessimistic scenario is a scenario where the company's growth is the same as industrial growth. The moderate scenario is a scenario where the company's growth is industrial growth plus the company's historical growth difference to industrial growth. An optimistic scenario is a scenario where the company's growth is industrial growth plus the company's historical growth difference to industrial growth, then added half of the difference (Neaxie & Hendrawan 2017). The pessimistic scenario is built on the assumption of consistent revenue growth of 11.18% for CPIN, 7.18% for JPFA, and 4.54% for MAIN. The moderate scenario was constructed with the assumption of revenue growth of 18.28% for CPIN, 8.52% for JPFA, and 6.75% for MAIN. The optimistic scenario is built on the assumption of revenue growth of 21.83% for CPIN, 11.18% for JPFA, and 11.18% for MAIN.

4.1 *DCF-FCFF, PER, and PBV valuation result*

The stock valuation using DCF-FCFF, PER, and PBV method in this research resulted in the share's intrinsic value as listed in Table 3.

5 CONCLUSION

The conclusions of this research are as follows:

a. Based on the analysis carried out on the optimistic scenario, it can be concluded that the intrinsic value of CPIN shares is IDR 11,816 with a PER value of 42.52 and a PBV value of 12.33. The intrinsic value of JPFA shares is IDR 18,171 with a PER value of 129.03 and PBV at a value of

Table 3. Valuation results.

		DCF-FCFF			PER			PBV		
Company	**Scenario**	Intrinsic Value	Price 2 Jan 2018	Valuation	Intrinsic Value	PER Industry Q1 2018	Valuation	Intrinsic Value	PBV Industry Q1 2018	Valuation
CPIN	Pessimistic	577	3,110	Overvalued	2.29	13.47	Undervalued	0.60	1.1	Undervalued
	Moderate	1,936		Overvalued	7.19	13.47	Undervalued	2.02	1.1	Overvalued
	Optimistic	11,816		Undervalued	42.52	13.47	Overvalued	12.33	1.1	Overvalued
JPFA	Pessimistic	2,087	1,300	Undervalued	15.37	13.47	Overvalued	2.43	1.1	Overvalued
	Moderate	3,400		Undervalued	25.70	13.47	Overvalued	4.13	1.1	Overvalued
	Optimistic	18,171		Undervalued	129.03	13.47	Overvalued	21.35	1.1	Overvalued
MAIN	Pessimistic	−468	734	Overvalued	−8.45	13.47	Overvalued	−0.62	1.1	Overvalued
	Moderate	−344		Overvalued	−5.97	13.47	Overvalued	−0.45	1.1	Overvalued
	Optimistic	−353		Overvalued	−5.69	13.47	Overvalued	−0.46	1.1	Overvalued

21.35. The intrinsic value of MAIN shares is IDR −353 with a PER value of −5.69 and PBV at a value of −0.46.

b. Based on the analysis carried out in the moderate scenario, it can be concluded that the intrinsic value of CPIN shares is IDR 1,935 with a PER value of 7.19 and a PBV value of 2.02. The intrinsic value of JPFA shares is IDR 3,400 with a PER value of 25.70 and PBV at a value of 4.13. The intrinsic value of MAIN shares is IDR −344 with a PER value of −5.97 and PBV at a value of −0.45.

c. Based on the analysis that has been done on the pessimistic scenario, it can be concluded that the intrinsic value of CPIN shares is IDR 577 with a PER value of 2.29 and a PBV value of 0.60. The intrinsic value of JPFA shares is IDR 2,087 with a PER value of 15.37 and PBV at a value of 2.43. The intrinsic value of MAIN shares is IDR −468 with a PER value of −8.45 and PBV at a value of −0.62.

REFERENCES

Damodaran, A. 1996. Investment Valuation Tools and Techniques for Determining the Value of Any Assets. United States of America: John Wiley & Sons Inc.

Damodaran, A. 2006. Damodaran on Valuation Second Edition. United States of America: John Wiley & Sons Inc.

Kontan.co.id. 2012. Harvesting Animal Feed Issuers' Profit. https://investasi.kontan.co.id/news/memanen-laba-emiten-pakan-ternak

Neaxie, L. V & Hendrawan, R. 2017. Stock Valuation Using Discounted Cash Flow and Relative Valuation Methods in Telecommunications Companies Listed on the Indonesia Stock Exchange for the 2017 Projection. Thesis of the Faculty of Economics and Business, Telkom University.

Sartono. 2010. Financial Management Theory and Application. Edisi 4. BPFE Yogyakarta.

Tandelilin, E. 2007. Investment Analysis and Portfolio Management. First edition, second printing. Yogyakarta: BPFE.

Tandelilin, E. 2010. Portfolio and Investment Theories and Applications. First edition. Yogyakarta: Kanisius.

Wira, D. 2014. Stock Fundamental Analysis. Jakarta: *Exceed Book*.

Synergizing Management, Technology and Innovation in Generating Sustainable and Competitive Business Growth – Hendayani et al (eds)
© 2021 Taylor & Francis Group, London, ISBN 978-0-367-68756-4

Earnings quality: Systematic risk, audit committee, IOS

M. Muslih & P.A. Muhdi
Faculty of Economics and Business, Telkom University, Bandung, West Java, Indonesia

ABSTRACT: This study aims to determine the effect of systematic risk, the number of audit committee meetings, audit committee expertise, and investment opportunity sets on the earnings quality in the infrastructure, utilities, and transportation companies in the 2014–2018 period listed on IDX. This study uses quantitative analysis methods with a population of 70 companies in the infrastructure, utilities, and transportation sectors listed on IDX in the 2014–2018 period. The samples produced were 50 samples with Non-probability sampling for 5 years period. The data in this study were analyzed using descriptive statistics and panel data regression using E-Views 10. The results showed that systematic risk, number of audit committee meetings, audit committee expertise, and investment opportunity sets contributed simultaneous to the earnings quality. Partially, the number of audit committee meetings contributed negatively, while systematic risk, audit committee expertise and investment opportunity sets do not have a significant contributed with earnings quality.

1 INTRODUCTION

Earnings information is expected to be a guideline in economic decision making for shareholders and other financial statement users. The importance of a company's earnings information makes some of the company's management to manipulate corporate earnings information (Risdawaty & Subowo 2015). The agency theory assumes that each individual is motivated to fulfill his interests. According to Jensen and Meckling (1976) management as a company organizer has broader access to internal information and company prospects than shareholders. This causes information asymmetry in the form of data manipulation that results in earnings that do not meet the requirements (Majidah et al. 2015).

Earnings quality is an important aspect to assess the health of a company's financial statements (Bellovary 2005). Earnings quality can be an indication of the ability of earnings information in responding to the market (Kusumawati & Wardhani 2018). To find out the level of earnings quality can use earnings response coefficient (ERC) indicators that measure directly the relationship of earnings information and investor response as in research conducted by Kusumawati and Wardhani (2018), Jaya and Wirama (2017), Nurhanifah and Jaya (2014).

Figure 1 shows the movement of earnings quality calculated using earnings response coefficient as an investor's response to company profits and cumulative abnormal return (CAR) as a market response to infrastructure, utilities, and transportation companies during the 2014–2018 period. In 2016, it indicated that earnings information was not significantly responded by the market, which was indicated by a negative value of CAR as a market response. Then in 2018, it shows that earnings information does not reflect quality earnings as indicated by the negative value of ERC as a proxy for earnings quality. To avoid making the wrong decision to make an investment, potential investors must also pay attention to other things that are not disclosed in earnings information such as systematic risk, Number of Audit Committee Meetings, Audit Committee Expertise, and Investment Opportunity Sets.

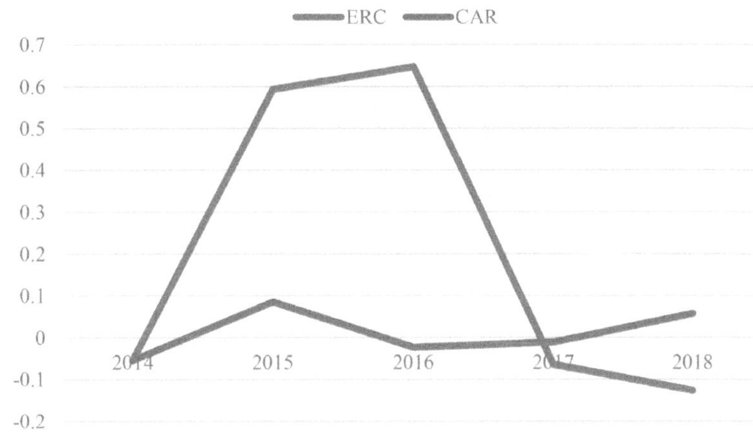

Figure 1. Graph of average earnings quality for the infrastructure, utilities and transportation sectors.

2 LITERATURE REVIEW AND RESEARCH HYPOTHESES

Systematic risk is the risk associated with changes that occur in the market as a whole, and will affect all companies that cannot be avoided or diversified (Tandelilin 2017). Companies that have high systematic risk, the information about earnings announcements will be less reacted by investors, so that it can cause ERC to be lower and the quality of earnings considered not good. The results of previous researchers by Lisdawati et al. (2016), Widayanti et al. (2014), and Hasanzade et al. (2013) stated that systematic risk contributed negatively to the earnings quality that is proxied by ERC.

Ha1: Systematic risk contributed negatively to the earnings quality

The audit committee in carrying out its supervisory function against management, must hold a regular meeting to monitor the process of preparing the company's financial statements. A frequency of meeting that frequently held by the audit committee will lead to better financial statements quality, which means earnings information reported also has higher quality (MM & Laksito 2017). This is reinforced in MM and Laksito's (2017) research, and Bala and Kumai (2016) stated that audit committee meetings contributed positively to the earnings quality that is proxied by ERC.

Ha2: The number of audit committee meetings contributed positively to the earnings quality

The audit committee characteristics involve monitoring the standards of financial reporting organization to increase effectiveness. Additionally, it can reduce agency conflict such as asymmetric information and agency cost. Thus, the greater the proportion of members who has expertise or educational background in accounting and finance, the financial reporting by management will be of higher quality. This is confirmed by previous researchers Chen and Kumal (2018) and Hamdan et al. (2013) stated the expertise of the audit committee or educational background in accounting and finance contributed positively to the earnings quality that is proxied by ERC.

Ha3: Audit committee expertise contributed positively to the earnings quality

IOS can be used as a basis for determining the classification of company growth in the future (Novianti 2012). When a company has a high IOS then quality of earnings will be increase, because most investors are interested in investing by hoping get a greater return in the future (Jaya & Wirama 2017). This is supported by previous researchers by Yasa et al. (2019), Nariman and Ekadjaja (2018) stated that IOS contributed positively to the earnings quality that is proxied by ERC.

Ha4: Investment opportunity sets contributed positively to the earnings quality

3 RESEARCH METHODS

Research data were obtained from annual reports of infrastructure, utilities, and transportation companies listed on IDX in the 2014–2018 period. This study uses quantitative analysis methods with a population of 70 companies in the infrastructure, utilities, and transportation sectors listed on IDX in the 2014–2018 period. The samples used in this study were 50 samples with non-probability sampling from 10 companies and 5 years research period.

In this study the dependent variable used is earnings quality (EQ) with ERC as an indicator with observations 5 days before and 5 days after the publication of the December 31 financial statements. The independent variable in this study was systematic risk (RISK) using the market model, audit committee meetings (MEET) using the number of audit committee meetings in one period, the audit committee expertise (EXPERT) using the proportion of members who had accounting or financial education backgrounds or had occupied important position in the financial sector, and Investment opportunity sets (IOS) using the MBVBA ratio. The equation of the panel data model analysis used in this study is as follows:

$$EQ = \alpha + \beta 1RISK + \beta 2MEET + \beta 3EXPERT + \beta 4IOS + \varepsilon \quad (1)$$

Information:

EQ	= Earnings Quality
RISK	= Systematic Risk
MEET	= Audit Committee Meeting
EXPERT	= Expertise of the Audit Committee
IOS	= *Investment Opportunity Sets*
α	= Constant
$\beta 1, \beta 2, \beta 3, \beta 4$	= Regression Coefficient
ε	= Error

4 ANALYSIS RESULTS AND DISCUSS

4.1 *Descriptive analysis*

Descriptive statistical test results are described as follows.

Table 1. Descriptive analysis results.

Variable	N	*Minimum*	*Maximum*	*The mean*	*Std. Deviation*
Earnings Quality	50	−1.2350	5,1280	0.1988	0.9573
Systematic Risk	50	−6.2310	3.0550	0.4070	1.6268
Number of Audit Committee Meetings	50	3,000	54.0000	12.5000	11.9300
Expertise of the Audit Committee	50	0.3333	1.0000	0.6930	0.2372
Investment Opportunity Sets	50	0.5375	3.0538	1.4773	0.6502

(a) The average earnings quality for infrastructure, utilities, and transportation companies in the 2014–2018 period listed on the IDX has a positive value of 0.1988 or received a good response (good news) to earnings information. (b) The average systematic risk for infrastructure, utilities and transportation companies in the 2014–2018 period listed on the IDX has a positive value of 0.4070 but far or less than one ($\beta < 1$). Systematic risk reflects that the sector is not sensitive (defensive) to market changes. (c) The average number of audit committee meetings in infrastructure, utilities and transportation companies in the period 2014–2018 listed on IDX was 12.5 or 13 times a year. This means the company is relatively effective in holding meetings or audit committee meetings. (d) The average audit committee expertise in infrastructure, utilities, and transportation companies for the period 2014–2018 listed on the IDX is 0.6930 or 69% of members who have financial and accounting expertise in one company. This reflects proportion of members who had accounting or financial education backgrounds or had occupied important position in the financial sector. (e) The average investment opportunity sets for infrastructure, utilities, and transportation companies in the period 2014–2018 on IDX amounted to 1.4773, reflecting high investment opportunities in this sector that will attract many investors by obtaining greater returns and can illustrate the company's growth potential in the future.

4.2 *Determination and simultaneous coefficient test*

Table 2. Determination and simultaneous coefficient test results.

R-Squared	0.280718	Mean dependent var	0.871095
Adjusted R-Squared	0.216782	S.D. dependent var	0.254700
S.E. of regression	0.225408	Akaike info criterion	−0.047166
Sum squared resid	2.286403	Schwarz criterion	0.144036
Log likelihood	6.179149	Hannan-Quin criter.	0.025645
F-statistic	4.390593	Durbin-Watson stat	1.695910
Prob(F-statistic)	0.004411		

Table 2 shows the adjusted r-squared of 0.21678 with a probability value (f-statistic) of $0.004411 < \alpha = 0.05$, meaning that systematic risk, the number of audit committee meetings, audit committee expertise, and investment opportunity sets are able to explain earnings quality of 21.7% and the rest are explained by other factors. Thus, systematic risk, the number of audit committee meetings, audit committee expertise, and investment opportunity sets contributed simultaneously to earnings quality.

4.3 *Partial test*

Table 3. Partial test results.

Variable	Coefficient	Std. Error	t-Statistics	Prob.
C	0.991126	0.202477	4.895005	0.0000
RISK	−0.024038	0.102503	−0.234512	0.8157
MEET	−5.663672	1.385003	−4,089285	0.0002
EXPERT	0.013912	0.235665	0.059034	0.9532
IOS	0.072860	0.184800	0.394264	0.6952

(a) RISK has no contributed to earnings quality. So that systematic risk is not a threat or a natural thing and is attached to a return as a return on investment that has been done, because investors also do not pay too much attention to systematic risk in assessing the quality of earnings on earnings information as a consideration in investment decisions. (b) MEET contributed negatively to the earnings quality. This illustrated that the company with the number of audit committee meetings that more often can result in earnings information reported by the company does not describe the real situation, so that the quality of earnings will be reduced and not responded well by investors. (c) EXPERT has no contributed on the earnings quality. This can explain that the selection of audit committee members who must have the ability in the field of accounting or finance is only formal or as a fulfillment of regulatory requirements only in the implementation of good corporate governance and cannot guarantee the quality of a company's earnings. (d) IOS does not affect earnings quality. This shows that investment opportunity sets cannot yet become a benchmark in determining the quality of earnings by investors for investment decisions.

5 CONCLUSIONS AND RECOMMENDATIONS

The results of this study indicate that the activities of the audit committee by carrying out regular meetings in carrying out governance mechanisms are determinants of earnings quality, although the level of contribution is low and can reduce the level of earnings quality, investors still respond. For further studies, it is recommended to develop this study using other governance variables such as BOC meetings as a determinant of earnings quality. Because the audit committee and the BOC are the company's internal control mechanisms that are directly related in making corporate decisions, so the activities or meetings that are conducted become a determining factor for the quality of earnings information for investors.

REFERENCES

Bala, H., Gugong, D., & Kumai, B. 2015. Audit Committee Characteristics and Earnings Quality of Listed Food and Beverage Firms in Nigeria. *International Journal of Accounting, Auditing, and Taxation Volume 2(8)*, 216–227.

Bellovary, J. L., Giacomino, D. E., & Akers, M. 2005. Earnings Quality: Its Time to Measure and Report. *The CPA Journal, Volume 75(11)*, 32–37.

Chen, S., & Komal, B. 2018. Audit Committee financial expertise and earnings quality: A meta-Analysis. *Journal of Business Research Volume 84*, 253–270.

Hamdan, A. M., Mushtaha, S., & Al-Sartawi, A. M. 2013. The Audit Committee Characteristics and Earnings Quality; Evidence from Jordan. *Australasian Accounting Business and Finance Journal, Volume 7(4)*, 51–80.

Handriani, E. 2020. Earnings Management and the Effect Characteristics of Audit Committee, Independent Commissioners: Evidence From Indonesia. *Research in World Economy, Vol. 11, No. 3*, 108–123.

Hasanzadel, M., Darabil, R., & Mahfoozi, G. 2013. Factors Affecting The Earnings Response Coefficient: An Empirical study for Iran. *European Online Journal of Natural and Social Sciences Volume 2(3)*, 2551–2560.

Jaya, K. A., & Wirama, D. G. 2017. Pengaruh Investment Opportunity Set, Likuiditas, dan Ukuran Perusahaan pada Kualitas Laba. *E-Jurnal Akuntansi Universitas Udayana Volume 21(3)*, 2195–2221.

Jensen, & Meckling. 1976. The Theory of The Firm: Manajerial Behavior, Agency Cost and Ownership Structure. *Journal of Financial and Economics, 3*, 305–306.

Kusumawati, H., & Wardhani, S. L. 2018. Analisis Determinan Yang Mempengaruhi Kualitas Laba Studi Pada Perusahaan Manufaktur Di Bursa Efek Indonesia (Periode 2012–2016). *MODUS Volume 30 (2)*, 17–37.

Lisdawati, Mulyadi, J., & Hermiyetti. 2016. Leverage, Beta, Growth Opportunities, Firm Size, dan Earnings Response Coefficient perusahaan Otomotif dan Komponennya. *Jurnal RIset Akuntansi dan Perpajakan Volume 3(1)*, 72–83.

M, R. R., & Laksito, H. 2017. Pengaruh Karakteristik Komite Audit Terhadap Kualitas Laba. *Diponegoro Journal of Accounting Volume 6(4)*, 1–11.

Majidah, Nazar, M. R., Muslih, M., & Anggraeni, G. 2016. Earnings Quality; Corporate Governance Perception Index, Intellectual Capital and Spiritual Values. *Advanced Science Letters, Vol. 22 No. 12.* 4338–4340(3).

Nariman, A., & Ekadjaja, M. 2018. Implikasi Corporate Governance, Investment Opportunity Sets, Firm Size, dan Leverage terhadap Earnings Quality. *Jurnal Ekonomi, Volume 23(1)*, 33–47.

Novianti, R. 2012. Kajian Kualitas Laba Pada Perusahaan Manufaktur yang Terdaftar di Bursa Efek Indonesia. *Accounting Analysis Journal Vol. 1 No. 2*, 1–6.

Nurhanifah, Y. A., & Jaya, T. E. 2014. Pengaruh alokasi pajak antar periode, investment opportunity sets, dan likuiditas, terhdapat kualitas laba. *Jurnal Ilmiah Wahana Akuntansi Volume 9(2)*, 109–133.

Risdawaty, I. M., & Subowo. 2015. Pengaruh Struktur Modal, Ukuran Perusahaan, Asimetri Informasi, dan Profitabilitas terhadap Kualitas Laba. *Jurnal Dinamika Akuntansi Volume 7(2)*, 109–118.

Soebyatko, B. B., Dewi, K., Mukhtaruddin, & Arsela, S. (2017. Investment Opportunity Set to Earnings Quality and Firm's Value: Corporate Governance Mechanism as Moderating Variable. *Corporate Ownership & Control, Vol.14, Issue 4(2)*, 435–448.

Surbakti, L. P., Shaari, H. B., & Bamahros, H. M. 2017. Effect of Audit Committee Expertise and Meeting on Earnings Quality in Indonesian Listed Companies: A Conceptual Approach. *Journal of Accounting and Finance in Emerging Economies, Volume 3, Issue 1*, 47–53.

Tandelilin, E. 2017. *Pasar Modal Manajemen Portofolio & Investasi.* Yogyakarta: PT Kanisius.
Widayanti, C. A., Vestari, M., & Farida, D. N. 2014. Faktor-Faktor yang mempengaruhi kualitas laba pada perusahaan high profile yang terdaftar di BEI. *Jurnal Dinamika Ekonomi & Bisnis, Volume 11(1)*, 46–64.
Yasa, G. W., Astika, I. B., & Widiariani, N. M. 2019. The Influence Of Accounting Conservatism, IOS, And Good Corporate Governance On The Earnings Quality. *Jurnal Ilmiah Akuntansi dan Bisnis*, 86–94.

Synergizing Management, Technology and Innovation in Generating Sustainable and Competitive Business Growth – Hendayani et al (eds)
© 2021 Taylor & Francis Group, London, ISBN 978-0-367-68756-4

The effect of the entrepreneurial competency on business success

L. Yuldinawati, S. Widyanesti, P. Wulansari, T.P. Avero & L.C. Apriliya
Faculty of Economics and Business, Telkom University, Bandung, West Java, Indonesia

ABSTRACT: Entrepreneurs are the main actors in economic growth. Entrepreneurship is a solution to reducing unemployment in Indonesia. The Bandung city government is organizing a new entrepreneur acceleration program in the city of Bandung from 2014–2018. In general, the constrain found that entrepreneurs still lack capability and knowledge in business. This study aims to determine the impact of entrepreneurial competence on entrepreneurial success and how much influence the entrepreneurial competence has on business success with the business environment as a moderator variable in entrepreneurship in Bandung. This research uses quantitative methods, with 100 samples using SEM-PLS analysis techniques. The results showed that entrepreneurial competence had a significant effect on business success.

1 INTRODUCTION

At this moment, the Indonesian population keeps on increasing. The increasing population is followed by the rising unemployment that shows the number of people that are not absorbed by employment, making the unemployment rate to increase (Novriansyah 2018). Entrepreneurship can be an alternative to solving unemployment (Herawaty 2016). Realizing the importance of entrepreneurs as the main actor in long-term sustainable economic growth, the government launches a program to accelerate the creation of new entrepreneurs by issuing mayor regulation No. 1090 the Year 2015 concerning the general guidelines in accelerating the creation of new entrepreneurs. There are five Regional Work Units (SKPD, Satuan Kerja Perangkat Daerah), which are included in the assignment list for achieving the target number of entrepreneurs. With the running of entrepreneurs accelerating program, done by five Regional Work Units (SKPD, Satuan Kerja Perangkat Daerah), some flaws still need to be fixed and improved so that the program can run as the government desires. According to the entrepreneurs' forum under the mayor in charge of supervising the program, it is found that training is not running effectively. So in 2019, the entrepreneurs accelerating program is replaced with a business assistance program for the new mayor period 2019–2024 (Tim Mentoring dan Evaluasi WUB 2019). In the assistance program, one of the benchmarks is entrepreneurs' competency. Entrepreneurs' competency is one of the benchmarks in achieving success in entrepreneurship because in general, a successful entrepreneur is the one who has competency. The success that is measured by competency can be seen from the business environment. Success is directly influenced by the business environment, the business environment is important, which proves that how a businessman runs his business was influenced by the environment where the business operates (Ahmad et al. 2010).

2 LITERATURE REVIEW

2.1 *Entrepreneurship*

Entrepreneurship leads to attitude and mentality of how someone is doing business (Basrowi 2016). Entrepreneurship is an active, creative, innovative, and detailed skill in seeing opportunities while always being open to accepting input and changes toward the positive direction that can make the business flourish (Saragih 2017).

2.2 *Entrepreneur*

An entrepreneur is a person who does his own business with all the ability that he has (Basrowi 2016). An entrepreneur is also a person who creatively and innovatively does his business activities, by developing an idea and process resources to seize opportunities (Suryana 2006).

2.3 *Entrepreneurial competency*

Entrepreneurial competency is defined as the characteristic of an individual such as knowledge, skills, and the ability to do business. Entrepreneurship competency covers strategic competency, conceptual competency, opportunity competency, relationship competency, learning competency, personal competency, ethical competency, and familism competency. (Ahmad et al. 2010).

2.4 *Business success*

The success of an entrepreneur can be divided into two, based on satisfaction of financial success and satisfaction with nonfinancial success (Ahmad et al. 2010).

2.5 *Business environment*

The business environment shows how a businessman runs their business at the place where their business operates. The business environment was divided into two, which are benign versus hostile business environment and stable versus dynamic business environment (Ahmad et al. 2010).

3 METHOD

This research uses a quantitative method with a causal investigation type. The population used is entrepreneurs fostered by five Regional Work Units (SKPD, Satuan Kerja Perangkat Daerah), with 100 people as samples. A non-probability technique did sampling by purposive sampling. In this research, primary data gathering is done by distributing a questionnaire and secondary data by literature study. Data processing was done by using SEM (structural equation modeling) with partial least square SEM.

4 DATA ANALYSIS AND RESULT

4.1 *Data analysis*

Out of 100 respondents, there were 58% male and 42% female. There are eight variable competency dimensions:

Based on Table 1, the relationship dimension had the highest value of 89.15%, while the lowest is in opportunity dimension as much as 83.12%. The business success variable is divided into two dimensions, satisfaction dimension with financial success 82.1%. The business environment dimension is divided into four parts (benign, hostile, stable, dynamic) with the purpose to see which environment is more dominant. It can be concluded that entrepreneurs organized by Bandung city government are doing business in a hostile and dynamic environment.

Table 1. Variable competency dimensions.

Dimensions	% Score
Strategic competency	86,15%
Conceptual competency	85,25%
Opportunity competency	83,12%
Relationship competency	89,15%
Learning competency	88,4%
Personal competency	84,42%
Ethical competency	86,68%
Familism competency	86,56%
Total	86,22%

4.2 *Result*

Evaluation to PLS model is done by evaluating the outer model and inner model to assess the validity and reliability of the model, and the inner model is used to predict that there is a relationship. Outer model evaluation in this research explains that all indicators have a loading factor of more than 0.5 to be stated as valid. Moreover, all latent variables have AVE (average variance extracted) more than 0.5 (AVE > 0.5), which means that discriminatory is valid. Then, all CR (composite reliability) value obtained are more than 0.7 (CR > 0.7) so that all variables in this research can be said to be reliable.

To test H1, which is entrepreneurial competency, has a significant influence toward business success, which results in path coefficient value between entrepreneurial competency toward business success has a positive sign as much as 0.761, which means the higher the competency, the more likely success will improve. Then based on R-square value (determinant coefficient) entrepreneurial competency has influence as much as 57.6%, and due to t-statistic value (17.661) bigger than t table (1.96), error rate 5% H1 is accepted.

To test H2, which is business environment significantly moderate, the relationship between entrepreneurial competency toward business success the R-square (determinant coefficient) obtained has influence as much as 61.2%, then due to t statistic (1.777) is smaller than t table (1.96), then the error rate H2 is rejected.

5 CONCLUSION

Based on the result, it can be concluded that entrepreneurial competency influences the business success in entrepreneurs organized by Bandung city government. Entrepreneurial competency has significant influence as much as 0.576 on business success. Entrepreneur competences have 57.6% influence, which means that there are 42.4% other factors that influence business success aside from entrepreneurial competency. In this research, we also found that the higher the competency, the higher the business success.

Business environment does not significantly moderate the relationship between the entrepreneurial competency and business success in entrepreneurs organized by Bandung city government. Based on this research, Bandung city government needs to select entrepreneurs that have good entrepreneurial competency as a base in entrepreneurship, which means to select entrepreneurs that are going to be organized for in the future, Bandung city government needs to pay attention to what kind of competency that the youth entrepreneurs already had and need to have referring to the tested competency indicator, especially ones that focused on the opportunity competency improvement.

For the next research, the researcher can investigate entrepreneurs organized by Bandung city government outside of Bandung as a comparison. Besides, that researcher might not only focus on entrepreneurs organized by Bandung city government but also on entrepreneurs in Indonesia.

REFERENCES

Ahmad, N.M., Ramayah,T., Wilson, C., & Kummerow, L. 2010. Is Entrepreneurial Competency and Business Success relationship Contigent Upon Business Environment? A study of Malaysian SMEs. *International Journal of Entrepreneurial Behaviour & Research.* Vol. 16, No.3, pp. 182–203.

Barsowi. 2016. *Kewirausahaan Untuk Perguruan Tinggi* (Cetakan ketiga). Bogor: Ghalia Indonesia.

Herawaty. 2016. Wirausaha Muda Dalam Peningkatan Pembangunan Pertanian. *Agrica Ekstensia.* Vol.10, No.2, hlm 81–87.

Novriansyah, M.A. 2018. Pengaruh Pengangguran dan Kemiskinan Terhadap Pertumbuhan Ekonomi di Provinsi Gorontalo. *Gorontalo Departement Review.* Vol 1, No.1.

Saragih, R. 2017. Membangun Usaha Kreatif, Inovatif dan Bermanfaat Melalui Penerapan Kewirausahaan Sosial. *Jurnal Kewirausahaan.* Vol.3, No.2, hlm 26–34.

Suryana. 2006. *Kewirausahaan Pedoman Praktis: Kiat dan Proses Menuju Sukses.* Jakarta: Salemba Empat

Tim mentoring dan Evaluasi WUB. 2018. Data Internal Tim Mentoring dan Evaluasi WUB.

Synergizing Management, Technology and Innovation in Generating Sustainable and Competitive Business Growth – Hendayani et al (eds)
 ISBN 978-0-367-68756-4

Job satisfaction and organizational commitment on employee performance in Gen Y

A. Ferdian & A.F. Meidina
School of Economics and Business, Telkom University, Bandung, West Java, Indonesia

ABSTRACT: This research was conducted at PT. Telekomunikasi Indonesia Internasional (TELIN) with a sample of Y-Generation group or commonly referred to as the Millennials Generation. The research objective is to determine how job satisfaction, organizational commitment, and employee performance in Generation Y group at TELIN and how job satisfaction and organizational commitment affect employee performance in Generation Y group partially or simultaneously. The sample of 122 employees the results of descriptive analysis shows that job satisfaction is included in the high category, organizational commitment is in the sufficient category, and employee performance is high. The result of hypothesis testing using the t-test shows that variable job satisfaction and organizational commitment partially affect employee performance. Simultaneous hypothesis testing with the F test shows that job satisfaction and organizational commitment simultaneously have a notable effect on employee performance.

1 INTRODUCTION

The growing number of Generation Y is both a challenge and an opportunity for companies. Therefore, companies must adapt to Generation Y people as their employees. In Indonesia Badan Pusat Statistik Republik Indonesia (BPSRI) publishes new workforce data according to (BPSRI, Millennial generation 2018) Generation Y will master employment in Indonesia. Employees with high job satisfaction certainly have high morale, so that their work performance will be maximal as well. Conversely, employees with low job satisfaction, causing poor work performance. They become not enthusiastic at work, and this will greatly affect the company. That is why employee job satisfaction is considered very important, especially to support company performance in competition in this globalization era (Sutanto 2013). The results of IBM's research stated that Generation Y (42 percent) had a desire to move from different company if their job did not match with their passion or expectations (Edukasi.kompas.com 2019).

Lack of existing commitment to employees will result in a decreased organizational commitment that can lead to low employee performance. He also mentioned that organizational commitment is the degree where employees believe and accept organizational goals, thus will remain or will not leave the organization. Reported (Okezone.com 2018) Generation Y is known as the generation that is not loyal when working in a company. Unlike the previous generation, companies need a different approach to make them loyal. Based on a survey by Deloitte, a global-scale consulting firm, money is not the only motivating factor for millennial workers. They also pay attention to diversity, an inclusive atmosphere, and work time flexibility. Based on previous research, employee performance has a relationship with job satisfaction as research (Novendri 2019), the outcome of the study showed that job satisfaction has a positive and notable effect on performance. Based on recently research (Putra 2016, 2018;, employee performance is affected positively by organizational commitment. Based on previous research, it can be determined that there is a relationship and the influence between Job Satisfaction, Organizational Commitment, and Employee Performance. It means that the better job satisfaction and organizational commitment are applied, the higher the employee's performance.

2 LITERATURE REVIEW

TELIN or PT. Telekomunikasi Indonesia Internasional serves international operator services and investments in the international telecommunications business and functions as Telkom's business arm to manage and develop its business lines abroad. Telin has been established by PT Telekomunikas Indonesia (Telkom) in 2007 and services more than 200 million retail customers (including wireless, Fixed-Broad Band and Other subscribers) as the main state telecommunication and network service provider in Indonesia (Pandevi 2019). Telin delivers a variety of high-quality international voice services, data services and commercial applications to wholesalers, companies, digital players and retail consumers in Indonesia, Singapore, Australia, Hong Kong, Hong Kong, Taiwan, USA and Myanmar (Charity et al. 2016).

The level of enjoyment that a person experiences with respect to his position or function in the company is job satisfaction. The level of individual happiness that the different facets of the job situation of the company where they job reward them in particular (Dewantoro & Purba 2018). The psychological person in the organization is then responsible for satisfying his task, regardless of the situation he experiences from his own environment. The level of happiness is one of the variables that influence job performance, and it eventually influences the productivity of the organization (Edison et al. 2016). And employee happiness is not enough to include rewards but also encouragement, appreciation of the performance of their managers and not monotonous environments, and opportunities for initiative and innovation (Damayanti & Cahyadi 2018).

Organizational commitment is a deep desire to be a participant of a corporate organization, to work for the desires and principles that the organization requires and embraces corporate values and objectives (Salim 2014). Through this view, the organization's commitment can be viewed as an attitude which shows its allegiance to an organization and as a continuous mechanism through which an individual communicates his interest in an organization (Siregar 2015). This, in other words, represents employee commitment to the company and an ongoing phase in which organizational members communicate their concern for the enterprise and its ongoing success and accomplishment (Bhatti & Qureshi 2007).

The cumulative significance of the employee performance is measured by the company from instances of various human activities over a typical period. One of the essential things in this description is behavior. Working success is, in particular, a series of several different activities over a long time (Fathonah & Panjaitan 2016). The second big principle is where the action is concerned; operating success comportments can contribute to the principles the organization requires (Nurhasan 2017). A variable which distinguishes a range of behaviors by different persons and between a range of behavior carried out at different times by the same entity. This distinction stems from the degree to which their impact leads (in all) to or deviates from the efficacy of organization. In other words, work output fluctuations are expected to be improvements in the company's behavior (Abrivianto 2014).

According to (Oktariani et al. 2017) companies engaged in the telecommunications and information technology industry, the presence of Generation Y can be considered a blessing. Generation Y joins the world of employment more and more (Qisthy & Sulistyo 2018). It's the human capital that businesses need, this millennial generation (Forbes 2015). Generation Y has a different character than Generation X, or especially the generation of baby boomers (Chandra & Dadang 2017). Companies may now create modifications and improvements, because the environment has evolved as well. Companies have to make improvements to the workplace if they choose to devote full to their human capital, the Y generation (Mahoney 2015). However, the organization does not only rely on generation Y, but neglect other generations (Onibala 2017). This Y generation still needs to be treated correctly because its character and operating style is not the same as the previous generation, he went on to claim (DeVaney 2015).

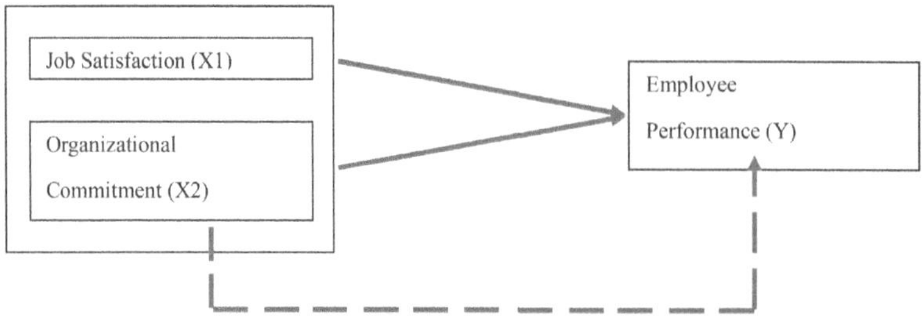

Figure 1. Framework.

The variable Job Satisfaction used is variable X1, Organizational Commitment is variable X2 and Employee Performance is variable Y. The framework of thought aims to show that Job Satisfaction and Organizational Commitment affects Employee Performance in Generation Y Group. will be used:

Based on the framework in this study, the hypotheses proposed in this research are job satisfaction and organizational commitment partially and simultaneously affect the performance of Generation Y group TELIN employees.

3 METHODOLOGY

A quantitative method with the type of causal research is applied in this study. Job satisfaction and organizational commitment are the independent variables, while the dependent variable is the employee performance. The population in this study used a Generation Y employee group of 172 employees. A simple random sampling technique is used in selecting 122 Generation Y employees with the Slovin formula (Sugiyono 2017). Descriptive analysis is chosen as the analysis technique, along with classic assumption test, partial hypothesis test (T-test), simultaneous hypothesis test (F test), and multiple linear regression analysis and coefficient of determination (Ghozali 2016).

4 RESULTS AND DISCUSSION

The job satisfaction level of Generation Y employees at TELIN is in the high category, with 77.35%. Moreover, the organizational commitment level of Generation Y employees at TELIN is in a sufficient category with a percentage of 67.04%. Furthermore, the performance of Generation Y employees at TELIN is in the high category, with a percentage of 80.56%. Job satisfaction and organizational commitment affect partially and simultaneously following the results of descriptive analysis. The overall variable job satisfaction, organizational commitment, and employee performance in Generation Y group are 70.9%, while other variables influence the remaining 29.1%.

The form of multiple linear regression equations is obtained: $Y = 0.053 + 0.443\ X1 + 0.469\ X2 + e$. The regression equation results imply that the regression coefficient for the independent variable X1 is shown positive, implementing a close relationship between Job Satisfaction (X1) and Employee Performance (Y). The regression coefficient of variable X1 of 0.443 indicates that each increase in Work Satisfaction (X1) of one unit will trigger an increase in Employee Performance (Y) of 0.443 units. The regression coefficient for the independent variable X2 is positive, initiating that there is a close relationship between Organizational Commitment (X2) and Employee Performance (Y). The regression coefficient of variable X2 of 0.469 indicates that each increase in Organizational Commitment (X2) of one unit will trigger an increase in Employee Performance (Y) of 0.469 units.

The relationship of independent variables is determined by using the T-test, namely job satisfaction and organizational commitment to employee performance that is the dependent variable.

Table 1. Multiple regression analysis.

Model	Unstandardized Coefficients B	Std. Error	Standardized Coefficients Beta	t	Sig.	Correlations Zero-order
(Constant)	.053	.185		.285	.776	
Job Satisfaction	.443	.050	.463	8.793	.000	.656
Organizational Commitment	.469	.044	.562	10.688	.000	.722

a. Dependent Variable: Employee Performance
Source: Data that has been processed by the author, 2020

Table 2. Simultaneous hypothesis tests.

ANOVA[a]

Model	Sum of Squares	df	Mean Square	F	Sig.
Regression	14.925	2	7.462	145.291	.000[b]
Residual	6.112	119	.051		
Total	21.037	121			

a. Dependent Variable: Employee Performance
b. Predictors: (Constant), Organizational Commitment, Job Satisfaction
Source: Data that has been processed by the author, 2020

In accordance to the data shown, it implies that the direction of the Job Satisfaction (X1) with Employee Performance (Y) is positive (note the value in the unstandardized column B), the value 0.443 means each progress in Job Satisfaction (X1) will also increase Employee Performance (Y). Afterward, the hypothesis is tested using the t-test by looking at the t count compared to t table (significance level $\alpha = 5\%$) the test criteria used were: The provisions previously stated, which obtained a t-count of 8.793 and t table of 1.980, so that t-count> t-table. This shows that there is a notable influence between Job Satisfaction on Employee Performance. The direction of the relationship between Organizational Commitment (X2) and Employee Performance (Y) is seen positive (note the value in the unstandardized column B). Then the authors tested the hypothesis using the t test by looking at the t count compared to t table (significance level $\alpha = 5\%$) the test criteria used were: The provisions previously stated, which obtained a t-count of 10.668 and t table of 1.980, so that t-count> t-table. This means that a significant influence is shown between Organizational Commitment on Employee Performance. F test is used to determine the relationship between job satisfaction and organizational commitment influence employee performance significantly. The following are results of the F test in this study.

With a value of $\alpha = 5\%$; $df1 = k = 2$; $df2 = n - k - 1 = 122 - 2 - 1 = 119$ obtained F table value of 3.072. Based on the calculation results obtained by Fcount is 145.291 with Ftable value of 3.072. The test criteria are, "reject Ho if Fcount > Ftable". Because of the test results obtained Fcount = 145.291 > Ftable = 3.072, then at $\alpha = 5\%$. Therefore, based on the results shown, it can be determined that Job Satisfaction and Organizational Commitment significantly influence Employee Performance. Analysis of the coefficient of determination is used to calculate the total effect of Job Satisfaction and Organizational Commitment on Employee Performance.

Based on the data above, it can be defined that the value of the correlation coefficient (R) is equal to 0.842 then the value of the coefficient of determination (R2) obtained a value of 0.709. This means that there is an influence between Job Satisfaction and Organizational Commitment on

Table 3. Coefficient of determination.

Model Summary[b]

Model	R	R Square	Adjusted R Square	Std. Error of the Estimate
1	,842[a]	,709	,705	,22663

a. Predictors: (Constant), Organizational Commitment, Job Satisfaction
b. Dependent Variable: Employee Performance
Source: Data that has been processed by the author, 2020

Employee Performance of 70.9%, while the remaining 29.1% is influenced by other variables that the researchers did not involve in this study.

Based on the results of the study note that the Generation Y group employees at PT. Telekomunikasi Indonesia Internasional (TELIN) feels that employees are satisfied to work within the company, and the company is able to accommodate the aspirations and desires, which is indicated in the variable employee job satisfaction. As for the organizational commitment variable, Generation Y of employees of TELIN is still not optimal in creating a comfortable atmosphere for employees. For the performance variable of Generation Y group employees, Generation Y group employees have done their jobs well, fulfilled the targets given, and the employees are trying to improve their performance following the company's goals continuously.

Based on the results of tests, job satisfaction and organizational commitment affect the performance of Generation Y employees at TELIN partially or simultaneously. TELIN can organize or provide training to support employees' capabilities and knowledge and create a design thinking training program that aims to provide a solution-based approach to solving problems, holding programs or events for creativity and innovation at TELIN with attractive rewards.

5 CONCLUSION

From the description above, it can be concluded as follows: Job satisfaction and organizational commitment affect the performance of Generation Y employees at TELIN partially or simultaneously. The influence of job satisfaction and organizational commitment to employee performance is 70.9%, while other variables influence the remaining 29.1%.

REFERENCES

Abrivianto, O. 2014. "Pengaruh Motivasi Kerja dan Komitmen Organisasional terhadap Kinerja Karyawan (Studi pada karyawan bagian HRD PT. Arthawena Sakti Gemilang Malang)".

Bhatti, K. K, & Tahir M. Q. 2007. "Impact of employee participation on job satisfaction, employee commitment and employee productivity." *International review of business research papers* 3, no. 2: 54–68.

Chandra, A & Dadang. 2017."Kepuasan kerja Generasi X dan Generasi Y terhadap komitmen kerja di Bank Mandiri Palembang", *Jurnal Aplikasi Bisnis dan Manajemen*, Vol.3 No.1.

Charity, D. S., and Edy Y. 2016. "Analisis Strategi Dalam Memasuki Pasar Internasional (Studi Kasus Pada PT Telekomunikasi Indonesia Dalam Ekspansi Di Myanmar)." *Jurnal Administrasi Bisnis* 32, no. 1 (2016): 18–26.

Damayanti, H. & Cahyadi. 2018. "Pengaruh Kepuasan kerja terhadap kinerja karyawan (Studi Kasus Karyawan Non Medis RS Al-Islam Wilayah Palembang).

Deloitte Indonesia Perspectives. 2019. "Generasi Milenial dalam Industri 4.0: Berkah Bagi Sumber Daya Manusia Indonesia atau Ancaman?". *Edisi Pertama*, September 2019 https://www2.deloitte.com/content/dam/Deloitte/id/Documents/about-deloitte/id-about-dip-edition-1-chapter-2-id-sep2019.pdf (accessed on September 24, 2020)

DeVaney, A.S. 2015. "*Understanding the Millennial Generation*", *Journal of Financial Service Professionals*.

Dewantoro & Purba .2017. "Pengaruh *Work Engagement* dan *Job Satisfaction* terhadap *Turnover Intention* (Perbandingan pada Generasi X dan Generasi Y)".
Edison, A, & Komariyah. 2016. "Manajemen Sumber Daya Manusia (Strategi dan Perubahan dalam Rangka Meningkatkan Kinerja Pegawai dan Organisasi)". Bandung: Penerbit Alfabeta, 2016.
Fathonah, H & Panjaitan. 2016. "Persepsi Kondisi Kerja dan Kinerja Karyawan Generasi Y", *Manajemen* IKM, Vol:11 No.2.
Forbes. 2015. *Millennials In The Workplace: They Don't Need Trophies But They Want Reinforcement.*
Gewati, M. 2019. "Di Dunia Kerja, Millenial dan Generasi Sebelumnya Ternyata Sama". *Kompas*, 14/04/2019. https://edukasi.kompas.com/read/2019/04/14/07000061/di-dunia-kerja-millenial-dan-generasi-sebelumnya-ternyata-sama?page=all (accessed on September 24, 2020)
Ghozali, I. 2016. Aplikasi Analisis Multivariete Dengan Program IBM SPSS 23 (Edisi 8). Cetakan ke VIII. Semarang: Badan Penerbit Universitas Diponegoro.
Jurnalis Inews. 2018. "Survei: Loyalitas Pekerja Milenial Tidak Bisa Dibeli dengan Uang". Okefinance, 18/05/2018. https://economy.okezone.com/read/2018/05/18/320/1899883/survei-loyalitas-pekerja-milenial-tidak-bisa-dibeli-dengan-uang (accessed on September 24, 2020)
Kerjasama Kementerian Pemberdayaan Perempuan dan Perlindungan Anak dengan Badan Pusat Statistik, 2018. "Profil Generasi Millenial Indonesia".
Mahoney, A. 2015. "*Commitment and Employee Development: Comparing Generation X and Y*"
Novendri, L. 2019. "Pengaruh Kepuasan Kerja Terhadap Kinerja Karyawan Milenial PT. Semen Padang Dengan Variabel Demografis Sebagai Moderator".
Nurhasan, R. 2017. "Kepuasan kerja dan Loyalitas Generasi Y", Jurnal Wacana Ekonomi, ISSN: 1412–5897.
Oktariani, H, & Sukandar. 2017. "Kepuasan Kerja Generasi X dan Generasi Y Terhadap Komitmen Kerja Di Bank Mandiri Palembang".
Onibala, T. 2017. "Karakteristik karyawan generasi langgas menurut pandangan para pimpinan", *Conference on Management and Behavioural Studies*, ISSN NO: 2541–3406.
Pandevi, E. M. 2019. "Ekspansi bisnis PT. Telekomunikasi Indonesia Internasional ke Singapura 2007–2018.", *Skripsi*.
Putra, Y. S. 2016. "*Theoritical Review*: Teori Perbedaan Generasi".
Putra, Y. S. 2018. "Perbedaan *Psychological Capital* Pada Karyawan Generasi Y dan Z serta Pengaruhnya Terhadap Komitmen Organisasi".
Qisthy, Mochammad & Sulistyo. 2018. "Pengaruh budaya organisasi dan kepuasan kerja Generasi Y terhadap *Organizational Citizenship Behaviour* (Studi pada karyawan Generasi Y PT. BPR Tunas Artha Jaya Abadi Kantor Pusat)", Jurnal Administrasi Bisnis (JAB): Vol.58 No.1, 2018.
Salim, V. C. 2014. "Hubungan antara dukungan supervisor terhadap keseimbangan kehidupan dan pekerjaan dengan komitmen organisasi: Sebuah studi terhadap generasi Y".
Siregar, S. 2015. "Pengaruh Kepuasan Kerja dan Komitmen Organisasi Terhadap Organizational Citizenship Behaviour (Perilaku OCB) Karyawan Kantor Distribusi PT. PLN (PERSERO) Distribusi Jawa Barat dan Banten".
Sugiyono. 2017. "Metode Penelitian Kuantitatif". Bandung: Penerbit Alfabeta.
Sutanto & Gunawan. 2013. "Kepuasan Kerja, Komitmen Organisasional dan *Turnover Intentions*".

Synergizing Management, Technology and Innovation in Generating Sustainable and Competitive Business Growth – Hendayani et al (eds)
© 2021 Taylor & Francis Group, London, ISBN 978-0-367-68756-4

The influence of individual, organization, and technology factors on knowledge sharing in Indonesian telecommunications company for the Kalimantan area

M.T.T. Taufik & F.P. Sary
School of Economics and Business, Telkom University, Bandung, West Java, Indonesia

ABSTRACT: This study aims to examine the effect of individual, organizational, and technological factors on knowledge sharing that refers to the analytical framework of Lin (2007), where the scope of this research is an Indonesian telecommunications company for the Kalimantan area. The research method used in this study is a quantitative research method with descriptive, verification, and causal research types. Data analysis techniques used are descriptive analysis and path analysis. This study involved a sample of 228 employees who filled out a questionnaire containing 37 questions. The sampling technique used in this research is Proportionate Cluster Sampling

1 INTRODUCTION

In the last five years, Indonesian telecommunications companies have experienced a decline in revenue trends, especially in the legacy business. This happened to one of them because of the shift in the era of the use of Technology, many that involve Internet-based digital platforms. Facing the challenges of the era, innovation and transformation into a digital telco company is an absolute must for companies to be able to reduce falling revenue that continues to fall. Transformation can occur if the company Manages the knowledge contained within the company. One of the advantages in Managing knowledge is to encourage corporate strategy (Dalkir 2005: 20). And Also conveyed by Lin (2007), a company that is adept at gathering and Integrating its knowledge is more likely to be unique, rare, and difficult To emulate by its competitors so that it has high potential in maintaining Its innovative ability. There are many conditions that affect employees in Conducting knowledge sharing activities, one of which is motivation and the Motivation of individuals (Lumbantobing 2011: 14). In addition, is the Importance of top management support for the knowledge sharing climate in Organizations (Macneil 2004), and also the capacity of the information System, which is stated as one of the enablers in the knowledge management Cycle (Lumbantobing 2011: 39). According to lin's theory, there are three Enablers that influence the dimensions of the process of knowledge sharing: Individual factors, organizational factors, and technological factors. These Three enablers will be examined for their effects on knowledge sharing, Through research focus on the Kalimantan area.

2 LITERATURE REVIEW

2.1 *Knowledge sharing*

According to Davidson and Voss (in Nawawi 2012: 2), knowledge management is a system that allows companies to absorb the knowledge, experience, and creativity of their employees for the improvement of the company. According to Lumbantobing (2011: 24), knowledge sharing is a systematic process in sending, distributing, and disseminating multidimensional knowledge and

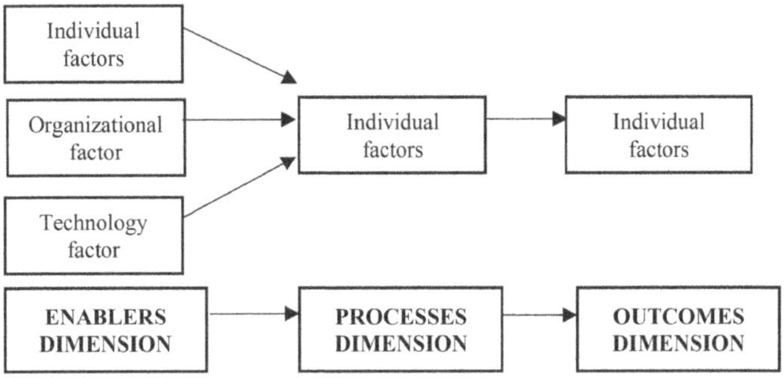

Figure 1. A general framework for studying knowledge sharing. Source: Hsiu-Fen Lin (2007).

context from a person or organization to other people or organizations that need it, through varied methods and media.

Knowledge sharing is explained by Hooff and Ridder (2004: 118) as a reciprocal process of the activity of exchanging knowledge by individuals, whether it is tacit or explicit knowledge, in order to create new knowledge, where the process consists of knowledge donating and knowledge collecting.

According to Lin (2007), enablers were identified as being a mechanism to foster individual and organizational learning as well as facilitating knowledge sharing activities within or across teams or work units. The three main dimensions in knowledge sharing consist of the enabler dimension, the process dimension, and the outcome dimension. In this study, researchers will focus on the relationship and influence between the individual, organizational, and technological factors as an enabler dimension and knowledge sharing as a process dimension. Lin (2007) divides knowledge sharing enablers into the following three factors:

1. Individual Factor
   a. Knowledge self-efficacy is defined as an assessment of individuals related to their ability to regulate the level of success of certain performance (Bandura 1986; in Lin 2007).
   b. Enjoyment in helping others, the pleasure of sharing will encourage a desire to share (sense of willingness).
2. Organizational Factor
   a. Top management support, involvement of top management will encourage positive employee intentions to engage and maintain knowledge sharing (Lin & Lee 2004; in Lin 2007).
   b. Organizational rewards, rewards from indicating that the organization appreciates employee attitudes (Cabrera & Bonache, in Lin 2007).
3. Technological Factor
   There are three indicators that can be used as a reference in correlation with knowledge sharing according to Al-Alawi et al. (2007: 26), which are:
   a. Existence of knowledge sharing technologies
   b. Effectiveness of knowledge sharing tools
   c. Comfort while using knowledge sharing technologies

3 RESEARCH METHODOLOGY

3.1 *Research model and hypothesis*

Based on the research model, these are the hypotheses:

H1: There is a total direct effect of individual, organizational and technological factors on knowledge sharing

H2: There is a direct effect of individual factor on knowledge sharing
H3: There is a direct effect of organizational factor on knowledge sharing
H4: There is a direct influence of technological factor on knowledge sharing

The research model used for the analysis is as follows:

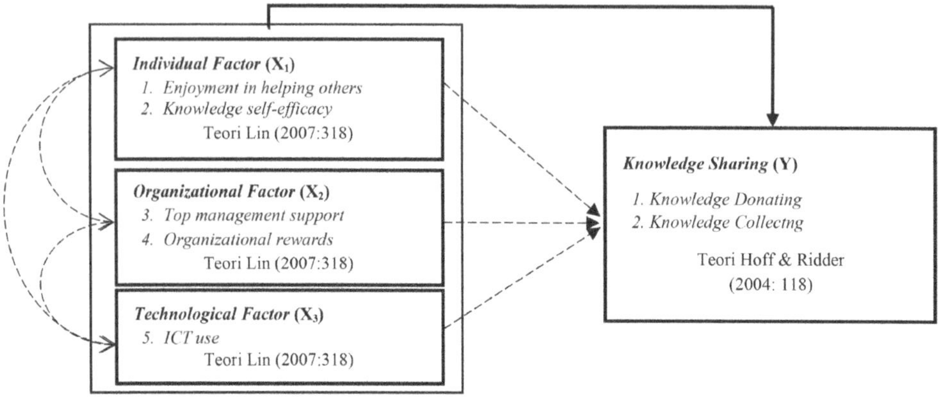

Figure 2. Research model.

4 DATA ANALYSIS AND RESULTS

This research uses descriptive analysis and path analysis with software SPSS for windows Proportionate Cluster Sampling technique because it is in accordance with geographical characteristics where the research is carried out divided into six different areas. The sample uses a population of permanent employees in Telkom Regional 6 with a total sample of 228 employees. This research uses a questionnaire containing 37 items with a five-point Likert scale. The result of validity test using SPSS software is valid because the value of items is greater than the value of r-table. The value of r-table is 0.361 for $n = 30$ and $\alpha = 0.05$ (two-tailed). Based on reliability test using Alpha Cronbach technique the item is reliable because the value of Cronbach's Alpha is greater than 0.7. The results of validity and reliability tests show that all items in the questionnaire are valid and reliable, so the data can be used for further statistical analysis.

The result of the F-test, as shown in Table 1, indicates that F_{count} (99,780) > F_{count} (2,64); the hypothesis "Individual factor, organizational factor, and technological factor simultaneously have a significant effect on knowledge sharing" is approved.

Based on Table 2, R^2 value is 0.572 or 57.2%, which means the value of the influence of the Individual factor, Organizational factor, and Technological factor variables simultaneously influences the knowledge sharing (Y) variable at PT. Telkom Indonesia Tbk. Regional 6 Kalimantan at 57.2%, while the remaining 42.8% is influenced by other factors not discussed in this study.

Result of the t-test conducted with the value of t_{table} is 1.960. Organizational factors variable has no significant effect on the variable Y because $t_{count} < t_{table}$ so the variables will be trimmed (deleted from calculation) in path analysis framework diagram as shown below.

Based on path analysis formula and the regression analysis calculation, the structural equation of path analysis is as follows:

$$Y = \rho yx1X1 + \rho yx3X3 + \rho y\varepsilon \quad (1)$$

$$Y = 0,442\,X1 + 0,431\,X3 + 0,435 \quad (2)$$

The result of path analysis calculation is shown in Table 5.

Table 1. Correlation Results Between Variables X1, X2, X3, and Y.

		Individual Factor	*Organizational Factor*	*Technological Factor*	*Knowledge Sharing*
Individual Factor	*Pearson Correlation*	1	.452**	.486**	.651**
	Sig. (2-tailed)		.000	.000	.000
	N	228	228	228	228
Organizational Factor	*Pearson Correlation*	.452**	1	.692**	.556**
	Sig. (2-tailed)	.000		.000	.000
	N	228	228	228	228
Technological Factor	*Pearson Correlation*	.486**	.692**	1	.645**
	Sig. (2-tailed)	.000	.000		.000
	N	228	228	228	228
Knowledge Sharing	*Pearson Correlation*	.651**	.556**	.645**	1
	Sig. (2-tailed)	.000	.000	.000	
	N	228	228	228	228

**. *Correlation is significant at the 0.01 level (2-tailed).*

Table 2. Result of F Test (Simultaneous test).

Model		*Sum of Squares*	*df*	*Mean Square*	*F*	*Sig.*
1	*Regression*	47.033	3	15.678	99.780	.000[b]
	Residual	35.196	224	.157		
	Total	82.229	227			

a. Dependent variable: Knowledge sharing
b. Predictors: (Constant), Technological factor, Individual factor

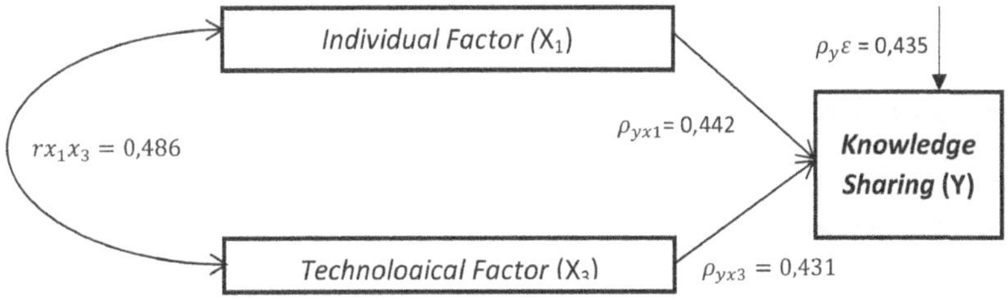

Figure 3. Path Analysis Model of Variable X1 and X3 to Variable Y.

Table 3. Result of KD or R^2 Test (value of simultaneous test).

Model	*R*	*R Square*	*Adjusted R Square*	*Std. Error of the Estimate*
1	.756[a]	.572	.566	.396388

a. Predictors: (Constant), Technological factor, Individual factor, Organizational factor

Table 4. Result of T-test (partial hypothesis test).

		Unstandardized Coefficients		*Standardized Coefficients*		
Model		B	Std. Error	Beta	*t*	*Sig.*
1	*(Constant)*	.203	.182		1.115	.266
	Individual Factor	.453	.054	.424	8.332	.000
	Organizational Factor	.111	.059	.116	1.892	.060
	Technological Factor	.337	.059	.359	5.706	.000

a. Dependent Variable: Knowledge sharing

Table 5. Indirect and direct effect of Variable X1 and X3 to variable Y.

		Non-direct effect		
Variable	Direct effect	X_1	X3	Total Effect
X_1	19,53%	0	9,258%	28,78%
X_3	18,57%	9,258%	0	27,83%
The total effect of variables X_1 and X_3 on the Y variable				56,5%
Effect of Other Variables on Y Variables				43,5%

5 CONCLUSIONS AND RECOMMENDATIONS

Based on analysis and calculations performed, individual factors, organizational factors, and technological factors simultaneously influence knowledge sharing in Telkom Indonesia Regional 6 Kalimantan. However, organizational factor variables have insignificant effect on the Y variable. Therefore a change in the path analysis framework involves only two variables, namely the individual factor variable and the technology factor.

The results of the calculation of path analysis, individual factor variables, and technology simultaneously affect knowledge sharing by 56.5%, while 43.5% are influenced by other factors. The partial hypothesis of the effect on knowledge sharing, individual factor variables have a value of 28.78% while the technology factor variable is 27.83%.

Advice for PT. Telkom Indonesia regional 6 Kalimantan in increasing knowledge sharing activities:

a. Maximizing individual factors activities that can increase familiarity between individuals or between units such as outdoor activities so as to foster trust between people.
b. Maximizing technological factors through increased capacity, improved user interface applications, increased application usage and also awareness of ICT facilities.
c. Maximizing knowledge sharing activities through socialization of the objectives and benefits of activities for the growth and sustainability of company performance.
d. The company can explore again the organizational factors which in this study are stated to have insignificant effect by communicating so that there is positive feedback expected by employees of the support of management for knowledge sharing activities.

This study only examined three variables that influence knowledge sharing. Therefore, it is suggested in subsequent studies to use other factors that are considered to influence knowledge sharing, such as organizational culture, positive attitude and innovation capability, or proceed to the outcomes dimensions based on Lin's previous framework diagram (2007).

REFERENCES

Al-Alawi, A. I., Al-Marzooqi, N. Y. & Mohammed, Y. F. 2007. Organizational Culture and Knowledge Sharing: Critical Success Factors. *Journal of Knowledge Management*, 11(2), 22–42. Retrieved from Emerald inside Journal Database.

Dalkir, K. 2005. Knowledge Management in Theory and Practice. McGill University, Montreal.

Hooff, B. van den & R, Jan A. de. 2004. Knowledge Sharing in Context: The Influence of Organizational Commitment, Communication Climate and CMC use on Knowledge Sharing. *Journal of knowledge management*, 8(6), 117–130. Retrieved from Emerald Inside Journal Database.

Lin, Hsu-Fen. 2007. *Knowledge Sharing and Firm innovation capability: An Empirical Study*. International Journal of Manpower. Vol. 28(3/4), pp. 315–332.

Lumbantobing, P. 2011. *Manajemen Knowledge Sharing Berbasis Komunitas*. Bandung, Indonesia: Knowledge management Society Indonesia.

MacNeil, C.M. 2004. *Exploring the supervisor role as a facilitator of knowledge sharing in teams*. Journal of European Industrial Training, Vol. 28 No. 1, pp. 93–102.

Nawawi, I. 2012. *Manajemen Pengetahuan (Knowledge Management) Teori dan Aplikasi dalam Mewujudkan Daya Saing Organisasi Bisnis dan Publik*. Bogor: Penerbit Ghalia Indonesia.

Synergizing Management, Technology and Innovation in Generating Sustainable and Competitive Business Growth – Hendayani et al (eds)
© 2021 Taylor & Francis Group, London, ISBN 978-0-367-68756-4

Business process reengineering of school committee in Indonesia

E.N. Sinaga
Student of Postgraduate of Universitas Terbuka, Indonesia

H.D.P. Sinaga
Student of Doctoral Program of the Diponegoro University, Semarang, Indonesia

ABSTRACT: Revitalization of the school committee's (SC) task to improve the quality of education is not in line with the expectations of the community, considering several cases were still occurring, such as the finding of 50% of SC were not functioning optimally, the existing number of illegal students, and several cases and complaints indicating the negligence of SC on their duties and functions. Based on the qualitative research, two conclusions are generated. First, the SC's business processes are not yet accountable and transparent. Second, the use of information technology and systems in the business process reengineering (BPR) of the SC will drive four important tasks of the SC accountably and transparently. It is expected that the state/regulator regulates the creation of the official website of each school in order to display all the reports of the duties and functions of the SC per semester.

1 INTRODUCTION

As human resources (HR) are the main capital in national development (Central Statistics Agency 2019) in Indonesia, the quality of education plays an important role in determining the future of the Indonesian nation and state. The urgency of strengthening the quality of education is undeniable given the statistics of the number of students in Indonesia for 2018/2019, as the next generation of the nation and state development in Indonesia is very large, which is from a total of 268.07 million inhabitants of Indonesia; 26.93 million people are students of the school elementary (SD) and its equivalents, 13.16 million people are junior high school (SMP) students and their equivalents, and 10.99 million are high school (SMA) students and their equivalents (Central Statistics Agency 2020). Of course, the quality of education in a school cannot be separated from the quality of educational services that are the joint responsibility of the stakeholders associated with the school. Stakeholders identified by Freeman (1984) are each group or individual that can influence or can be influenced by the achievement of organizational goals, so that in the scope of school education, the existence of these stakeholders should be able to accommodate the wishes of every organization that must implement sustainable business processes, which are able to produce much better quality outputs (Kumar et al. 2019, 55).

One of the stakeholders that must exist in every school in Indonesia is the school committee, as Article 1 number 2 of the Minister of Education and Culture Regulation (Permendikbud) No. 75 of 2016 concerning school committees has defined the school committee as an independent institution consisting of parents/guardians of students, school community, as well as community leaders who care about education. Consideration of Permendikbud No. 75 of 2016 which seeks to revitalize the duties of school committees to improve the quality of education is still not in line with what is expected by the community. The research reported by the Directorate General of Primary and Secondary Education in 2009 showed that 50% of the Education Board and school committees were not functioning optimally (Okezone 2014). Education observers from the North Sumatra Education Consultation Institute revealed that one of the factors that caused the outbreak of illegal/stealth students in SMA/SMK Negeri (High Schools) in North Sumatra was the lack of public control due to the malfunctioning of the school committee as it should because the school committee should be the frontline to oversee the implementation education in schools (Medan Bisnis 2018). Civil Society Coalition for Educational Transformation considers Permendikbud No. 75 of 2016 is no better than Kepmendiknas No. 044/U/2002 because the Permendikbud no longer mentions the purpose of the existence of the school committee to create a transparent, accountable, and democratic climate so that the implementation and service of education are of higher quality in each educational unit as it has been affirmed in the Minister of Education (HukumOnline 2017). Then, according to the Malang Corruption Watch Advocacy, a number of cases and complaints in the city of Malang indicated that the school committee was negligent in carrying out its main duties and functions, starting from supervising the use of the school operational assistance budget and special budget funds (Radar Malang 2019).

Responding to the duties of school committees, which are still not fully maximized despite the rapid development of information, communication, and technology that should be one of the important strategies in strengthening the functions and duties of school committees to continuously improve the quality of education, it is necessary to open public information in limiting all forms of abuse of authority and in supervising the use of the education budget by considering the rights of each related stakeholder to obtain access and information (Sinaga & Bolifaar 2020) through business process reengineering (BPR) of the school committee in Indonesia. Thus, this study will attempt to answer two main problems in improving and strengthening the functions and duties of the school committee and at the same time in order to fulfill one of the objectives of the state in the preamble of the 1945 Constitution in a transparent and accountable manner, namely to educate citizens. First, how is the school committee's business process at the moment? Second, how is the reengineering of the school committee's business processes in improving the quality of education accountably and transparently in Indonesia?

2 LITERATURE REVIEW

Various facts about the non-existence of the school committee in improving the quality of education require further study related to the business process so far. There are indeed some previous studies on school committees. Sawaludin (2012), who concluded that school committee management (with a case study in SMK 1 Tanjung) did not have a planning program that was analyzed for service quality, did not have an organization in service quality, had not yet maximally mobilized service quality, and had not maximally controlled quality service. However, this previous research has not provided a solution for how an ideal/adequate school committee business process is in improving the quality of education that is accountable and transparent. Then, the study of Sinaga (2017) concluded that there was a significant difference in the implementation of the role of school committees in SMAN 1 and SMAN 2 in Balige District, which had an impact on improving the quality of education, where the quality of education at SMAN 2 Balige was higher than SMAN 1 Balige. This previous research only focused on the role of school committees in the quality of education, not yet reaching the school committee's business processes in improving the quality of education that is accountable and transparent. Furthermore, Ratnaningtyas and Setiyani (2017), who conducted cluster sampling to determine the effectiveness of the role and effectiveness of school committees in financial management in Semarang City High Schools, concluded that the school committee as a supervisory body for managing school financial management in Semarang City High Schools was effective, where the school committee is still involved in the school program and continues to oversee the running of school financial management, although its function is slightly reduced in the financial section because the school funds are financed by the school operational assistance fund (BOS).

The previous research only focused on the role of school committees in financial management, not yet reaching the school committee's business processes in improving the quality of accountable and transparent education. Therefore, further investigation is needed regarding the implementation of the BPR system of school committees in improving the quality of education in Indonesia given that many studies state that BPR is a management approach aimed at increasing the efficiency and effectiveness of processes in public organizations, across public organizations, from public organizations to businesses, and from public organizations to citizens (Lucas 2016). Reengineering defined by Hammer and Champy (1993) as *"the fundamental rethinking and radical redesign of business processes to achieve dramatic improvements in critical, contemporary measures of performance, such as cost, quality, service, and speed"* shows that BPR is an approach or business management strategy that focuses on analyzing business processes, reimagining strategies, integrating the use of information technology (IT), and redesigning business processes to achieve increased efficiency, waste reduction, and improved performance (Susanto et al. 2019). BPR breakthrough closely related to IT will open a new dimension of the reorganization process considering that efforts to focus more on IT will design and mechanize the business processes of school committees in Indonesia to simplify implementation and will also eliminate forms of work that do not add value (Bhaskar 2016).

Furthermore, regarding the BPR, which is the main solution to increase productivity and quality and at the same time streamline costs (as long as organizations can identify success and failure factors in implementing it), it had been scientifically reviewed by several scholars, such as Lucas (2016), Bhaskar (2018), and Mohapatra (2013). Lucas's study (2016) found that the public sector would be effective and efficient in service delivery if the BPR was implemented, where BPRs became a tool for radical improvement in all aspects of its performance in providing services to the public. Bhaskar (2018) summarized the success and failure factors of BPRs based on various literature reviews, academic points of view, and interview. Success factors include readiness, courage, and willingness to make changes, using the best methodology and framework, shared working environment, commitment, and top management support, aligning BPR strategies with IT capabilities, training systems, education, and fair rewards, less bureaucratic structure, culture, adequate financial support, focus on functions and tasks while maintaining effective communication, and proper analysis of business needs. Failure of BPR can occur due to factors including inadequate preparation, lack of suitable and effective BPR framework and methodology, inadequate availability of reliable advanced technology, unclear and unrealistic strategies and scope, incomplete BPR implementation, incomplete communication effective, poor leadership and lack of top management commitment, lack of collaborative work, the insufficient authority given to BPR teams, lack of innovation in the redesigned process, many stakeholders who are resistant to change, and lack of training and education (Bhaskar 2018). Thus, in order for the BPR to be successful, it is sufficient to implement the five BPR methodologies mapped by Mohapatra (2013): preparation for reengineering, map and analyze as-is process, design to-be process, implement reengineered process, and improve process continuously.

The use of BPR in radically improving school committees in Indonesia is inseparable from the existence of any group or individual that can influence or can be influenced by the achievement of school committee functions so that it is sufficient to apply stakeholder theory in implementing sustainable business processes, which are able to produce high levels of service and the quality of output is much better (Kumar et al. 2019). Stakeholder theory will deal with three interrelated problems that arise in an organization: how value is created, how to link ethics and capitalism, and how to help managerial thinking in connecting explicitly to values and ethics better, in correlating a business environment, a group, and individuals (Parmar et al. 2010). Stakeholder theory is very important in decision-making techniques in school committees considering the normative justification of stakeholder principles relating to the common good, risk, ethics, and the principle of fair play (Phillips et al. 2003), given the tendency for decision making in a group or an individual not necessarily accurate and/or fair. The presence of stakeholders will increasingly show that the implementation of the duties and functions of school committee members based on good faith will be common good in resisting the arbitrary actions of a particular individual or group (Bonnafous-Boucher & Porcher 2010).

3 METHODOLOGY

Regarding the urgency and importance of describing, evaluating, and reengineering the school committee's business processes in improving the quality of accountable and transparent education in Indonesia through the BPR, this study must rely on certain values in dealing with existing problems, ideally by using qualitative research (Macfarlane 2010) by sourcing the secondary data. This qualitative research includes a series of interpretive techniques that attempt to describe, solve problems, and translate certain phenomena (Cooper & Schindler 2014), in the form of maximization of school committees who already have legal standing in Indonesian legislation. Secondary data is data that has been available, which refers to data that has been collected and analyzed by certain parties whose data is reliable, appropriate, and sufficient with the context of the problem to be studied in this study (Kothari 2004). Sources of library data are in the form of binding primary legal materials (such as applicable laws and regulations in Indonesia), secondary legal materials that can explain primary legal materials (such as textbooks, scientific journals, international seminar results), and tertiary legal materials that can support existing explanations on primary and secondary legal materials (such as dictionaries, encyclopedias, official and trusted websites). Further, the secondary data in the form of primary, secondary, and tertiary materials will be analyzed using unobtrusive methods, namely content analysis, document analysis, and comparative analysis of history and its rules (Leavy 2017).

4 ANALYSIS AND DISCUSSIONS

4.1 *Overview and legality of school committees in Indonesia*

School committees, which number at least 5 people and at most 15 people in each school and who may not concurrently serve as committee members in other schools in Indonesia, are functioning to improve the quality of educational services that must be carried out cooperatively, democratically, and be independent, professional, and accountable (Article 1 number (2) and Article 2 of Permendikbud No. 75 of 2016). The elements of the school committee (up to a maximum of 100% of members meet) are in accordance with Article 4 (1) and (2) of Permendikbud No. 75 of 2016 and must consist of elements of at most 50% parents/guardians of students who are still active at the school concerned, at most 30% community leaders who have work and life behaviors that can be role models for the local community, and/or members/administrators of organizations or community groups concerned with education, not including members/management organizations of professional educators and administrators of political parties, and at most 30% of education experts, such as retired educators, and/or people who have experience in the field of education.

School committee members who are elected accountably and democratically through a parent/guardian meeting of students have a management board consisting of a chairman, secretary, and treasurer who are elected from and by members through consensus and/or through voting to be later determined by the principal (Article 6 and Article 7 of Permendikbud No. 75 of 2016) a term of office of at most three years and can be reelected for one term of office.

4.2 *Current school committee business processes in Indonesia*

Once inaugurated, the school committee must draw up a statute and bylaws that contain at least the names and places of residence, basis, objectives and activities, membership and management, rights and obligations of members and management, finance, work mechanisms and meetings, changes to the statutes and by-laws, and the dissolution of the organization (Article 7 paragraph (4)

Permendikbud No. 75 of 2016). The four important tasks of the school committee are: (1) giving consideration in determining and implementing education policies related to school policies and programs, school income and expenditure plans/school work plans and budget (RAPBS/RKAS), school performance criteria, criteria educational facilities in schools, and the criteria for collaboration with other parties; (2) raising funds and other educational resources from the community both individuals/organizations/business world/industry and other stakeholders through creative and innovative efforts; (3) supervising education services in schools in accordance with statutory provisions; and (4) following up complaints, suggestions, criticisms, and aspirations from students, parents/guardians, and the community as well as the results of the school committee's observations of school performance (Article 3 of the Ministry of Education and Culture Regulation No. 75 of 2016). Then, in Article 9 Permendikbud No. 75 of 2016 regulates the implementation of functions and duties that must coordinate with the relevant school in coordinating and consulting with the provincial education council/district/city education council, provincial/district/city education offices, and other stakeholders.

School committees that in carrying out their functions to improve the quality of education services must be carried out cooperatively, democratically, independently, professionally, and accountably, apparently the business process has not yet referred to the functions and ways of carrying out these functions as the general characteristics of the public sector in the form of reluctance, risk stability, dependency on public budgets, and the absence of incentives have hampered business processes (Ghatari et al. 2014), which should be transparent and accountable. Although Article 13 of Permendikbud No. 75 of 2016 has regulated that school committees are required to submit reports to parents/guardians of students, the community, and school principals through periodic meetings at least one time in one semester in the form of school committee activities reports and reports on the results of fundraising. Funding and other educational resources from the community, but access to information on each component of the four important tasks of the school committee per semester for three years of membership does not meet transparent and accountable qualifications. In this case, the government should pay special attention to the "process" in the organization of school committees by trying to find solutions to improve and accelerate the organization's processes through various tools and techniques that have developed in strategic management so far, one of which is through reengineering business processes (Jamali et al. 2011) on school committee organizations. Thus, the responsibility of the four important tasks of school committees throughout Indonesia is compiled by the central government, in this case, the Ministry of Education and Culture, through its official website in a transparent and accountable manner, so that competent stakeholders can monitor and evaluate the results of reporting and accountability of the school committee. This is in line with the idea of Bhaskar (2016), which confirms that information and technology are important enablers of BPRs, where with the existence of technological information it will be possible for BPRs to flow: (1) a shared database (information is available in many places simultaneously and also a job can be done simultaneously); (2) telecommunications network (which allows the Ministry of Education and Culture organization to maintain central operations control and also decentralized at the same time, where the telecommunications network allows school committees, schools, district/city education offices, provincial education offices, parents/guardians of students, and the public to access and input information); (3) decision support tools (which allow decision making to be part of the participation of each competent stakeholder); (4) wireless, Android, and laptop data communication (which allows committee members to work independently); (5) automatic identification (which allows tracking of every use of user names that can decide and determine the results of the implementation of tasks both at school and when assignments are in the field.

4.3 *Business process reengineering of school committee in improving the quality of education in Indonesia*

A business process redesign is needed to achieve changes that can align school committee performance improvement with improving the quality of education services in schools through BPR.

Table 1. Matrix of the mapping and steps for BPR implementation on school committees.

Mapping	Steps	Implementation on BPR of School Committees
Preparation for reengineering	*Build cross-. functional team, identify customer-driven objective, and develop strategic purpose.*	Because the BPR of the school committee is for SD and equivalent, the SMP and equivalent, and SMA and its equivalent throughout Indonesia, where the autonomy of school management is currently divided among the regency/city governments, the provincial government, and the Ministry of Religion, the cross-functional team and the integration of the use of ICTs are centralized at the Ministry of Education and Culture. The aim is to ensure accountability of all school committee tasks (in the form of consideration, RAPBS/RKAS, school performance criteria, educational facilities criteria, criteria for school collaboration with other parties, fundraising and other educational resources, supervision of education services in schools, and follow-up complaints, suggestions, criticisms, and aspirations from students, parents/guardians, and the community as well as observations of the school committee on school performance) whose reports must be made per semester can be published transparently on the official website of the school, relevant local government, and central government (Ministry of Education and Culture).
Map and analyze As-Is process	*Create activity and process models, simulate and perform, and identify disconnects and value adding process.*	It is the most important reengineering step, which shows that a fundamental process change has taken place, whereby the activity and process model that can add value creation has been through the feedback process and must be the result of active participation of the school committee with the school, parents/guardians of students, and related education agencies. Furthermore, the results of these activities are sent or uploaded on the official website, which is centralized at the Ministry of Education and Culture.
Design To-Be process	*Benchmark process, design and validate To-Be processes, and perform trade-off analysis.*	One concrete example of benchmarks in starting BPR is PT. Garuda Indonesia, due to reengineering, increased its load factor from 61.6% during the second semester of 2008 to 68.6% in the first semester of 1999 (Indrajit 2016). Furthermore, the results of the uploading of school committees to the government website will be a benchmark for other school committees, so that between school committees can transfer knowledge to improve each other's performance in the future.
Implement reengineered process	*Evolve . implementation plan, prototype, and simulate transition plans, initiate training programs, and implement transition plan.*	All relevant stakeholders must be responsible for minimizing the disruption of ICTs operations and supporting any smooth reengineering process. This, among others, can be done through education and training programs, making detailed schedules, tasks, and responsibilities of each school committee member. In addition, the government must think of operational funds, permanent space for school committees in related schools, and several employees who assist the operation of school committee members, given the function to be produced by school committee members is to improve the quality of education services in related schools.
Improve process continuously	*Initiate ongoing . measurement, review performance against target, and improve process continuously*	Accountability of all committee tasks through its reporting per semester will be seen transparently on the official website of the education office, the Ministry of Religion, and the Ministry of Education and Culture, so that it can be a means of monitoring and evaluation for stakeholders who are competent with the functioning of the school committee in improving the quality of education services in their schools.

Sources: Developed from Mohapatra (2013) and Bhaskar (2016).

Certainly, the willingness of every competent stakeholder to influence and be influenced by the objectives of the BPR of the school committee is necessary so that fundamental changes based on the BPR of the school committee can run regularly and orderly in improving the quality of education, including in balancing existing obligations (such as the obligation to carry out research, provide services, and ensure effective teaching) and choose best mechanisms and approaches for evaluating schools (Wirawan et al. 2020). Considering that school committee organizations need to increase their productivity in improving the quality of schools through business processes that must undergo fundamental and systematic changes, the business processes must be efficient, effective, and innovative processes (Jamali et al. 2011) without ignoring the use of innovative IT applications so that management can be flexible, team-oriented, and coordinated across functions, so that it is recognized that this reengineering process requires considerable investment (Bhaskar 2016) and even requires time that is not fast (Ghatari et al. 2014).

As for the reengineering process of school committees to result in process improvements, drastic cost reductions after BPR implementation, and increased productivity of school committee tasks and functions, it is important to apply the five BPR methodologies mapped by Mohapatra (2013). Preparation for reengineering of the school committee is based on a description of the current school committee's business processes based on applicable laws, raising questions about the need and benefits of BPR for education stakeholders, which will provide benchmarks for existing processes and processes school committee reengineering. Next, map and analyze the As-Is process based on adequate resources to be allocated in accordance with the results of the process, including identifying obstacles to the process of adding value to be carried out. Furthermore, to design a process to be done through several steps, such as conducting a comparison stage in the framework of process improvement and implementation, then conducting a trade-off analysis of the feasibility of the alternatives so that the best alternative is found. The fourth step in the form of reengineering process is the most difficult stage because it will face a lot of resistance, where improvement programs in organizational processes must be able to align these things (such as organizational structure, IT infrastructure, business policies, and procedures) with their implementation so that a design is produced that can help the organization move to the desired To-Be process. And the fifth step in the form of continuous process improvement can be done through efforts to always monitor the process and record the progress of activities and actions. The impact of empirical reengineering can be carried out by subsequent empirical studies through metric-based measurements by taking feedback from specific stakeholders concerned. Conducting stakeholder surveys and progressively reviewing performance against clear targets can help in continuously improving the process. The following Table 1 is a matrix in the form of a summary mapping of the five BPR methodologies of school committees developed from the thoughts of Mohapatra (2013) and Bhaskar (2016).

5 CONCLUSIONS

This study produces two main conclusions. First, the business process in carrying out the duties of school committees in Indonesia is not yet transparent and accountable, whereas the function of school committees that must improve the quality of education services in their schools cannot be monitored and evaluated by the relevant stakeholders. Second, the state (also as the regulator) must integrate ICTs in BPRs in order to produce efficient, effective, and accountable process improvements and productivity of school committees' tasks and functions. In order for the output in the form of reports and accountability per semester through the implementation of the BPR built on the school committee to be monitored and evaluated transparently by the relevant stakeholders, the state must create the official website of each centralized school as well as the official website to the respective Regions Education Office and to the Ministry of Education and Culture. Indeed, the biggest obstacle in building a school committee BPR lies in the budget, but considering the urgency of the BPR in implementing the duties and functions of the school committee and the mandate of the 1945 Constitution, the state/regulator can do it in stages for certain schools based on certain parameters.

REFERENCES

Bhaskar, H.L. 2016. A critical analysis of information technology and business process reengineering. *International Journal of Productivity and Quality Management* 19(1): 98–115.

Bhaskar, H.L. 2018. Business process reengineering framework and methodology: a critical study. *International Journal of Services and Operations Management* 29(4): 527–556.

Bonnafous-Boucher, M. & Porcher, P. 2010. Towards a stakeholder society: Stakeholder theory vs theory of civil society. *European Management Review* 7(4): 205–216.

Central Statistics Agency 2019. *Potret Pendidikan Indonesia: Statistik Pendidikan 2019*. Katalog BPS: 4301008. Jakarta: Badan Pusat Statistik. Available at: https://www.bps.go.id/publication/download.html?nrbvfeve=MWRlYjU4OGVmNWZkYmZiYTMzNDNiYjUx&xzmn=aHR0cHM6Ly93d3cuYnBzLmdvLmlkL3B1YmxpY2F0aW9uLzIwMTkvMTEvMjkvMWRlYjU4OGVmNWZkYmZiYTMzNDNiYjUxL3BvdHJldC1wZW5kaWRpa2FuLXN0YXRpc3Rpay1wZW5kaWRpa2FuLWluZG9uZXNpYS0yMDE5Lmh0bWw%3D&twoadfnoarfeauf=MjAyMC0wMy0wNSAxMzoyMTowNA%3D%3D. Accessed on March 3, 2020.

Central Statistics Agency 2020. *Statistik Indonesia 2020*. Katalog: 1101005. Jakarta: Badan Pusat Statistik. Available at: https://www.bps.go.id/publication/download.html?nrbvfeve=NmU2NTRkZDcxNzU1MmU4MmZiM2MyZmZl&xzmn=aHR0cHM6Ly93d3cuYnBzLmdvLmlkL3B1YmxpY2F0aW9uLzIwMjAvMDIvMjgvNmU2NTRkZDcxNzU1MmU4MmZiM2MyZmZlL3N0YXRpc3Rpay1pbmRvbmVzaWEtLXBlbnllZGlhYW4tZGF0YS11bnR1ay1wZXJlbmNhbmFhbi1wZW1iYW5ndW5hbi5odG1s&twoadfnoarfeauf=MjAyMC0wMy0wNSAxMjo1ODoxNQ%3D%3D. Accessed on March 3, 2020.

Cooper, D.R. & Schindler P.S. 2014. *Business Research Methods*. New York: McGraw-Hill/Irwin.

Freeman, R. E. 1984. *Strategic Management: A Stakeholder Approach*. Boston: Pitman Publishing.

Ghatari, A.R., Shamsi, Z. & Vedadi, A. 2014. Business process reengineering in public sector: ranking the implementation barriers. *International Journal of Process Management and Benchmarking* 4(3): 324–341.

Hammer, M. & Champy. J. 1993. *Reengineering the Corporation: A Manifesto for Business Revolution*. London: Harper Collins Publisher.

HukumOnline 2017. Koalisi Pendidikan Kritik Wewenang Baru Komite Sekolah. Available at: https://www.hukumonline.com/berita/baca/lt58831a069976d/koalisi-pendidikan-kritik-wewenang-baru-komite-sekolah/. Accessed on March 3, 2020.

Indrajit, R.E. 2016. *Business Process Reengineering*. Yogyakarta: Preinexus.

Jamali, G., Abbaszadeh, M.A., Ebrahimi, M. & Maleki, T. 2011. Business Process Reengineering Implementation: Developing a Causal Model of Critical Success Factors. *International Journal of e-Education, e-Business, e-Management and e-Learning* 1(5): 354–359.

Kothari, C.R. 2004. *Research Methodology: Methods & Techniques*. New Delhi: New Age International (P) Ltd., Publishers.

Kumar, K., Zindani, D. & Davim, J. P. 2019. *Industry 4.0: Developments towards the Fourth Industrial Revolution*. Singapore: Springer Nature Singapore Pte Ltd.

Leavy, P. 2017. *Research Design: Quantitative, Qualitative, Mixed Methods, Arts-Based, and Community-Based Participatory Research Approaches*. New York and London: The Guilford Press

Lucas, T. 2016. The Application Of Business Process Re-Engineering Systems To Enhance Service Delivery In The Public Sector. European Journal of Research in Social Sciences 4(7). Available at https://www.idpublications.org/wp-content/uploads/2016/06/Full-Paper-THE-APPLICATION-OF-BUSINESS-PROCESS-RE-ENGINEERING-SYSTEMS-TO-ENHANCE-SERVICE-DELIVERY-IN-THE-PUBLIC-SECTOR.pdf. Accessed on April 2, 2020.

Macfarlane, B. (2010). *Values and virtues in qualitative research*. In Savin-Baden, M. & Major, C.H, New Approaches to Qualitative Research: Wisdom and Uncertainty. Oxon: Routledge, 19–27.

Medan Bisnis 2018. Kasus Siswa Ilegal, Fungsi Komite Sekolah Dipertanyakan. Available at http://www.medanbisnisdaily.com/news/online/read/2018/01/28/22690/kasus_siswa_ilegal_fungsi_komite_sekolah_dipertanyakan/. Accessed on March 3, 2020.

Mohapatra, S. 2013. *Business Process Reengineering: Automation Decision Points in Process Reengineering*. New York: Springer Science+Business Media.

Okezone 2014. Komite Sekolah Belum Berfungsi Maksimal. Available at: https://news.okezone.com/read/2014/11/26/65/1071066/komite-sekolah-belum-berfungsi-maksimal. Accessed on March 3, 2020.

Parmar, B.L., *et al.* (2010). Stakeholder Theory: The State of the Art. *The Academy of Management Annals* 4(1): 403–445.

Phillips, R., Freeman, R.E. & Wicks, A.C. 2003. What Stakeholder Theory is not? *Business Ethics Quarterly*, 13(4): 479–502.

Radar Malang 2019. Kinerja Komite Sekolah Masih Memprihatinkan. Available at: https://radarmalang.id/kinerja-komite-sekolah-masih-memprihatinkan/. Accessed on March 3, 2020.

Ratnaningtyas, K. & Setiyani, R. (2017). Efektifitas Komite Sekolah Sebagai Badan Pengawas Manajemen Keuangan Sekolah pada SMA Negeri Se-Kota Semarang. *Economic Education Analysis Journal* 6(2): 571–582.

Sawaludin. 2012. Analisis Manajemen Komite Sekolah Dalam Meningkatkan Kualitas Pelayanan Pendidikan di SMKN 1 Tanjung Kabupaten Lombok Utara. Jakarta: Suatu Tugas Akhir Program Magister pada Program Pascasarjana Universitas Terbuka. Available at: http://repository.ut.ac.id/1327/. Accessed on March 5, 2020.

Sinaga, D. 2017. Analisa Peran Komite Sekolah Dalam Peningkatan Mutu Pendidikan Di Kecamatan Balige Kabupaten Toba Samosir (Studi Komparatif SMA Negeri 1 Balige dan SMA Negeri 2 Balige). *Sosiohumaniora* 19(2): 159–166.

Sinaga, H.D.P. & Bolifaar, A.H. 2020. Blockchain Adoption for Plea Bargaining of Corporate Crime in Indonesia. *ICBCT'20: Proceedings of the 2nd International Conference on Blockchain Technology*, March 2020: 115—119. DOI: 10.1145/3390566.3391680.

Susanto, H., Leu, F-Y. & Chen, C.K. 2019. *Business Process Reengineering: An ICT Approach*. Florida: Apple Academic Press, Inc.

Wirawan, A., Saraswati, R., Sa'adah, N. & Sinaga, E.N. 2020. Preventing Corporate Corruption through Strengthening Accounting Education in Higher Education. *Test Engineering and Management* 83(March-April): 11767–11779.

Synergizing Management, Technology and Innovation in Generating Sustainable and Competitive Business Growth – Hendayani et al (eds)
© 2021 Taylor & Francis Group, London, ISBN 978-0-367-68756-4

The role of E-WOM in social media on purchase intention on the Shopee e-commerce platform in Indonesia

S. Rimadias, Y. Annaba, A.S. Herlambang, A. Muladi & H.E. Dharma
Faculty of Economic, STIE Indonesia Banking School, Indonesia

ABSTRACT: This research aims to measure the influence of e-WOM (electronic word of mouth) participation compiled by intrinsic and extrinsic motives to the purchase intention as well as its implications and also to understand how e-WOM influences the online shopping patterns of customers. This research is categorized as survey research with descriptive analysis method by taking samples and using questionnaires as main data. The model was tested using a quota sample of 150 undergraduate students in Indonesia and single cross-sectional survey. The respondents are choosing by non-probability and convenience sampling techniques. The results of analyses in this research were tested using structural equation modeling (SEM). The results show only two of five hypotheses failed to be rejected and have significant effect. The results show that e-WOM on social media has an essential role in driving increased purchase intention on the Shopee e-commerce platforms in Indonesia.

1 INTRODUCTION

The use of the Internet for business transaction activities is known as electronic commerce (E-commerce). E-commerce can occur between business organizations and consumers, including the use of the Internet and the World Wide Web for the sale of products and services for consumers (Doolin et al. 2005). The use of the Internet for business transactions has been considered as an important thing, which is marked by the increasing use of e-commerce transactions in Indonesia (DailySocial & Veritrans 2012). The rapid growth in e-commerce is caused by Asian consumers, especially Indonesia, who are highly dependent on purchasing products online. This is explained in the data table of website visitors and e-commerce application downloaders in Indonesia on the iPrice Indonesia website in 2020, which shows that more and more foreign and local e-commerce continues to experience rapid development in 2020, one of which is Shopee, and Shopee also is ranked first as the most downloaded online shopping application. E-commerce sites in Indonesia try to encourage their customers to produce more e-WOM (electronic word of mouth), the reason being that consumers produce information available to potential customers with trust (Gauri et al. 2008). E-WOM is considered as the right marketing strategy to attract new customers and retain existing customers. Researchers have recognized the increasing importance of e-WOM in e-Business. This is what makes e-WOM the basis for finding out information, making decisions to buy, and shaping the image of a brand in the eyes of consumers (Yoo et al. 2013).

This study adopts the results of research conducted by Yoo et al. (2013), who successfully explored the influence of e-WOM participation on e-Loyalty in e-commerce. Based on Yoo et al's. (2013) research, both intrinsic and extrinsic motivation influence e-WOM. On the one hand, intrinsic motivation triggers behavior by reason of interest, pleasure, and satisfaction caused by the behavior itself. Extrinsic motivation is followed by reasons for compensation obtained from the results of external activities. These intrinsic and extrinsic motivations simultaneously influence individual intentions, thus affecting purchase intention. Consumer decisions to download e-commerce applications in Indonesia are generally thought to be influenced by several factors, including the role of

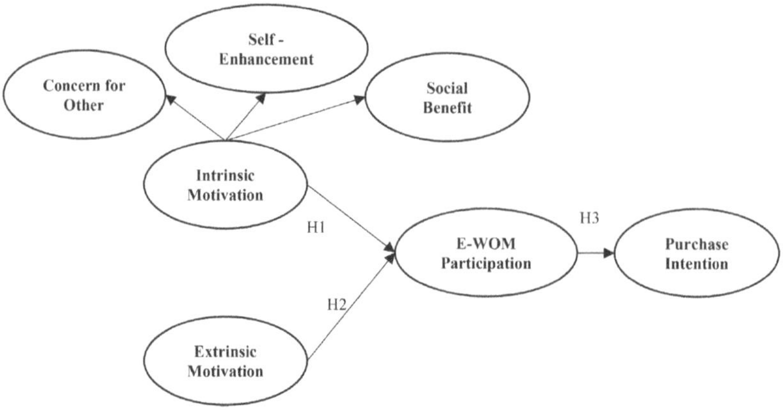

Figure 1. Conceptual framework, Yoo et al. (2013).

e-WOM on social media. This study seeks to examine the role of e-WOM in social media toward purchase intention in the Shopee e-commerce platform in Indonesia.

2 LITERATURE REVIEW

2.1 *Consumer motivation*

Someone's motivation comes from within yourself not because someone else is asking you to do something. Motivation can be described as the strength within the individual that drives them to react (Chen & Xie 2008). Motivation is divided into two, namely, intrinsic and extrinsic motivation. On the one hand, intrinsic motivation triggers behavior by reason of interest, pleasure, and satisfaction caused by the behavior itself. Extrinsic motivation is followed by reasons for compensation obtained from the results of external activities. These intrinsic and extrinsic motivations simultaneously influence individual intentions.

2.1.1 *Intrinsic motivation*

Intrinsic motivation is a factor that affects e-WOM positively because intrinsic motivation associates the values of happiness, friendship, and a sense of fun as a benefit for them. Furthermore, collecting information from five product categories within 12 weeks revealed that consumers had more attention to trust the results of reviews or other consumer explanations in the form of e-WOM than information provided by a salesperson because other consumers have consumed the product first. So, the higher the motivation of someone, the higher the e-WOM produced (Yoo et al. 2013).

Concern for other customers refers to emotional bonds that vary depending on the level of welfare and consumption patterns of customers (Yoo et al. 2013). Self-enhancement is motivation that makes others feel good about what is a decision for themselves and to get recognition in the partition to do e-WOM (Yoo et al. 2013), and for the social benefit obtained by consumers when other consumers interact with other customers using e-WOM (Yoo et al. 2013). The benefits made are by giving suggestions and comments on goods that have been purchased properly and correctly.

2.1.2 *Extrinsic motivation*

Extrinsic motivation refers to the facilities provided by sellers to give someone enthusiasm or motivation to review a variety of products with compensation given in the form of incentives, vouchers, or gifts of certain items. With this compensation consumers have a way to review a matter through short messages to get and disseminate information from a product. This is what makes e-WOM the basis for knowing information, making decisions to buy and shape the image of a brand in the eyes of consumers (Yoo et al. 2013). The higher extrinsic motivation provided by companies and sellers will encourage an increase in the number of positive e-WOMs.

2.2 *e-WOM participation*

Electronic word of mouth communication (e-WOM) or communication by word of mouth is an electronic communication process in the form of providing recommendations both individually and in groups of a product or service that aims to provide information personally (Schiffman & Kanuk 2000). E-WOM can provide valuable input for a brand because e-WOM is often the most honest and candid opinion of consumers. E-WOM influences how products and services can be purchased, customer perceptions can be formed, and new trends that can form. Consumer reviews as one form of e-WOM are important for potential customers, who may be hesitant to buy if they only read product information available (Kotler & Keller 2009).

Empirical results indicate that information characteristics, consumer behavior, and technological factors have a positive influence on consumer purchase intentions (Yoo et al. 2013). E-WOM involvement has a significant positive effect on consumer purchase intentions (DailySocial & Veritrans 2012). The emergence of e-WOM has changed the way customers interact with other customers and how they engage with the business, and then consumer reviews are also important for potential customers, who may be hesitant to buy if they only read the product information available (Kotler & Keller 2009).

2.3 *Purchase intention*

Consumer buying interest is how likely a consumer is to buy a brand or how likely is a consumer to move from one brand to another (Schiffman & Kanuk 2000). Consumer behavior is usually preceded and influenced by many external stimuli, both in the form of marketing stimuli and stimuli from the environment. The stimulation is then processed in accordance with his personal characteristics, before the purchase decision is finally taken. The personal characteristics of consumers used to process these stimuli are very complex, and one of them is motivation to buy. In summary, the results show that perceived value and social awareness factors influence customer purchasing decisions and behavioral intentions (Chen et al. 2018). In the decision process, the stages that are passed by online buyers are introduction of needs, information seeking, and evaluation of alternatives, buying decisions, and behavior after purchase. Empirical results indicate that information characteristics, consumer behavior, and technological factors have a positive influence on consumer purchase intentions (Chen et al. 2018).

3 METHODOLOGY

3.1 *Sample and data collection*

The criteria for determining the sample in this study were respondents who were Shopee consumers in Indonesia who download the application. For statistical methods with SEM programs, the appropriate sample size is between 100 to 200 (Hair et al. 2010).

Data collection is carried out by means of a questionnaire survey technique for registered respondents through a systematic list of questions with easy-to-understand answers. Statement indicators are measured with a Likert scale of 1–5, where scale 1 shows the perception of Strongly Disagree (STS) and scale of 5 Very Agree (SS). The results of the questionnaire survey were then processed by researchers with the statistical method using the structural equation model (SEM) analysis method with AMOS 21 software.

3.2 *Survey instrument*

The survey instruments include information on consumer profiles, information collected about gender, age, and occupation. E-WOM response is a communication process in the form of providing recommendations both individually and in groups of a product or service measured using three indicators adopted from the measurement indicators (Yoo et al. 2013).

Extrinsic motivation response, which is something that is obtained through self-observation, or through suggestions, suggestions or encouragement from others, is measured by using three indicators adopted from the measurement indicators (Yoo et al. 2013). Intrinsic motivation response, which is the desire to act due to internal motivating factors, is measured using six indicators adopted from the measurement indicators (Yoo et al. 2013). Purchase intention response, which is the intention of a person to buy a certain product, is measured using three indicators adopted from the measurement indicators (Heijden et al. 2003).

4 RESULT

Research results in accordance with the data processing methods that have been described are as follows. Sample respondents in this study were 150 respondents, with the percentage of men 6% while the percentage of women was 94%. Respondents in this study were mostly people who were still students, amounting to 80% of the total respondents, with expenditures of less than Rp 1,000,000.

The results showed extrinsic motivation had a positive influence on e-WOM participation. The majority of respondents in this study were students or students seen from the data of 150 students. Students and students who in fact do not have any other source of income other than the gift of their parents, therefore tend to be fond of something related to incentives, in other words the higher the extrinsic motivation they get, the higher the effort they spend on doing reviews or word of mouth on a particular item or brand. From the results of intrinsic motivation, research shows a positive influence on e-WOM participation. The higher intrinsic motivation arises because of oneself, the higher the consumer's encouragement to provide recommendations or reviews of a product even without the encouragement of the seller or externally being asked to do it. This is driven by concern for other consumers, self-enhancement, and social benefits, which is reinforced by the assumption that consumers trust the results of reviews from previous buyers to decide to buy a product compared to information provided by sales (Yoo et al. 2013). Users are also happy to provide recommendations for products they have purchased at Shopee on their social media because they associate the value of happiness, friendship, and a sense of fun as a benefit they receive even though they are not getting any "reward." From the results of e-WOM participation, research shows it can have a positive influence on purchase intention. Stimulus from outside the consumer, both in the form of marketing stimuli and stimuli from the environment, are processed in accordance with their personal characteristics, before finally a purchase decision is taken. The personal characteristics of consumers used to process these stimuli are very complex, and one of them is motivation to buy. It can be concluded that the better or positive an e-WOM review is given, the better and greater the consumer's purchase intention.

4.1 *Validity test and reliability test*

A variable can be said to have good validity if the standardized loading factors $\geq$0.50 and ideally $\geq$0.70 (Heijden et al. 2003). Furthermore, a construct has good reliability if the value of construct reliability (CR) $\geq$0.70 and variance extracted (EVA) $\geq$0.50. All indicators in this study have a factor loading of $\geq$0.5, which explains all indicators declared valid and all variables are able to measure what is actually measured. The results of this study also explain that the reliability of AVE and CR measurements that have met the requirements and is thus known that the indicators formed are able to explain latent variables.

Table 1. Output regression weights.

Hypothesis	Path	Estimation	P	Conclusion
1	*WOM <– IM*	0,813	***	Supported Data
2	*WOM <– EM*	0,369	0,005	Supported Data
3	*WOM <– PI*	0,210	0,022	Supported Data

4.2 *Estimate*

At the estimation stage, the data must be reevaluated. To conduct an evaluation, there are stages that must be passed, as follows.

4.3 *Sample size*

The sample size used in this study amounted to 150 that met the required amount of data in the SEM method.

4.4 *Overall model test*

In the goodness of fit (GOF) measurement, 1,761 calculation results are obtained, which means that the CMIN/df match level $\leq$5.00 (good fit) so that the conclusion of the model is good fit.

4.5 *Hypothesis testing results in structural model (Structural Model Fit)*

The overall model is the overall influence between constructs in which there are exogenous latent variables and endogenous variables. Analysis of the overall model relates to the coefficients or parameters that show the effect of latent variables on other latent variables, according to the conceptual framework of the study. Then, in the analysis of the overall model the significance level is known by looking at the p value. If the estimated parameter values show results that are in accordance with the hypothesis and the level of significance $p < 0.05$, the hypothesis proposed means that the data is supported. However, if the estimated parameter values show the results are not in accordance with the hypothesis and the level of significance $p > 0.05$, then the hypothesis proposed means that the data is not supported.

Based on Table 1, there are three hypotheses that are proven to be accepted, namely H1, H2, and H3. Overall, the variables that make up the hypothesis have a significant effect.

5 DISCUSSION AND IMPLICATION

Based on this research, input can be given to sellers on the Shopee platform. Specific samples that dominated in this study were students. What drives them to do e-WOM is the benefits in the form of gifts, incentives, giveaways or vouchers that encourage e-WOM, which in turn can increase consumer buying interest. Besides that, sellers can also encourage e-WOM through intrinsic motivation by creating a special forum for buyers to stay in touch and exchange information on a product or service that they like. The higher and better quality of e-WOM, it will have an impact on increasing purchase intention. This means that the more and more positive reviews in the assessment column Shopee and social media, the purchase interest will increase. The seller can develop a more mature strategy so that consumers can be more interested in buying marketed products. The results show that e-WOM on social media has an essential role in driving increased purchase intention on Shopee e-commerce platforms in Indonesia. Furthermore, the results of the study illustrate that both extrinsic motivation and intrinsic motivation have a positive effect on e-WOM participation.

Limitations in this study are that the majority of respondents are students or college students so the results of the study describe their behavior. Future research needs to target different respondents who will produce different results.

REFERENCES

Chen, C. C., Hsiao, K. L., & Wu, S. J. 2018. Purchase Intention in Social Commerce. Library Hi Tech.

Chen, Y., & Xie, J. 2008. Online Consumer Review: Word-of-Mouth as a New Element of Marketing Communication Mix. Management Science, 54(3), 477–491.

DailySocial, Veritrans, 2012. E-Commerce in Indonesia. Presentation. DailySocial & Veritrans.

Doolin, B., Dillon, S., Thompson, F., & Corner, J. L. 2005. Perceived risk, the Internet shopping experience and online purchasing behavior: A New Zealand perspective. Journal of Global Information Management (JGIM), 13(2), 66–88.

Gauri, D. K., Bhatnagar, A., & Rao, R. 2008. Role of Word of Mouth in Online Store Loyalty. Communications of the ACM, 51(3), 89–91.

Green, P.E., Krieger, A.M., 1991. Segmenting Markets with Conjoint Analysis. Journal of Marketing, Volume 55, pp. 20–31.

Hair, J. F., Anderson, R. E., Babin, B. J., & Black, W. C. 2010. Multivariate data analysis: A global Perspective (Vol. 7).

Kotler, P., & Keller, K. L. (2009). Marketing Management. Organization (Vol. 22)

Schiffman, L.G & Kanuk, L. 2000. Consumer Behavior. (2nd Ed.). New Jersey: Prentice-Hall, INC.

Van der Heijden, H., Verhagen, T., & Creemers, M. 2003. Understanding Online Purchase Intentions: Contributions from Technology and Trust Perspectives. European Journal of Information Systems, 12(1), 41–48.

Yoo, C. W., Sanders, G. L., & Moon, J. 2013. Exploring the Effect of e-WOM Pparticipation on e-Loyalty in e-commerce. Decision Support Systems, 55(3), 669–678

Yusuf, A. S., & Busalim, A. H. 2018. Influence of e-WOM Engagement on Consumer Purchase Intention in Social Commerce. Journal of Services Marketing.

Synergizing Management, Technology and Innovation in Generating Sustainable and Competitive Business Growth – Hendayani et al (eds)
© 2021 Taylor & Francis Group, London, ISBN 978-0-367-68756-4

The effect of human resources development toward work performance at the Department of Population and Civil Registration of Bandung city

G. Saputra
Faculty of Economics, Garut University, Garut, Jawa Barat, Indonesia

I. Sumiati
Faculty of Social and Political Sciences, Pasundan University, Jawa Barat, Indonesia

H. Rismanto & D.A. Kurniawan
Faculty of Economics, Garut University, Garut, Jawa Barat, Indonesia

ABSTRACT: Human resources (HR) are workers or employees in an organization that have an important role in achieving organizational goals. The purpose of this research is to prove the influence of HR development on work performance in the Department of Population and Civil Registration of Bandung. This research uses a quantitative approach, data was gathered through survey questionnaires that were distributed to 36 respondents; a stratified random sampling which the result shows that there is a significant influence between HR development toward work influence of 76.2%. The finding of research is expected to be considered in the HR development program, especially in Department of Population and Civil Registration of Bandung.

1 INTRODUCTION

The success of an organization is largely determined by the quality of the people who work in it. Rapid environmental changes require their ability to capture the phenomenon of change, analyze their impact on the organization, and prepare steps to deal with these conditions. Then job satisfaction, job involvement, psychological empowerment, organizational commitment, perceived organizational support, and engagement which determine the clear directions in the job or organization so that clear task requirements are well observed to avoid confusion will further increase the productivity (Astorga et al. 2016).

Individual potential through actuality. The form of work actuality and the potential of each individual is accompanied by giving trust so that it can create a sense of pleasure, a sense of sincerity to carry out their duties and responsibilities optimally. And then the final need is the self-transcendence need, which is the need to go beyond one's self. This need could manifest itself through spirituality, deep meditation, peak experiences, flow, social activism, or using one's fully realized potential to make the world a better place (D'Souza 2018).

Forward progress of the organization is very dependent on employee performance at work. Education and training of employees is a natural thing to do for optimal performance and high work productivity so that employees can be assessed as achieving. Achievements or contributions are made by employees in carrying out their duties and responsibilities and functions as a community service. In addition, work performance is restricted as a result of work behavior.

2 LITERATURE REVIEW

2.1 *Human resources development*

HR becomes an important part to get attention because it plays a very important role for improving the performance or progress of a company. Performance is basically what employees do or don't do that affects how much their contribution to the agency or organization including quality service is presented (Dipang 2013). HR development is very necessary because it has important aspects for increasing HR productivity and also has certain goals which must be achieved for the progress of a company or social service organization (Arifah et al. 2015). According to Labola (2019), HR development is a strategic and comprehensive approach to managing people, workplace culture, and the environment to effectively contribute and be productive to the goals and objectives of the organization. The development of an organization's human resources has a direct impact on the career development, talents, and resilience of employees at work and provides a new paradigm for the organization in developing its human resources (Labola 2019).

The purpose and benefits assessment according to what Wilson built (2012: 232), the purpose of these are performance assessment:

1. Evaluation between individuals in the organization assessment performance can aim to evaluate the performance of each individual in the organization. This purpose is able to provide benefits in determining if the number and kind of compensation is the right of for every individual in the organization.
2. Capacity building in the structure of each individual performance evaluation at the organization was beneficial to the development of employees. For every individual in the structure, performance for employees who have low performance needs to be good in development through education and training
3. Various systems maintenance system in the structure, that is any subsystem related between one other subsystem. One subsystem which does not function well will offended another subsystem. Hence, system are needed to properly nourish an organization.
4. Documentation performance evaluation will benefit as a basis of a follow-up in a position of employees in the future. Benefit assesses performance here pertaining to decisions management.

2.2 *Work performance*

At work, every employee wants to feel satisfaction. Both in the environment, co-workers and satisfaction in terms of work, so it needs to be considered in the performance of each employee in each contribution. Job satisfaction is undeniably considered as one of the major considerations in assessing the efficiency and effectiveness of any business organizations. As a matter of fact, businesses nowadays under modern management perspective duly take into consideration the employees' personal needs, wants, and desires to be a very good indicators for achieving job satisfaction. Ideally, logic commands that when an employee is satisfied with his job, that will make him happy, and when he is happy, he will likely become a successful employee (Jalagat 2016). In order to utilize HR fully and augment organizational success, an effective employee performance management system is imperative for a business organization. The performance-driven objective is expected to be aligned with the organizational policies so that the entire process moves away from being event driven to become more strategic and a people centric perspective (Pradhan & Jena 2017). In fact, an abundance of resources such as infrastructures or physical facilities are made meaningless without the support of qualified human resources that directly affect the continuity of the business operations. Within the framework of the professionals, good employee performance mirrors the ability to contribute through their works, leading to the behavioral achievement that is in accordance with the goals of the company (Muda et al. 2014).

3 METHODOLOGY

3.1 *Research characteristics*

This research was conducted using a quasi-quantitative approach, quantitative deductive-fold research that is describing general-to-specific research. Viewed from the level of research, this research has multiple verification because it tests hypotheses. The research method used is the explanatory survey method, one of the research methods that can be categorized in theoretical research and is usually applied in non-exact fields, including in the fields of social science and public administration. The source of data and information can be done through surveys, interviews, questionnaires, and relevant documents. This method not only explains or illustrates the empirical facts found in the field but will also explain the analysis of influence either partially or simultaneously between variables that are the focus of research.

Field studies and field research is how to obtain data by doing research directly on objects that are being investigated. It consists of the following:

1. Observation of nonparticipant's technique data collection by means of a direct observation in the population and civil registration of Bandung, but researchers were not directly involved in the process of work done by employees in the population and civil registration of Bandung.
2. Interview technique data collection was done by using the method integration directly to respondents, that is to the secretary agency and head of governance HR development in the population and civil registration of Bandung.
3. Chief technique data collection was done by means of giving sets of questions that were closed, which means that all had an alternative answer that had already been provided previous to getting information by using scale ordinal, namely by providing a score on the question as positive and negative question. Chiefly this is to an end and information surrounding matter in the population and civil registration of Bandung city. Target questionnaire was for 36 respondents, 111 employees, population and civil registration of Bandung city with using a technique sampling stratified random sampling.

3.2 *Research data analysis*

It consists of two variables of HR and work performance. It is reliable and the valid instruments are absolute requirement to get results that are valid and it is reliable, for measuring validity and reliability: instruments are as follows:

A. The validity of the data analysis used by researchers to process data is using correlation analysis rank Spearman to test the validity of its data by using the following formulas

$$rs = \frac{\Sigma_{i-1}^{n} R(X_i)R(Y_i) - n\left(\frac{n+1}{2}\right)^2}{\sqrt{\left[\Sigma_{i-1}^{n} R^2(X_i) - n\left(\frac{n+1}{2}\right)^2\right]\left[\Sigma_{i-1}^{n} R^2(Y_i) - n\left(\frac{n+1}{2}\right)^2\right]}} \quad (1)$$

Information:

rs = a correlation coefficient rank Spearman

r (x_i) = rank at x data ke-i r

(y_i) = rank in y data ke-i n = many sample

B. Reliability test performed to obtain the data collectors accuracy (instrument) used reliability test instruments performed with the formula alpha. A method for reliability internally analyze reliability of a measuring instrument from once, measurements of the formula used is alpha. Steps sought value reliability with the alpha, that is as follows:

$$r_{11} = \left(\frac{k}{k-1}\right) \cdot \left(1 - \frac{\Sigma S_i}{S_t}\right) \quad (2)$$

Information:

r_{11} = The reliability
ΣS_i = The number of variant a score every item
S_t = Variant total
k = The number of items

Then tested with reliability test instruments performed with the formula correlation Pearson product moment to technique split two, start end, namely:

$$r_b = \frac{n(\Sigma XY) - (\Sigma X)\cdot(\Sigma Y)}{\sqrt{[n.\Sigma X^2 - (\Sigma X)^2].[n.\Sigma Y^2 - (\Sigma Y)^2]}} \quad (3)$$

The price of the new b r _ shows half. reliability test Therefore, called r. reliability tests used to find the whole recipe Spearman, brown, namely:

$$r_{11} = \frac{2.r_b}{1 + r_b} \quad (4)$$

4 RESULT AND DISCUSSION

4.1 *Validity and reliability tests*

The formula used in this validity test is the Spearman rank correlation formula. Based on the calculation results, it can be seen that the HR development indicator concluded that from 24 items, 1 item was the result of the reliability calculation with the help of statistical product and service solution (SPSS) description of the reliability level of the questionnaire data which can be seen in the following Table 1: Reliability of HR Development Variables for Work Performance. Based on the table, it shows that the alpha standardized items are HR development variables and achievement variables the reliability index standard, meaning that the data is declared reliable and can be seen to represent or at least approach the measured variable. HR development indicators as an analytical tool are used to measure the achievement variable as appropriate.

From the three preceding tables, the following can be described.

Based on the value of R in the table above, it is known that the magnitude of the regression coefficient between X and Y is 0.755 and the magnitude of r square is 0.762 (obtained from the square of 0.755). In this study, variable X contributes to influence

4.2 *Determination coefficient test*

The coefficient of determination is a statistical analysis used to find out how much influence the development of HR has on work performance. Calculation of the coefficient of simultaneous determination can be known as follows:

$$\text{KD} = rs^2 \times 100\% \quad (5)$$

Table 1. Regression test.

Model	R	R Square	Adjusted R Square	Std. Error of the Estimate
1	,873[a]	,762	,755	5,531

Table 2. ANOVA.

ANOVA^a

Model		Sum of Squares	Df	Mean Square	F	Sig.
1	Regression	3,328,998	1	3,328,998	108,832	,000^b
	Residual	1,040,002	34	30,588		
	Total	4,369,000	35			

a. Dependent Variable: PrestasiKerja
b. Predictors: (Constant), PSDM

		Unstandardized Coefficients		Standardized Coefficients		
Model		B	Std. Error	Beta	t	Sig.
1	(Constant)	19,227	6,862		2,802	,008
	PSDM	0,788	,076	,873	10,432	,000

a. Dependent Variable: Prestasi Kerja

Where:
KD: how far changes in the variable Y are influenced by the variable X = the square of the correlation coefficient.

$$KD = 0.873^2 \times 100 = 76,2\%$$

The development of human resources has a close influence to improve work performance in the Department of Population and Civil Registration in Bandung. The magnitude of the change in work performance that can be explained by the development of human resources through a linear relationship between human resource development with work performance of 76.2% means it has a close relationship.

5 DISCUSSION

Developing human resources are intended to improve work performance of employees because basically employees are someone who had a role in controlling, make use of the entire available resources. In organization, the principle is of development of human resources that can measure covering both/poor work performance.

The quality of work is an outcome that can be measured by the level of efficiency and effectiveness of someone. Employees work in achieving its objectives. The quality of work in the Population and Civil Registration Department in the city of Bandung shows it is optimal, which it happens because it is still a weak mechanism and the work at every unit of work which is not organized in a system is integrated, effective, and efficient. As in the procedures for employees to provide services, like in the service delivery service birth certificates, which are not yet done optimally.

The quantity of work to be demonstrated through the results and speed in finishing the job, the results of a job in the Department of Population and Civil Registration in the city of Bandung can be said it is not optimal, that it still lacks understanding of the main tasks and functions of employees on getting the job done. In a procedure to complete maybe birth certificates, it should take time of about three days but is completed within five days to a week.

6 CONCLUSION

There is a lack of innovation of employees in the Department of Population and Civil Registration in Bandung city in developing their abilities. The population and civil registration department in the city of Bandung tends to be content with knowledge and ability owned now so in implementing and completed his ability and only relies they owned and have no desire to develop the ability of new and broader approaches. Human resource participants have different backgrounds, as primary school, the incongruity between educational background to work, the work experiences and their age. This would make it difficult for and impeded the due exercise grasp, and the reason for them is for lessons given differently. To improve behavior, employees in the Department of Population and Civil Registration in the city of Bandung have strict monitoring that is conducted by the leader of the department head and secretary. Development activities of training and education are gradual and continuous by adjusting responsiveness owing to employees, so that employees understood correctly on training and education.

The limited number of this research is still a limitation. Researchers hope that they receive this, that the lack of improvement in order to research will come of the limitations:

1. Research is quite a limited time, a limited number of researchers to maximize for finding data respondents, because not all respondents are prepared to provide a short time to filling out the questionnaire.
2. There is lack of research using a questionnaire, that they should come to the answer to be given by the sample is not showing their nature.
3. A period of research it was only a month so that it cannot be known for the unjust in the long run.

REFERENCES

Arifah, S., Zainuddin, M., & Gutama, A. S. 2015. Pengembangan Sumber Daya Manusia di Lembaga Organisasi Pelayanan Sosial (Studi Kasus Mengenai Pelatihan Karyawan di Aksi Cepat Tanggap Jakarta Selatan). Prosiding Penelitian dan Pengabdian kepada Masyarakat, 3(3), 395.

Astorga, Eriberto R. and Martinez, Hazel S. and Vertucio, Herbert D. 2016. *Multi-factorial Dimension of Employees Productivity of Selected Private Tertiary Educational Institution in Manila*. Universal Journal of Psychology 4(2): 63–80, 2016. DOI: 10.13189/ujp.2016.040201

Dipang, L. 2013. Pengembangan sumber daya manusia dalam peningkatan kinerja karyawan pada PT. Hasjrat Abadi Manado. Jurnal EMBA: Jurnal Riset Ekonomi, Manajemen, Bisnis dan Akuntansi, 1(3).

D'Souza, J. F 2018. *The SAGE Encyclopedia of Lifespan Human Development.* Sage Reference: 1921–1922, 2018. DOI: http://dx.doi.org/10.4135/9781506307633.n714

Fery Yanuar Martedy. 2018. Pengaruh Budaya Organisasi dan Gaya Kepemimpinan terhadap Motivasi Kerja serta Dampaknya pada Kepuasan Kerja Karyawan (Studi Kasus di BAWASLU Pusat). Jurnal Administrasi Bisnis (JAB)|Vol. 57 No.1 April 2018| administrasibisnis.studentjournal

Handayaningrat, S. 2001. *Pengantar Studi Ilmu Administrasi dan Manajemen.* Jakarta: *Haji Masagung.*

Jalagat, R. 2016. Job performance, job satisfaction, and motivation: A critical review of their relationship. *International Journal of Advances in Management and Economics*, 5(6), 36–42.

Labola, Y. A. 2019. Konsep Pengembangan Sumber Daya Manusia Berbasis Kompetensi, Bakat dan Ketahanan dalam Organisasi. Jurnam Manajemen & Kewirausahan, 7(1), 28–35.

Muda, I., Rafiki, A., & Harahap, M. R. 2014. Factors influencing employees' performance: a study on the Islamic Banks in Indonesia. *International journal of business and social science*, 5(2).

Pradhan, R. K., & Jena, L. K. 2017. Employee performance at workplace: Conceptual model and empirical validation. Business Perspectives and Research, 5(1), 69–85.

Sumiati, Imas. 2015. *Pengantar Statistik.* Bandung: UNPAS.

Synergizing Management, Technology and Innovation in Generating Sustainable and Competitive Business Growth – Hendayani et al (eds)
© 2021 Taylor & Francis Group, London, ISBN 978-0-367-68756-4

The effect of entrepreneurial traits on business motivation for people with disabilities

M.K. Putri, G. Anggadwita & N. Kamila
Telkom University, Bandung, West Java, Indonesia

ABSTRACT: The Social Rehabilitation Organization for People with Visual Sensory Disabilities (BRSPDSN) is a rehabilitation and social protection center for people with disabilities—in this case, people who are blind. In this institution there are some clients who want to become entrepreneurs, but it is very difficult for them to compete, because the clients do not have the quality of entrepreneurship to build a business and motivation for entrepreneurship. The purpose of this study is to determine the impact of entrepreneurial characteristics on client entrepreneurial motivation at this institution. This study uses causality method by multiple linear regressions. Our respondents are 100 clients with a minimum age of 17 years and above. The results are that only self-esteem and result orientation influences entrepreneurship motivation partially, while simultaneously all independent variables influence entrepreneurship motivation. This research suggests improving a client's self-esteem through increasing meeting intensity in order to check business plan results previously and future visions.

1 INTRODUCTION

Entrepreneurs need a strong mentality. Entrepreneurs are people who have entrepreneurial traits such as self-confidence in what they do, dare to take a risk that they will get, have leadership in themselves to lead their own company, and so on. People with disabilities have physical limitations that make it difficult for getting opportunities to get a job in a company.

Based on the phenomenon collected through interviews, it is known that many people with disabilities in the Social Rehabilitation Organization for People with Visual Sensory Disabilities (BRSPDSN) Wyata Guna Bandung are lacking the motivation for entrepreneurship. In order to become a successful entrepreneur, one must have the following characteristics and attitude in confidence; be task-oriented and get results; take risks; have leadership; have originality; be oriented to the future (Meredith in Suharyadi et al. 2007: 9). This research has the aim of knowing entrepreneurial traits that influence entrepreneurial motivation.

2 LITERATURE REVIEW

2.1 *Entrepreneurship*

According to Sukirman (2017: 116), entrepreneurship is a creative and innovative ability that is used as the basis and resources to find opportunities for success. So entrepreneurship is a process of searching for a profitable opportunity, but it must be based on various considerations and strong mentality in dealing with any risks that might occur.

2.2 *Entrepreneurial characters and attitude*

To become a successful entrepreneur, one must have the following characteristics and attitudes (Meredith in Suharyadi et al. 2007: 9):

1. Confidence: An entrepreneur must have high self-confidence.
2. Task-oriented and results: An entrepreneur must focus on tasks and results.
3. Dare to take risks: This is the first thing you need to get started.
4. Leadership: Successful entrepreneurs are determined by their ability to lead.
5. Originality: This is a characteristic.
6. Oriented to the future: Having foresight is the ability that is usually there for successful entrepreneurs.

2.3 *Entrepreneurial motivation*

Motivation according to Kreitner and Kinicki in Wibowo (2016: 322) is a psychological process that evokes and directs behavior toward achieving goals. Robbins in Wibowo (2016: 322) argues that motivation is a process that causes the intensity, direction, and continuous effort of the individual toward achieving goals.

3 RESEARCH METHODOLOGY

The characteristics of this study use quantitative methods, with the aim of research being the type of casual research and the type of causal investigation. The population in this study were blind persons over the age of 17 years at this institution, as many as 100 people. The sampling technique in this study used quota sampling. In this study, samples were taken according to a population of 100 people. This study uses primary data obtained through questionnaires with Likert scale measurements where each instrument on the questionnaire is accompanied by five possible answers. This questionnaire has questions in the research variables according to the state of the object of the study. Secondary data sources from this study are derived from books, journals, website articles, online news, previous research, and other relevant sources.

4 RESULT AND DISCUSSION

The data analysis method used in this study is a descriptive analysis to describe the characteristics of respondents and research variables. In the study, the authors used descriptive analysis of the independent and dependent variables which were then classified into the total score of respondents. This study has one independent variable, namely entrepreneurial traits, and has six subvariables, namely confidence (X1), task-oriented and results (X2), risk-taking (X3), leadership (X4), originality (X5), and oriented to the future (X6) and the dependent variable is entrepreneurial motivation (Y). This study examines classic assumptions which consist of normality test and homogeneity tests and testing hypotheses consisting of t (partial) test.

4.1 *Sample characteristics*

Respondents studied in this study were people who are blind in the Wyata Guna BRSPDSN, as many as 100 people. After checking 100 questionnaires, it can be seen that both the respondent's profile information and the question items are completely answered and there are no double answers so that all questionnaires can be used. The profile of the respondents observed was gender and age. Based on the research, it is known that the highest number of respondents who answered the questionnaires were 64 people or 64%, while the rest were women, as many as 36 people or 36%. The majority of respondents in this study were aged 16 to 20 years, as many as 67 people.

Table 1. Descriptive analysis of the nature of entrepreneurship.

Entrepreneurial Traits							
		Answer Category					
	Indicators	STS	TS	KS	S	SS	Average
1	I am sure that I am capable of running this business	1	5	10	47	37	3.31
2	I am sure that I am able to compete with normal people	0	6	13	29	52	3.42
3	The majority of failures are caused by poor planning	1	7	10	56	26	3.19
4	I am sure when starting this business	1	6	13	58	22	3.15
5	I am sure that the business will not betray the result	0	8	10	35	47	3.37
6	I go through this business because I want to help others	0	3	20	52	25	3.19
7	All problems in the business always have a way out if I am diligent in living it	1	4	11	31	53	3.45
8	I used to wake up earlier than other people	0	6	27	46	21	3.06
9	I work harder than other people	0	6	27	35	32	3.14
10	I am involved in this business because it is purely from my initiative	0	5	17	31	47	3.36
11	I know the risks in this business well	0	5	12	46	37	3.32
12	I am sure I can lead others	0	7	25	44	24	4.08
13	Others trust what I say	0	7	25	51	17	3.02
14	New ideas always appear in my brain every day	0	7	16	55	22	3.14
15	I always have new ideas every day	0	5	23	56	16	3.06
16	I always get new opportunities regulary	0	3	17	63	17	3.15
Frequency		4	90	276	735	495	
Percentage of Each Choice		0%	6%	17%	46%	31%	
The Trend of Variable Like Entrepreneurship		23%			77%		
Average Value of Entrepreneurial Traits							**3.21**

4.2 *Descriptive analysis*

The research subjects observed in this study were entrepreneurial traits, which were seen from the indicators of self-confidence, task and outcome orientation, risk-taking, leadership, originality, and future orientation that were seen through the lowest, maximum, the average, and the tendency of the respondent's answers.

4.3 *Verification analysis of causality*

4.3.1 *Normality test*

The normality test in this study uses the asymp.sig (2-tailed) value Kolmogorov-Smirnov. Data is considered normal if the value is sig > 0.05. Data normality test can be seen as follows:

Based on the picture above it can be seen that the sig value is >0.05. This means that the data pattern has formed a linear line because the residuals do not significantly affect the data prediction model linearly. Data with a linear pattern means that in general the independent variables, entrepreneurial traits, can produce positive or negative changes in entrepreneurial motivation values.

4.3.1.1 Homogeneity test

Based on the research, each group of respondents is having a homogeneous pattern in answering statement items on the variables of entrepreneurial traits and entrepreneurial motivation. That is, in general, when a client answers entrepreneurial traits, the answer influences the same assessment of entrepreneurial motivation.

Table 2. Descriptive analysis of entrepreneurial motivation.

Entrepreneurial Motivation						
	Answer Category					
Indicators	STS	TS	KS	S	SS	Average
1 I want entrepreneurship because of economic factors	1	12	23	51	14	2.94
2 I want entrepreneurship because I have many dependents	0	9	9	26	56	3.43
3 I am an entrepreneur because I want to be free of depending on other people	0	10	20	40	30	3.12
4 I want entrepreneurship because I want to buy many things that I want	1	1	18	17	63	3.52
5 I want entrepreneurship because I want to be recognized that people who have physical disabilities have the same abilities as normal people	0	3	9	39	49	3.47
6 I want entrepreneurship because entrepreneurship has more challenges	0	5	18	45	32	3.23
7 I want entrepreneurship because my hobby is channeled	0	4	10	34	52	3.47
8 I am an entrepreneure because I want to prove that physical limitations are not a barrier	0	3	9	32	57	3.57
9 I am an entrepreneure because I want to use my abilities optimally to help others	1	3	10	39	47	3.42
Frequency	3	50	126	323	400	
Percentage of Each Choice	0%	6%	14%	36%	44%	
The Trend of Entrepreneurial Motivation Variable	20%			80%		
Average Value of Entrepreneurial Motivation						**3.35**

Table 3. Normality test.

One-Sample Kolmogorov-Smirnov Test		
		Unstandardized Residual
N		100
Normal Parameters[a,b]	Mean	0E-7
	Std. Deviation	3.89337207
Most Extreme Differences	Absolute	.090
	Positive	.045
	Negative	−.090
Kolmogorov-Smirnov Z		.896
Asymp. Sig. (2-tailed)		.398

4.3.1.2 The result of the coefficient of determination

Based on the research, the effect of all variables in entrepreneurial traits together on entrepreneurial motivation in people who are blind in Wyata's BRSPDSN produces a value of 73.1%, while the remaining 26.9% is influenced by other variables that are not examined in this study.

Based on Table 4, it can be seen that only the confidence variable and task orientation and results have a significant effect on entrepreneurship motivation, while the risk-taking variables, leadership, originality, and orientation in the future have no significant effect on entrepreneurial motivation.

Table 4. t test results.

Coefficients[a]

Model		Unstandardized Coefficients		Standardized Coefficients		
		B	Std. Error	Beta	t	Sig.
1	(Constant)	−9.399	3.132		−3.001	.003
	PD_Total	.612	.226	.232	2.705	.008
	Orientation_Total	1.049	.244	.502	4.299	.000
	Dare_taking_risks11	1.362	.821	.144	1.659	.100
	Leadership_Total	.167	.389	.032	.429	.669
	Original_Total	.463	.390	.075	1.187	.238
	Orientation_future_16	−.279	.769	−.024	−.363	.718

a. Dependent Variable: Construct Motivation

Table 5. Equation of multiple linear regression.

Coefficients[a]

Model		Unstandardized Coefficients		Standardized Coefficients		
		B	Std. Error	Beta	t	Sig.
1	(Constant)	−9.399	3.132		−3.001	.003
	PD_Total	.612	.226	.232	2.705	.008
	Orientation_Total	1.049	.244	.502	4.299	.000
	Dare_taking_risks11	1.362	.821	.144	1.659	.100
	Leadership_Total	.167	.389	.032	.429	.669
	Original_Total	.463	.390	.075	1.187	.238
	Orientation_future_16	−.279	.769	−.024	−.363	.718

a. Dependent Variable: Construct_Motivation

4.3.2 *F test results*

Based on the research, all variables in entrepreneurial traits together have a significant effect on entrepreneurial motivation in people who are blind in Wyata Guna BRSPDSN.

4.3.3 *Equation of multiple linear regression*

The multiple linear regression equation is a linear regression research model with more than one independent variable.

Based on Table 5, the multiple linear regression equation in this study is:

Entrepreneurial Motivation = −9,399 + 0,612 (Confidence) + 1,049 (Orientation on Tasks and Results) + 1,362 (Dare to Take Risks) + 0,167 (Leadership) + 0,463 (Originality) – 0,279 (Future Orientation).

The explanation of this equation can be seen as follows: The constant value of −9.399 means that constant entrepreneurial motivation in people who are blind in the Wyata BRSPDSN without the involvement of entrepreneurial traits variables is −9.399.

5 CONCLUSION

Based on the processing and analysis results that have been done before, the conclusion of this study is the mapping of entrepreneurial traits in people who are blind in Wyata's BRSPDSN. For the 100 people, the biggest value is in item number 7, which is about fortitude and perseverance. This situation requires self-acceptance from respondents so that they believe that one way to overcome limitations is steadfastness and perseverance, while items that have the lowest average value are number 13 regarding the ability to influence others. The limitations that exist in the respondent make the ability to influence others to be reduced. Entrepreneurial properties that influence the motivation of people who are blind in Wyata Guna BRSPDSN are partially significant is an attitude of confidence and orientation to tasks and results, but simultaneously all the independent variables have a significant effect with a determination coefficient of 73.1%, while the remaining 26.9% is influenced by other variables not examined in this study.

REFERENCES

Era, R. 2020. *The Effect of Business Capital, Length of Business and Entrepreneurship Attitude to the Income and Welfare of the Family Women of Batik Craftsmen in Danau Teluk Jambi City.* Jurnal Studi Ekonomi dan Bisnis Islam.Jambi.

Jamaludin, A. & Arifin, Z. & Priyono. 2020. *The Effect of Learning Entrepreneurship towards Studen Motivation of STIE YPBI Jakarta.* International Journal of Engineering Technologies and Management Research. Jakarta.

Ncube, F. 2020. *Factors Enhancing Member Commitment toTrade Unions in The Hospitality in Zimbabwe.* Journal of Business Administration Research. Zimbabwe.

Nguyen, D.D. & Le, T.M. & Kingsbury, A.J. 2020. *Farmer Participation in the Lychee Value Chain in Bac Giang Province, Vietnam.* Journal of Agribusiness in Developing and Emerging Economies. Vietnam.

Robbins, S. 2007. *Essentials of Organizational Behavior Edisi Terjemahan.* Jakarta: Erlangga.

Saleh, H. & Hudaya, A. 2019. *The Application of Entrepreneurship Program at Packet C PKBM Assolahiyah.* Bandung: Empowerment.

Sugiyono. 2017. *Metode Penelitian Kuantitatif, Kualitatif, dan R&D.* Bandung: Alfabeta.

Suharyadi. & Arissetyanto, N. & Purwanto, S.K. & Faturohman, M. 2007. *Kewirausahaan.* Jakarta: Salemba.

Sukirman. 2017. Jiwa Kewirausahaan dan Nilai Kewirausahaan Meningkatkan Kemandirian Usaha Melalui Perilaku Kewirausahaan. *Jurnal Ekonomi dan Bisnis , 20* (1), 113–132.

Ulfa, N.F. & Sensuse, D.I. & Ruldeviyani, Y. 2019. *Analysis of Factors Affecting the Success of the Use of Academic Information Systems on Lecturer Users: A Case Study of Sriwijaya University.* International Conference on Advanced Computer Science and Information Systems (ICACSIS). Bali.

Wibowo. 2016. *Manajemen Kinerja.* Raja Grafindo Perkasa: Jakarta.

Synergizing Management, Technology and Innovation in Generating Sustainable and Competitive Business Growth – Hendayani et al (eds)
© 2021 Taylor & Francis Group, London, ISBN 978-0-367-68756-4

Gap analysis of multigenerations' digital competence

R. Wahyuningtyas & V.M. Fajriani
Telkom University, Bandung, West Java, Indonesia

M.R. Chaudhuri
Xavier Business School, St.Xavier's University, Kolkata, West Bengal, India

Y.M. Yusoff
Universities Malaysia, Terengganu, Malaysia

ABSTRACT: Every company needs a strategy to survive in the current digital era. This study aims to identify and analyze the digital competence of Generation X, Generation Y, and Generation Z employees. The method in this study is descriptive by using a quantitative method approach. Operational variables of this research are information, communication, content creation, security, and problem resolution. Data collection was carried out using a questionnaire that was distributed to 238 employees.

1 INTRODUCTION

Intense competition between banks in Indonesia, both state-owned and private, coupled with the number of banks now acquiring each other to strengthen their participation in the banking world to remain stable, advanced the fulfillment of the need for assistance to get the assistance provided. One issue that then arose was the development of the company into digital banking through technology that increased financial efficiency and improved service and operational quality. It shows that digital application users in large banking companies in Indonesia are still below 70% (Internal report of X company, 2019). The Millennial generation is considered already familiar with technology in the organization. The current condition faced by the company is that employees come from several different generations. Bank X, as one of the biggest companies in Indonesia, in its digital banking transformation certainly demands its human resources, especially of the frontlines in today's digital competencies. This study will identify the gaps that exist with today's digital banking transformation compared between diverse generations at the Bank X.

2 LITERATURE REVIEW

2.1 *Digital competence*

Digital competence is defined as an ability to understand and utilize information from various digital sources displayed through computers (Belshaw 2011). Digital competency according to Martin and Grudziecki (2006) has three stages of development, namely the first level of development is for basic competencies (skills, knowledge, attitude), the second level is for the professional level, while the third level is digital transformation where the ability is in creativity and innovation. Ferrari (2013) classifies digital competencies based on five competency areas, namely information, communication, content creation, safety, and problem solving. The information dimension covers the area of competence in the form of the ability to identify, discover, retrieve, store, organize, analyze, and assess the relevance and purpose of digital information. The communication dimension covers areas of competence in the form of communication skills in a digital environment, sharing information online, collaborating through digital tools, and participating in communities and networks. The content creation dimension covers the areas of competence in the form of the ability to create and edit new content, integrate and recompile previous knowledge and content, produce expression creativity, and produce media and programming. The safety dimension covers competency areas in the form of personal protection capabilities, data protection and digital identity protection, and security measures, safe and sustainable use. The problem-solving dimension covers the areas of competence in the form of the ability to identify digital needs, the determination of digital information facilities that are appropriate to the needs, conceptual problem solving through digital means, creative use of technology, and technical problem solving.

2.2 *Generation group*

Schullery (2013) states that people from the same generation have similar generational experiences such as the culture, politics, economics, world events, natural disasters, and technology, so that they form the same views, values, choices, and beliefs. The distribution of generations includes the Silent Generation or traditionalists, which is the generation born 1925–1945; Baby Boomers, 1946–1964; generation X, 1965–1981; and Millennials or Generation Y, 1982–1999. Workers are currently dominated by three generations of generations, namely the generations of Baby Boomers, Generation X, and Generation Y (Hernaus & Vokic 2014). Pratidhina (2016) found that job characteristics among generations are different significantly.

Based on the previous explanation, the theoretical framework in this study is shown in Figure 1.

Hypothesis in this study is as follows:

H_0: Condition when the required competence is the same as existing (current) competence of employees from X, Y, and Z generations.

H_1: Condition when required competence is not the same as existing (current) competence of employees from X, Y, and Z generations.

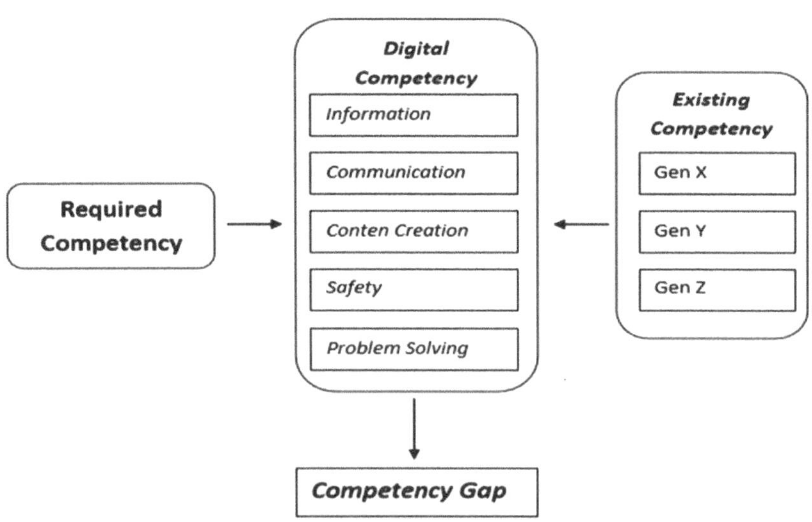

Figure 1. Theoretical framework.

3 METHODOLOGY

This research focuses on the digital competence of employees in Bank X from different generations. The sample consists of 238 frontlines from Generations X, Y, and Z. Data collection used literature studies, interview,s and surveys. This study looks at the gap competence through comparison between current digital competences with required digital competence among employees of Bank X. The results of the interview resulted in digital competency that was expected and prioritized to branch employees in the form of a proficiency level of 21 digital competencies, which would then be compared with the results of questionnaires distributed to existing employees who would later show the gaps. In this study, researchers used a different t-test, Independent Sample t-Test testing with an average different test method. Digital competency gaps generated from this study will be categorized into three categories. The following is the presentation of the digital gap category according to Aisyah (2017):

1. Current Competence = Required Competence
2. Current Competence > Required Competence
3. Current Competence < Required Competence

Competency gap comparisons are seen from each determined dimension so that the dimensions that are most dominant need development/development and grouping of competency gaps will be divided into:

1. Digital competency gaps in total respondents for each generation
2. Digital competency gaps for each area and indicator competence

4 RESULT AND DISCUSSION

To get an overview of digital competence condition for the company, questionnaires and interviews were filled with the criteria of Level 1: Foundation if calculated values are between 1.00–1.67; Level 2: Intermediate if calculated values are between 1.68–2.34; Level 3: Continued if calculated values are between 2.35–3.00. From the results of data processing, the results obtained are related to current competency (CC) and required competence (RC) for each dimension can be seen in Figures 2 through 6. The results of data processing show that there are several indicators that

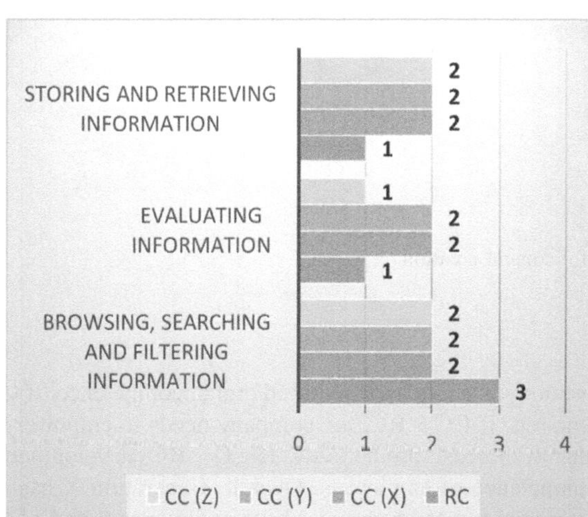

Figure 2. CC and RC for information.

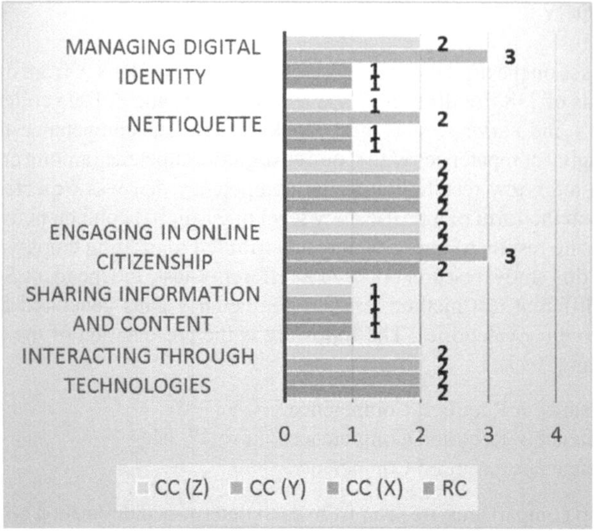

Figure 3. CC and RC for communication.

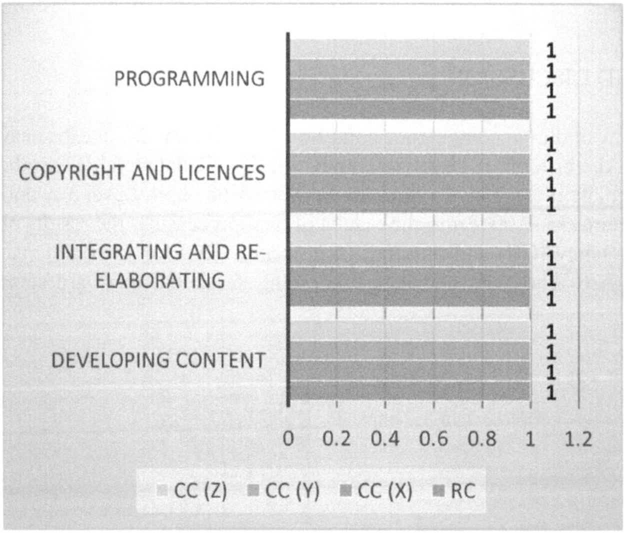

Figure 4. CC and RC for content creation.

exceed, equal, and have not yet reached the required digital competence. If CC = RC, competency development is not required. If CC > RC, the company needs to empower employees to support other activities in order to increase productivity. If CC < RC, development steps are needed to improve the digital competence of employees. Overall, Generation X has digital competence at Level 1, which means employees are aware and have an understanding of the digital dimension. Generation Y has digital competence at Level 2, which means employees are able to use the aspects in digital dimension. Whereas Generation Z also has digital competence at Level 1, which is still

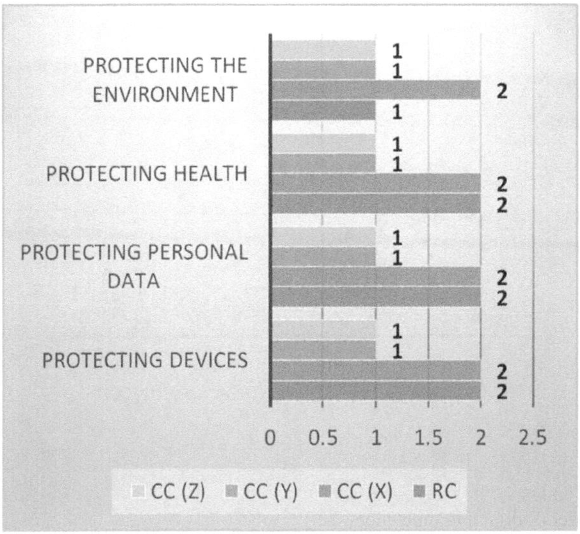

Figure 5. CC and RC for safety.

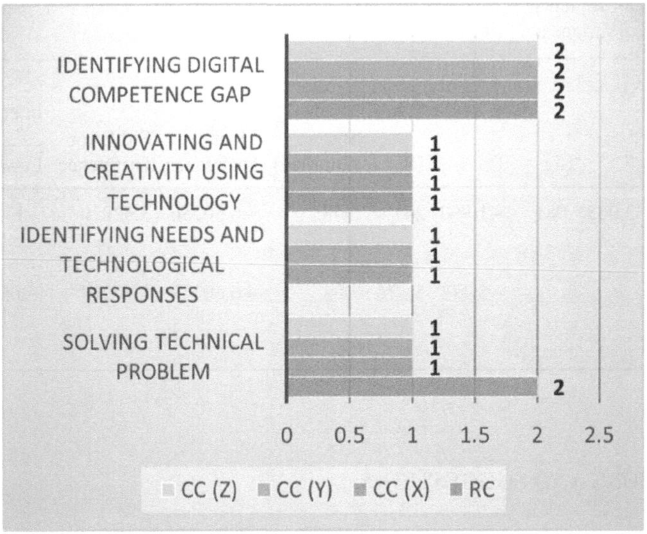

Figure 6. CC and RC for problem solving.

at the foundation stage. Then the results of hypothesis testing to determine whether there is a significant difference between required and current digital competence between generations is as in Table 1.

From Table 1, it can be seen that the calculated significance value of 0.048 < 0.05. Based on the hypothesis testing criteria, it is concluded that Ho is rejected and Ha is accepted, meaning that there is a difference between required competence and current competence of employees for Generations X, Y, and Z.

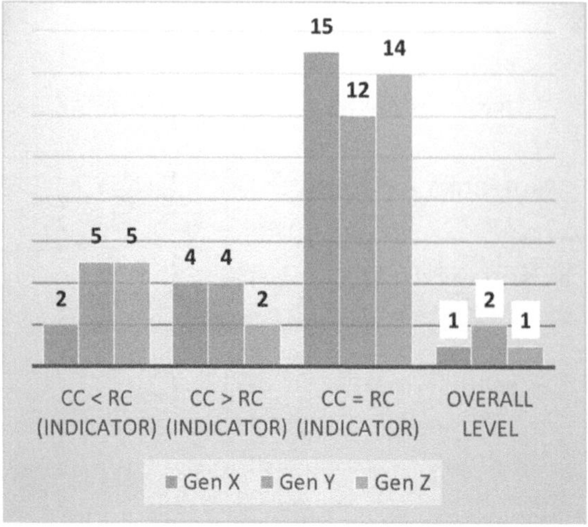

Figure 7. Overall level of digital competence.

Table 1. Hypothesis testing.

		Levene's Test for Equality ofVariances		T-test for Equality of Means						
									95% Confidence Interval of Difference	
		F	Sig	T	Df	Sig (2- tailed)	Mean Difference	Std Error Difference	Lower	Upper
Value	Equal Variances Assumed	3.065	.081	−1.990	241	.048	−6.60756	3.32020	−13.14788	−.06725
	Equal Variances Assumed			−5.113	5.376	.003	−6.60756	1.29234	−9.86054	−3.35458

5 CONCLUSIONS AND SUGGESTIONS

Regarding the analysis of digital competence gap among generations, conclusion and suggestion for Bank X are as follows:

a There are two indicators from two dimensions of digital competence for X generation that are still below the expectations and requirements set by management, that is, information and problem solving. Browsing, searching, and filtering information as indicators for information dimensional has not met the standards. Problem solving related to solve technical problems also has not met required competence.
b There are five indicators from three dimensions of digital competence for X generation that are still below requirements. Information related to browsing, searching, and filtering information does not meet the standards desired by management. Safety dimension for protecting devices, protecting personal data, and protecting health also has not met required competence. Indicators

of problem solving related to solving technical problems fall into the not competent yet, so they need development.

c There are five indicators from three dimensions of digital competence for Z generation that are still below expectations set by management. Indicators from the information dimension such as browsing, searching, and filtering information does not meet the standards. Protecting devices, protecting personal data, and protecting health as indicators of safety have not met required competence. Problem solving indicators such as solving technical problems fall into the not competent yet.

d Based on the results of the research on the partial hypothesis test, the calculated significance value was 0.046 less than the 0.05 significance level, so it was concluded that there were differences between required competence with current digital competence between Generations X, Y, and Z

e Socialization and education are needed related to all media owned by the company in the search for management information. It also needs controlling processes related to customer transactions.

g Companies can provide training to protect personal work devices, understand risks, minimize online threats, and know the safety and security standards of these devices.

f Provide training to employees on how to secure computer equipment, personal data information, and health protection when using digital media, as well as providing guidance in order to resolve common technical problems.

h Top level management needs to understand the development of information and digital technology both inside and outside the company, especially related to electronic transaction information laws and regulations in force in Indonesia.

REFERENCES

Aisyah, N. S. 2017. *Pengukuran dan analisis kesenjangan kompetensi digital untuk mendukung visi perusahaan di unit research divisi digital service PT. Telekomunikasi Indonesia*. Tesis. Fakultas Bisnis dan Menejemen. Universitas Telkom: Bandung

Ferrari, A. 2013. *DIGCOMP: A Framework for Developing and Understanding Digital Competence in Europe*. European Commission

Hernaus, T. & Vokic, N.P. 2014. *Work Design for Different Generational Cohorts: Determining common and idiosyncratic job characteristics*. Journal of Organizational Change Management, Vol. 27 (4), pp. 615–641

Martin, A. & Grudziecki J. 2006. *DigEuLit: Concepts and Tools for Digital Literacy Development. Innovation in Teaching and Learning in Information and Computer Sciences*. Vol. 5, Issue 4, pp. 249–267, doi: 10.11120/ital.2006.05040249.

Pratidhina, G. 2016. *Komparasi Job Characteristics Antar Kelompok Generasi (Baby Boomers, Generasi X, Dan Generasi Y): Studi Kasus Di Kantor Telkom Regional II Jakarta*. Tesis. Fakultas Bisnis dan Manajemen: Universitas Telkom

Synergizing Management, Technology and Innovation in Generating Sustainable and Competitive Business Growth – Hendayani et al (eds)
 ISBN 978-0-367-68756-4

Influence of the government's role to the quality of private higher education and the impact on graduate quality

S. Borges & R. Wahyuningtyas
School of Economics and Business, Telkom University, Bandung, West Java, Indonesia

ABSTRACT: The foreign workers influx is happening in Timor-Leste, which makes the job market more competitive for university graduates. Hence, the government and universities in Timor-Leste are obliged to improve human resources' quality so that graduated students are able to compete in the global and national markets. This research aims at discovering the effect of government's role on the private higher education quality and its impact on graduates' quality in private higher education in Timor-Leste. The data were collected using a questionnaire consisting of 98 statements involving 786 lecturers from eight private higher education as the population, and 265 lectures as the samples. The findings show that (1) the government's role significantly influences the higher education quality; (2) the higher education quality significantly influences the graduates' quality; and (3) the government's role and the higher education quality simultaneously influence the graduates' quality in private higher education in a significant way.

1 INTRODUCTION

One feature of globalization in Timor-Leste today is the influx of foreign workers from various countries. The foreign workforce has replaced the resources produced by universities in Timor-Leste. Globalization makes competition in the economic field harder and tighter, but always within the scope of cooperation. In that competition, the victory will be determined by the quality of human resources. A nation that can fix itself by increasing the quality of its human resources will most likely be able to compete in such healthy competition (Kadarisman 2011: 1). This has become a major challenge for the government and universities in Timor-Leste to improve the quality of human resources so that they can compete in the global and national markets in Timor-Leste.

Most universities in Timor-Leste currently face problems related to the very limited quality of human resources. This can be seen from the average condition of lecturers in private universities in Dili, Timor-Leste, of the total number of 786 lecturers in eight private universities in Dili, Timor-Leste, 53% had undergraduate education qualifications, 43.6% with Master degree qualifications, and 3.4% lecturers with Doctoral degree qualifications. Whereas for public universities in Dili, Timor-Leste, there was only one university named the National University of Timor-Leste with a total number of 405 lecturers with 20.4% with Bachelor degree, 73.6% with Master degree, and 6% with Doctoral degree.

Arwildayanto (2013: 19) states that the central point determining the quality of college graduates is the quality of the lecturers themselves. For this reason, university lecturers must have one higher level of academic ability from the student in the education program they teach and each lecturer must have a professional certificate.

In addition, the results of the National Agency for Academic Assessment and Accreditation (ANAAA) in 2017 and 2018 involving nine experts in Quality Assurance Higher Education from four countries such as BAN-PT Indonesia, AACCUP Philippines,MQA Malaysia, and TEQSA Australia, and an assessment panel consisting of three members each, two citizens and one international who was assigned as a team leader, showed that of the 33 study programs in all universities in

Timor-Leste, almost 76% were accredited C and 12% were accredited B and 12% non-accredited. This is a major problem and challenge for universities in Dili, Timor-Leste. Therefore, how can they improve the quality of education to be better in order to produce human resources who are ready to compete in the future?

Based on the raised issues above, the following research questions are proposed:

1. How much influence does the role of government have on the quality of private tertiary institutions in Dili?
2. How much influence does the quality of private tertiary institutions have on the quality of graduates in Dili?
3. How much influence does the role of government have on the quality of private tertiary institutions and its impact on the quality of graduates in private tertiary institutions in Dili?

2 LITERATURE REVIEW

2.1 *Role of government*

The role of the government in tertiary education is significant in making policies to determine the quality of education, since government policy is the cornerstone of regulation to achieve its goals. Responsive policy is a product of democratic law that follows the principle of openness between the people and the government. Determination of government education policies must be in accordance with national policies. According to Matondang (2010), national development in the field of education is an effort to educate the nation and improve the quality of human resources in realizing an advanced, just, and prosperous society.

2.2 *Quality higher education*

Higher education is the final terminal for someone who has the opportunity to learn at the highest level through school education (Dardjowidjojo 1991: 42). Higher education institution is an education unit that organizes higher education, which can be in the form of academic, polytechnic education, high school, or university. How the government, other departments, or the community conducts education to form a strong student personality is strongly influenced by: (1) The role of the organizer (government, foundations, and leaders of universities); and (2) The academic community (lecturers and students, as well as facilities and infrastructure). Everything is an integrated system in the organization of higher education. In college, students get an education, both in terms of intelligence, skills and mental. Thus, the role of higher education is needed to form a strong student personality.

2.3 *Quality graduates*

Sudradjad (2005: 17) affirms that quality education is able to produce graduates who have the ability in both academic and vocational competencies, which are based on personal and social competencies, and noble moral values as their life skills. Sudradjad further states that quality education is capable of producing whole integrated people who are able to neutralize faith, knowledge, and charity.

2.4 *Research framework*

Samium (2015) in Widiasworo (2018: 71) explains that the research framework is a temporary explanation of a phenomenon that is the object of the problem. This research examined the influence of the government's role on the quality of private higher education and the impact on the quality of graduates. The variables are the government's role as an independent variable (X), quality of private universities as an intervening variable (Y), and the impact on the quality of graduates as a variable (Z).

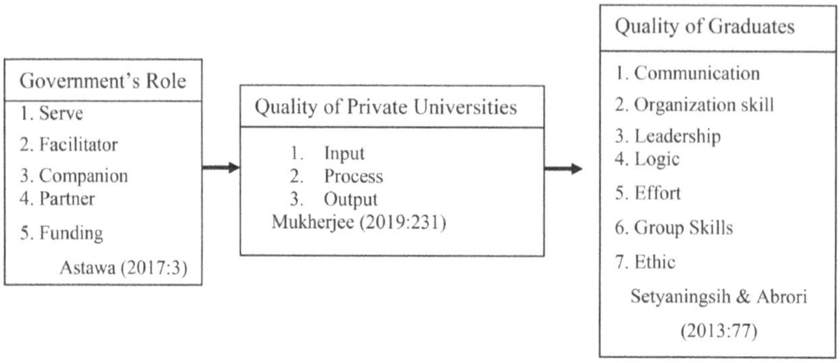

Figure 1. The variables.

3 METHODOLOGY

This research is descriptive and quantitative statistical research methods. Sugiyono (2019: 21) states that in the narrow sense, statistics can be interpreted as data, but in a broad sense, statistics can be interpreted as tools for analysis and tools for making decisions.

The population was lecturers at eight private universities, namely Universidade Da Paz, Universidade Dili, Universidade Oriental Timor Lorosae, Dili Institute of Technology, Institute of Business, Institute Superior Cristal, InstitutoProfissional De Cannossa, and InstitutoCiencias Da Saude. Of the eight universities, there were 786 lecturers. The sample obtained in this research, with a confidence level of 95% and an error rate of 5% and using the Slovin formula, was 265 lecturers. This study employs the convenience sampling technique conducted in tertiary institutions, in which the questionnaires were developed using Google Forms. In addition, since the population of this study is not homogeneous, proportionate stratified random sampling technique was used to take and determine the number of samples. The population was stratified but disproportionate, because the number of stratified population starts from Bachelor, Master, and Doctor degrees. Data analysis techniques used in this research were simple linear regression and multiple linear regression techniques to examine the effect of the role of government on the quality of private universities and the influence of the role of government and the quality of private universities on the quality of graduates.

4 FINDINGS AND DISCUSSION

4.1 *The model 1 regression analysis for the influence of government role variable on the quality of private universities*

Analysis of the regression model 1 was used to find out how significant the influence of variable X (the role of government) on variable Y (quality of graduates). The test results showed that the amount of R square (R^2) was 0.093. From the number 0.093, it can be interpreted that the influence of the government's role on the quality of private universities was 9.3% while the remaining 90.7% was an influence from other variables not included in this research as in Table 1.

In addition to the R Square results above, the results of a simple linear regression test for the role of government variable on the quality of college graduates indicate that there was a significant effect of the role of government variable on the quality of college graduates variable. The test results obtained a t-test value of 5.197, which was greater than the t-table value of 1.96725 with a significance of 0,000 $< \alpha = 0.05$ as in Table 2. Therefore, based on the research hypothesis criteria, H0 was rejected and Ha was accepted.

Table 1. The model summary of the influence of government's role toward the quality of private universities.

Model	R	R Square	Adjusted R Square	Std. Error of the Estimate
1	0.305	0.093	0.090	9.208

Predictors: (Constant), Government's Role

Table 2. Coefficient value for government's role variable on the quality of private universities.

Model		Unstandardized Coefficients		Standardized Coefficients		
		B	Std. Error	Beta	T	Sig
1	(Constant)	19.044	21.265		0.896	0.371
	Government's Role	2.099	0.404	.305	5.197	0.000

Dependent Variable: Quality of private universities

Table 3. The model summary of the influence of government's role and the quality of private higher education toward the quality of graduates.

Model	R	R Square	Adjusted R Square	Std. Error of the Estimate
1	0.722a	0.522	0.518	2.674

Predictors: (Constant), Quality of private universities, government's role

The result of this research is in accordance with the research conducted by Asiyail (2015) entitled "Improving Quality Higher Education in Nigeria: The Roles of Stakeholders," which found that government could influence the improvement of the quality of higher education by ensuring relevant funding policy by establishing proper funding of universities in the country. In addition, the findings of this research are in line with research by Jesy, Anjuandi, and Yosafat (2018) entitled "The Role of Local Governments in Quality Educational Development in the Lampung Region of Indonesia," which states that in improving education, the role of government is needed to ensure that education runs well and to produce a quality human resource.

4.2 *The model II regression analysis for the influence of government role and quality of private universities variables on the quality of graduates*

The results of the model II regression analysis as in the model summary in Table 3 showed an R Square (R^2) value of 0.522. This showed that there was an influence of the government's role and the quality of private universities variables on the quality of graduates by 52.2%. The remaining 47.8% was the contribution or influence of other variables not included in the research.

In addition to the results of R Square above, the results of multiple linear regression tests for the role of government and the quality of private higher education variables on the quality of graduates showed a significant influence. The test results obtained a calculated F value of 142.996 with a significant value of 0,000 $< \alpha = 0.05$. With a calculated F value of 142.996 > F table 3,870. Then, based on the hypothesis of the research, H0 was rejected and Ha was accepted. Therefore, it can be concluded that there was a significant influence from the role of government and the quality of private universities variables toward the quality of graduates with a percentage of 52.2%. The influence of other variables can be calculated by the formula of $(1 - r^2)$ or $(1 - 0.522) = 0.478$ or equal to 47.8%.

Table 4. Anova with F and Sig for the influence of government's role and the quality of private higher Education toward the quality of graduates.

Model		Sum of Squares	Df	Mean Square	F	Sig.
1	Regression	2044.906	2	849.384	142.996	.000b
	Residual	1873.751	262	11.938		
	Total	3918.657	264			

a. Dependent Variable: Quality of Graduates
b. Predictors: (Constant), Quality of private universities, government's role

The aforementioned results show that the government's role and the quality of higher education influenced the quality of graduates. It is in accordance with the results of research conducted by Cao and Li (2015), who concluded that to get good quality in private tertiary institutions, the role of government and the quality of private tertiary institutions should have a good impact on the quality of graduates. Moreover, the results of this research are also similar with research conducted by Koespiadi et al. (2015), which concluded that the quality of higher education influenced the quality of graduates. Similarly, the results of research conducted by Asmawi (2005) on strategies to improve the quality of quality graduates in higher education show that there was an influence of the quality of higher education on the quality of graduates. Lastly, the results of research of Stanciu and Banciu (2012) entitled "Quality of Higher Education in Romania: Are Graduates Prepared for the Labor Market?" show that the quality of higher education influenced the quality of graduates.

5 CONCLUSION AND SUGGESTIONS

According to the results of data analysis and discussion, the conclusions of the research can be drawn as follows:

1. The government's role had a significant effect on the quality of private universities with a significance value of $0.000 < \alpha 0.05$.
2. The quality of private colleges in Dili, Timor-Leste had a significant effect on the quality of graduates with a significance value of $0.000 < \alpha 0.05$.
3. The role of government and the quality of private universities had significant effect on the variable of quality of graduates simultaneously.

Therefore, according to the results of data processing and analysis in Section IV and the conclusions above, there are several suggestions for this research for the role of government and the quality of private universities variables toward the quality of graduates as follows:

1. The government through the Ministry of Higher Education needs to help and support facilities and build infrastructure to every private university and provide financial assistance to every private university to conduct research to improve the quality of private universities.
2. The government through the Ministry of Higher Education needs to provide scholarships for private universities to increase the qualifications of lecturers to Master and Doctoral levels.
3. To produce output or quality of graduates who are ready to compete in the global market, universities need to select prospective students who excel at the time of the input process or the process of admission of new students.

REFERENCES

Arwildayanto. 2013. Higher Education Human Resource Management. Bandung: Alfabeta

Asmawi, M. R. 2005. Strategy Improve Quality Graduates At University. Department of Administrative Sciences, State Administration Studies Program, Faculty of Social and Political Sciences, Sheikh Islamic University-Yusuf, Tangerang – Banten 15118, Indonesia.

Astawa, T. N. I. 2017. Understanding the Role of Society and Government in the Advancement of Education Quality in Indonesia. Journal of Quality Assurance Institute of Quality Assurance, Institute of Hindu Dharma Negeri Denpasar.

Basuki, W. 2017.Management of Vocational and Vocational Technology Education. Jakarta: BumiAskara.

Burns, R. 2017. Education In Timor-Leste: Envisioning Thefuture, *Journal Of International And Comparative Education, Independent Education Consultant.*

Education for All. 2015. National Review, Ministry Education of Timor Leste, Dili.

Jesy O. Anjuandi, S. & Yosafat, B.S. 2018. The Role of Local Governments in Quality Educational Development in the Regions Lampung Indonesia.

Koespiadi, Mudjanarko, S.W. &Kurniawan, F. 2015. Quality Improvement of Higher Education Graduates to Meet the Needs of the Construction Services Market in Indonesia. Civil Engineering Study Program, Narotama University.

Labour Market Outlook Timor-Leste; Edition 7. 2017. Democratic Republic of Timor Leste, Secretariat of State for Youth and Labor National Directorate for Labor Market Information.

Labour Market Outlook Timor-Leste; Edition 8. 2018. Democratic Republic of Timor Leste, Secretariat of State for Youth and Labor National Directorate for Labor Market Information.

Macpherson, R. 2011. *Educational Administration and Management in Timor Leste, Language and Capacity Building Challenges In A Post-Conflict, International Journal of Educational Management.*

Masram&Mu'ah. 2017. Professional Human Resource Management. Surabaya, PondokJatiSidoarjo

Mukherjee, S. P. 2019. *Quality in Higher Education, India Studies in Business and Economics.*

Murti, R. W. & Prasetio. 2018. Influence of Lectures' Competence Academic Achievement of Faculty Economics and Business Telkom University.

National Education Strategic Plan.2011-2030. Ministry of Education and Culture Republic Democratic of Timor Leste.

Prasetyo, W. M. R. Suharnomo & Mahfudz. 2017. Human Resource Development Strategy in 5 Higher Education Institutions to Face Global Competition, (Studies at Universities in the City of Semarang).

Rahardjo, S. 2017: http://www.spsssindonesia.com/2017/03/path analysis test method.

Setiawati, L. 2012.Effectiveness of Higher Education Management Development, Universitas Pendidikan Indonesia Bandung.

Setyaningsih, I. & Abori, M. 2013. Analysis of Graduation Quality Based on Graduation User Satisfaction Level.

Sugyiyono. 2018. Management Research Methods. Bandung. Alfabeta

Sugiyono. 2019. Statistics for Research. Bandung. Alfabeta

Synergizing Management, Technology and Innovation in Generating Sustainable and Competitive Business Growth – Hendayani et al (eds)
© 2021 Taylor & Francis Group, London, ISBN 978-0-367-68756-4

Role of CEO in talent management to develop new leaders in the IR 4.0.

T. Priyanto
Graduate School of Gadjah Mada University, Yogyakarta, Indonesia

Indrawati
School of Business and Management, Telkom University, Bandung, West Java, Indonesia

A.S.A. Susetyo
Telkom Corporate University, Bandung, Jawa Barat, Indonesia

ABSTRACT: Many published research papers show talent management has highly significant positive correlation with the organization performance. The talent management complexity increased over the last decade, especially in the Industrial Revolution 4.0 (IR 4.0) era. Many experts agree that IR 4.0 may blur the line between people and technology, where technologies may replace people's role in the organization. As talents have an important role in securing organization performance, therefore, talent management should come to the attention of the top management, especially the chief executive officer (CEO). This paper presents the conceptual studies, which focus on the CEO roles in talent management to develop new leaders in the IR 4.0 era. The paper is qualitative research based on literatures review of scientific articles and reports of reputable organizations. This paper finds that the proposition states that there is a strong correlation between the role of the CEO and talent management, which then supports the organization performances.

1 INTRODUCTION

IR 4.0 is changing life, and due to Covid-19; the revolution is coming sooner as now need physical distancing. IR 4.0 stands for "fourth industrial revolution," which is a term referring to rapid trans-formations in the design, production, implementation, operation, and service impacted by digitalization, artificial intelligence, Internet of things (IoT), and cloud computing (Barton et al. 2020). All of these digital technologies advancements are changing the way in managing and leading an organization, which then causes more volatility, uncertainty, complexity, and ambiguity (VUCA).

In dealing with this new environment, it requires changing mindset, culture, leadership competencies, and style. The new leadership is called as leadership 4.0 or digital leadership, which is changing in managing and leading organization and leading talent to achieve its business objectives, which then also affects all processes in talent management (TM).

Talent management is a process from finding or attracting, selecting, improving, to maintaining the best talents to meet the company's needs today and in the future (Wolor et al. 2020). Many published articles show that talent development is positioned to ensure the success of company performance and excel in any changing environment. The CEO, who has the highest position in the company, typically deals with very high level strategic decisions and those that lead the company's overall growth. He/ she sets the tone, vision, and envision culture of their organizations (Kenton 2020) and determines the competences of all talent to embrace current and future business environment. Therefore, the CEO emphasizes four essential roles: envisioning, nominating, enabling, and managing crisis (Shekshnia 2018).

Envisioning is the first step of addressing the economic, technological, social, and political forces dominating the IR 4.0. This step aims to develop the company to be able to adapt its strategies, structures, processes, people, and technology to deliver better results (Ellis 2020). In the view of talent management, the CEO should envision the required talents and their competencies, then nominating and enabling the talents to achieve the company's goals. In addition, the CEO has to prepare all people to be ready with the changes as part of talent management processes.

2 LITERATURE REVIEW

2.1 *Industry Revolution 4.0*

Experts believe that the IR 4.0 will be the basis of revolutionary change of all industries that forge them many ways. Firstly, it may push companies to implement an open innovation business model. Secondly, it may force companies to expand an open innovation culture. Finally, it may force companies to expand the feedback loop of an open platform businesses model (Lee et al. 2018).

In view of new leadership 4.0, it needs cross hierarchical, team-oriented, and cooperative with focus strongly on innovation with implementing design thinking methodology to solve complex problems and find desired solutions (Oberer & Erkollar 2018). WEF showed that leaders should have intelligence on understanding context, reflect a moral code, tap into the social and emotional, and generate solutions, embrace technology, and drive transformations (Barton et al. 2020). Leadership should also have four principles, namely, focus on systems rather than technologies, empower our societies to master technologies and act to counter a fatalistic and deterministic view of progress, prioritize futures by design rather than default and collaboration between all stakeholders. These four principles must play as a central role in the integration of the transformative technologies (Schwab 2016).

Companies need to prepare to embrace VUCA in many measures. Firstly, companies may put a significant investment in capabilities required to leverage the opportunities that the digital economy offers. Secondly, companies may need to do a rapid business transformation adopting agile, intelligent, yet automated platforms in the cloud enabling superior customer experience and value. In addition, companies may also need to reimage the internal functions to increase agility, rise value, and enhance stakeholder experience across the value chain (Muriithi et al. 2017).

2.2 *Talent management*

Talent management is an HR function focusing on attracting and recruiting, training and development, carrier development, talent mobility, and succession planning. To ensure that talent will support performance, talent management must be integrated and harmonized with organizational objectives and strategies. In addition, talent management has also to relate the expected culture and people in the organization (Wolor et al. 2020).

2.2.1. Talent attraction is activities to attract talent with required qualifications who are future leaders of the organization. The source of talent can come from within and outside the organization. The way to get the best prospective employees is by how the company makes a good and positive image to the community including public relations strategies, company branding, company introduction, corporate social responsibility and promotion (Wolor et al. 2020).

2.2.2. Recruiting is a process for finding talent to be employed by organizations with required qualifications who are future leaders. If it is internal recruitment, the talent has already had insight and knowledge about the business processes of the company. However, if the organization wants to make a new change, resources from outside the organization are better to influence the existing norm (Wolor et al. 2020).

2.2.3. Training and development (T&D) is a process to develop people and talent with required competencies to catch up with the new trend in technology, businesses, leadership, and management in coping with VUCA and IR. T&D should provide programs that will improve the technical skills, strategic knowledge, and enhance attitude and performance of employees (Promsri 2019). T&D is to ensure their achievement on key trends, agility, artificial intelligence (AI), and using culture as a competitive advantage. Mentoring and coaching are also methodologies to develop talent to have more experiences and to improve skills.

2.2.4. Retaining is a process of maintaining talent to remain in the organization. There are two strategies in retaining talent, namely, intrinsic incentives and extrinsic incentives (Wolor et al. 2020). Intrinsic incentives refer to money that can satisfy employees in physiological matters such as attractive compensation packages and additional incentives. Extrinsic incentives refer more to things outside of money related that can be satisfying in psychological terms such as insurance and other non-cash remuneration, and flexible working hours (McKinsey 2018). Career improvement opportunities, organizational culture, and work life balance is also reducing the rate of employee turnover.

2.2.5. Carrier development, succession planning, and talent mobility are processes which will retain top talent. Succession planning is for promoting talent to have higher responsibility and position, talent mobility is a process to provide talent to have more experiences.

3 METHODOLOGY

This paper is qualitative research based on a literature review of various scientific articles taken from journal and prominent research and articles related to the theme of this paper that help in facing IR 4.0 from a talent management point of view and the CEO role in talent management.

The main objective of this qualitative research is to provide the reviews about the framework, analysis, and solution of the talent management strategic model that improves the organization performance and embraces the Industrial Revolution 4.0 challenges. After an in-depth review of the literature for analysis, the author selected several as the main focus.

4 DISCUSSION

Based on literatures, the following terminologies are becoming important in HR: agility, mindset, innovation, openness and digital technology, design thinking and these will push leadership style in the context fast cross hierarchical, team oriented, cooperative approach with focus through innovation (Oberer & Erkollar 2018). The challenge is how to make these terminologies become living in the organization.

On the other side, the role of CEO sets the tone, vision, culture, and nominating people and enabling them to be a team. To be successful, today's CEOs and executives maintain three key components: 1) right strategy, 2) operations to execute the strategy, and 3) having the best people to execute those operations (HR.com 2012).

Envisioning capability of the CEO is the first key to determine the success of the company, and the CEO has to be able to see the future and should be able to bring all leaders to be in his vision in anticipating VUCA and IR 4.0. Following setting the vision, the CEO should decide the strategy to achieve organizations' objectives. Having understood the role of CEO and talent management, the conceptual role of the CEO in talent management in embracing IR 4.0 is showed in Figure 1.

Two roles of CEO are acknowledged, which are setting the tone for vision, culture, competencies and leadership and supporting all processes of talent management. Culture, competencies, and

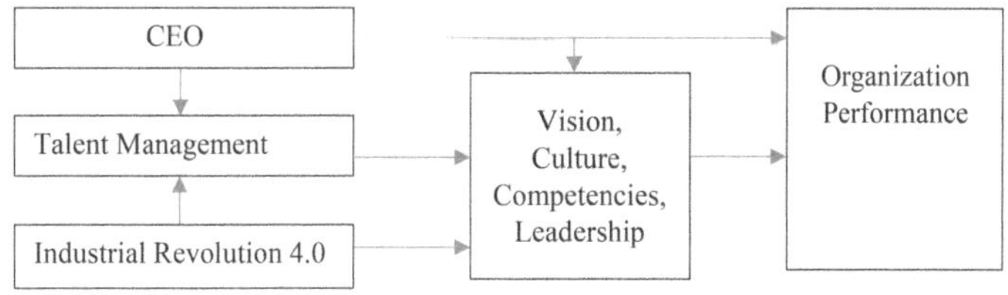

Figure 1. Conceptual role of CEO in talent management.

leadership have to be developed and groomed to ensure the organization is able to embrace the new era IR 4.0. Then, the CEO has to ensure that all processes will guarantee the result as planned.

Involvement of the CEO in talent management processes can be in the whole processes; however, the CEO may join on the steps which are considered as crucial. This role of CEO is shown by Michael D. Ruslim in his book when Astra did not reduce the budget for learning even during the recession in 2008–2009 (Ruslim 2011). CEO Telkom shows that he was involved from selecting people, placing people, walking around, direct interviews for one layer under C level (Rasyid 2015; Yahya 2013). In general, the involvement of CEO in talent management is as follows:

Talent attraction: In this activity, the CEO could be the role model and also ambassador of the company to attract talent with special qualifications who are future leaders of the organization. The source of talent can come from within and outside the organization.

Recruiting: The CEO can be involved during selecting talent for critical positions and future leaders who have to be fit with culture and also having capabilities to execute company strategy. Two approaches can be implemented which are from within or outside the organization. Inside source will provide talent who already have insight and knowledge about the organization, and outside organization source will be used when the organization wants to make a new change (Wolor et al. 2020).

Training and development is a process to develop people and talent competencies to catch up with the new trend in technologies, businesses, leadership, and management. Joining training and development, talents may improve their technical skill, strategic knowledge, as well as enhance their attitude and performance (Promsri 2019). This process is having the most involvement from the CEO, which is usually during the leadership development for future leaders. The CEO who has the vision is also involved in identifying skill gaps and creating employee development programs to address it, including agility.

Supporting the above statements, the recent PWC's research in 2019 showed that 79% of CEO globally agitated about the lack of essential skills of their employees that may hinder companies' future growth, while the previous PWC's research in 2014 showed that 63% of CEO intention over employees' skill increased over the last 5 years as the emerging technologies introduction (PwC 2019).

Following PWC, the recent Deloitte's research found that 83% of learning and development professionals said that the executive involvement in learning is not an encounter. However, this should be part of the company strategy, where the CEO's championship across the organization is required. Although only 27% of learning and development professionals reported that their CEOs actively champion the learning, the CEOs spend their time in soft skill learnings 20% more than the employees. Therefore, compounding the executive content may be the right tactic to increase the CEO's championship in the training and development. The direct involvement of the CEO in leadership programs may increase employee engagement. It may also inspire employees to attend the course as of immediacy and relevancy as they think that the CEO's leadership advice is relevant to their career advancement (LinkedIn Learning 2020).

Retaining, Succession Planning and Talent Mobility: These three processes usually are implemented at the same time as they have all talent list and data and sometimes these processes are called carrier development. The CEO is always leading talent meetings, especially for one layer under C-level, a critical position and top talent. In this process, intrinsic incentives and extrinsic incentives should be decided. Career improvement opportunities, organizational culture, and work life balance have to be managed to reduce the rate of employee turnover.

Retention also could be implemented using assigning talent to be talent mobility, which talent is able to have more experiences from other units, organization, or other business area. In this process, talent may still be in the same level but having more challenging tasks or new areas of working. If they are promoted, then it becomes a succession plan to create future leaders.

To ensure the future business which requires agility and digital leadership, the talent should be the right talent with the right learning and experience for the right strategic initiatives in the right time. Having said this, it is very crucial that CEO's have a role in talent management. This concern has shown by McKinsey, that the talent-driven organization needs a central brain trust consisting of the CEO, chief financial officer, and chief human resources officer as people allocation is as powerful as financial allocation to make sure the company has the right talent to meet the challenges of the future, and the CEO is the pivotal role (Barton 2020).

5 CONCLUSION

This study reveals that the CEO role is very critical in talent management in facing IR 4.0. The top down approach in transformation is inevitable, starting from defining the vision to determining the culture, competencies, and leadership. In performing this, the CEO must warrant the alignment with other senior management, especially the chief financial officer and the chief human resources officer.

The CEO must ensure that the company's vision is well communicated and understood by all levels of the organization, so that all staff have the same vision in achieving organizational goals.

The involvement of the CEO in the talent management process is inevitable. Research has found that the CEO involvement is most tortuous in training and development processes. However, how much time is used by the CEO in each talent management process, the impact on talent management, and how its influence on achieving the company's goals still needs further study.

REFERENCES

Barton, D., Carey, D., Charan, R., 2020, An agenda for the talent- first CEO, https://www.mckinsey.com/business-functions/organization/our-insights/an-agenda-for-the-talent-first-ceo, downloaded May 2020.

Ellis, R.K., 2020, Does your company have what it needs to compete in the Fourth Industrial Revolution? https://www.td.org/magazines/td-magazine/revolution-40.

HR.com, 2012, Driving Successful HR Leadership: Talent Management's Role in Core Business Strategy, www.hr.com

Kao, J., 2020, These six intelligences will drive smart leadership in disrupted times, https://www.weforum.org/agenda/2020/03/six-essential-intelligences-shape-smart-leadership-in-disrupted-times/, downloaded May 2020.

Kenton, W., 2020, Chief Executive Officer (CEO), https://www.investopedia.com/terms/c/ceo.asp, downloaded May 2020

Lee MH., Yun J.J., Pyka, A., Won, DK., Kodama, F., Schiuma, G., Park, HS., Jeon, J., Park, KB., Jung, KH., Yan, MR., Lee, SY., Zhao, X., 2018, How to Respond to the Fourth Industrial Revolution, or the Second Information Technology Revolution? Dynamic New Combinations between Technology, Market, and Society through Open Innovation, Journal of Open Innovation: Technology, Market, and Complexity.

LinkedIn Learning, 2020. 4th Annual 2020 Workplace Learning Report, L&D in a new decade: taking the strategic long view. https://learning.linkedin.com/content/dam/me/learning/resources/pdfs/LinkedIn-Learning-2020-Workplace-Learning-Report.pdf.

McKinsey, 2018, The CEO of Guardian Life on talent in an age of digital disruption March 20, 2018 | Video, https://www.mckinsey.com/business-functions/organization/our-insights/the-ceo-of-guardian-life-on-talent-in-an-age-of-digital-disruption.

Muriithi, F.W., Makau, M.S., 2017, Talent Management: A Conceptual Framework from Review of Literature and a Research Agenda, Journal of Human Resource Management 2017; 5(6): 90–94.
Oberer, B., Erkollar, A., 2018, Leadership 4.0: Digital Leaders in the Age of Industry 4.0, International Journal of Organisational Leadership, www.aimijournal.com
Promsri, C., 2019, Training Program Analysis for Leadership 4.0 in Fourth Industrial Revolution, East African Scholars Journal of Economics, Business and Management, Abbreviated Key Title: East African Scholars J Econ Bus Manag, Volume-2 | Issue-9 | Sept-2019 |.
PWC Global, 2019, Talent Trends 2019: Upskilling for a Digital World part of PwC's 22nd Annual Global CEO Survey trends series. https://www.pwc.com/gx/en/ceo-survey/2019/Theme-assets/reports/talent-trends-report.pdf.
Rasyid, A., 2015, Telkom 3010 Inside Story Telkom Value Creation, Penerbit Kompas ISBN 978 979 709 913 8
Ruslim, M.D., 2011, Lead By Heart, page 236, Gramedia, ISBN: 978-979-22-7027-3.
Schwab, K., 2016, Four leadership principles for the Fourth Industrial Revolution, https SEE-C-14 #21 Revised (3)://www.weforum.org/agenda/2016/10/four-leadership-principles-for-the-fourth-industrial-revolution/ downloaded May 2020.
Shekshnia, S., 2018, Leadership & Organisations, The Four Essential Roles of a CEO https://knowledge.insead.edu/leadership-organisations/the-four-essential-roles-of-a-ceo-8591downloaded May 2020.
Wolor, CW., Khairunnisa, H., Purwana, D., 2020, Implementation Talent Management To Improve Organization's Performance In Indonesia To Fight Industrial Revolution 4.0, International Journal of Scientific & Technology Research Volume 9, Issue 01, January 2020.
Yahya, A., 2013, Great Spirit & Grand Strategy, Gramedia, ISBN 979-979-22-7621-3.

Synergizing Management, Technology and Innovation in Generating Sustainable and Competitive Business Growth – Hendayani et al (eds)
© 2021 Taylor & Francis Group, London, ISBN 978-0-367-68756-4

Optimal stock portfolio establishment using PEG and Tobin's Q ratio with active and passive strategy approach in JKLQ45 index 2013–2018 period

S. Lestari & D. Rahadian
Telkom University, Bandung, West Java, Indonesia

ABSTRACT: In this study, the formation of a portfolio will be formed based on the financial ratio of price earning to growth (PEG) and Tobin's Q. Formation of the portfolio will also be built based on active annual, semi-active, and passive strategies. After the portfolio is formed, an evaluation of the portfolio's performance will be carried out. The results showed that the PEG medium portfolios on passive and active annual strategies generate low risk with profits above the average portfolio and market. Tobin's Q portfolio is also able to provide a relatively high return on the active semester and active quarter strategy, which is above both the average portfolio and even the market. The results of the portfolio performance evaluation in this study are that the Sharpe Index's best ranking is the active quarterly strategy, while the best performance index ranking in Jensen Index is the annual active strategy.

1 INTRODUCTION

Index one is a good performance index with uses of 45 issuers with liquidity with high market capitalization and liquidity (Indonesia Stock Exchange Index Guide Book 2010).

Based on in Figure 1, it shows that the closing price has fluctuated with a positive tendency to increase from 2013 to 2018. The Index opened at 761.26 in January 2013 and continued to fluctuate with an increasing tendency, and in December 2018 it closed at the 982.73 level.

Figure 1. Graph of closing price of JKJKLQ 45 Index for 2013–2018.
(Source: Adapted in id.investing.com accessed August 20, 2019)

Based on Figure 2, it can be seen that the movement of stock returns in the JKLQ 45 index has fluctuations. The highest performance was recorded in December 2017 with a figure of 8.790%, while the lowest performance was in April 2015 with a figure of −9.615%. This shows that the range of the JKLQ 45 Index return is within that range.

Based on Figure 3, the graph comparison of average return of JKLQ 45 and IHSG in 2013–2018, it can be seen that the JKLQ 45 Index has an average return below IHSG. The average JCI return was 0.51%, while for JKLQ 45 itself, it was only 0.46%. This indicates that the return generated by JKLQ 45 is still below the return generated on the CSPI.

According to Tandelilin (2014: 115), to reduce the risk of investing, investors need to "diversify" the portfolio. Investors need to form a portfolio through the selection of a combination of several assets such that risks can be minimized without reducing the expected return on investment (Tandelilin 2014: 115).

In compiling several portfolio alternatives, many financial ratios approaches can be used. One of them is using the price earning to growth (PEG) ratio. In Damodaran (2012: 344), it is mentioned that the PEG ratio is a function of risk, growth potential, and the company's payment ratio. Not only the PEG ratio, but you can also use Tobin's Q ratio to create a good portfolio alternative. Tobin's Q is one indicator variable that measures a company's performance from an investment perspective and has been tested in various situations to top management.

After determining the strategy, in this study according to Tandelilin (2014: 488), performance appraisal of the portfolio is also used, the aim is to identify whether the portfolio formed can provide a return under the risk to be borne by investors.

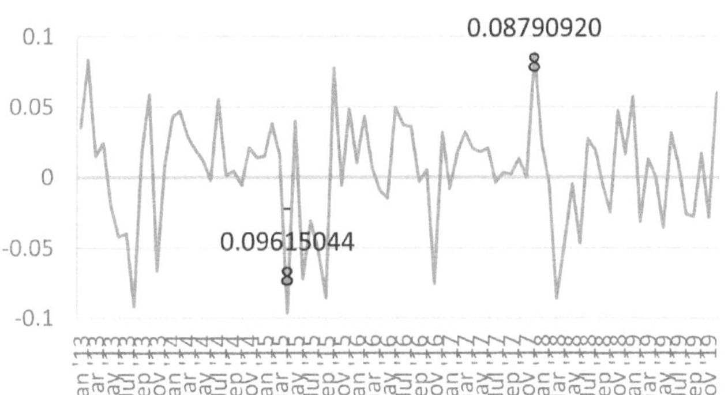

Figure 2. JKJKLQ 45 Return Index 2013–2019.(Source: Adapted on id.investing.com August 20, 2019)

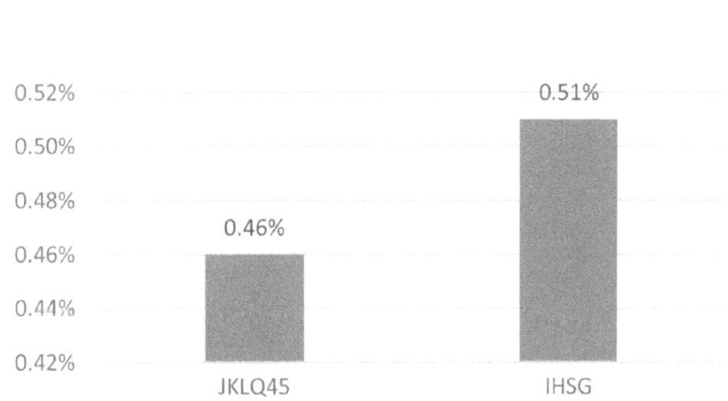

Figure 3. Comparison of average JKLQ 45 and IHSG returns 2013–2018.
(Source: Adapted on id.investing.com October 20, 2019)

2 RESERCH METHODOLOGY

This research used quantitative research methods. The population in this study is all listed companies listed on the JKLQ 45 Index listed on the Indonesia Stock Exchange (IDX). In this study, the sampling technique used was the purposive sampling technique. Data analysis techniques in this study were carried out with the following stages: 1) Initial calculation; 2) Use of PEG and Tobin's Q in portfolio formation; 3) Determination of weighting of portfolios; 4) Calculation of portfolio expected return and portfolio risk; 5) Evaluation of portfolio performance using Sharpe and Jensen indexes.

3 RESEARCH RESULTS

Based on Table 1 the total value of accumulated returns on the passive strategy is 58.680%. There are four portfolios with return values above both the average total and the IHSG as the market. The high PEG portfolio with the highest return (rank 1), followed by the low Tobin's Q portfolio, the medium Tobin's Q portfolio, and the medium PEG portfolio in the fourth position. While the total average value of accumulated risk in the passive strategy is 22.0760%, where the overall portfolio is formed riskier than the CSPI as the market, there is one portfolio with a risk value below the total average risk, namely the PEG medium portfolio (rank 2). The portfolio with the highest risk for a passive strategy is a high PEG portfolio. Next to the annual active strategy, the total value of the average return (return) on the annual active strategy is 68.442%.

There are five portfolios with a return value above the total average and above the market average (CSPI), there is a low PEG portfolio with the highest return value (rank 1) followed by four other portfolios. While the total average value of accumulated risk in the strategy, annual active is equal to 21,748%. The overall portfolio formed is riskier than the average market index (CSPI). But there are two portfolios with a risk value below the total average risk, namely the medium PEG portfolio and Tobin's high.

Based on Table 2, the total average return on the active semester strategy is 63.384%, in which the portfolio as a whole has a return above the average total and above the IHSG except for JKLQ 45 portfolios, including ranking by ranking, that is, the low Tobin's Q portfolio (rank 1), the medium Tobin's Q portfolio (rank 2), the low PEG portfolio (rank 3), all the time, the medium PEG portfolio, the high PEG portfolio, and the high Tobin's Q portfolio. As for the total average value of accumulated risk in the semester active strategy is 22.162%. The entire portfolio formed is riskier than the CSPI, whereas the portfolio most at risk is the medium Tobin's portfolio.

Table 1. Annual passive and active portfolio strategy return and risk ranking.

	Pasif				AktifTahunan			
	Return Portfolio		Risk Portfolio		Return Portfolio		Risk Portfolio	
Passive Portfolio	Accumulation Return	Ranking	Accumulation Risiko	Ranking	Accumulation Return	Ranking	Accumulation Risiko	Ranking
Low Tobins Q	76,53%	2	23,56%	4	77,62%	2	24,73%	6
Medium Tobins Q	73,01%	3	24,35%	6	76,27%	4	23,78%	5
High Tobins Q	42,39%	6	22,76%	3	73,22%	5	20,82%	2
Low PEG	45,17%	5	24,34%	5	63,84%	6	23,65%	4
Medium PEG	68,83%	4	19,54%	1	82,54%	1	20,05%	1
High PEG	79,74%	1	26,11%	7	77,55%	3	24,91%	7
JKLQ 45	40,60%	7	21,86%	2	53,15%	7	21,93%	3
CSPI	43,18%		14,09%		43,18%		14,11%	
Sum Average	58,68%		22,08%		68,42%		21,75%	

Table 2. Ranking returns and portfolio risks for active and semester and quarterly strategies.

	Active Semester				Active Quartal			
	Return Portfolio		Risk Portfolio		Return Portfolio		Risk Portfolio	
Active Portfolio	Accumulation Return	Ranking	Accumulation Return	Ranking	Accumulation Return	Ranking	Accumulation Return	Ranking
Low Tobin's Q	76,83%	1	24,90%	6	74,96%	1	26,08%	6
Medium Tobin's Q	73,71%	2	26,55%	7	74,05%	2	23,69%	4
High Tobin's Q	64,26%	6	21,00%	1	66,51%	3	22,71%	3
Low PEG	73,45%	3	22,31%	3	63,81%	5	21,94%	2
Medium PEG	72,48%	4	23,69%	5	52,52%	6	25,17%	5
High PEG	67,66%	5	22,78%	4	65,46%	4	27,37%	7
JKLQ 45	37,64%		21,96%	2	41,86%	7	19,89%	1
CSPI	41,05%	7	14,11%		41,39%		14,13%	
Sum Average	63,38%		22,16%		60,07%		22,62%	

Furthermore, the total average return on the active quarter strategy is 60.069%, where there are five portfolios with a return value above the average total and above the IHSG, including the low Tobin's Q portfolio with the highest return value (ranking 1), then the medium Tobin's Q portfolio (rank 2), the high Tobin's Q portfolio (rank 3), and high PEG portfolio (rank 4), and low PEG portfolio. The total average value of accumulated risk in the active quarter strategy is 22.621%, where the entire portfolio formed is riskier than IHSG as the market, but there are two portfolios with a risk value below the total average risk, namely JKLQ 45 portfolio has the lowest risk value (rank 2), followed by a high Tobin's Q portfolio (rank 3), whereas the portfolio with the highest risk is a high PEG portfolio.

4 CONCLUSSION

Overall results of the calculations and the evaluations in this study showed that portfolios formed from stocks in the JKLQ 45 Index using Tobin's Q and PEG ratios were able to produce higher returns than the JKLQ 45 Index. However, the risk resulted was also higher. According to the principle of high-risk high-return. Portfolios formed with a composition containing LQ4 Index shares are able to produce a portfolio composition with good return performance with a certain level of risk (efficient portfolio).

This study uses two indexes to measure portfolio performance, which are Sharpe and Jensen, where in this study, investors can invest in the JKLQ 45 Index using the annual active strategy on the Sharpe Index or the quarter active strategy on the Jensen Index. The Sharpe Index's measurement is using the annual active strategy. The medium PEG portfolio provides the best performance compared to other portfolios. Whereas the Jensen Index uses the active quarter strategy, the portfolio that provides the best performance is the Tobin's Q low portfolio.

In addition, the medium PEG portfolio is able to provide relatively high returns on passive and active annual strategies. In the passive and active annual strategy, the PEG medium portfolio produces relatively low risk with returns above the average portfolio and market (CSPI). In addition to the medium PEG portfolio, Tobin's Q's low portfolio is also able to provide relatively high returns on the semester active strategy and quarter active strategy, where the result is above the average portfolio and also the market (CSPI). Returns are generated by other portfolios, but the risk resulted was also higher. The result of this study is in accordance with the investment principle of high-risk high-return. Tobin Q's low portfolio is able to provide relatively high returns with also generated risks.

5 SUGGESTION

The results of this study can be used as a reference on how to form/optimize an optimal portfolio. Investors use financial ratios, including Tobin's Q and PEG ratios in forming the portfolio composition. In addition, the results of this study can be used as a material consideration for investors in determining the composition of shares in their portfolio.

REFERENCES

Bursa Efek Indonesia. 2010. *Buku Panduan Indeks Harga Saham Bursa Efek Indonesia*. Jakarta: Bursa Efek Indonesia.

Bursa Efek Indonesia. 2019. Annual Report Bursa Efek Indonesia Tahun 2019. [*Online*]. Tersedia: https://www.idx.co.id/en-us/about-idx/annual-report/. [07Agustus 2019]

Damodaran, A. 2012. *Investment Valuation: Tools and Techniques for Determining the Value of Any Assets*. New York: John Wiley & Sons, Inc.

Investing.com. 2018. IDX JKLQ 45 (). [*Online*]. Tersedia: https://id.investing.com/indices/idx-.[07 Agustus 2019]

Tandelilin, E. 2014. *Portfolio dan Investasi Teori dan Aplikasi*. Yogyakarta: Kanisius.

Synergizing Management, Technology and Innovation in Generating Sustainable and Competitive Business Growth – Hendayani et al (eds)
© 2021 Taylor & Francis Group, London, ISBN 978-0-367-68756-4

Financial distress analysis on telecommunication companies in 2013–2017 periods (empirical studies in Asia Pacific)

F.T. Kristanti & R.A. Syahputra
Telkom University, Bandung, West Java, Indonesia

ABSTRACT: This study aims at determining the predictions of financial distress in telecommunications companies in the Asia Pacific during the period of 2014–2017. This study employed a quantitative approach by involving telecommunications companies in the Asia Pacific as the population meeting the requirements to be samples. Determination of samples was conducted by purposive sampling technique. The data analysis method used was logistic regression analysis. The variables used were financial risk (FR), operating risk (OR), profitability (PR), lending interest rate (LR), and inflation rate (IN). The results show that (1) PR had a negative effect on financial distress, (2) the ratio of FR, OR, LR, and IN did not have a positive effect on financial distress, indicated by a positive regression coefficient, and the resulting significance value was greater than required, >0.05.

1 INTRODUCTION

According to the 2018 Mobile Economy report released by the GSM Association (GSM Association 2017), cellular technology and its derivatives had contributed 4.5% to global gross domestic product (GDP). Nominally, this contribution provides added value of USD 3.6 trillion. It is estimated that in 2022, the contribution of this sector will reach USD 4.6 trillion, along with productivity and efficiency improvements marked by the implementation of mobile services and M2M/IoT solutions. In 2017, the cellular industry ecosystem created 29 million jobs (direct and indirect), and contributed to public sector funding with a value of nearly USD 500 billion collected from taxes and USD 25 billion through frequency spectrum tenders (GSM Association 2018).

A high level of competition in the telecommunications industry triggers operators to compete in adopting new technologies and network expansion to increase capacity. Anther factor triggering the level of risk is economic condition. The uncertainty and increasing competition environment cause companies that do not adapt to these factors to experience financial distress and will lead to company bankruptcy. There is a difference in definition between bankruptcy and financial distress according to Platt and Platt (2006). Financial distress is a condition where the following three factors are met, namely, negative EBITDA, negative EBIT, and negative net income.

However, it is still unclear when is the beginning or end of financial distress. Formerly, Platt and Platt (2002) defined financial distress as a condition in which a company's finances are unhealthy or in crisis. Elloumi and Guyie (2001) categorize companies with financial distress if they experience negative net income for two consecutive years. Bankruptcy is not always the case, but when it becomes real, it can have a direct impact on companies, both economically and socially (Kristanti & Herwany 2017).

The purpose of this study was to determine the variables of financial risk, operational risk, profitability, lending interest rate, inflation and financial distress in telecommunications companies in the Asia Pacific, in the 2013–2017 period.

2 LITERATURE REVIEW

Financial distress is a condition where a company faces a certain financial problem. According to Platt and Platt (2002), financial distress is defined as a stage of decline in financial conditions that occurred before the bankruptcy or liquidation. According to Wruck (1990), financial distress is a situation where cash flow operations are inadequate to meet current liabilities such as debt trade or interest costs (Aiyabei 2002). Some research on bankruptcy focuses on the use of financial ratios as a predictor of financial distress. Altman (1968) used the Z score as a tool to predict bankruptcy probability. Ohlson (1980), Zmijewski (1984), and Lau (1987) used the same prediction model but with different financial ratios.

2.1 *Financial perspective*

Boritz (1991) describes the process of financial distress that begins with an incubation period conditioned by poor economic conditions and management, which takes the wrong financial decisions. In this situation, companies experiencing negative earnings per share (EPS) in the long run are considered to be in financial distress. Kristanti et al. (2016) state that the variables of gender diversity, independent board, and leverage significantly influenced the likelihood of financial distress in family firms in Indonesia, while the operational risk, size, profitability, price book value (PBV), and auditor quality variables did not have any effect. Chrisitidis and Gregory (2010) found that working capital over total assets, total liabilities over total assets, cash flow over total assets, earnings before interest and tax over share capital, quick assets over current assets and funds from operations over total liabilities had a significant effect on financial distress. In addition, Parker et al. (2002) conducted a study with components of financial variables to identify the condition of financial distress. Their study concluded that liquidity, profitability, and size had a significant effect on financial distress.

2.2 *Macroeconomy impact*

Alifiah (2014) used macroeconomic variables and financial ratios, with the conclusion that debt ratio, total assets turnover ratio, working capital ratio, net income ratio, net income to total asset ratio, and base lending rate affect financial distress. Based on these findings, this study replicated the study conducted by Parker et al. (2002), and by adding macroeconomic environment variables, as studies conducted by Alifiah (2014) and Tsai et al. (2009). In terms of macroeconomic variables, Inekwe et al. (2017) argue that GDP had a positive effect on financial distress, contrary to Alifiah's analysis (2014), stating that the GDP variable did not have an effect on financial distress. Alifiah also analyzed the effect of lending rate, which had a positive impact on financial distress, as which was in accordance with Tsai et al. (2019). However, this analysis was disputed by research conducted by Bhattacharjee and Han (2014), which concluded that the lending rate did not have effect on financial distress.

3 RESEARCH METHODOLOGY

3.1 *Data sample*

In this study, the data were collected from the financial statements of the telecommunication operator in the Asia Pacific and other reliable sources, over the period 2013–2017. The sample was a part, the number, and characteristics possessed by the population, based on these characteristics: (1) A wireless telecommunications company incorporated in the GSM Association (GSMa) and operated in the 2014–2017 periods; (2) Listed on the respective country's stock exchanges; (3) The biggest market share in the country of origin; and (4) Had completed financial statements in the 2014–2017 period. The study involved 14 operators from 14 countries: Telstra (Australia), China

Mobile (China), SmarTone (Hong Kong), Reliance Communication (India), XL Axiata (Indonesia), NTT Docomo (Japan), SK Telecom (South Korea), Maxis (Malaysia), Spark (New Zealand), Globe Telecom (Philippines), Starhub (Singapore), FarEasTone (Taiwan), TrueMove H (Thailand), and Turk Telecom-Oger Telecom (Turkey).

3.2 *Variables and measurement variables*

Dependent variable (Y) is a variable that is influenced by independent variables. This study used a logistic regression approach, because the independent variable was a combination of continuous and categorized variables (Kristanti et al. 2016). This study used logit analysis, an approach that used the dependent variable as the logarithm of two possibilities: (1) if the company experiences financial stress and (0) if it does not (Alifiah 2014).

To represent this idea, the following model is used:

$$Y_i = \alpha + \beta_1 X_1 + \beta_2 X_2 + \mu I \quad (1)$$

where X_i = explanatory variable; $Y_i = 1$, if there is a Financial Distress; $Y_i = 0$, if there is no Financial Distress.

Then, the equation can be written in the logistic regression function as follows:

$$\ln(P/1 - P) = \alpha + \beta_1 X_1 + \beta_2 X_2 + \mu I \quad (2)$$

Thus, the probability of Financial Distress can be described in the equation:

$$P = \frac{1}{1 + e^{(\alpha + \beta_1 X_1 + \beta X_2 + \ldots \beta n X n)}} \quad (3)$$

The independent variable (X) is the variable affecting the dependent variable. The independent variables for this study are:

a. X_1, Financial risk was measured by comparing total debt with total assets. This ratio was used to test the extent to which companies used money, borrowed from third parties (VanHorne & Wachowicz 2016).
b. X_2, Operating Risk showed the ability of sales of total assets used. It was expected that the possibility of going bankrupt would decrease, when the ratio of assets to total sales decreased. Parker et al. (2002) found that operation risk is less than one hazard ratio, the likelihood that a company suffering from financial distress will decrease, although not significantly.
c. X_3, Profitability showed the company's ability to recover from financial distress. Profitability was measured by the ratio of return of sales. The profitability ratio was expected to have a negative correlation with financial distress; in other words, an increase in the profitability ratio would reduce the risk of being exposed to financial distress (Parker et al. 2002).
d. X_4, Lending interest rate was the reference interest rate used by the private sector to finance short- and medium-term business activities. Lending interest rate would change. Adjusting to the market, it was related to the policies of the central banks of each country.
e. X_5, Inflation was the tendency of rising prices of goods and services in general that took place continuously. Inflation could also be interpreted as a decrease in the value of money against the value of goods and services in general (BPS 2020).

4 ANALYSIS AND RESULT

4.1 *Descriptive analysis*

Descriptive analysis aims at finding out the data picture of research results. In this study, descriptive analysis was based on minimum, maximum, and average values, where the values were used to show the characteristics of the variables used in this study.

Table 1. Descriptive statistic.

Variable	N	Minimum	Maximum	Mean	Std. Deviation
Financial Risk (FR)	70	.229152913	12.1400376	1.104920919	1.964064107
Operating Risk (OR)	70	.0806671721	16.23731766	1.948898352	1.998245780
Profitability (PR)	70	−.0941962708	.387189512	.1520710740	.0971136583
Lending Interest Rate (LR)	70	1.044750000	12.6625000	6.049963036	3.009559107
Inflation (IN)	70	−.9004249630	11.14431108	2.648638750	2.606198728
Valid N (listwise)	70				

FR variables indicating the extent to which companies used third-party money to generate profits, and obtained a minimum value of 0.2291 and a maximum value of 12.1400 while the average value of financial risk 1, 1049 and the standard deviation value of 1.9651 from the results, it was seen that the average value > standard deviation means that the distribution of financial risk data did not have any gaps and the mean value could be used as a representation of the whole data.

OR variable showed the ability of sales of the total assets used. It was expected that the possibility of going bankrupt would decrease. When the ratio of assets to total sales decreased, it would be obtained that a minimum value of 0.0807 and a maximum value of 16.2373; while the average value of OR was 1.9489 and a standard deviation of 1.9982 from the results it was seen that the average value < standard deviation, which means that the OR data distribution was heterogeneous and there was a gap between the minimum value and the maximum value, That made the mean value have a poor representation of the entire data.

PR showed the company's ability to recover from financial distress. Profitability was measured by the ratio of return of sales. A high ratio value showed the company's ability to generate profits and be able to carry out debt obligations. Minimum value of −0.0942 and a maximum value of 0.3872 while an average value of 0.1521 profitability and a standard deviation of 0.0971 from the results it is seen that the average value > standard deviation means that the profitability data distribution did not have any gaps and the mean value could be used as a representation of the whole data.

LI variables are the reference interest rates used by the private sector to finance short- and medium-term business activities. LR would change. Adjusting to the market, it was related to the central bank policy of each, a minimum value of 1.0447 and a maximum value of 12.6625, while the average value of LR profitability was 6.0499 and the value standard deviation of 3.0096 from the results was seen that the average value > standard deviation means that the LR data distribution did not have any gaps, and the mean value could be used as a representation of the whole data.

IN variable, which is a process of increasing prices generally and continuously (related) related to market mechanisms that could be caused by various factors, among others, increased public consumption, excess liquidity in the market that triggers consumption or even speculation, to include also the result of an uneven distribution of goods. It obtained a minimum value of −0.9004 and a maximum value of 11.1443, while the average value of Inflation 2.6486 and a standard deviation of 2.6062 from the results it is seen that the average value > standard deviation means that the inflation data distribution did not have a gap and the mean value could be used as a representation of the whole data.

In this study, the Y variable used nominal scale data that value 1 indicated the condition of financial distress, and value 0 indicated the condition that did not experience financial distress. From Table 2, it shows the condition of samples that experienced financial distress by 10% and samples that did not experience financial distress by 90. The data shows that indications of financial distress occurred in Indonesia, India, Thailand, and Turkey, which were seen from negative EPS values in the long-run research time

Table 2. The number of samples in the dependent variable.

Variable	Frequency	Percent
Not in the condition of financial distress	63	90%
In the condition of financial distress	7	10%
Total	70	100%

Table 3. Variables in the equation.

	B	S.E.	Wald	df	Sig.	Exp(B)	
Step 1[a]	Financial Risk (FR)	1.174	.607	3.748	1	.053	3.236
	Operating Risk (OR)	1.241	.906	1.876	1	.171	3.459
	Profitability (PR)	−50.049	25.254	3.928	1	.047	.000
	Lending Interest Rate (LR)	.546	.375	2.125	1	.145	1.727
	Inflation (IN)	.149	.417	.128	1	.720	1.161
	Constant	−8.945	4.820	3.445	1	.063	.000

a. Variable(s) entered on step 1: Financial risk, operating risk, *profitability*, *lending interest rate*, *inflation*.

4.2 *Result and discussion*

According to Santoso (2017), logistic regression is basically the same as discriminant analysis, the difference is only in the type of data from the dependent variable in the form of a binary variable (nominal data) using the data of an independent variable whose size is known.

The logistical equations used in this study are:

$$Ln\frac{FD}{1-FD} = \beta 0 + \beta 1X1 + \beta 2X2 + \beta 3X3 + \beta 4X4 + \beta 5X5 + \mathrm{e} \tag{4}$$

Therefore, the results of processing the statistical data are in Table 3:

The following regression model could be drawn:

$$Ln\frac{FD}{1-FD} = -8.945 + 1.174FR + 1.241RP + (50.049)PR + 0.546LR + 0.1491N + \mathrm{e}$$

whereas $n\frac{P}{(P-1)}$ = Log from the comparison between financial distress possibility and non–financial distress possibility; $\beta 0 - \beta 7$ = Regression coefficient; FR = Financial risk; OR = Operating risk; PR = *Profitability*; LR = *Lending Interest Rate*; IN = *Inflation*; e = error term

Financial risk did not have a positive effect on financial distress. Therefore, the hypothesis was rejected. This study was in accordance with research conducted by Kristanti and Herwany (2017), where the results of research with components of financial variables to identify the condition of financial distress could be formulated into six variables: financial risk (leverage), size, liquidity, return on assets (ROA), price earnings ratio (PER), and price book value (PBV). This study concluded that financial risk (leverage), operational risk, profitability, ROA, PER, and PBV variables did not affect financial distress.

There was no significant effect of operating risk on the condition of financial distress. The results of this analysis were in line with research conducted by Kristanti and Effendy (2017), which showed that the operational risk variable did not significantly affect financial distress.

There was a significant effect of profitability on the condition of financial distress. The regression coefficient value of −50.049 indicated a negative influence. This shows that profitability affected financial distress. Therefore, the hypothesis was accepted. This is in line with research conducted by Lee (2014), who conducted the research with components of financial variables to identify the condition of financial distress that could be formulated into six variables: profitability, leverage, efficiency and valuation.

The profitability variable, measured by the return of sales instrument, showed the company's ability to recover from financial distress. Parker et al. (2002) concluded that this variable had significantly positive effect on financial distress. There was no significant effect of lending interest rate on the condition of financial distress. This shows that the lending interest rate did not have a positive effect on financial distress. In a study conducted by Alifiah (2014), analyzing the effect of lending rate that had a positive impact on financial distress, was the same thing that had been stated by Tsai et al. (2009). Inflation did not significantly influence the condition of financial distress. This shows that inflation did not have positive effect on financial distress. Therefore, the hypothesis was rejected.

5 CONCLUSION AND RECOMMENDATION

The results of this study indicate that profitability had a significant effect on the condition of financial distress in telecommunications companies in the Asia Pacific region; thus, business actors in this sector needed to be aware of financial ratio parameters, especially in the profitability ratio category. As a predictor of financial distress, an increase in the profitability ratio increased the company's endurance against the risk of financial distress.

Furthermore, Lee (2014) clarified financial ratios in several categories. The Profitability category includes EBIT margin, return on equity, and return in assets. Profitability was also used to measure the ratio between earnings and sales. Profitability is describing the company's ability to recover from financial distress conditions. For the government as regulator, the profitability ratio could be considered in making laws and regulations that protected all stakeholders from the possibility of financial distress.

REFERENCES

Aiyabei, J. 2002. Financial Distress: Theory, Measurement & Consequence. *The Eastern Africa Journal of Humanities & Sciences, 1*(1), 61–68.

Alifiah, M. N. 2014. Prediction of Financial Distress Companies in the Trading and Services Sector in Malaysia Using Macroeconomic Variables. *Procedia – Social and Behavioral Sciences. 129,* 90–98. doi: 10.1016/j.sbspro.2014.03.652

Altman, E. 1968. Financial Ratios, Discriminant Analysis and the Prediction of Corporate Bankruptcy, *23*(4), 589–609. doi: 10.2307/2978933

Bhattacharjee, A., Han, J. 2014. Financial Distress of Chinese firms: Microeconomic, Macroeconomic and Institutional Influences. *China Economic Review,* 30, 244–262. doi: 10.1016/j.chieco.2014.07.007

Biro Pusat Statistik, Inflasi. https://www.bps.go.id/subject/3/inflasi.html#subjekViewTab1, May 31, 2020,

Boritz, J. 1991. The going concern assumption: Accounting and auditing implications. Toronto, Canada: Canadian Institute of Chartered Accountants (Research Report).

Chrisitidis, A. Chih-Ying., Gregory, A. 2010. Some New Models for Financial Distress Prediction in the UK. Xfi – *Centre for Finance and Investment Discussion Paper* no: 10/04

Elloumi, F., Guiyie, Jean-Pieree. 2001. *Financial Distress and Corporate Governance: A Survival Analysis.* Corporate Governance.

GSM Association. 2017. Global Cellular Market Trends and Insight Q3 2017.

GSM Association. 2018. The Mobile Economy 2018.

Inekwe, J. N., Jin, Y., Valenzuela, M. R. 2017. The effects of Financial Distress: Evidence from US GDP growth. *Economic Modelling,* (72), 8–21. doi: 10.1016/j.econmod.2018.01.001.

Pereira, C. P. J. E. 2013. Corporate Bankruptcy of Portuguese Firms. Zagreb International Review of Economics and Business, Faculty of Economics and Business, University of Zagreb, vol. 16(2), pages 39–56, May.

Kristanti, F.T., Effendi, N. 2017. A Survival Analysis of Indonesian Distressed Company Using Cox Hazard Model. *Int. Journal of Economics and Management* 11 (S1): 155–167.

Kristanti, F. T., Herwany, A. 2017. Corporate Governance, Financial Ratios, Political Risk and Financial Distress: A Survival Analysis. *Acc. Fin. Review* 2 (2) 26–34.
Kristanti, F. T., Rahayu, S., & Huda, A. N. 2016. The Determinant of Financial Distress on Indonesian Family Firm. *Procedia-Social and Behavioral Sciences*, Vol. 219.
Lau, A. Hing-Ling. 1987. A Five-State Financial Distress Prediction Model. *Journal of Accounting Research* Vol. 25, No. 1 (Spring, 1987), pp. 127–138.
Lee, Ming-Chan. 2014. Business Bankruptcy Prediction Based on Survival Analysis Approach. *International Journal of Computer Science & Information Technology* (IJCSIT) Vol 6, No 2, April 2014
Ohlson, J. 1980. Financial Ratios and the Probabilistic Prediction of Bankruptcy. *Journal of Accounting Research. 19*, 109–131.
Parker, S., Peters, G. F., & Turetsky, H. F. 2002. Corporate governance and corporate failure: a survival analysis. *The international journal of business in society.*
Platt, H.D., Platt M.B. 2002. Predicting corporate financial distress: reflection on choice-based sample bias. *Journal of Economics and Finance, 26*(2), 184–197.
Platt, H. and M. B. Platt. 2006. Understanding Differences between Financial Distress and Bankruptcy. *Review of Applied Economics, 2*(2), 211–227.
Santoso, S. 2017. Statistik Multivariate dengan SPSS. Jakarta, PT. Elex Media Komputindo
Tsai, Bi-Huei., Lee, Cheng-Few., Sun, L. 2009. The Impact of Auditors' Opinions, Macroeconomic and Industry Factors on Financial Distress Prediction: An Empirical Investigation. *Review of Pacific Basin Financial Markets and Policies* Vol. 12, No. 3
Van Horne, J. C., Wachowicz, Jr, J. M. 2016. *Prinsip-Prinsip Manajemen Keuangan* [Principles of Finance Management]. Jakarta: Penerbit Salemba Empat.
Wruck, K. H. 1990. Financial Distress, Reorganization, and Organizational Efficiency. *Journal of Financial Economics*, 27, 419–444.
Zmijewski, M. 1984. Methodological Issues Related to Estimation of Financial Distress Prediction Models. *Journal of Accounting Research*, 22, 59–82.

Synergizing Management, Technology and Innovation in Generating Sustainable and Competitive Business Growth – Hendayani et al (eds)
© 2021 Taylor & Francis Group, London, ISBN 978-0-367-68756-4

Fraud pentagon analysis in detecting fraudulent financial statement (study on mining sector companies listed in the Indonesia Stock Exchange period of 2014–2018)

A. Nurbaiti & N. Romadhona
Faculty of Economics and Business, Telkom University, Bandung, West Java, Indonesia

ABSTRACT: Fraudulent financial statements are one type of fraud that often occurs in Indonesia. The occurrence of fraudulent financial statements will cause a company's internal conflicts and also harm the external parties in making decisions. This study aims to detect fraudulent financial statements using fraud pentagon analysis in the form of factors of pressure, opportunity, rationalization, capability, and arrogance in mining sector companies listed on the Indonesia Stock Exchange period of 2014–2018. The sample of this study used purposive sampling, which was 31 company samples. Data analysis method in this research is logistic regression analysis using SPSS 25 software. The result showed that simultaneously the pressure, opportunity, rationalization, capability, and arrogance affect the fraudulent financial statement. Meanwhile, partially test result pressure, opportunity, rationalization, and capability have no effect and arrogance has a positive effect on fraudulent financial statement.

1 INTRODUCTION

In making a decision to invest in a company, the first thing that investors will do is analyze the company with significant and careful consideration. Financial statements can be taken as a reference by investors as external users. However, there are still many companies that falsify financial statements because the company wants to look good by the external users of financial statements who are interested to invest in the company. Cressey (1953) first introduced the factors used to detect fraudulent financial statement, which are called the fraud triangle, namely, pressure, opportunity, and rationalization. The fraud triangle theory was developed into the fraud diamond theory by Wolfe and Hermanson (2004) by adding one indicator, namely capability. Fraud diamond theory is deemed necessary to be developed and adapted to the times, so fraud diamond theory is adjusted by Crowe Howarth LLP (2011) to become a fraud pentagon theory by adding one indicator, namely, arrogance.

Based on a survey conducted by the Association of Certified Fraud Examiners (ACFE) Indonesia in 2016, it was concluded that fraudulent financial statement was one of the most detrimental types of fraud in Indonesia. The case of PT Timah Persero Tbk (TINS) in the first semester of 2015 was one example of a case of fraudulent financial statements in Indonesia. PT Timah Persero Tbk conducted fictitious financial statements by saying that the efficiency of the strategy had led to positive performance. Even though the real condition that happened in the first semester of 2015 was loss of Rp59 billion. Based on the case of fraud that occurred, this study aims to determine the fraud pentagon analysis in detecting financial reporting fraud in the mining sector companies in the 2014–2018 period.

2 LITERATUR REVIEW

2.1 *Fraudulent financial statement (Y)*

According to the Association of Certified Fraud Examiners (ACFE) in Tessa and Harto (2016), fraudulent financial statement is defined as follows: The deliberate misrepresentation of the financial condition of an enterprise accomplished through the intentional misstatement or omission of amounts or disclosures in the financial statements in order to deceive financial statement users. In this study, fraudulent financial statement is proxied by f-score. Code 1 if f-score > 1.00, code 0 if f-score < 1.00.

2.2 *Pressure (X_1)*

According to Tuanakotta (2010), someone who commits embezzlement or fraud has an urgent financial need. The pressure is in the form of the need for money. The higher of leverage ratio of the company will make the higher of credit risk, also the higher the impact on the risk of high losses as well. Company's manager will try to manipulate financial statements by reducing the leverage ratio of the company so that the company's debt looks small (Agustina & Pratomo 2019). The pressure factor in this study is proxied by external pressure, which is calculated by the leverage ratio. The leverage ratio is calculated by total debts divided by total assets.

2.3 *Opportunity (X_2)*

Opportunity is a chance that someone has to commit fraud. According to the American Institute of Certified Public Accountants (2002), ineffective monitoring is a condition where the internal control system doesn't operate effectively, giving the opportunities to commit fraud. Ineffective monitoring is calculated as a percentage of the number of independent commissioners (BDOUT).

2.4 *Rationalization (X_3)*

According to Tuanakotta (2010), rationalization is a form of seeking justification for the violations that have been done. Nature of industry is the ideal state of a company in the industry. Account receivables can be a benchmark for the ideal state of a company. Accounts receivable is related to estimates of uncollectible receivables whose amounts are subjective, so that management can use the account as a tool to manipulate financial statements (Faradiza 2019). In this study, the ratio of total receivables used as proxies can be calculated by receivable t divided by sales t minus receivable t-1 divided by sales t-1.

2.5 *Capability (X_4)*

Capability is the ability by fraudsters to penetrate internal controls in a company, develop a sophisticated embezzlement strategy, and be able to control social situations that are able to bring profit to them by influencing others to cooperate with them (Faradiza 2019). In this study the competency factor is proxied by the change of directors (DCHANGE) as measured by dummy variables; code 1 is given if the company changes the forms of directors in the study period, while code 0 is given if the company does not change the forms of directors.

2.6 *Arrogance (X_5)*

Arrogance is the nature of a lack of conscience as an attitude of superiority or the presence of arrogance in someone who believes that internal control can't be enforced personally (Agustina & Pratomo 2019). Baningrum (2017) states that the number of chief executive officer (CEO) photos displayed in a company's annual report can represent the level of arrogance or superiority possessed by the CEO. In this research, arrogance is measured using the frequency of the number of CEO's pictures or photos appearing in the company's annual report.

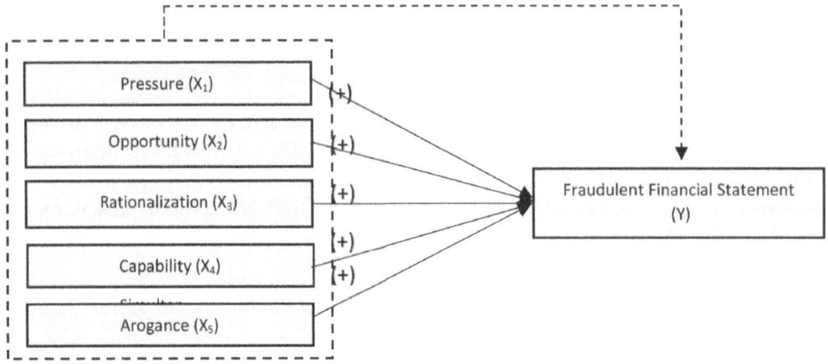

Figure 1. Conceptual framework.

2.7 *Conceptual framework*

2.7.1 *Effect of pressure on fraudulent financial statement*

Pressures is an impulse form within humans to commit fraud. This pressure is based on financial needs or problems or just because of greed (Ulfah et al. 2017). According to Tuanakotta (2010), someone who commits fraud and embezzlement of money because of the pressure, that pressure might be an urgent need that must be fulfilled. The company manager might see instability in their company; it can be a pressure for managers, then they might commit a fraudulent financial statement so the company will look good for the external funding sources, namely, investor or creditor.

2.7.2 *Effect of opportunity on fraudulent financial statement*

Opportunity is a condition where someone has the opportunity to commit fraud. Ineffective monitoring is ineffective or the company's internal control system is not functioning properly (Agusputri & Sofie 2019). The failure of the internal control system within the company provides an opportunity for management to commit fraudulent financial statement. This opportunity will be used as well as being possible for management to maximize their actions in committing fraud.

2.7.3 *Effect of rationalization on fraudulent financial statement*

Rationalization is a form of seeking justification for the violations that have been done. The perpetrators of fraud believed that their actions didn't break the rules and are not fraud, but they considered this right to something that they have done (Ulfah et al. 2017). In this study, rationalization is proxied by the nature of the industry, which is the ideal condition of a company. The ideal condition of a company is achieved by showing the company's best ability to achieve its goals. Basically, investors are more interested to investing in companies with ideal or good conditions in an industry (Agusputri & Sofie 2019).

2.7.4 *Effect of capability on fraudulent financial statement*

Competence or ability can be interpreted as the position or role of a person in an organization what makes them commit fraud (Hermanson & Wolfe 2004). Competence means the ability of fraud perpetrators to penetrate internal controls in the company, develop strategies, and control situations to benefit themselves by influencing others (Faradiza 2019).

2.7.5 *Effect of arrogance on fraudulent financial statement*

Arrogance is a superiority of someone who believes that internal policies don't affect him. An arrogant person tends to desire praise and recognition for every outcome he has achieved (Crowe 2011). In this study, arrogance was proxied by the frequency number of CEO pictures appearing in annual reports. This shows that the more CEO photos displayed in the annual report the higher arrogance of a CEO as shown by displaying his position and role in a company. The CEO who wants to maintain his position will use all means to get it even if he has to commit fraud in order to improve the performance of the company to keep looking good (Vivianita & Indudewi 2018).

3 RESEARCH METHODOLOGY

This research is a quantitative research. The population used in this study is mining sector companies listed in the Indonesia Stock Exchange 2014–2018. The sample technique used in this study was purposive sampling in order to obtain 31 sample companies with a five-year research period. Regression analysis used in this study is logistic regression analysis.

4 RESULT AND DISCUSSIONS

4.1 *Simultaneous test*

Based on Table 1, the result of the overall significance level of independent variables is 0.048 or smaller than 0.05 as the level of significance determined. It means that the independent variables simultaneously are pressure, opportunity, rationalization, capability, and arrogance that affect the dependent variable fraudulent financial statement.

4.2 *Partial Test*

Based on the data in Table 2, the effect of partial influence percentage of pressure, opportunity, rationalization, competence, and arrogance to detecting fraudulent financial statement is as follows:

X_1, LEVERAGE sig of 0.124 > 0.05 then pressure has no effect
X_2, BDOUT sig of 0.834 > 0.05 then opportunity has no effect
X_3, RECEIVABLE sig of 0.570 > 0.05 then rationalization has no effect
X_4, DCHANGE sig of 0.242 > 0.05 then capability/competence has no effect
X_5, CEOPIC sig of 0.030 < 0.05 then arrogance has positive effect

Table 1. Omnibus test of model coefficients.

		Chi-square	Df	Sig
Step 1	Step	11.183	5	.048
	Block	11.183	5	.048
	Model	11.183	5	.048

Table 2. Variables in the equation.

		B	S.E.	Wald	df	Sig.	Exp (B)
Step 1[a]	LEV	−3.005	1.953	2.366	1	.124	.050
	BDOUT	.873	4.152	.044	1	.834	2.394
	RECEIVABLE	−.416	.733	.322	1	.570	.660
	DCHANGE	−1.339	1.145	1.368	1	.242	.262
	CEOPIC	.180	.083	4.706	1	.030	1.197
	Constant	−2.489	1.872	1.767	1	.184	.083

4.3 *Discussion*

Obtain output that forms a logistic regression equation as follows:

$$\text{Ln}\frac{Fraud}{1 - Fraud} = -2,489 - 3,005\text{LEV} + 0,873\text{BDOUT} - 0,416\text{REC} - 1,339\text{DCHANGE} + 0,180\text{CEOPIC}$$

Based on the equation, this can be described as follows.

The constant value of −2,489 has the meaning that if the pressure, opportunity, rationalization, capability, and arrogance have a zero value, it will reduce the probability of companies to do fraudulent financial statement by 0.083 times.

Based on Table 2, leverage has no effect in detecting fraudulent financial statement and has a negative direction regression coefficient value equal to -3.005, which means that it is contrary to the hypothesis that saying if the higher of leverage ratio of the company will make the higher of credit risk, also the higher the impact on the risk of high losses as well, management will try to manipulate financial statements by reducing the leverage ratio of the company.

Based on Table 2, BDOUT has no effect in detecting fraudulent financial statements and has positive direction regression coefficient value equal to 0.873, which means that the number of independent commissioners can reduce the probability occurrence of fraudulent financial statement.

Based on Table 2, RECEIVABLE has no effect in detecting fraudulent financial statements and has negative direction regression coefficient value equal to -0.416, which means that it is contrary to the hypothesis that saying if accounts receivable is related to estimates of uncollectible receivables, so that management can use the account receivable as a tool to manipulate financial statement.

Based on Table 2, DCHANGE has no effect in detecting fraudulent financial statements and has negative direction regression coefficient value equal to -1.333, which means that it is contrary to the hypothesis that saying if a change of board of director makes a new board of directors it needs to adapt with the situation in the company, so there's a probability occurrence of fraudulent financial statement.

Based on Table 2, CEOPIC affects detecting fraudulent financial statements and has a positive direction regression coefficient value 0.180, which means that the photos of a CEO in annual reports can detecting the occurrence of fraudulent financial statement.

5 CONCLUSSION AND SUGGESTION

5.1 *Conclusion*

1) The leverage ratio as a proxied of pressure can't detect fraudulent financial statement.
2) The number of independent commissioners as a proxied of opportunity can reduce the occurrence of fraudulent financial statement.
3) The receivable ratio as a proxied of rationalization can't detect fraudulent financial statement.
4) The change of board of directors as a proxied of capability can't detect fraudulent financial statement.
5) The photos of a CEO in annual reports as a proxied of arrogance can detecting the occurrence of fraudulent financial statement.

5.2 *Suggestion*

Future research can use a more diverse research sample in other sectors and add the number of years of research to get better results.

REFERENCES

Agustina, R. D., & Pratomo, D. 2019. Pengaruh Fraud Pentagon dalam Mendeteksi Kecurangan Pelaporan Keuangan. JIMEA, Jurnal Ilmiah MEA (Manajemen, Ekonomi dan Akuntansi), Vol. 3 No.1.

AICPA (American Institute of Certified Public Accountant), SAS No. 99. 2002. Consideration of Fraud in a Financial Statement Audit. New York: AICPA.

Association of Certified Fraud Examiners Indonesia Chapter. 2017. Survai Fraud Indonesia 2016. Jakarta: ACFE Indonesia Chapter.

Faradiza, S. A. 2019. Fraud Pentagon dan Kecurangan Laporan Keuangan. Jurnal Ekonomi dan Bisnis, Fakultas Ekonomi dan Bisnis Islam, Universitas Islam Negeri Sunan Kalijaga Yogyakarta.

Howarth, C. 2011. Putting The Freud in Fraud: Why The Fraud is No Longer Enough. Crowe Howarth.

Setiawati, E., & Baningrum, R. M. 2018. Deteksi Fraudulent Financial Reporting Menggunakan Analisis Fraud Pentagon: Studi Kasus Pada Perusahaan Manufaktur yang Listed di BEI Tahun 2014–2016. Jurnal Riset Akuntansi dan Keuangan Indonesia, 91–106.

Tessa G, C., & Harto, P. 2016. Fraudulent Financial Reporting: Pengujian Teori Fraud Pentagon Pa-da Sektor Keuangan dan Perbankan di Indonesia. Simposium Nasional Akuntansi XIX, 1–21.

Tuanakotta, T. M. 2010. Akuntansi Forensik dan Audit Investigatif Edisi 2. Jakarta: Salemba Empat.

Synergizing Management, Technology and Innovation in Generating Sustainable and Competitive Business Growth – Hendayani et al (eds)
© 2021 Taylor & Francis Group, London, ISBN 978-0-367-68756-4

The effects of tax burden, company size, and bonus mechanism on transfer pricing

Kurnia, D.W. Hapsari & O.D. Sartika
Telkom University, Bandung, West Java, Indonesia

ABSTRACT: Transfer pricing is a policy to determine the transfer price of transactions between the company and other parties that have special relationship. It must be consistent with arm's length principle so they will not be abused by the company that is maximizing their profit. This research aims to determine the simultaneous and partial influence between tax burdens, company size, and bonus mechanism on transfer pricing in various industrial subsectors of manufacturing companies listed on the Indonesia Stock Exchange for 2016–2018. The samples are 19 companies within three years of research, so 57 total companies were obtained. The analysis technique used in this study is logistic regression analysis using SPSS 25. The result shows tax burden, company size, and bonus mechanism simultaneously have a significant effect on transfer pricing. Meanwhile, only company size has a positive effect on transfer pricing partially.

1 INTRODUCTION

The globalization forces Indonesia to be more responsive to various changes. Entering the era of the industrial revolution 4.0 and increasingly sophisicated technological developments, Indonesia is demanded to be responsive to these technological changes (Wicaksananingtyas & Sari 2019). The globalization of economy, business, and investment enriches the growth and development of multinational companies. Multinational companies benefit from the economy's scale on the goods they produce or sell, expanding market share, and increasing effeciency in supply chain management. To strengthen their business base, multinational companies establish subsidiaries, business branches, or business representatives in various countries in order to strengthen the strategic alliances for the growth of their product's export and import market share in various countries. These operations, which are carried out in various countries, will cause tax differences among countries and pose a risk for tax administration. The differences in tax burden among countries will trigger the companies to deviate the transfer pricing, which can result in improper prices, costs, or rewards for transactions made among companies with a special relationship. Transfer pricing is a determinant of transaction prices made among companies that have a special relationship. Transfer pricing can be misused by companies that persue maximum profits. Multinational companies use subsidiaries or branches in low-tax countries as an opportunity to avoid taxes, as was done by PT Toyota Motor Manufacturing Indonesia (TMMI). They shift its tax obligations in countries that have high tax rates to countries that have low tax rates. TMMI was suspected of playing transaction prices with special parties and increasing the burden through improper royalty payment. They also sell cars to related parties in Indonesia (TAM) and Singapore (TMAP) below the cost of production, thereby reducing business circulation (Sugiharto 2014).

The amount of tax burden that must be paid by the company is the motivation of the company to conduct transfer pricing in order to reduce the tax burden. The company utilizes differences in tax rates among countries to minimize the tax burden thourgh transfer pricing. Transfer pricing is carried out by shifting profit from companies in high tax countries to low tax countries. This is in line with research conducted by Yulia et al. (2019), which states that tax burden has a significant effect on transfer pricing. The higher the amount of tax burden that must be paid by the company will encourage companies to reduce the tax burden through transfer pricing. As stated by Nurjanah et al. (2016), that the size of the company has an essential role for investors because companies with large total assets will bring investors to invest in the company. Therefore, it will encourage the directors to manage profits through transfer pricing. This practice is carried out so that the company can maintain stability and increase company profits in order to attract investors to invest funds and convience creditors to get loans. This is in line with research conducted by Waworuntu and Hadisaputra (2016) and Marisa (2017), which states that company size has a significant effect on transfer pricing. There is a tendency for management to do the transfer pricing to maximize bonuses if bonuses are based on profits. The management can choose accounting procedures that can manage earnings from future periods to current periods. This is in line with research by Saifudin and Putri (2018), which states that the bonus mechanism has a significant effect on transfer pricing.

2 LITERATURE REVIEW

2.1 *Agency theory*

According to Jensen and Meckling (1976), agency theory explains how conflict arises from differences in interests between management (agent) and the shareholders (principle). This conflict arises as a result of information asymmetry between the principle and the agent where individual goals are prioritized over company goals.

2.2 *Transfer pricing*

According to the Minister of Finance Regulation Number 213 Year 2016 regarding the type of additional documents and/or information mandatory to be kept by taxpayers who conduct transactions with related parties and its procedures, transfer pricing means the determination of price in related party transactions.

2.3 *Tax burden*

According to the Law Number 28 Year 2007 of the Republic of Indonesia concerning general provisions and tax procedures, a tax is a mandatory contribution to a state that is owned by a personal taxpayer or a company/institution which is forceful under the law with no direct compensation and is used for public interest for the greatest prosperity of the people.

2.4 *Company size*

Company size is a values that indicates the size of the company (Yulia et al. 2019). Companies with sizeable total asset values indicate that companies are relatively more stable and able to generate profits compared to companies with smaller assets (Melmusi 2016).

2.5 *Positive accounting theory*

Positive accounting theory explains the processes that use accounting capabilities, understanding, and knowledge as well as the use of accounting policies that are most suitable for dealing with certain conditions in the future (Hery 2017). This theory can predict management behavior in giving bonuses. If the remunerations received are based on bonuses, then management will try to maximize profits so that they will increase the bonuses they receive.

Table 1. Omnibus test of model coefficients.

		Chi-square	Df	Sig.
Step 1	Step	17.559	3	.001
	Block	17.559	3	.001
	Model	17.559	3	.001

2.6 *Bonus mechanism*

According to Hartati et al. (2015), a bonus mechanism is a one of the accounting calculation strategies that aim to maximize the receipt of compensation by the management or directors by maximizing the company's overall profits.

3 METHODOLOGY

This study is a descriptive study conducted to determine the value of variables without making comparisons or relation with other variables (Siregar 2017). This study uses a quantitative research methodology to examine particular populations or samples. The populations used in the research were manufacturing companies of various industrial subsectors, which were listed on the Indonesia Stock Exchange and the panel data from 2016–2018. This study used purposive sampling as a sampling techinque with specific criteria. Therefore, there were 19 companies of various industrial subsectors where the research criteria were found. This study used logistic regression analysis with the help of the SPSS 25 application. The transfer pricing was proxied using a dichotomous approach, with a condition if the company makes sales transactions to a party with a special relationship, it wil be given a value of 1 and 0 for the opposite. The tax burden was measured using the current effective tax rate (CETR), which is the comparison between the current tax burdens against taxable income (Romdhon et al. 2019). The size of the company was proxied by using the Log natural of the total assets. Ln total assets were used to reduce excessive data fluctuations without changing the proportion of the actual value (Khairunisa et al. 2017). The bonus mechanism was measured using the bonus component approach using the net profit trend index as a proxy for this study. The net profit trend index was calculated based on the percentage of the achievement of net profit in the current year against the previous year's net profit (Ernawati et al. 2019).

4 RESULT AND DISCUSSION

This study uses descriptive statistical analysis and logistic regression analysis. Based on the sample selection criteria, the companies that met the criteria consisted of 19 companies within three years, so as many as 57 samples of various industrial subsector companies were obtained. This study has six outlier data so that it is improved to 51 samples.

Simultaneous testing results showed a significance level of 0.001. It can be concluded that the significance value is smaller than 0.05, so that the tax burden, company size, and bonus mechanism have a significant effect on transfer pricing simultaneously.

The tax burden has a regression coefficient of −3.762 with a significance level of 0.109, which is higher than 0.05. This means that the tax burden did not affect the transfer pricing and contradicts with H_1. This is possible in minimizing the tax burden that can be done through tax management (Mispiyanti 2015). Tax management can be done through tax planning by minimizing the tax burden legally or not violating the tax regulations, such as utilizing weakness (the gray area) of laws and tax regulations. The results are in line with Saifudin and Putri (2018), Melmusi (2016), and Mispiyanti (2015), which state that the tax burden does not affect transfer pricing.

Table 2. Variable in the equation.

		B	S.E.	Wald	Df	Sig.
Step 1	Tax burden	−3.762	2.347	2.569	1	.109
	Company size	.789	.330	5.709	1	.017
	Bonus mechanism	−.005	.035	.020	1	.887
	Constant	−20.052	9.380	4.570	1	.033

A regression coefficient of 0.789 is obtained with a significance level of 0.017 on the company size. So the size of the company had a significant effect on the positive direction of transfer pricing. This result supports H_2, big companies tend to do transfer pricing practices to maintain stability and increase company profits. Companies with large total asset ownership indicate that the company has good prospects in a relatively long period (Amelia et al 2017). This will encourage directors to manage earnings through transfer pricing. Transfer pricing is done so that companies can maintain stability and increase company profits. If the company is stable, it will attract investors and convince credictors to provide loans to the company. The results of this study are in line with Sulistyowati and Kananto (2019), Waworuntu and Hadisaputra (2016), and Nurjanah et al. (2016) which states that company size has a significant effect on transfer pricing.

The bonus mechanism has a regression coefficient of −0.005 with a significance level of 0.887, which is higher than 0.05. So this variable did not affect the transfer pricing. This result contradicts to H_3, the size of the profits obtained by the company does not affect management decisions in transfer pricing to maximize bonuses. As stated by Ernawati et al. (2019) in maximizing corporate profits, companies can use a more proper method than using transfer pricing. This is because the directors need to maintan their values and reputation in front of the community and be responsible for their performance results. In addition, high company profits do not guarantee that directors or managers will receive high bonuses because the company will continue to consider other factors and review performance in previous years. The results of this research are in line with Ernawati et al. (2019), Sulistyowati and Kananto (2019), and Refgia et al. (2017) which states that the bonus mechanism does not significantly influence transfer pricing.

5 CONCLUSION

Based on the results of this study, it is known that the tax burden, company size, and bonus mechanism variables significantly influenced the transfer pricing of manufacturing companies in various industry subsectors listed on the Indonesia Stock Exchange from 2016–2018 simultaneously. The company size had a significant effect on the positive direction of transfer pricing partially, while the tax burden and bonus mechanism did not affect transfer pricing.

REFERENCES

Amelia, M. V., Pratomo, D., & Kurnia. 2017. Pengaruh Kepemilikan Institusional dan Kepemilikan Manajerial dengan Variabel Kontrol Ukuran Perusahaan dan Leverage Terhadap Penghindaran Pajak. *E-Proceeding of Management ISSN: 2355–9357, 4*(2), 1510–1515.

Ernawati, D. W., Candrawati, T., & Ratnawardhani, E. A. 2019. Determinan Praktik Transfer Pricing Pada Perusahaan Utilitas, Infrastruktur dan Telekomunikasi. *Seminar Nasional Gabungan Bisnis & Sosial Polinema.*

Hartati, W., Desmiyawati, D., & Julita, J. 2015. Tax Minimization,Tunneling Incentive dan Mekanisme Bonus terhadap Keputusan Transfer Pricing Seluruh Perusahaan yang Listing di Bursa Efek Indonesia. *Simposium Nasional Akuntansi XVIII Medan.*

Hery. 2017. *Teori Akuntansi*. Jakarta: PT Grasindo.

Jensen, M. C., & Meckling, W. H. 1976. Theory of The Firm: Managerial Behavior, Agency Costs and Ownership Structure. *Journal of Financial Economics*, (3), 305–360. https://doi.org/10.1002/mde.1218
Khairunisa, K., Hapsari, D. W., & Aminah, W. 2017. Pengaruh Kualitas Audit, Corporate Social Responsibility dan Ukuran Perusahaan Terhadap Tax Avoidance. *Journal Riset Akuntansi Kontemporer (JRAK), 9*(1), 36–43.
Marisa, R. 2017. Pengaruh Pajak, Bonus Plan, Tunneling Incentive, dan Ukuran Perusahaan Terhadap Transfer Pricing. *Jurnal Akuntansi AKUNESA, 5*(2).
Melmusi, Z. 2016. Pengaruh Pajak, Mekanisme Bonus, Kepemilikan Asing dan Ukuran Perusahaan Terhadao Transfer Pricing Pada Perusahaan yang Tergabung Dalam Jakarta Islamic Index dan Terdaftar di Bursa Efek Indonesia Periode 2012–2016. *Jurnal EKOBISTEK Fakultas Ekonomi, 5*(2), 1–12.
Mispiyanti. 2015. Pengaruh Pajak, Tunneling Incentive dan Mekanisme Bonus Terhadap Keputusan Transfer Pricing. *Journal of Accounting and Investment, 16*(1).
Nurjanah, I., Isnawati, H., & Sondakh, A. G. 2016. Faktor Determinan Keputusan Perusahaan Melakukan Transfer Pricing. *Jurnal SNA*.
Refgia, T., Ratnawati, V., & Rusli, R. 2017. Pengaruh Pajak, Mekanisme Bonus, Ukuran Perusahaan, Kepemilikan Asing, dan Tunneling Incentive Terhadap Transfer Pricing (Perusahaan Sektor Industri Dasar dan Kimia yang Listing di BEI Tahun 2011–2014). *Jurnal Online Mahasiswa Fakultas Ekonomi Universitas Riau, 4*(1), 543–555.
Republik Indonesia. 2007. *Undang-Undang Republik Indonesia Nomor 28 Tahun 2007 Perubahaan Ketiga Atas Undang-Undang Nomor 6 Tahun 1983 Tentang Ketentuan Umum dan Tata Cara Perpajakan*. Jakarta: Republik Indonesia.
Romdhon, M., Pansuri, C., & Rahayu, R. 2019. Effective Tax Rate and Book-Tax Difference Based on Industrial Sectors Companies on the Indonesia Stock Exchange. *Review of Integrative Business and Economics Research, 8*(4), 6722.
Saifudin, & Putri, L. S. 2018. Determinasi Pajak, Mekanisme Bonus, dan Tunneling Incentive terhadap Keputusan Transfer Pricing pada Emiten BEI. *AGREGAT: Jurnal Eknomi Dan Bisnis, 2*(1), 32–43. https://doi.org/10.22236/agregat
Saraswati, A. R. G., & Sujana, I. K. 2017. Pengaruh Pajak, Mekanisme Bonus, dan Tunneling Incentive Pada Indikasi Melakukan Transfer Pricing. *E-Jurnal Akuntansi Universitas Udayana ISSN: 2302–8556, 19*(2), 1000–1029.
Septiyani, R. P. P., Ramadhanti, W., & Sudibyo, Y. A. 2018. Some Factors That Affect Transfer Pricing Decision. *SAR (Soedirman Accounting Review): Journal of Accounting and Business, 3*(1), 21. https://doi.org/10.20884/1.sar.2018.3.1.1158
Siregar, S. 2017. *Metode Penelitian Kuantitatif Dilengkapi dengan Perbandingan Perhitungan Manual & SPSS*. Jakarta: Kencana.
Sugiharto, D. 2014. Prahara Pajak Raja Otomotif. Retrieved September 18, 2019, from Investigasi.tempo.co website: https://investigasi.tempo.co/toyota/
Sulistyowati, S., & Kananto, R. 2019. *The Influences of Tax, Bonus Mechanism, Leverage and Company Size Through Company Decision on Transfer Pricing. 73*(Aicar 2018), 207–212. https://doi.org/10.2991/aicar-18.2019.45
Waworuntu, S. R., & Hadisaputra, R. 2016. Determinants of Transfer Pricing Aggressiveness in Indonesia. *Pertanika Journal Social Sciences & Humanities, 24*, 95–110.
Wicaksananingtyas, C. A., & Sari, S. P. 2019. Pengaruh Effective Tax Rate, Nilai Tukar, Tunneling Incentive, dan Mekanisme Bonus Terhadap Harga Transfer. *The 9th University Research Colloqium 2019 Universitas Muhammadiyah Purworejo*.
Yulia, A., Hayati, N., & Daud, R. M. 2019. The Influence of Tax, Foreign Ownership and Company Size on the Application of Transfer Pricing in Manufacturing Companies Listed on Idx During 2013–2017. *International Journal of Economics and Financial Issues, 9*(3), 175–181. https://doi.org/10.32479/ijefi.7640

Synergizing Management, Technology and Innovation in Generating Sustainable and Competitive Business Growth – Hendayani et al (eds)
© 2021 Taylor & Francis Group, London, ISBN 978-0-367-68756-4

Financial performance, sustainability reporting, and its impact to firm value: Evidence from Asia sustainability reporting rating

M. Romdhon, R.A. Fadilah, L. Nurlaela & W. Ningsih
Department of Accounting, Garut University, Garut, Indonesia

ABSTRACT: This study investigates the association between (1) financial performance and sustainability reporting, and (2) sustainability reporting and firm value. This research was conducted using panel data, ordinary least squares regression, and the observations for companies in developing countries based on Asia sustainability ranking report in the database from 2017 to 2018. The findings of this study showed that profitability is positively associated with financial statements disclosure, sustainability reporting, and also supports on firm value. Our study contributes to the sustainability issue in the context of emerging markets, unlike the majority of prior studies which highlighted developed markets.

1 INTRODUCTION

Environmental damage has been a serious problem in recent years. Economic activities are carried out in various parts of the world. One of the economic factors that make environmental problems is companies. The company's activities in seeking and increasing profits are considered as exploitation and have an impact on natural resources and human resources, and this causes demands from the community toward the company to provide social responsibility. Companies develop the 3P concept launched by Elkington (1988), namely, People, Planet, and Profit or which is called the triple bottom-line concept. This is the beginning concept of the disclosure development. The information about social responsibility showed on sustainability reporting.

Sustainability report disclosure is one of the important things for every organization. Sustainability reporting has become popular, particularly in the last decade, emerging as a result of the evolution of environmental and corporate social responsibility reports (Jones et al. 2016; Uyar & Kuzey 2017). Sustainability reporting is useful for stakeholders to make a decision for companies and also becomes a media that supports companies to give the information about performance in all aspects, such as economic, social, and environmental. Many organizations move from the traditional reporting (it is only financial aspects) to a more modern reporting with financial and non-financial aspects (social and environmental dimensions).

In its reporting, an organization can use the framework from the Global Reporting Initiative (GRI) (GRI 2013). GRI has been very successful in terms of its level of adoption, completeness, prestige, and visibility since the beginning of 1999 (Brown et al. 2009). Before this framework was developed, the format of the environmental, social responsibility, or sustainability report used by the company was not based on a globally agreed framework; thus the format of the report varies and is difficult to compare. Therefore, GRI provides a common basis for sustainability reporting (Ortiz & Marín 2014). Research studies show that now the framework is most commonly used among companies in many countries (Chen et al. 2015; KPMG 2013; Michelon et al. 2015). In addition, GRI provides rich resources to guide users throughout the implementation process. Lock and Seele (2016) found that standardization through the GRI framework improves the quality of corporate social responsibility reports.

Previous studies focused only for developed countries or on a global scale. And the purpose of this study is to know whether finance encourages the disclosure of sustainability reporting and whether sustainability reporting has an impact on increasing company value. Previous research was conducted in Turkey, and only discussed about developed countries. Developing countries and developed countries are different. For example, developing countries have a greater gap in their protection enforcement in terms of environmental protection or human rights legislation compared to developed countries (Graham & Woods 2006).·In addition, the influence of stakeholders (civil society, media, consumers, campaigns) in developing countries may be less influential than in developed countries. Therefore, researchers want to know this context in developing countries in Asia, to explore and report sustainability reporting by joining the Asian sustainability reporting ranking.

2 LITERATURE REVIEW AND HYPOTHESIS

Among the theories pertaining to sustainability reporting, the dominant ones are the agency, legitimacy, stakeholder, and signaling theories (Reverte 2009; Ruhnke & Gabriel 2013). Fama and Jensen (1983) state that agency costs appear due to the conflicts of interests and information asymmetry between insiders and outsiders; hence, sustainability reporting plays a significant role in reducing this asymmetry. According to Deegan (2002), a company needs to gain legitimacy in the sense of a social "license to operate" to reach the necessary resources to carry out its activities; thus, sustainability reports are the tools of legitimizing a business, and demonstrate that it is staying within the acceptable boundaries of society. Stakeholder theory posits that a business organization needs to maintain good relations with all stakeholders, rather than merely with its shareholders, and must satisfy their informational needs through sustainability reports (Lourenço & Branco 2013; Reverte 2009).

2.1 *Financial performance*

The variables in this study were developed from research by Kuzey and Uyar (2017), which in this study classifies factors that are considered to be able to influence the sustainability reports. The availability of resources using profitability and free cash flow is one of the factors used. This variable can reflect financial performance because it is considered to have more power to encourage sustainable reporting. Legendre and Coderre (2013) find that a company's adoption of the GRI framework is positively related to profitability. Aksu and Kosedag (2006) estimate a positive relationship between free cash flow, transparency, and disclosure, because companies tend to reduce the negative impact of holding cash.

H1 a. Profitability positively associated with GRI-based sustainability reports.

H1 b. Free cash positively associated with GRI-based sustainability reports.

2.2 *Firm value*

Lo and Sheu (2007) and Anam et al. (2011) find that there was a positive relationship between disclosure and firm value based on signaling theory, which is that transparency and disclosure increased firm value (Anam et al. 2011). Environmental and social performance were positively associated with firm value (Bachoo et al. 2013; Berthelot et al. 2012; Guidry dan Patten 2010; Lo dan Sheu 2007).

H2. Sustainability reporting positively associated with firm value.

3 DATA AND RESEARCH DESIGN

3.1 *Data and sample selection*

Asia sustainability reporting rating is an award for sustainability reports compiled by organizations or companies not only in Indonesia but also several other countries in Asia consisting of 56 organizations from five countries, namely, Indonesia, Malaysia, the Philippines, Bangladesh, and Singapore. We start with 51 firm-year observations listed in Asia sustainability reporting rating from 2017–2018. Data was collected from Thomson Reuters EIKON. We dropped 25 firm observations with no available data, then we were left with 52 observations from 26 firms. This observation includes four countries: Indonesia, Malaysia, Philippines, and Bangladesh.

3.2 *Research design*

3.2.1 *Proxy of financial performance*

Following Uyar and Kuzey (2017), we employ profitability and free cash flow as measurements of financial performance. We set a return on assets (ROS) as a proxy for profitability and free cash flow from cash from operation divided by capital expenditure.

3.2.2 *Proxy of sustainability reporting*

Following Uyar and Kuzey (2017), we set a dummy variable to measure SR, where SR equals 1 if (the company published by GRI-sustainability report guidelines); and 0 otherwise.

3.2.3 *Control variable*

For control variables, we follow the reaserch of Uyar and Kuzey (2017). We control financial performance with size, leverage, and industry. There is a significant positive association between firm size and sustainability reporting (Artiach et al., 2010; Liu & Anbumozhi, 2009; Lourenço and Branco, 2013; Reverte 2009). Larger corporations are expected to publish higher quality sustainability reports and adopt higher-level GRI application levels to legitimate their operations. There is strong industry influence upon sustainability reporting (Skouloudis et al. 2014). Liu and Anbumozhi (2009) argue that environment-sensitive industries are inclined to disclose environmental issues since they are likely to harm the environment, and as such are prone to stricter regulation.

We test our hypothesis by using the following model:

$$\text{SREPGRI} = \beta_0 + \beta_1\text{FCF} + \beta_2\text{ROA} + \beta_3\text{IND} + \beta_4\text{SIZE} + \beta_5\text{LEV} + \varepsilon \quad (1)$$

$$\text{TOBINQ} = \text{B0} + \beta_1\text{SREGPRI} + \beta_2\text{FCF} + \beta_3\text{ROA} + \beta_4\text{SIZE} + \beta_5\text{IND} + \beta_6\text{LEV} + \varepsilon \quad (2)$$

4 RESULT AND DISCUSSION

Model 1, ROA positively associated with sustainability report, which is a variable with a significance of 1%. The companies that have good financials will support sustainability, because it requires a lot of cost (Braam et al. 2016). SIZE has a significance level of 5%. Larger firms are more likely to publish a sustainability report than smaller firms (Kansal et al. 2014; Nazari et al. 2015). Leverage is positively associated with sustainability report with a significance of 10%, which means that the greater debt pushes them using sustainability reporting to make creditors trust the company. Industry and free cash flow are not associated with sustainable reporting, which explains that companies that have a higher risk in the sector of the environment are not positively associated with the sustainability report, even though the company is engaged in having a higher risk to the environment that is not a driver for the company to make a sustainability reporting, and also companies that have free cash flow are not positively associated, because of the company using the company's internal expansion funds.

Model 2 show that a sustainability report has a positive relationship with a significance of 1%, and publishing sustainable report has an impact to increase the value of the company. This study reconfirms previous findings from Kuzey and Uyar (2017) that a sustainable report has a positive relationship with firm value. Free cash flow, size, leverage, and industry have a significant relationship to the value of the company.

5 CONCLUSIONS

This study aimed at investigating the financial performance of sustainability reporting practices by listed Asia sustainability reporting ranking in developing countries. Sustainability reporting is related with firm value. The study makes a significant contribution to the sustainability issue in the context of emerging markets, unlike the majority of prior studies, which highlighted developed markets. We assume that sustainability reporting might be a tool of overcoming this issue and contributes to the transparency of these markets.

The study has some theoretical implications. The findings support legitimacy, agency, and signaling. This research supports the size variable, automatically supports theories of legitimacy (Kolk & Perego 2010), the larger companies require more legitimacy and higher resources (Kansal et al. 2014; Liu & Anbumozhi 2009; Lourenço & Branco 2013), and incurred lower reporting costs (Jennifer Ho & Taylor, 2007). ROA supports signaling theory, which reviews a signal that a company has profits that will need to do ongoing reporting. And leverage supports agency theory, because there is agreement from creditors regarding the ability and sustainability of the company with the existence of sustainability reports that will be easier for creditors associated with the company directly without additional agency costs due to lack of information available from the company.

Implications for the company are this sustainability reporting can increase the value of the company by adding and reporting through sustainability reports so that investors who care about the environment or sustainability of the company will attract investors and will improve on markets that are supported efficiently. The industry does not have an impact, because regulations about industry are still weak. This paper has several limitations. Firstly, the dataset refers to only the two years between 2017 and 2018, since Asia sustainability reporting is a relatively hot topic. Secondly, determinant of sustainability reporting is not only financial performance but also from other aspects.

REFERENCES

Aksu, M. & Kosedag, A. 2006. Transparency and Disclosure Scores and their Determinants in the Istanbul Stock Exchange. *Corporate Governance: An International Review,* vol. 14, no. 4, pp. 277–296.

Anam, O.A., Fatima, A.H. & Abdul Rashid Hafiz Majdi. 2011. Effects of intellectual capital information disclosed in annual reports on market capitalization. *Journal of HRCA: Human Resource Costing & Accounting,* vol. 15, no. 2, pp. 85.

Braam, G.J.M., Uit de Weerd, L., Hauck, M. & Huijbregts, M.A.J. 2016. Determinants of corporate environmental reporting: the importance of environmental performance and assurance. *Journal of Cleaner Production,* vol. 129, pp. 724–734.

Brown, H.S., de Jong, M. & Levy, D.L. 2009. Building institutions based on information disclosure: lessons from GRI's sustainability reporting. *Journal of Cleaner Production,* vol. 17, no. 6, pp. 571–580.

Cormier, D., Magnan, M. & Van Velthoven, B. 2005. Environmental disclosure quality in large German companies: Economic incentives, public pressures or institutional conditions? *European Accounting Review,* vol. 14, no. 1, pp. 3–39.

Deegan, C. 2002. The legitimising effect of social and environmental disclosures – a theoretical foundation. *Accounting, Auditing & Accountability Journal,* vol. 15, no. 3, pp. 282.

Elkington, Jhon. 1988. Cannibas With Forks: The Triple Bottom Line in 21th Century Business.

Fama, E.F. & Jensen, M.C. 1983. Separation of Ownership and Control. *The Journal of Law & Economics,* vol. 26, no. 2, pp. 301–325.

Graham, D. & Woods, N. 2006. Making corporate self-regulation effective in developing countries. *World Development,* vol. 34, no. 5, pp. 868–883.
GRI. 2013. Global Reporting Initiative G4. http://www.Globalreporting.org.
Jennifer Ho, L. & Taylor, M.E. 2007. An Empirical Analysis of Triple Bottom-Line Reporting and its Determinants: Evidence from the United States and Japan. *Journal of International Financial Management & Accounting,* vol. 18, no. 2, pp. 123–150.
Jones, P., Hillier, D. & Comfort, D. 2016. Materiality and external assurance in corporate sustainability reporting: An exploratory study of Europe's leading commercial property companies. *Journal of European Real Estate Research,* vol. 9, no. 2, pp. 147–170.
Kuzey, C. & Uyar, A. 2017. Determinants of sustainability reporting and its impact on firm value: Evidence from the emerging market of Turkey. *Journal of Cleaner Production,* vol. 143, pp. 27–39.
Kolk, A. & Perego, P. 2010; 2008. Determinants of the adoption of sustainability assurance statements: an international investigation. *Business Strategy and the Environment,* vol. 19, no. 3, pp. 182–198.
KPMG. 2013. KPMG International Survey of Corporate Responsibility Reporting 2013. KPMG International Cooperative.
Legendre, S. & Coderre, F. 2013. Determinants of GRI G3 Application Levels: The Case of the Fortune Global 500: Determinants of GRI G3 Application Levels. *Corporate Social Responsibility and Environmental Management,* vol. 20, no. 3, pp. 182–192.
Liu, X. & Anbumozhi, V. 2009. Determinant factors of corporate environmental information disclosure: an empirical study of Chinese listed companies. *Journal of Cleaner Production,* vol. 17, no. 6, pp. 593–600.
Lo, S. & Sheu, H. 2007. Is Corporate Sustainability a Value-Increasing Strategy for Business?. *Corporate Governance: An International Review,* vol. 15, no. 2, pp. 345–358.
Lock, I. & Seele, P. 2016. The credibility of CSR (corporate social responsibility) reports in Europe. Evidence from a quantitative content analysis in 11 countries. *Journal of Cleaner Production,* vol. 122, pp. 186–200.
Nazari, J.A., Herremans, I.M. & Warsame, H.A. 2015. Sustainability reporting: external motivators and internal facilitators. *Corporate Governance,* vol. 15, no. 3, pp. 375–390.
Ortiz, E. & Marin, S. 2014. Global Reporting Initiative (GRI) as recognized guidelines for sustainability reporting by Spanish companies on the IBEX 35: Homogeneity in their framework and added value in the relationship with financial entities. *Intangible Capital,* vol. 10, no. 5.
Reverte, C. 2009. Determinants of Corporate Social Responsibility Disclosure Ratings by Spanish Listed Firms. *Journal of Business Ethics,* vol. 88, no. 2, pp. 351–366.
Ruhnke, K. & Gabriel, A. 2013. Determinants of voluntary assurance on sustainability reports: an empirical analysis. *Journal of Business Economics,* vol. 83, no. 9, pp. 1063–1091.
Skouloudis, A., Jones, N., Malesios, C. & Evangelinos, K. 2014. Trends and determinants of corporate non-financial disclosure in Greece. *Journal of Cleaner Production,* vol. 68, pp. 174–188.

Synergizing Management, Technology and Innovation in Generating Sustainable and Competitive Business Growth – Hendayani et al (eds)
© 2021 Taylor & Francis Group, London, ISBN 978-0-367-68756-4

Financial literacy and consumptive behavior of housewives in DKI Jakarta

A. Krisnawati & N. Fauziah
Faculty of Economics & Business, Telkom University, Bandung, West Java, Indonesia

ABSTRACT: This study aims to assess whether there is a significant effect of financial literacy on consumptive behavior of housewives in DKI Jakarta. This quantitative research was conducted with a descriptive analysis technique using simple linear regression. The sample in this study is determined by applying purposive sampling technique. T-test results indicate that financial literacy has a significant negative effect on the consumptive behavior of housewives in DKI Jakarta. The results of this study indicate that the level of financial literacy of housewives in DKI Jakarta is classified as good. However, the level of consumptive behavior is classified as poor. This finding is distinctive, so that it can provide implications for further researchers to conduct a qualitative research that can better explain the reasons of the results of this study.

1 INTRODUCTION

Knowledge in financial management is important for all human beings, including the smallest social unit in society, i.e. family. Poor knowledge of financial management can certainly affect human's behavior in determining decisions. According to the National Survey of Financial Services Authority (OJK) in 2016, the financial literacy rate of Indonesian women is only 22.5%, this figure is lower than the level of financial literacy rate of male at 33.2%.

According to Hadisubrata (1990), a family is the smallest social unit in society consisting of father, mother, and unmarried children. Housewives have an important role in managing family finance. Families who have good finance can meet their material needs properly. It shows the role of the housewife as a manager in family finance. Although financial problems are a concern for all family members, yet the greatest responsibility in managing family finance is in housewives.

Based on data from OJK, DKI Jakarta is a province with a high level of literacy. However, it does not guarantee that all DKI Jakarta people have good financial literacy knowledge. According to Bisnis.com article (12/10/19), Nizhomy Rahman, Head of Subdivision of Financial Education Implementation of OJK, stated that out of 100 people, only 29 people have financial literacy. It shows that there should be more efforts to educate people in order to increase their financial literacy due to the low level of financial literacy in DKI Jakarta particularly, and Indonesia generally.

According to the Central Statistics Agency (BPS) in 2018, there were 2,735,080 households living in DKI Jakarta, including in the Thousand Islands, South Jakarta, East Jakarta, Central Jakarta, West Jakarta, and North Jakarta. The Cost of Living Survey by the Central Statistics Agency (BPS) places DKI Jakarta as one of the provinces with the most expensive cost of living in Indonesia of Rp7,500,000. As DKI Jakarta is a central representative of Indonesia, therefore it is important to have financial knowledge for housewives who are the financial managers of families so that they can truly establish prosperous families in Indonesia.

Based on the findings of a shopping search engine pioneer and a price comparison platform, Priceza, quoted from Marketeers.com article (accessed on January 22, 2020), in 2015 to 2017

Jakarta was ranked first as the most active online shopper with a percentage level of 41.94%. It shows that internet penetration in big cities in Indonesia is indeed quite high and evenly distributed. As quoted by the Indonesian Internet Service Providers Association (APJII), internet penetration in urban areas reached 72.4% in 2017.

Urban culture has been attached to life in big cities in Indonesia, one of which is Jakarta. Lifestyle that was not previously referred to as culture has now penetrated to all people who are living in the city of Jakarta. Therefore, the City of Jakarta was chosen as the object of research because it reflects a fairly high level of consumption so that research on financial literacy and consumptive behavior will be needed.

This research aims to answer the following questions: (1) What is the level of financial literacy of housewives in DKI Jakarta?; (2) What is the level of consumptive behavior of housewives in DKI Jakarta?; (3) Does financial literacy significantly affect the consumptive behavior of housewives in DKI Jakarta?

2 LITERATURE REVIEW

Knowledge, beliefs, and skills of the community to manage finance well can certainly suppress the consumptive behavior of the community. This knowledge can be called as financial literacy. According to the Program for International Student Assessment (PISA) (2012), financial literacy is knowledge and understanding of financial concepts that are used to make effective financial choices. In choosing an effective need, there are many factors that support and worsen the selection of needs, one of which is the education factor.

Consumptive is the nature of human's behavior who like to spend something outside of their true needs. According to Dikria and Mintarti (2016), consumer behavior can be interpreted as a tendency to buy or consume goods those are actually less necessary and not based on rational considerations, because individuals are more concerned with wants than needs. A study conducted by Lina and Rosyid (1997) describes several indicators of consumer behavior, these indicators are impulsive buying, wasting, and looking for pleasure.

This research refers to several previous studies. Research conducted by Sari et al. (2019) also shows that there is a significant influence between financial literacy on consumptive behavior of housewives, there is a significant influence between lifestyle on consumptive behavior of housewives, and there is a significant influence between financial literacy and lifestyle on consumptive behavior of housewives. Behavior of money management has a relationship with saving management which leads to consumer behavior. Research conducted by Allgood (2012) shows that financial literacy and self-assessment affect financial behavior. A study conducted by Watung (2018) also shows that financial literacy, social environmental factors, and cultural factors are related, influencing, and positively contributing to student consumption behavior in the Economic Education School of Economics, State University of Manado, financial literacy is related, influencing, and positively contribute to student consumption behavior in the Economics Education School of Economics, State University of Manado.

3 RESEARCH METHODS

This research applies a quantitative method, and based on its purpose, this research is categorized as verification study. Based on the time frame, this study belongs to the type of cross sectional, because it is carried out at a certain time period to process, analyze, and draw conclusions from the data obtained. The type of investigation in this study belongs to causal investigation, because it describes a cause-effect relationship (Indrawati 2015: 117).

This study has two types of research variables, namely independent variable and dependent variable. The independent variable used in this study is financial literacy, while the dependent variable used in this study is consumptive behavior. The data collection method applied in this study is a survey by distributing questionnaires. The questionnaire was created using an ordinal measurement scale, which is a Likert scale with five categories. In the financial literacy variable, the Likert scale category of "strongly disagree" gets score 1, the category of "disagree" gets score 2, the category of "neutral" gets score 3, the category of "agree" gets ascore 4, and the category of "strongly agree" gets score 5. Whereas the variable of consumptive behavior applies vice versa, the category of "strongly disagree" gets score 5, the category of "disagree" gets score 4, the category of "neutral" gets score 3, the category of "agree" gets score 2, and the category of "strongly agree" gets score 1.

This study applies non-probability sampling technique, i.e. purposive sampling. The population in this study are housewives in DKI Jakarta, amounting to 2,735,080 people. The level of trust in this study is 95% and the significance level is 5%. By applying the Slovin formula, the results of calculation of the number of samples amounted to 399.94 respondents or rounded to 400 respondents.

4 DISCUSSION

The results of this study indicate that the level of financial literacy of housewives in DKI Jakarta is 82.99%, this figure is included in good categories. The dimension of financial literacy knowledge is 84.41% and the dimension of advanced financial literacy knowledge is 81.72%. It shows that housewives in DKI Jakarta have good financial literacy. However, it is found that consumptive behavior of housewives in DKI Jakarta is in the bad category, which is 42.89%. It shows that despite having a good level of financial literacy, housewives in DKI Jakarta have high level of consumptive behavior.

Consumptive behavior of housewives in DKI Jakarta can be affected by several factors including age, level of education, and income. Based on the characteristics of respondents, it is known that the highest number of respondents was at the age of 31–40 years as many as 163 people with a percentage of 41%. The people with an age range of 31–40 are productive people, so that they have a tendency to behave consumptively. Furthermore, it is also known that the highest number of respondents is 214 people with bachelor-degree education or 53.5%. The people with bachelor-degree education mostly have good knowledge in accessing technology including in using e-commerce so that they tend to make transactions easier and will increasingly encourage consumptive behavior. The results of this study also show that the highest number of respondents, which is 148 people or 37%, earn Rp10,000,001 up to Rp15,000,000 per month. Housewives with high income tend to consume not only to meet basic needs but also to meet a high lifestyle so that they have consumptive behavior.

The result of simple linear regression analysis shows that the value of the regression coefficient (b) is negative, i.e. −1.045. It shows that every increase in financial literacy by one unit will result in a decrease in consumer behavior by 1,045. Based on hypothesis testing results, it is known that t-statistic is in the area of negative influence so that t-statistic 14.046 > t-table 1.966 with a significance value of 0.000 less than 0.05. Then H0 is rejected and H1 is accepted, which means the financial literacy variable significantly affects the consumption behavior variable of housewives in DKI Jakarta. The result of this study confirms the result of research conducted by Fattah et al. (2018) which states that financial literacy has a significant negative relationship to consumptive behavior.

The magnitude of the effect of financial literacy on consumptive behavior is tested using a coefficient of determination which results in a coefficient of determination of 33.1%. It shows that financial literacy has an effect of 33.1% on consumer behavior. While the remaining 66.9% is influenced by other variables those are not examined in this study. Based on research conducted by Dewi et al. (2017), it is stated that family environment, peers, and self-control influence consumer behavior. While according to Sari et al. (2019), a factor that influences consumer behavior is lifestyle.

5 CONCLUSIONS AND IMPLICATIONS FOR FURTHER RESEARCH

Financial literacy of housewives in DKI Jakarta is 82.99% which is classified in the good category, it means that Housewives in DKI Jakarta have good financial literacy. Consumptive behavior of housewives in DKI Jakarta is 42.89% which is included in the bad category, it means that housewives in DKI Jakarta have high-level of consumptive behavior. In this study it was found that financial literacy has a significant negative effect on consumer behavior in housewives in DKI Jakarta. These findings provide an implication for further research that it is suggested to conduct a qualitative research to support the results of this study with better explanations.

REFERENCES

Allgood, S. W. B. 2012. The Effects of Perceived and Actual Financial LIteracy on Financial Behavior. *Economic Inquiry*, 1–53.

Badan Pusat Statistik. 2019, Desember. *Rumah Tangga (dalam ribuan) dan Rata-rata Banyaknya Anggota Rumah Tangga Menurut Kabupaten/Kota di Provinsi DKI Jakarta, 2010 dan 2018.* Retrieved from Badan Pusat Statistik DKI Jakarta: https://jakarta.bps.go.id/dynamictable/2019/09/17/59/3-1-3-rumah-tangga-dalam-ribuan-dan-rata-rata-banyaknya-anggota-rumah-tangga-menurut-kabupaten-kota-di-provinsi-dki-jakarta-2010-dan-2018-.html.

Dewi, N., Rusdarti, & Sunarto, S.T. 2017. Pengaruh Lingkungan Keluarga, Teman Sebaya, Pengendalian Diri dan Literasi Keuangan terhadap Perilaku Konsumtif Mahasiswa. Journal of Economic Education, 29–35.

Dikria, O., & Mintarti, S. U. 2016. Pengaruh Literasi Keuangan dan Pengendalian Diri terhadap Perilaku Konsumtif Mahasiswa Jurusan Ekonomi Pembangunan Fakultas Ekonomi Universitas Negeri Malang Angkatan 2013. *Jurnal Pendidikan Ekonomi*, 128–139.

Fattah, F. A., Indriayu, M., & Sunarto. 2018. Pengaruh Literasi Keuangan dan Pengendalian Diri Terhadap Perilaku Konsumtif Siswa SMA Muhammadiyah 1 Karanganyar. *Jurnal Pendidikan Bisnis dan Ekonomi*, 11–21.

Hadisubrata. 1990. *Keluarga Dalam Dunia Modern.* Jakarta: PT. BPK Gunung Mulia.

Indrawati. 2015. *Metode Penelitian Manajemen dan Bisnis: Komvergensi Teknologi Komunikasi dan Informasi.* Bandung: PT. Refika Aditama.

Lina & Rosyid, H. F. 1997. Perilaku Konsumtif berdasarkan Locus of Control pada Remaja Putra. *Psikologika*, 24–28.

Otoritas Jasa Keuangan. 2019, September. *Survei Nasional Literasi dan Inklusi Keuangan 2016.* Retrieved from Otoritas Jasa Keuangan: https://www.ojk.go.id/id/berita-dan-kegiatan/siaran-pers/Documents/Pages/Siaran-Pers-OJK-Indeks-Literasi-dan-Inklusi-Keuangan-Meningkat/17.01.23%20Tayangan%20%20Presscon%20%20nett.compressed.pdf.

PISA. 2012. *Financial Literacy Assesment Framework.* OECD Publishing.

Sari, E. C., Ismanto, B., & Luhsasi, D. I. 2019. Perilaku Konsumtif Literasi Keuangan dan Gaya Hidup Ibu Rumah Tangga. *Jurnal Ecodunamika.*

Watung, S. R. 2018. The Influence o FInancial Literacy, Social Environment Factors, and Cultural Factors to Consumptive Behavior, (Urvey on Faculty of Economics Students, Manado State University-Indonesia). *International Journal of Scientific Research and Management.*

Synergizing Management, Technology and Innovation in Generating Sustainable and Competitive Business Growth – Hendayani et al (eds)
© 2021 Taylor & Francis Group, London, ISBN 978-0-367-68756-4

Earnings response coefficient: Evidence from Indonesia

Cahyaningsih & P. Hanifa
Telkom University, Bandung, West Java, Indonesia

ABSTRACT: This study examines whether market reactions to earnings announcements vary in the infrastructure, utilities, and transportation industry. Specifically, this study investigates the effect of growth opportunity, leverage, and financial quality on the earnings response coefficient. This study analyzes 30 firm-year observations from 10 firms over the period 2015–2018. This study finds growth opportunity has a positive effect on the earnings response coefficient, while leverage has a negative effect on the earnings response coefficient. Meanwhile, financial quality has no effect on the earnings response coefficient.

1 INTRODUCTION

An issue of accounting and finance describes the relationship between earnings reported by the companies and their stock returns (Ball & Brown 1968; Kormendi & Lipe 1987). Earnings information is the most responded to by investors because it describes the company's performance, but earnings information can be biased because earnings management and financial statements are not reported in a timely manner, and not all information is disclosed by the company (Cahyaningsih et al. 2011). This study measures earnings quality using earnings response coefficient (ERC). Theoretically, ERC can be defined as changes in stock prices caused by changes in current earnings (Collins & Kothari 1989) and are used to measure unexpected returns in response to unexpected earnings reported by the company (Scott 2015).

The market reacts differently to good or bad news from companies, one of which is earnings information. PT. Citra Marga Nusaphala Persada Tbk. (CMNP) showed an increase in earnings in 2018 by 21% compared with 2017, but the CMNP stock price fell to Rp1,310 per share (Binsasi 2018). In addition, PT. Adi Sarana Armada Tbk. (ASSA) in the third quarter of 2018 gained earnings of 45.46% from the same period in the previous year, but closing price of ASSA's stock was in the same position with the previous day at Rp268 per share (Hadi 2018). Unlike the condition experienced by PT. Telecommunication Indonesia Tbk. (TLKM) in the third quarter of 2018, the company's earnings decreased 29%, but the stock price rose 0.82% at a price of Rp3,680 per share (Franedya 2018). The phenomenon that occurs in CMNP, ASSA, and TLKM showed that the earnings information is not sufficient as a reference for investors in making decisions. This study focused on three variables that could be considered by investors, including growth opportunity, leverage, and financial quality.

2 LITERATURE REVIEW AND HYPOTHESIS DEVELOPMENT

2.1 *Growth opportunity and earnings response coefficient*

Growth opportunity is the company's prospect in generating profits in the future (Scott 2015). The company's success in completing the current project can provide a signal to the market that the company is also able to identify and obtain additional successful projects in the future, so that the company is considered as a growing company. Companies that have the potential to grow will provide a good signal for investors. Company growth illustrates the success of a company in taking advantage of opportunities. The higher the growth opportunity of the company, the higher the opportunity for the company to earn profits in the future. The market will assess the possibility of the company's growth, which is reflected by the formation of stock prices as the expectation of obtaining the value of benefits in the future (Collins & Kothari 1989; Hasanzade et al. 2014). Therefore, companies that have high growth opportunities will be responded to positively by the market so that the earnings response coefficient also increases.

H1: The higher the growth opportunity, the higher the earnings response coefficients

2.2 *Leverage and earnings response coefficient*

Leverage is a measuring tool to assess the level of debt that finances a company's assets (Musthafa 2017: 75). Companies that have a high degree of leverage indicate that most of the company's assets are financed with debt. Earnings information delivered by companies that have high leverage is less trusted by investors, since investors assume that the company will prioritize its profits for debt payments rather than making dividend payments (Cahyaningsih 2009; Dewi & Putra 2017). Therefore, companies that have high leverage will be responded to negatively by investors so the earnings response coefficient will also decrease.

H2: The higher the leverage, the lower the earnings response coefficient

2.3 *Financial quality and earnings response coefficient*

Submission of financial statements is expected to provide useful information for potential investors and creditors as well as other users in making investments, loans, and other similar decisions that rationally (Riahi & Belkaoui 2011: 233). Information that is useful for decision making is relevant and reliable information. Qualitative characteristics of information are said to be relevant if the information has feedback value, predictive value, and timeliness (Hery 2017: 43). Timeliness can be used as a way to measure the financial quality of a company (Mosa et al. 2019). Companies that do not report financial statements in timely manner indicate that there is an information disruption. Information disruption can be in the form of management behavior to improve financial statements so that they look good. Therefore, companies with good financial quality are shown by timely financial statements that will be responded to positively by investors so ERC will also increase.

H3: The higher the financial quality, the higher the earnings response coefficient

3 RESEARCH METHODS

3.1 *Sample*

This was a quantitative study that used secondary data in the form of financial statements and company stock prices. This study used a purposive sampling method with the criteria of companies in the infrastructure, utilities, and transportation industries that were consistently listed on the Indonesia Stock Exchange for the 2015–2018 period, used the rupiah currency, presented complete financial information, and generated positive earnings; thus, a sample size consisted of 10 companies was obtained. This study used 30 firm-year observations data after excluding several outliers.

3.2 *Variables*

The dependent variable in this study was ERC that was measured by the slope coefficient in the regression of stock returns on unexpected earnings (Scott 2015). The independent variables in this study were growth opportunity (GO) as measured by market-to-book value (MBV), leverage (LEV) as measured by debt-to-asset ratio (DAR), and the financial quality (FQ) as measured by timeliness

Table 1. Descriptive statistics.

Information	Earnings Response Coefficient (ERC)	Growth Opportunity (GO)	Leverage (LEV)	Financial Quality (FQ)
Continuous Variables				
Mean	0.09184	1.77034	0.48947	
Maximum	0.75416	4.43342	0.87361	
Minimum	−0.57329	0.39758	0.07497	
Standard Deviation	0.24518	1.25659	0.22373	
Dummy Variables				
Timely				15
Not Timely				15
Observation	30	30	30	30

as a dummy variable that takes a value of 1 if the company reported timely financial statements ($\leq$90 days) and 0 if the company did not report timely financial statements ($>$90 days). This study estimated the panel data regression model as follows:

$$ERC_{it} = \alpha + \beta_1 GO_{it} + \beta_2 LEV_{it} + \beta_3 FQ_{it} + \varepsilon \quad (1)$$

where ERC_{it} = Earnings response coefficient of company i in year t; GO_{it} = Growth opportunity of company i in year t; LEV_{it} = Leverage of company i in year t; and FQ_{it} = Financial quality of company i in year t.

4 RESULTS AND DISCUSSIONS

4.1 *Descriptive statistics*

Table 1 showed descriptive statistics of continuous variables (i.e., ERC, GO, and LEV) and a dummy variable (i.e., FQ). ERC obtained a mean (standard deviation) of 0.09184 (0.24518). The maximum value of ERC owned by PT. Telekomunikasi Indonesia Tbk. (TLKM) in 2017 was 0.75416. This value indicated that investors provided a positive response by 0.75416 to the earnings information obtained by TLKM in 2017. The minimum value of ERC owned by PT. Jasa Marga Persero Tbk. (JSMR) in 2016 was −0.57329. This value indicated that the investors provided a negative response by −0.57329 to the earnings information obtained by JSMR in 2016. GO obtained a mean (standard deviation) of 1.77034 (1.25659). The maximum value of GO owned by PT. Tower Bersama Group Tbk. (TBIG) in 2018 was 4.43342. This value indicated that the market valued TBIG at 4.43342 times above the book value of equity. The minimum GO value owned by PT. Adi Sarana Armada Tbk. (ASSA) in 2015 was 0.39758. This value indicated that the market valued ASSA at 0.39758 times above the book value of equity. LEV obtained a mean (standard deviation) of 0.48947 (0.22373). The maximum value of LEV owned by TBIG in 2018 was 0.87361. This value indicated that the amount of TBIG assets financed by debt was 0.87361. The minimum value of LEV owned by PT. Pelayaran Nelly Dwi Putri Tbk. (NELY) in 2017 was 0.07497. This value indicated that the amount of NELY assets financed by debt was 0.07497. The dummy variable, namely, FQ, indicated that half of the sample (50%) consisted of companies that reported timely financial statements, and the rest (50%) consisted of companies that did not report timely.

4.2 *Regression results*

Table 2 showed that growth opportunity (GO) had a positive effect on earnings response coefficient ($p < 0.05$), which provided support for H1. Thus, the higher the growth opportunity of a company, the higher the earnings response coefficient. The result is consistent with our conjecture that

Table 2. Panel regression results.

Variables	Coefficient	Std. Error	t-Statistic	Prob.
Intercept	0.1701	0.0993	1.7131	0.0986
GO	0.1048	0.0329	3.1865	0.0037
LEV	−0.5097	0.1840	−2.7699	0.0102
FQ	−0.0286	0.0786	−0.3632	0.7194
Adjusted R^2	0.2748			
F-statistic	4.6637			0.0098

companies that have the potential to grow will provide a good signal for investors. High growth opportunity reflects the company's ability to take advantage of opportunities. The higher the opportunity for the company to grow shows that the company has a great opportunity to generate profits in the future. This result is consistent with the studies conducted by Collins and Kothari (1989) and Hasanzade et al. (2014). Table 2 also reported that leverage (LEV) had a negative effect on earnings response coefficient ($p < 0.05$), which provided support for H2. Thus, the higher the company's leverage, the lower the level of earnings response coefficient. The result is consistent with our conjecture that companies that have high leverage will provide a bad signal for investors. A company with high leverage is less trusted by investors since the company will prioritize its earnings for debt payments rather than making dividend payments. This result is consistent with the study conducted by Cahyaningsih (2009) and Dewi and Putra (2017). This study also found that financial quality (FQ) had no effect on earnings response coefficient ($p > 0.05$), which provided rejection to H3. This result is not consistent with our conjecture because companies that reported timely financial statements did not provide a good signal for investors. Companies that did not report timely financial statements did not indicate any disruption in information or poor financial quality. This result is consistent with the study conducted by Mosa et al. (2019).

5 CONCLUSIONS

This study investigates the effect of growth opportunity, leverage, and financial quality on earnings response coefficient. Based on the samples that consisted of 10 companies of infrastructure, utilities, and transportation industries listed on the IDX during the 2015–2018 period, this study found evidence that the higher the growth opportunity, the higher the earnings response coefficients. The results of this study also indicated that the higher the leverage, the higher the earnings response coefficients, but financial quality had no effect on earnings response coefficient. This study also reported that the coefficient of determination obtained was only 27.5%. The further researchers are expected to be able to test other variables that are estimated to have an effect on ERC, such as systematic risk, accounting conservatism, and earnings management. This study has several practical implications, namely, for company management and investors. The company management is expected to increase the company's ability to obtain long-term profits. In addition, companies with high levels of leverage are expected to maximize the use of debt to generate profits. Investors are expected to use information on the level of growth opportunity and leverage of the company in making investment decisions.

REFERENCES

Ball, R., & Brown, P. 1986. An Empirical Evaluation of Accounting Income Numbers. *Journal of Accounting Research*, 159–178.

Binsasi, K. R. 2018. *Saham Citra Marga Nusaphala Persada Kurang Likuid Meski Punya Prospek Positif.* Kontan.co.id [online]. Available: https//www.kontan.co.id/news/saham-citra-marga-nusaphala-persada-kurang-likuid-meski-punya-prospek-positif [10 November 2019].

Cahyaningsih. 2011. The Effect of Leverage, Price-to-Book-Value, and Size toward Earning Response Coefficient with Corporate Social Responsibility Disclosure as an Intervening Variable. *Proceedings The 2th International Research Symposium in Service Management*. 26–30 Juli 2011 in Yogyakarta.

Cahyaningsih, Martina, & Isynuwardhana. 2011. The Effect of Good Corporate Governance Mechanism, Corporate Social Responsibility Disclosure, Earnings Management, and Corporate Characteristic toward Earning Response Coefficient. *Proceedings the Twenty-Third Asian-Pacific Conference (APC) on International Accounting Issues*. 16–19 Oktober 2011 in Beijing, China.

Collins, D., & S. Kothari. 1989. An Analysis of International and Cross-Sectional Determinants of Earnings Response Coefficients. *Journal of Accounting and Economics*, 11, 143–181.

Dewi, A. P., & Putra, I. P. 2017. Pengaruh Leverage dan Ukuran Perusahaan terhadap Earnings Response Coefficient. *E-Jurnal Akuntansi Universitas Udayana, 19*(1), 367–391.

Franedya, R. 2018. *Laba Anjlok 20% Harga Saham Telkom Menguat 0,82%.* CNBC Indonesia [online]. Available: https//www.cnbcindonesia.com/market20180300925O7-17-6266/laba-anjlok-20-saham-telko m-menguat-082 [10 November 2019].

Hadi, P. S. 2018. *Omzet Naik, Saham ASSA Masih Stagnan.* Bisnis.com [online]. Available: https://market.bisnis.com/read/20181024/190/852884/omzet-naik-saham-assa-masih-stagnan# [10 Februari 2020].

Kormendi, R., & Lipe, R. 1987. Earning Innovations, Earnings Persistence, and Stock Returns. *Journal of Business*, 323–345.

Mosa, F. W., Maslichah, & Mawardi, M. 2019. Pengaruh Pengungkapan CSR, Timeliness, Debt to Equity terhadap Earning Response Coefficient. *Jurnal Ilmiah Riset Akuntansi,* 08(1), 26–35.

Musthafa. 2017. *Manajemen Keuangan*. Yogyakarta: ANDI.

Scott, W. R. 2015. *Financial Accounting Theory Seventh Edition.* Toronto: Pearson.

Synergizing Management, Technology and Innovation in Generating Sustainable and Competitive Business Growth – Hendayani et al (eds)
© 2021 Taylor & Francis Group, London, ISBN 978-0-367-68756-4

Integrated invoice and accounting system design for food sector SMES using OpenERP with Quickstart Methodology

H. Panduwiyasa, W. Puspitasari & M. Saputra
School of Industrial and System Engineering, Telkom University, Bandung, West Java, Indonesia

ABSTRACT: Optimization of business processes is an important thing that must be solved efficiently. However, many small medium enterprises (SME) in the food sector industry are not completely aware of the potential for savings presented by technologies and digital business tools to manage data transactions. Problems that arise in the SMEs' accounting information system and invoicing are when they do not implement the technology to integrate the invoice data from one to another division. On the other side of problems, paper invoices have been causing high costs and slow processing times. To overcome it, SMEs need a system that effectively resolves the high price of invoice processing operations. One of the best solutions is to implement open source ERP systems. Considering the problem, OpenERP was chosen by this research as open source ERP software that can help SMEs to improve the integrated invoice system and the accounting cycle automation based on Quickstart methodology.

1 INTRODUCTION

SMEs are known to be the majority businesses in most countries and play a major role in most economies of developing countries (Kumar 2017). SMEs represent approximately 90% of businesses and more than 50% of employment worldwide (World Bank 2020). Majority of SMEs in Indonesia engaged in five area, consist of food and beverage 44.9%; wooden crafts 19.9%; textiles 14.4%; nonmetal minerals 6.9%; and furniture 3.5% (BPS 2018). As the largest sector of SMEs, increased production indexes and technology efficiency are needed to maintain optimal profits (Harahap 2018). Only 16% of SMEs in ASEAN are digitally integrated (Bain 2018). Most systems of SMEs are not integrated and paid the high cost in invoice processing, due to the ignorance of implementing digital technology as the challenges of industrial revolution 4.0 (ERIA 2019). Enterprise-level business process invoice and receipt at cost of US $2.07, while the SMEs are approximately at the cost of US $10 (Hung & Vignesh 2019). As the SMEs need to have an agile, thrifty, and flexible system in the field of accounting and invoice management, it could be done by implementing enterprise resource planning (ERP) (Justenhoven et al. 2017). OpenERP is the solution, with the Quickstart methodology which is adaptable to be implemented as an integrated accounting and invoice processing system (Hendarsyah 2019).

2 LITERATURE REVIEW

2.1 *Enterprise resource planning (ERP)*

Enterprise resource planning (ERP) is a complex set of comprehensive system applications that are designed to integrate and manage all business functions within a company (Ullah et al. 2018). ERP helps business activities including all operational needs based on the Internet services and data share (Luís et al. 2015). Benefits of ERP for companies consist of several things which

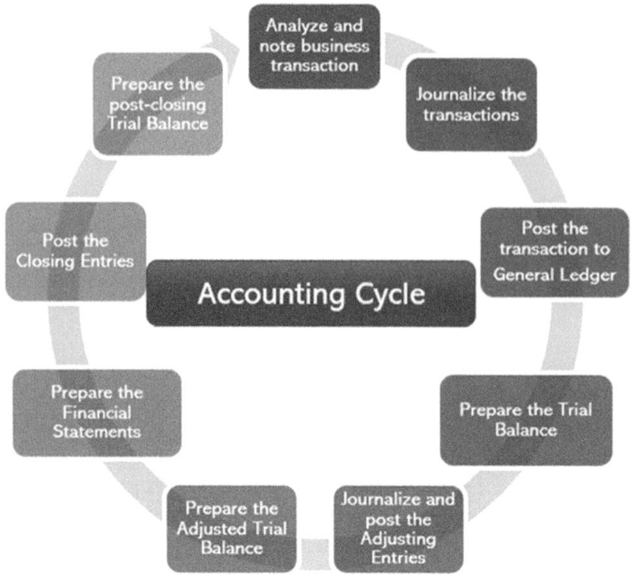

Figure 1. Accounting cycle (Weygandt. 2016).

include increasing system effectiveness and data integration between departments (Ociepa et al. 2017).

2.2 *OpenERP*

OpenERP (previously TinyERP, and now Odoo) is an open-source ERP system software that supports business goals, is adaptive, and is able to integrate information and data between one module with another (Pramana et al. 2019). Odoo became a platform with real-time services that covers all business areas within modular systems (Kendengis & Santoso 2018). OpenERP uses Python language and PostgreSQL as a database management system (Devkota 2016). OpenERP/Odoo has three-tier architecture, namely data tier as database management system, logic tier as the server that contains the processes of the software being run optimally, and presentation tier as the interface that connects the web with the server (Nafianto 2019)

2.3 *Accounting cycle*

The accounting cycle is a function cycle to collect, identify, record, process, store, communicate, and produce financial reports from transaction data for the company (Weygandt et al. 2016). There are nine phases of the accounting cycle.

Based on Figure 1, the accounting cycle can be explained as follows:

1. Analyze and note business transaction
2. Journalize the transactions
3. Post the transaction to general ledger
4. Prepare the trial balance
5. Journalize and post the adjusting entries
6. Prepare the adjusted trial balance
7. Prepare the financial statements
8. Post the closing entries
9. Prepare the post-closing trial

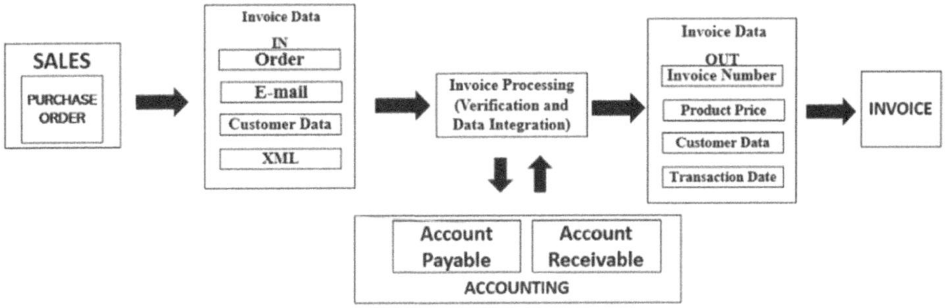

Figure 2. Invoice pprocessing system (Tater et al., 2018).

2.4 *Invoice processing system*

A process of data integration and communication is carried out by the system from one to another division to produce the invoice as the proof of transaction (Tater et al. 2018).

Invoice processing aims to record, save, and recap transactions conducted by companies, both debt or receivable activities, internal and external, which include cash inflows and outflows from the company's treasury system (Bezuglov 2018). Invoice processing has six phases, which start from receipt of the transaction, which occurs when the buyer has purchased a product from the seller and entered into a transaction with the seller. A good receipt occurs when the seller has recorded and entered data from the purchase order given by the buyer. When product data has been received to the system and agreed to be paid by the buyer, an invoice will be posted. After the invoice has been processed, the buyer must pay for the product they bought from the seller. The seller can provide an invoice as valid proof of payment after payment is made. Furthermore, invoice data will be evidence for the accounting ledger, which must be adjusted before being recorded in the general ledger and financial statements. Finally, when the data has been adjusted in the financial statements, the invoice system transaction ends (Neuvonen 2015).

3 RESEARCH METHODOLOGY

3.1 *Quickstart*

Quickstart is a development methodology of the OpenERP/Odoo system which is prioritizing its flexibility and is adaptive to every type of business process that exists (Matavya 2017). There are four stages of Quickstart methodology, starting with the kick-off call stage, where the company/SMEs give an explanation to the client related to how the system is applied to the business. Then, the system is carried out through a series of analysis of existing business processes, owned by the SME, to determine the business targeting process of the system that will be applied. After the analysis has been done, configuration and customization are carried out to develop the application by adjusting the needs of business processes and GAP analysis to the SME. Finally, after all requirements and analyses are fulfilled, the implementation of the system has been completed for the client (SME) (Gupta 2019).

4 ANALYSIS AND DESIGN

4.1 *Use case diagram*

Use case diagrams are used to determine the functions and limitations that exist in an information system and access rights that can be exercised by certain types of users (Drechsler et al. 2016). Regarding the accountant's use case diagram, there are eight main functional openERP/Odoo

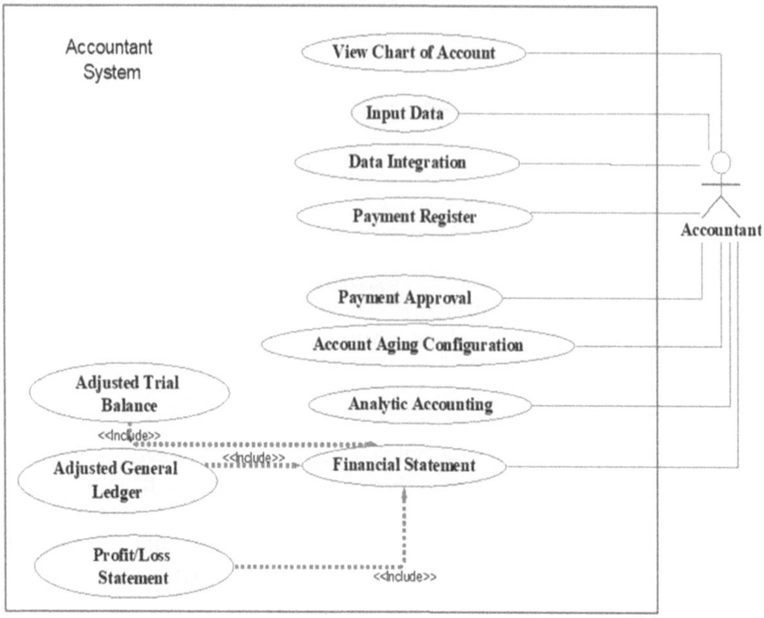

Figure 3. Use case diagram of accountant in OpenERP.

systems for the accountant, starting with the accountant creating, viewing, and editing the SME chart of account (CoA). The accountant can also do data integration, payment registration, payment approval, invoice processing, and accounting analytics. In developing the openERP/Odoo feature, the accountant can also configure the account aging related to payables/receivables made between SMEs and customers. The accountant can also process the invoice and financial statement, which consists of trial balance, general ledger, and profit loss statement that can be printed in PDF format by the openERP/Odoo system.

4.2 *Chart of account OpenERP/Odoo*

Chart of account is a list of accounts and the account numbers that identify their location in the ledger (Weygandt 2016).

For this research, the default chart of account that was created from openERPb, as can be seen in Table 1, consists of 14 types, namely, receivable, payable, bank and cash, current assets, other income, income, expenses, cost of revenue, non-current assets, prepayments, fixed assets, current liabilities, non-current liabilities, and equity.

4.3 *System architecture design*

The system architecture design as target of this research is the implementation of the openERP/Odoo-based ERP system in the accounting and invoice management modules, where each division can be integrated and produces master data that are connected. The implementation of Odoo in the accounting and invoicing management module system, in the food or culinary SME sector, aims to ensure that the financial and budget control processes that occur every time there is data coming in, from the sales, inventory, and purchasing sections, can recap well. This system creates an organized business process environment and automates various business needs effectively and efficiently.

Table 1. OpenERP chart of account.

Code	Name	Type	Code	Name	Type	Code	Name	Type
101200	Account Receivable	Receivable	101700	Liquidity transfers	Current Assets	102000	Non-Current Assets	Non-Current Assets
111100	Account Payable	Payable	101600	Opening Income Account	Other Income	103000	Prepayments	Prepayments
101401	Bank	Bank and Cash	201000	Foreign Exchange Gain	Income	100000	Fixed Asset Account	Fixed Assets
101501	Cash	Bank and Cash	200000	Product Sales	Income	111300	Receive and Profit/Loss Account	Current Liabilities
101300	Tax Paid	Current Assets	212300	Bank Fees	Expenses	111200	Tax Received	Current Liabilities
101130	Stock interim Account (Delivered)	Current Assets	212100	Purchase of Equipment	Expenses	111000	Current Liabilities	Current Liabilities
101120	Stock interim Account (Received)	Current Assets	211000	Foreign Exchange Loss	Expenses	112000	Non-Current Liabilities	Non-Current Liabilities
101110	Stock Valuation Account	Current Assets	220000	Expenses	Expenses	300200	Dividends	Equity
101000	Current Assets	Current Assets	210000	Cost of Revenue	Cost of Revenue	300100	Capital	Equity

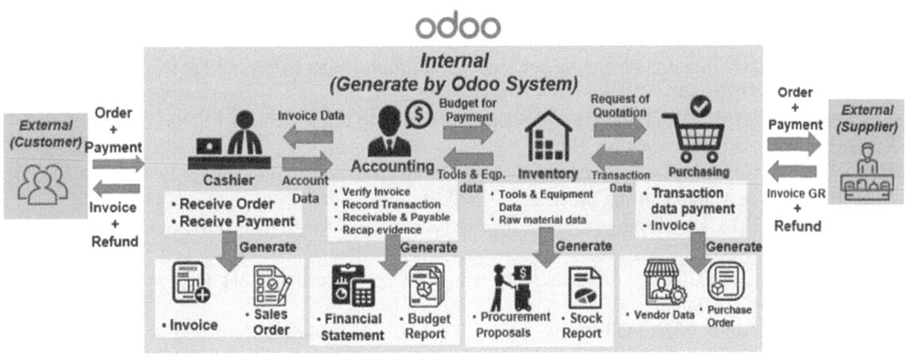

Figure 4. SMEs' business model target.

5 CONCLUSION

As the result of ppenERP implementation in the food sector, SMEs' accounting information system, the SMEs can process financial reports that are integrated with any department, either for inventory to plan the number of items that need to be purchased for the next day or with sales to easily monitor the daily income. OpenERP also provides a system for processing invoices in the food sector SMEs, being able to record and monitor transaction evidence in real time, effectively and efficiently. OpenERP allows food sector SMEs to reduce paper waste and resources, including to save long-term financial assets by generating invoices in e-invoice types, or PDFs that can be sent by email.

REFERENCES

Badan Pusat Statistik. 2018. Klasifikasi Baku Lapangan Usaha Indonesia (KBLI) Indonesian Business Field Standard Classification, Pg. 21–23.

Bain & Company.Inc. 2018. Advancing Towards ASEAN Digital Integration. A framework for digital integration. Page: 38–39.

Bezuglov, Ilya. 2018. Optimization of Invoice Handling Accounts Payable. Finland: Metropolia University of Applied Sciences. Page: 1–35.

Devkota, A. 2016. Business Information Technology. In O. U. of, OpenERP guidebook for small and medium enterprises. Finland: Oulu University of Applied Sciences. Page. 10–11.

Drechsler, Hevner, et al. 2016. A Four-Cycle Model of IS Design Science Research: Capturing the Dynamic Nature of IS Artifact Design page 12–33.

Economic Research Institute for ASEAN and East Asia. 2019. Final Report: Study on MSMEs Participation in the Digital Economy in ASEAN, Nurturing ASEAN MSMEs to Embrace Digital Adoption, page: 2–5. ASEAN, South East Asia.

Gajjar. Mantavya. 2017. Odoo 10 Implementation Cookbook, "Quickstart Implementation Methodology" Chapter 2.

Gupta, Abhimanyu. 2019. Generation of Multiple Conceptual Models from User Stories in Agile, Ghent University, Belgium.

Harahap, A. 2018. Analysis of Micro and Small Industry Development in Indonesia. International Journal of Scientific & Technology Research. Vol 7, Issue 4, page: 1–2.

Hendarsyah, S. P. 2019. Perancangan Sistem ERP Smart UKM Berbasis Model Layanan Pada Proses Accounting Dengan Metode Service Oriented Architecture, Bandung, Telkom University.

Hung, S., K. Vignesh. 2019. Your Complete Guide to Accounts Payable Transformation: How Can Digital Enablement Make the AP Process Learner, Faster, and Smarter". Everest Group Research.Page: 1–19.

Justenhoven, P., Sechser, J., Loitz, R. 2017. Digital Audits of Financial Statement: Study on the use of technology in finance and accounting. PricewaterhouseCoopers (PwC), Page: 12–13.

Kendengis Y., Santoso, L. 2018. Integration Between ERP Software and Business Intelligence in Odoo ERP: Case Study A Distribution. Advance In Natural And Applied Sciences. Petra Christian University, page 16–21. Indonesia.

Kumar, Ruchira. 2017. Targeted Financing For Sme's And Employment Effects: What Do We Know And What Could Be Done Differently?, World Bank Group, Page. 5–6.

Luís, S., Castro, F., et al. 2015. Planning and Scope Definition to Implement ERP: The Case Study of Federal Rural University of Rio de Janeiro, Brazil.

Nafianto, Chandratya. 2019. Development of Flexible Production Scheduling By Applying Gantt Chart to the ERP Open Source Manufacturing Module.

Neuvonen, Juuso. 2015. Developing purchase invoice processing through workflow automation. Page 12–15, Finland.

Ociepa – Kubicka., et al. 2017. Advantages of using enterprise resource planning systems (ERP) in the management process, Poland.

Odoo Official Website. 2020. Odoo Accounting Feature and benefit. Retrieved April 7, 2020, from https://www.odoo.com/page/accounting-features.

Pramana Nyoman B., Bayupati I Putu., Purnawan I Ketut. 2019. Implementation of Odoo for Managing Safety Stock in Clothing Retail Industry. International Journal of Computer Applications, Vol 177(23):46–53. December 2019.

Rao, Sujata., Kudtarkar, K. 2018. Implementation of Odoo ERP for Business Applications. Somaiya International Conference on Technology and Information Management (SICTIM 2018). PP: 32–33 Mumbai, India.

Tater, T., Dechu, S., Mani, S. Maurya, C. 2018. Prediction of Late Payment of Invoices in Account Payable Business Process. 16th International Conference (ICSOC 2018), Hangzhou, China, November. Page: 12–15. Proceeding.

Ullah, Abrar., Baharun.RB., Nor KMD., Yasir.M. 2018 Overview of Enterprise Resource Planning (ERP) System in Higher Education Institutions (HEIs), Page 1–21.

Weygandt Jerry J, Kimmel Paul D., Kieso. 2016. Accounting Principles, Twelfth edition. WILEY sales. Chp.4 Completing the Accounting Cycle, page. 166–167.

World Bank. 2020. Small and Medium Enterprises (SMEs) Finance: Improving SMEs'access to finance and finding innovative solutions to unlock sources of capital. Overview. Retrieved April 7, 2020. From https://www.worldbank.org/en/topic/smefinance.

Synergizing Management, Technology and Innovation in Generating Sustainable and Competitive Business Growth – Hendayani et al (eds)
© 2021 Taylor & Francis Group, London, ISBN 978-0-367-68756-4

Profit planning at Paseban Garut Hotel using profit volume cost analysis

D.F.L. Hamdah, C.H. Pansuri, H.S. Hanifah & S.N. Diyani
Faculty of Economics, Garut University, Garut, Jawa Barat, Indonesia

ABSTRACT: The purpose of this study was to determine the profit and loss planning process at Hotel Paseban Garut using profit volume costs. This research uses descriptive qualitative method. The data techniques used are library research and field research. Data processing techniques are with qualitative data processing. Data processing is done by way of data reduction, data presentation, and data collection. The research was conducted at Hotel Paseban Garut. Based on the results of research and discussion, it can be seen that when the contribution margin is greater than fixed costs, the sales of Hotel Paseban Garut can exceed the breakeven point; in other words, the hotel is in a safe condition so that when the company experiences a decrease in sales to the breakeven point, the hotel does not gain or lose. The results of the calculation of the margins of Hotel Paseban Garut show the level of hotel security, which means that it has a safe distance from experiencing losses.

1 INTRODUCTION

Increasing competition among companies makes the hotel management be demanded to do their job well, as basically the performance of hotel managers determines the success or failure of a company and the profits generated by the company can be a measure of success or failure of the manager performance. Success in business performance requires the involvement of every manager (Pueters & Gudergan 2019). One of the management functions performed by managers in an effort to achieve goals is planning about the description of activities to be carried out in the future, such as planning earnings to achieve the expected profit.

Company management must know whatever revenue targets that must be achieved in order for the company to achieve profit. One of the efforts that companies can do so that planning runs effectively can use tools in the form of cost-profit analysis that can reduce management to avoid cost, volume, and profit relationships. The conventional analysis tool of volume earnings with analytical terms is widely used in decision making (Fong Ching Yuan 2009).

Paseban Hotel is one of the hotel service industries in Garut Regency. Based on the results of research interviews conducted with the managers of Hotel Paseban Garut, in the face of very fierce competition regarding the goal of the amount of profit to be achieved, Hotel Paseban has not conducted a profit volume cost analysis. In addition, Paseban Hotel has not classified the costs of its business activities into fixed costs and variable costs. This condition is not in line with what Hasen and Mowen (2011: 4) stated, that profit volume cost analysis is a very useful tool for planning for management and consideration in decision making.

As for Carter's statement (2009: 72), in the calculation of cost volume profit analysis, costs must be separated into fixed costs and variable costs. Based on these phenomena, this study aims to determine the profit planning at Paseban Garut Hotel using the cost of profit volume.

2 LITERATURE REVIEW

2.1 *Cost volume profit analysis*

Profit volume cost analysis is a very useful tool for planning for management and consideration in making decisions for companies to get the desired profit. Samryn (2012) mentions the assumption of cost volume profit analysis, that is:

- The selling price is constant along the relevant range.
- Costs are linear in each relevant range and are divided into elements of variable costs and fixed costs accurately.
- In companies that produce and sell many products, the sales mix is constant.
- In a manufacturing company, the inventory level does not change in the sense that the difference between the initial inventory level and the ending inventory period is not significant.

The following are the basics in analyzing the cost of profit volume according to Samryn (2012):

- Contribution Margin: The contribution margin formula uses sales less variable costs; the change in the contribution margin will always move proportionally to changes in sales and variable costs.
- Breakeven Point: The breakeven point is the level of activity in which the company does not make a profit and does not suffer losses.
- Margin of Safety (Margin of Safety): Security margins are excess sales from budgeted sales or realization above the breakeven point; the calculation results show the amount up to how much the sales could fall until the breakeven results.

2.2 *Profit planning*

Earnings planning is a description of the activities that will be carried out in the future to be able to get the desired profit. As for-profit planning, according to Carter (2009: 4), namely, "Development of an operational plan to achieve company goals." One of the calculations of cost volume profit analysis used for earnings planning is profit target analysis. This is based on a statement regarding the analysis of profit targets according to Samryn (2012: 179), namely, "In the application of the volume and profit costs relationship is basically the same as the break-even analysis. The difference only lies in the amount of profit calculated in the formula."

2.3 *The relationship between cost volume analysis and profit planning*

The analysis of the relationship between the cost of profit volume and profit planning can be used to base the calculation of contribution margins, breakeven points, profit targets, and safety margins. One of the cost volume profit analysis formulas that is often used for profit planning is profit target. This is based on the statement regarding the analysis of profit targets according to Garrison, Noreen, and Brewer (2016: 222), namely, "One of the main uses in the analysis of profit volume costs, by estimating the sales volume needed to achieve a certain profit."

The analysis of cost of profit volume according to Hasen & Mowen (2011: 4), namely, "One very useful tool for planning and decision making."

3 METHODS

3.1 *Characteristics and research stages*

This research is a descriptive qualitative reserch. Sources of data used are primary and secondary data, while the primary data in this study are direct interviews with managers and corporate finance about planning tools and cost classification. The secondary data used is the financial statement

Table 1. Contribution margin calculation.

	2016		2017		2018	
	Rp	%	Rp	%	Rp	%
Bed Room	248.512.250		279.652.366		265.474.919	
Hall	14.141.249		30.456.665		41.186.119	
Mess & Bungalow	15.375.249		27.194.166		32.304.520	
Canteen	79.324.475		91.070.425		77.585.500	
Total	357.353.223	71,7	426.373.622	71,3	416.551.058	70,5

Table 2. Breakeven point calculation.

Year	Breakeven	Sales
2016	362.957.880	498.110.000
2017	370.731.461	598.330.000
2018	374.944.318	591.000.000

document of the Paseban Garut Hotel from 2016–2018. The data was obtained through library research techniques and field interviews. The data processing technique in this research is data analysis. The data that has been collected was then analyzed using qualitative descriptive methods by reducing data, presenting data, and drawing conclusions.

3.2 *Conceptual framework and hypotheses*

This study has one research variable, namely, the cost of profit volume.

4 RESULTS AND DISCUSSION

4.1 *Results of calculation of profit volume costs*

4.1.1 *Contribution margin*

Paseban Garut improved in 2018 due to competition in selling prices between hotels, but sales obtained in 2018 can increase hotel costs, or in other words, the hotel is safe.

4.1.2 *Breakeven point*

The calculation results in Table 2 can be seen if the company has decreased sales until it is at the breakeven point, then the company is in a state of not getting profit and not suffering losses. In addition, from the results of the above research it can be seen that hotel sales are above the break-even point, which means that the Hotel Paseban Garut was able to cover the costs incurred during 2016–2018.

4.1.3 *Safety margins*

The calculation of the safety margin (margin of safety) of Paseban Garut Hotel in 2016 shows a level of security of Rp.135,152,120 or 27.1%, in 2017 shows a level of security of Rp.227,598,539 or 38%, and in 2018 shows a level of security amounting to Rp.216,055,682 or 36.5%, which means that during the sale of the Paseban Garut Hotel it does not go down until it reaches the security level, the Paseban Garut Hotel still earns profit or has a safe distance to not suffer losses.

4.1.4 *Analysis of profit targets*

Calculation of profit target analysis produces an income target in 2016 that must be achieved at Rp.420,500,415 to get a profit of Rp.41,258,000 as planned, in 2017 that must be achieved at Rp.475,003,226 to get a profit of Rp.74,716,500 as planned, and in 2018 what must be achieved is Rp.494,078,482 to get a profit of Rp.119,666,000 as planned.

The results of research on the cost of profit volume at the Hotel Paseban Garut are that the hotel is able to cover the costs that occur during 2016–2018. Even though the breakeven point during 2016–2018 was achieved, the number is still very high. It can be seen by seeing the margin of safety during 2016–2018 is very small so that the Paseban Garut Hotel is vulnerable to losses. The hotel sector is very vulnerable to strategic disturbances from outside (Xu & Zhang 2020) and in accordance with what was stated by Garrison, Noreen, and Brewer (2016), namely, the higher the safety margin, the lower the risk of not returning capital.

Others than the Paseban Garut Hotel can benefit more than the planned profits each year. Even though in 2018 there was a decrease in profit from the previous year, the hotel still got a profit exceeding the target because hotel sales did not experience a very large decline from the previous year.

5 CONCLUSION

From the results of the research conducted, the author can reject that profit by using the cost that can estimate the results of the contribution that is greater than the fixed costs or income that the hotel earns which can cover fixed costs so that the hotel can make a profit every year. The results from the breakeven point of sales obtained by the hotel are still in a safe condition because every year hotel sales can exceed the breakeven point. The results of the Paseban Garut Hotel security margin each year have a safe distance to not suffer losses.

REFERENCES

Carter, W. K. 2009. *Akuntansi Biaya.* Jakarta: Salemba Empat.

Darminto, D. P. 2011. *Analisis Laporan Keuangan.* Yogyakarta: UPP STIM YKPN.

Duyo, S. F. 2013. Analisis Cost Volume Profit Untuk Perencanaan Laba Pada Hotel Sintesa Peninsula Manado. *Jurnal EMBA*, 603–610. https://ejournal.unsrat.ac.id/index.php/emba/article/view/2128.

Firdaus, & Wasilah. 2014. *Akuntansi Biaya.* Jakarta: Salemba Empat.

Garrison, R., Noreen, E., & Brewer, P. 2016. *Akuntansi Manajerial.* Jakarta: Salemba Empat.

Hasen, & Mowen. 2011. *Akuntansi Manajerial.* Jakarta: Salemba Empat.

Henry, S. 2012. *Akuntansi Manajemen.* Riau: Star Gate Publishing.

Jumingan. 2011. *Analisis Laporan Keuangan.* Jakarta: Bumi Aksara.

Kembi, L. D., Sondakh, J. J., & Tirayoh, V. Z. 2014. Perencanaan Laba Berdasarkan Analisis Biaya Volume Laba Pada PT. Multi Food Manado. *EMBA*, 354–362. https://ejournal.unsrat.ac.id/index.php/emba/article/view/6274.

Koraag, J. F., & Ilat, V. 2016. Analisis Cost Volume Profit Untuk Perencanaan Laba Pada Pabrik Tahu Ibu Siti. *Berkala Ilmiah Efisiensi*, 803–812. https://ejournal.unsrat.ac.id/index.php/jbie/article/view/13576.

Mulyadi. 2010. *Akuntansi Biaya.* Yogyakarta: STIE YKPN.

Munawir. 2007. *Analisis Laporan Keuangan.* Yogyakarta: Lyberty.

Nazir. 2011. *Metode Penelitian.* Bogor: Ghalia Indonesia.

Rudianto. 2013. *Akuntansi Manajemen.* Jakarta: Erlangga.

Samahati, R. B. 2013. Analisis Biaya Volume Laba Sebagai Alat Bantu Perencanaan Laba Pada Hotel Sedona Manado. *EMBA*, 1009–1018. https://ejournal.unsrat.ac.id/index.php/emba/article/view/2306.

Samryn, L. M. 2012. *Akuntansi Manajemen.* Jakarta: Kencana.

Sihombing, S. B. 2013. Analisis Biaya Volume Laba Sebagai Alat Bantu Perencanaan Laba PT.Bangun Wenang Beverages Company. *EMBA, 1*(3), 181–188. https://ejournal.unsrat.ac.id/index.php/emba/article/view/1955.

Sofyan. 2011. *Analisis Kritis atas Laporan Keuangan.* Jakarta: Rajawali.

Sugiyono. 2017. *Metode Penelitian Kuantitatif, Kualitatif dan R&D.* Bandung: Alfabeta.

Swastha, B. 2014. *Manajemen Penjualan.* Yogyakarta: BPFE.

Synergizing Management, Technology and Innovation in Generating Sustainable and Competitive Business Growth – Hendayani et al (eds)
© 2021 Taylor & Francis Group, London, ISBN 978-0-367-68756-4

The effect of inflation, BI rate, exchange rate, earnings per share, return on assets, debt to equity ratio on stock return SOE in the infrastructure sector, subsectors of construction listed in Indonesia Stock Exchanges 2015–2018

A. Iradianty & Y.F.D. Listiawan
Telkom University, Bandung, West Java, Indonesia

ABSTRACT: This research examines the effect of inflation, BI rate, exchange rates, earning per share (EPS), return on assets (ROA), debt-to-equity (DER) on the return of shares in state-owned enterprises subsector construction in the period 2015–2018. The method in this study used quantitative methods with secondary data sources used. Sample data retrieval techniques used purposive sampling techniques. The results of this study were obtained simultaneously from all dependent variables against the independent variables and partial research on inflation variables, the BI rate, exchange rates, and DER effect on return shares, but not with EPS and ROA variables that do not affect the return of shares.

1 INTRODUCTION

Financial market has a strategic role as a source of funding in economic activity, a media for transmitting monetary and fiscal policy, and financial system stability. Financial market is one of the economic growth indicators, where the money supply in the country can be seen in this market, not only the amount of local currency (Indonesian Rupiah) but also the amount of foreign currency circulating in our country, and it affects the exchange rate between countries. Financial market also includes government savings from tax revenues and spending, or called government expenditures, such as personnel expenditure, goods expenditure, grant expenditure, fuel subsidies and non-fuel subsidies, payment of domestic debt interest and foreign debt, and infrastructure development.

The Indonesian government is currently active in the development of infrastructure to support the activities of its people, such as the construction of toll roads, bridges, railway lines, dams, new airports and housing, flats and homes dedicated to low-income communities. The availability of this new infrastructure is expected to increase the number of investors which in turn will open new jobs and reduce the number of unemployed, both in industry, tourism, or other areas. This project is carried out by private companies and state companies engaged in infrastructure in accordance with the guidelines for the procurement procedures. This research will take the object of government companies or called BUMN (Badan Usaha Milik Negara) subsector of contraction listed on the Indonesia Stock Exchange from 2015 to 2018.

According to UU numbers 19 of 2003, SOE is a business entity from all or part of its capital sourced from the state through direct investments originating from separated state assets. SOE in a country is expected to be able to increase the welfare of the community in social and economic terms. The growth of SOE in a country describes the condition of progress of a country, because one of the state's revenue sources is derived from BUMN. Growth of a country is said to be seen from the development of existing infrastructure. Significant infrastructure growth can help economic equality, development equitable, or new employment. It indirectly affects the economic growth of a country. This study took subsectors of construction (sector infrastructure) in SOE. The construction subsector is an important part of the country's economic growth. So, it is very tempting to invest in the financial market with the object of the infrastructure industry.

According to Halim (2015), investment is an investor's decision on some of the current funds for the purpose of obtaining profit (return) in the future. Return shares is the yield gained from the investment, the stock return is a change in the price value of the share T-Previous period. An investor to maximize the investment profit usually performs analysis with macroeconomic analysis; a tool used as an analysis tool among others is inflation, BI rate, and the rupiah exchange rate. Investors in investing, in addition to using factors above the fundamental analysis of the company, also used before investing, is to calculate the ratio of profitability and ratio of the company's leverage. In this study, the profitability ratio used is using the return on asset (ROA) and earning per share (EPS) ratios. Meanwhile, the leverage ratio is debt to equity ratio (DER).

The study of previous research conducted by Jatiningtyas and Iradianty (2016) uses the dependent variable return stock inflation, interest rates, exchange rate, ROA, and DER as independent variables, obtaining the simultaneous results of inflation variables, interest rates, rupiah, ROA, and DER exchange rate that do not significantly affect the return of shares. This result is backed by the same research results of Aulia and Iradianty (2016), which examines the dependent variable is the return of shares and the independent variable of inflation, interest rate, exchange rate, ROE, and CR resulting in an independent variable of inflation, interest rates, value exchange. ROE and CR do not have any simultaneous effect on the return of shares. This is in contrast to the research conducted by Adnan and Iradianty (2018) using the dependent variable return stock inflation, interest rates, exchange rate, ROA, DER as independent variables, obtaining the simultaneous results, variable inflation, interest rates, Rupiah exchange rate, ROA and DER effect on the return of shares. These results were a gap from research conducted on previous research.

2 LITERATURE REVIEW

Shares according to Fahmi (2015) The shares are a sign of a sheet of paper listed as a nominal value, the name of the company, and is discussed with the rights and obligations described by the shareholders. Return stock Tandelilin (2017) Return is the result gained when investing. Stock is influenced by ROA (Adnan 2018), but not affected by inflation, rate of return, the exchange rate (Aulia & Iradianty 2016; Jatiningtyas & Iradianty 2016). The second variable is inflation, inflation is the overall and continuous increase in prices. Inflation Rate Empirical evidence suggests a negative relationship between inflation rate and stock prices (Mankiw et al. 2013) because high and varying inflation rates generate more uncertainty, and thus the demand for minimum return will also rise which will decrease the market valuation (Khan & Khan 2018).

BI Rate According to the official website of Bank Indonesia, BI 7-Day (Reserve) Repo Rate is a new policy interest rate that can affect the capital market sector, Bank sectors, and rill sectors quickly. This Variable as the interest rate is chosen because the effect of interest rate is positive nevertheless bad news has a strong impact on the stock market, as Federal Reserve raises interest rate more (less) than expectations then it is contemplated bad (good) news to the stock market (Khan & Khan 2018). Other variables, the Indonesian Rupiah exchange rate is the value used between a person buying a country's currency with foreign currency (Mankiw et al. 2013). Currency is regularly incorporated as an investment in the asset portfolio, and knowledge about the impact of the exchange rate on the stock market is important for the performance of fund portfolios (Khan & Khan 2018).

Earning per Shares (EPS) is a large net profit of a company given to investors who have shares of the company (Tandelilin 2017). The success of management in administrating the capital can be seen from its success in generating profit because with the profits obtained, the management can improve the welfare of the stakeholders (Yuliza 2018). EPS formula is net income after interest and taxes divided by the numbers of shares. Next variable is Return on Asset (ROA), ROA is the benchmark of a company capable of profiting from all the assets owned by the related company (Hery 2017). ROA measures the profitability relative to funds invested in the company by common stockholders, preferred stockholders, and suppliers of debt financing (Warrad 2015). It can be calculated as ROA is net income divided by average total assets.

Debt to equity ratio (DER) is one of the financial ratios included in the leverage ratio group. This ratio illustrates the ability of a company to suffice all obligations owned with existing assets data and methodology (Hery 2017). DER is the ratio used by companies to assess the company's equity from the company's debt, the higher the value of DER, meaning the smaller the number of assets financed by the owner of the company, and the greater the value of DER, meaning the greater the number of assets financed by the owner of the company (Suntoyo 2013).

This research based on the method of research will use quantitative research methods. Based on research objectives, this research is grouped as a verification study, at the time of implementation of this research using times series research. Based on the involvement of researchers in this research, the author has no transparency, namely with secondary data. This research samples using SOE subsector construction companies listed on the Indonesian Stock Exchange and has a complete financial report of each of its periods. Based on the criteria above, this study had a sample of companies to be researched; the four companies are as follows: (1) PT Adhi Karya, Tbk. (ADHI); (2) PT Pembangunan Perumahan, Tbk. (PTPP); (3) PT Wika Karya, Tbk. (WIKA); (4) PT Waskita Karya, Tbk. (WSKT).

3 RESULT AND DISCUSSIONS

Inflation, BI rate, the exchange rate, EPS, ROA, and DER simultaneously affect significantly the return of shares registered in the SOE subsector construction period 2015–2018. Judging from the results, the results are described as (a) The inflation variable probability value has a value of 0.0159. It is concluded that the inflation variable affects partially toward the stock return. (b) The probability value of the BI rate variable has a value of 0.0264. It can be concluded that the BI rate variable affects partially against the stock return. (c) Probability value. A variable exchange rate of the rupiah has a value of 0.2102. It can be concluded that the rupiah exchange rate variable does not affect partially on the return of the stock. (d) Variable probability value EPS has a value of 0.1026. It can be concluded that the EPS variable does not affect partially on the stock return. (e) The probability value of the ROA variable has a value of 0.4951. It can be concluded that ROA variables do not affect partially on the stock return. (f) The DER variable probability value has a value of 0.0172. It can be concluded that the DER variables affect partially on the stock return.

4 CONCLUSION

Based on the results of the research discussed, it can be concluded as follows: Inflation, BI rate, exchange rates, EPS, ROA, and DER simultaneously affect significantly the return of shares. Partially inflation, BIRrate, Rupiah, and DER exchange rates affect the return of shares, and vice versa, EPS and ROA do not affect the return of the shares registered in the SOE subsector construction period of the years 2015–2018.

REFERENCES

Adnan, M. & Iradianty, A. 2018. Efek Inflasi, Tingkat Suku Bunga, Nilai Tukar Rupiah, Rasio Tingkat Pengembalian Aset (ROA), dan Rasio Tingkat Pengembalian Utang (DER) terhadap Return Saham. eProceedings of Management, Vol 5, No 3.

Ali, M. A., Kalim, U., Raza, H., Ali, H. A., Rehman, M., & Ullah, M. I. 2017. The Relationship Between ROA, ROE, ROCE and EPS Ratios with Break-up Values of Shares of Karachi-Pakistan Fuel and Energy Listed Companies, 1–8.

Anwaar, M. 2016. Impact of Firms' Performance on Stock Returns (Evidence from Listed Companies of FTSE-100 Index London, UK), 1–10.

Aulia, P.G., Yunita, & Iradianty, A. 2016. Pengaruh Inflasi, Tingkat Suku Bunga, Nilai Tukar Mata Uang, ROE Dan CR Terhadap Return Saham (Studi Pada Perusahaan Rokok yang terdaftar di BEI Periode 2012–2015), eProceedings of Management, Vol 3, No 1.

Duke, S. B., Ikenna, N., & Nkamare. 2015. Impact of Dividend Policy on Share Price Valuation in Nigerian Bank, 156–170.

Hery. 2017. Analisis Laporan Keuangan. Jakarta: Grasindo.

Jatiningtyas, N. & Iradianty, A. 2016. The Effect Inflation, Interest Rate, Exchange Rate, Return on Assets (ROA), and Debt Ratio (DER) on Stock Return (Case study on Telecommunication Subsector listed in Indonesia Stock Exchange Period 2011–2015). Proceeding of International Seminar & Conference on Learning Organization.

Khan, J. & Khan, I. 2018. The Impact of Macroeconomic Variables on Stock Prices: A Case Study of Karachi Stock Exchange. Journal of economics and Sustainable Development, 9(13).

Mankiw, N. G., Quah, E., & Wilson, P. 2013. Pengantar Makro Ekonomi.Jakarta: Salemba Empat.

Mugambi, M., & Okech, T. C. 2016. Effect of Macroeconomic Variables on Stock Returns of Listed Commercial Banks in Kenya, 390–418.

Musallam, S. R. 2018. Exploring the Relationship between Financial Ratios and Market Stock Returns, 101–116.

Sunyoto, D., 2013. Fundamentals of Corporate Financial Management. 1st print. CAPS (Center of Academic Publishing Service). Jakarta.

Tandelilin, E. 2017. Pasar Modal Manajemen Portofolio dan Investasi.Yogyakarta: Kanisius.

Warrad, L. 2015. Return on Asset and Return on Equity effect of Net Operating Cycles: Jordanian Study. Research Journal of Finance and accounting. SSN 2222-1697 (Paper) ISSN 2222–2847 (Online) Vol.6, No.14 (2015).

Yuliza, A. 2018. The effect of Earnings per share and Firm Size to Stock Price LQ45 Company Listed in Indonesia Securities. (2018). International Journal Engineering & Technology, 7 (4.9) 247–249.

Synergizing Management, Technology and Innovation in Generating Sustainable and Competitive Business Growth – Hendayani et al (eds)
© 2021 Taylor & Francis Group, London, ISBN 978-0-367-68756-4

The analysis of stock index cointegration in ASEAN-5 Countries, China, Japan, and India capital markets over the period of 2015–2019

I. Yunita & S.R.D. Riverdhan
School of Economics and Business, Telkom University, Bandung, West Java, Indonesia

ABSTRACT: The interaction and interdependence among markets have a vital role to the analysis of predictability, portfolio diversification, and asset allocation. To analyze international portfolio, cointegration test is needed. This research aims to conduct a cointegration analysis of stock index in ASEAN-5 Countries, China, Japan, and India, both in groups and in pairs in 2015–2019. The method used is the Johansen Cointegration test. It is found that there is cointegration of stock price indexes in ASEAN-5 countries in 2015–2019. There is also cointegration between the ASEAN-5 with China, Japan, and India in 2015–2019. Moreover, the paired cointegration shows that there is cointegration in all 28 pairs identified and that no country that dominates the capital market in Asia. It is concluded that there are long- and short-term relationships between those eight indexes as it creates long-term equilibrium and short-run deviations between assets during the period of 2015 until 2019.

1 INTRODUCTION

The capital market is an institution that plays an essential role in the progress of a country (Agyei-Ampomah 2011). The capital market has an important role in the economy of a country because the capital market performs two main functions, first as a means for business funding and second as a means for companies to get funds from the investor community (Mailangkay 2013). In investing, an investor must consider several things in advance, one of which is the historical price of shares and the country's stock price index (Sunariyah 2011).

Cointegration analysis is aimed at identifying a tendency of a short- and long-run relationship between capital markets (Lee & Isa. 2014). This is of utmost importance for both investors and policymakers. For investors, the previous studies have indicated that cointegration analysis is critical in diversifying portfolios to achieve efficient capital allocation. For the policymakers, cointegration analysis is vital to study the range of financial products that can be broadened in order to strengthen domestic capital markets (Chien et al. 2015).

In the recent decade, Asian stock markets are exhibiting increasing importance on the world economic stage. There are almost 20,000 companies listed in Asia's stock markets as of 2012, compared to over 10,000 in the Americas and a total of 13,300 in Europe, Middle-East, and Africa (Lipinsky & Ong 2014). ASEAN has foster serious economic cooperation with China, along with other strong economic alliances like Japan and India. For example, ASEAN and China signed an agreement to establish an ASEAN-China Free Trade Area (ACFTA) in 2002 (Ong & Habibullah 2012). The collective economic size of ASEAN-5 (Indonesia, Thailand, Philippines, Malaysia, and Singapore), Japan, China and India has the potential to offer a significant opportunity to diversify its export and imports. However, due to the diversity in cultural and social condition, there is a need to examine the cointegration in ASEAN-5, China, Japan and India.

The study conducted by Hendrawan and Gustyana (2011) tested in pairs and groups for research objects using indexes from ASEAN-5 countries, Hong Kong, Japan, South Korea, and China and showed the results that there was cointegration both in groups and in pairs, except for seven test pairs for cointegration namely Indonesia-Japan, Hong Kong-Japan, Malaysia-South Korea, Malaysia-Japan, South Korea-Japan, Japan-Philippines and Japan-Singapore which showed no cointegration. Further research by Rajwani and Mukherjee (2013) showed that the Indian stock market was not integrated with one of the Asian markets either in pairs or groups and concluded that the Indian market was not sensitive to dynamics in markets in the long run. However, different results were shown by Seth and Sharma (2015), who said that there was a cointegration in pairs between India and other Asian countries. Due to the time-varying result, it is important to analyze the recent cointegration in these countries. Therefore, to complement the previous studies, this paper aims to conduct cointegration tests both in pairs and in groups in the ASEAN-5 countries, China, Japan, and India for the period of 2015–2019.

2 RESEARCH METHODOLOGY

The data used in this research is secondary data downloaded from the Wall Street Journal, which is the index data of daily closing share price of IHSG, SET, PSEI, STI, KLSE, SSE, Nikkei 225, NIFTY50. First, the descriptive analysis is conducted. In the descriptive analysis, the data is processed to provide an overview of standard deviation, skewness, and kurtosis (Sekaran 2011). Second, stationarity test is conducted as the requirement of cointegration test. A random process data is categorized as stationary if the mean and variance are constant over time and covariant between the two data sets coherently depends only on the lag between the two that time period. To test the stationarity, a unit root test is used (Widarjono 2013). Third, the cointegration tests are conducted using the Johansen test Method (Johansen 1988). After the group cointegration, a paired cointegration test is conducted for the capital market ASEAN-5 countries, China, Japan, and India. This paired test aims to identify which country is the most dominant among the other capital markets.

3 RESULT AND DISCUSSION

3.1 *Descriptive analysis*

Descriptive analysis is used to provide summaries about the sample and the measures. Overall, the standard deviation value of each index is low, which means data are clustered around the mean. It is seen that Indonesia, Japan, Philippine, Thailand and Singapore are negatively skewed while Malaysia and India are normally distributed, and China is positively skewed. Then, the value of kurtosis that draws the value that represents the level of the curve of a curve is found. It is seen that Philippine and China stock index are leptokurtic, which is the condition of a very pointed curve, while the rest are platicurtic, which is a flat curve.

3.2 *Stationarity analysis*

Table 1 shows the result of the stationarity level test on the data of stock price indexes in Indonesia, Malaysia, India, Japan, Philippines, Thailand, China, and Singapore. It shows that the probability value of each index is greater than 0.05, which means the data is not stationary. To proceed to the cointegration test stage, stationary data is needed, so a first difference is performed to get stationary data. After performing a first level difference on each index, it is known that each index (i.e., JSX, KLSE, Nikkei, NIFTY50, PSEI, SET, SSEC, and STI) has a value of Probability <0.05. It can be concluded that the data is stationary at level one of the differences.

3.3 *Cointegration on the stock price index in ASEAN-5 countries (JSX, KLSE, PSEI, SET, and STI)*

When conducting the cointegration test, the level of significance is employed, as seen in Table 2. In that table, it can be seen that the value of Trace Statistics is bigger than Critical Value, which

Table 1. Stationarity level and first level difference result.

		Stationarity Test Result		First Level Difference	
Country	Index	ADF	Probability	ADF	Probability
Indonesia	JSX	−1.331129	0.6168	−30.36305	0
Malaysia	KLSE	−2.188401	0.2108	−27.23902	0
India	NIFTY50	−0.535225	0.8816	−31.44787	0
Japan	NIKKEI225	−1.707519	0.4271	−30.3052	0
Philippines	PSEI	−2.707728	0.0730	−30.6727	0
Thailand	SET	−1.556729	0.5044	−29.66981	0
China	SSEC	−2.210884	0.2026	−16.83115	0
Singapore	STI	−1.843094	0.3596	−29.50336	0

Source: Data processed (2020).

Table 2. Cointegration test in groups of five stock price indexes.

Unrestricted Cointegration Rank Test (Trace)				
Hypothesized		Trace	0.05	
No. of CE(s)	Eigenvalue	Statistic	Critical Value	Prob.**
None*	0.233108	979.6652	69.81889	0.0001
At most 1*	0.221877	739.7347	47.85613	0.0001
At most 2*	0.192963	512.9473	29.79707	0.0001
At most 3*	0.176095	319.1420	15.49471	0.0001
At most 4*	0.147288	144.0376	3.841466	0.0000
Trace test indicates 5 cointegrating eqn(s) at the 0.05 level				

*denotes rejection of the hypothesis at the 0.05 level
**MacKinnon-Haug-Michelis (1999) p-values
Source: Data processed (2020).

indicates that there is cointegration among ASEAN-5 countries' stock price indexes. This result is in accordance with Ong and Habibullah's (2012) research that found the economic interdependence and comovement occur in ASEAN-5 countries. The result of this research has proven previous studies findings that the combination of diverse economic structures in ASEAN-5 countries forms a comparative advantage to the markets (Chien et al. 2015; Ong & Habibullah 2012). The diverse economic structures are shown by Thailand's reliability on tourism, Singapore's achievement in financial services and technology, Malaysia's comparative advantage in manufactured electrical related apparatus, and manufacturing industries, and Indonesia and the Philippines' dependent on agricultural and agro-based produce. Chien et al. (2015) found that there is a regional financial integration in ASEAN-5 and China between 1994 and 2002. This research complements it by presenting cointegration in the five countries between 2015 and 2019.

3.4 *Cointegration on stock price indices in ASEAN-5 countries, China, Japan and India (JSX, KLSE, PSEI, SET, STI, SSEC, Nikkei225, and NIFTY50)*

After examining the cointegration among the five ASEAN countries, the cointegration test on the ASEAN-5 stock price index, China, Japan, and India is conducted. Table 3 indicates the cointegration testing with the same significance level of 5% with stationary data from the previous step. It can also be seen that the Trace Statistic are bigger than the Critical Value, which means there

Table 3. Cointegration test in groups of eight stock price indexes.

Unrestricted Cointegration Rank Test (Trace)

Hypothesized		Trace	0.05	
No. of CE(s)	Eigenvalue	Statistic	Critical Value	Prob.**
None*	0.246916	1505.853	159.5297	1.0000
At most 1*	0.223854	1249.498	125.6154	1.0000
At most 2*	0.212751	1020.411	95.75366	0.0001
At most 3*	0.189624	804.1648	69.81889	0.0001
At most 4*	0.181200	614.0923	47.85613	0.0001
At most 5*	0.160711	433.3686	29.79707	0.0001
At most 6*	0.143478	274.9875	15.49471	0.0001
At most 7*	0.138701	134.9797	3.841466	0.0000

Trace test indicates 8 cointegrating eqn(s) at the 0.05 level

*denotes rejection of the hypothesis at the 0.05 level
**MacKinnon-Haug-Michelis (1999) p-values
Source: Data processed (2020).

is cointegration between JSX, KLSE, PSEI, SET, STI, SSEC, Nikkei225 and also NIFTY50. The presence of cointegration on stock price indexes in ASEAN-5 Countries, China, Japan, and India (JSX, KLSE, PSEI, SET, STI, SSEC, Nikkei225, and NIFTY50) implies that there are long- and short-term relationships between those eight indexes as it creates long-term equilibrium and short-run deviations between assets during the period of 2015 until 2019. This is in line with Hendrawan and Gustyana (2011), who found that there is a long-term equilibrium in ASEAN-5 countries and Hongkong, Japan, South Korea, and China from 2000 to 2010. The result of this research is also supported by Ong and Habibullah (2012) that the ASEAN-5 coalition has a cointegrating condition, and it is improved when China is included in ASEAN-5. Cointegrated markets indicate a move towards financial stability and cannot deviate too far from their long-run goal. However, Batareddy et al. (2012) suggested that this equilibrium needs to be relooked at and rebalanced from time-to-time because assets correlation is a time-varying concept. This is especially important because there is the presence of structural breaks that may happen in a period of time, as what is found in previous research by Rajwani and Mukherjee (2013).

3.5 *Paired cointegration anaylsis in stock price indixes in ASEAN-5 countries, China, Japan, and India*

Cointegration testing in pairs is done by testing the integration of stock price indexes between the two countries. From the index of eight countries, 28 pairs were obtained for cointegration testing. Using Johansen's integration test at a significance level of 5%, Table 4 shows the result that each pair has a Trace Statistics value that is bigger than the Critical Value, which means that in all index pairs, there is a cointegration in pairs. This result shows that there is a long-term interdependence in all pairs of indexes. Because the results show that all countries cointegrate in pairs, it is concluded that there is no dominant country among the ASEAN-5 (i.e., Indonesia, Malaysia, the Philippines, Singapore, and Thailand), China, Japan, and India in 2015 to 2019. A few years before the period of this study, different results were derived from the previous study of Hendrawan and Gustyana (2011). They found that China was dominant because of market capitalization in 2010.

Attention can be given to the fact that all pairs with ASEAN-5 countries are integrated into this research in both developed countries (Japan) and developing countries (India and China). This was a different case with Hendrawan and Gustyana (2011), who found that in its ASEAN-5's bivariate

Table 4. Paired cointegration test of eight stock price index.

No.	Index	Trace Statistic	Critical Value	Indication
1	JSX-KLSE	395.058	15.49471	Cointegrated
2	JSX-NIFTY50	408.8524	15.49471	Cointegrated
3	JSX-NIKKEI225	371.9816	15.49471	Cointegrated
4	JSX-PSEI	419.9285	15.49471	Cointegrated
5	JSX-SET	391.4744	15.49471	Cointegrated
6	JSX-SSEC	340.8294	15.49471	Cointegrated
7	JSX-STI	360.8097	15.49471	Cointegrated
8	KLSE-NIFTY50	197.2965	15.49471	Cointegrated
9	KLSE-NIKKEI225	360.2874	15.49471	Cointegrated
10	KLSE-PSEI	393.3406	15.49471	Cointegrated
11	KLSE-SET	395.9486	15.49471	Cointegrated
12	KLSE-SSEC	346.0475	15.49471	Cointegrated
13	KLSE-STI	362.6694	15.49471	Cointegrated
14	NIFTY50-NIKKEI225	364.714	15.49471	Cointegrated
15	NIFTY50-PSEI	408.6364	15.49471	Cointegrated
16	NIFTY50-SET	365.5794	15.49471	Cointegrated
17	NIFTY50-SSEC	342.1151	15.49471	Cointegrated
18	NIFTY50-STI	363.093	15.49471	Cointegrated
19	NIKKEI225-PSEI	366.3747	15.49471	Cointegrated
20	NIKKEI225-SET	342.7768	15.49471	Cointegrated
21	NIKKEI225-SSEC	316.5234	15.49471	Cointegrated
22	NIKKEI225-STI	322.2138	15.49471	Cointegrated
23	PSEI-SET	379.7293	15.49471	Cointegrated
24	PSEI-SSEC	345.3904	15.49471	Cointegrated
25	PSEI-STI	365.0141	15.49471	Cointegrated
26	SET-SSEC	314.3065	15.49471	Cointegrated
27	SET-STI	350.5715	15.49471	Cointegrated
28	SSEC-STI	295.0502	15.49471	Cointegrated

Source: Data processed (2020).

integration analysis for a period of 2000–2010, there were four pairs that were not integrated. These were Indonesia-Japan, Malaysia-Japan, Japan-Philippines, and Japan-Singapore. It can be seen that Japan was not integrated with four of ASEAN-5 countries a decade before. The finding from this paper (shown in Table 4) implies that in recent years, Japan markets are more integrated to ASEAN-5 than almost ten years ago. This can be influenced by the increasing market capitalization of Japan over the years.

4 CONCLUSIONS

Based on the result and discussion on the cointegration test of the stock price index in the capital markets of ASEAN-5 countries, China, Japan, and India, it is concluded that there is a cointegration of stock price indexes in ASEAN-5 countries, China, Japan, and India in 2015–2019. According to the paired cointegration test analysis, there is no country that dominates the capital market in ASEAN-5 and China, Japan, and India in 2015–2019. This is different from previous studies that conducted their research in a decade before. For future research, it is critical that further research takes a longer period so that the cointegration between exchanges at a longer time period can be analyzed. In addition to a longer period, it is also advisable to take a different object or add research objects from European or American countries to see the link between Asian and European or American exchanges. Finally, different methods to compare results between methods, for example, the Engel-Granger (EG) method, can also be employed to offer a diverse interpretation.

REFERENCES

Agyei-Ampomah, S. 2011. Stock market integration in Africa. *Managerial Finance, 37*(3), 242–256.

Bungin, B. 2013. *Penelitian Kualitatif*. Jakarta: Kencana.

Chien, M. S., Lee, C. C., Hu, T. C., & Hu, H. T. 2015. Dynamic Asian stock market convergence: Evidence from dynamic cointegration analysis among China and ASEAN-5. *Economic Modelling, 51*, 84–98.

Dantes, N. 2012. *Metode Penelitian*. Yogyakarta: ANDI.

Darmawan, D. 2013. *Metode Penelitian Kuantitatif*. Bandung: PT Remaja Rosdakarya.

Hendrawan, R., & Gustyana, T. T. 2011. Kointegrasi Bursa-Bursa Saham di Asia. *Jurnal Keuangan dan Perbankan, 15*(2), 159–167.

Johansen, S. 1988. Statistical Analysis of Cointegrating Vectors. *Journal of Economic, Dynamics and Control, 12*(2), 131–154.

Lee, Siew Peng & Isa, M. 2014. Stock market integration and the impact of the subprime financial crisis: A Malaysian perspective. *Asian Journal of Business and Accounting, 7*(1), 29–54.

Lipinsky, F., & Ong, L. L. 2014. Asia's Stock Markets: Are There Crouching Tigers and Hidden Dragons? *IMF Working Papers,* 14(37), 1.

Mailangkay, J. 2013. Integrasi Pasar Modal Indonesia dan Beberapa Bursa Di Dunia (Periode Januari 2013–Maret 2013). *EMBA, 1*(3), 722–731.

Ong, H. B., & Habibullah, M. S. 2012. Is China compatible with ASEAN-5? A gradual cointegration analysis. *Journal of Economic Studies, 39*(3), 356–367.

Rajwani, S. & Mukherjee, J. 2013. Is the Indian stock market cointegrated with other Asian markets?. *Management Research Review, 36*(9), 899–918.

Santosa, B. 2012. Integrasi Pasar Modal Kawasan Eropa. *Jurnal Ilmu Ekonomi dan Sosial, 1*(2), 166–173.

Sekaran, U. 2011. *Metodologi Penelitian untuk Bisnis*. Jakarta: Salemba Empat.

Seth, N., & Sharma, A. K. 2015. International stock market efficiency and integration: Evidences from Asian and US markets. *Journal of Advances in Management Research, 12*(2), 88–106.

Sujarweni, W., & Endrayatno, P. 2012. *Statistika untuk Penelitian*. Yogyakarta: Graham Ilmu.

Sunariyah. 2011. Pengantar Pengetahuan Pasar Modal. Yogyakarta: UPPSTIM YKPN.

Widarjono, A. 2013. *Ekonometrika*. Yogyakarta: UPP STIM YKPN.

Synergizing Management, Technology and Innovation in Generating Sustainable and Competitive Business Growth – Hendayani et al (eds)
© 2021 Taylor & Francis Group, London, ISBN 978-0-367-68756-4

The quality of financial statements in the public sector

Wahyuningsih, E. Kusmiati & S. Marlina
Faculty of Economics, Universitas Garut, Garut, West Java, Indonesia

ABSTRACT: This study aims to analyze the factors that affect the quality of financial statements in the Garut District Health Office. Factors analyzed were human resource competencies and the application of regional financial accounting systems. This research uses the verification method. Sampling was done through purposive sampling of as many as 25 people. The results showed that the quality of financial statements was significantly influenced by human resource competencies and the application of regional financial accounting systems. Human resource competency is measured by knowledge, individual abilities, and work attitudes, while the application of the regional financial accounting system is measured by recording, summarizing, and reporting.

1 INTRODUCTION

The financial statements are the output of the accounting system that is useful for providing information to those who will make that information the basis for making decisions (Bokšová et al. 2015). In Indonesia, the Regional Government Financial Report (LKPD) receives an assessment in the form of an opinion from the Financial Supervisory Agency (BPK). As regulated in Act Number 15 of 2004 concerning the Audit of State Financial Management and Responsibility, there are four opinions given by the examiner, namely, Unqualified Fair Opinion (WTP), Unqualified Opinion (WDP), Unqualified Opinion (TW), and Statement of Refusing Opinion or Not Giving Opinion (TMP).

In a pre-research interview, the head of the Regional Financial and Asset Management Agency (BPKAD) of Garut Regency said that "... although Garut Regency received a Fair Opinion without Exception (WTP) in 2015, the presentation of financial statements from the elements of each SKPD in Garut Regency is still not good because of the lack of human resource competence in presenting financial reports. This causes the preparation of financial statements that are presented not in accordance with Government Accounting Standards (SAP)." On the other hand, the head of finance of the Garut District Health Office said that "the presentation of the financial statements of the Garut District Health Office is still in the process of improving quality, although in reality most of the employees who present financial reports do not come from accounting graduates."

Some research that confirms that the presentation of financial statements is not good is influenced by the lack of human resource competence (Adhikari & Gårseth-nesbakk 2016; Anggriawan & Yudianto 2018; Arifuddin et al. 2019; Mardinan et al. 2018), as well as the application of regional financial accounting systems that are not good (Andrian et al. 2018; Cîrstea 2014; Poudel et al. 2014; Rahman et al. 2015).

The purpose of this study is based on the facts and literature mentioned above, namely, analyzing the factors that influence the quality of financial statements. More specifically, the factors under study are human resource competencies and regional financial accounting systems.

2 LITERATURE REVIEW

2.1 *Quality of financial statements*

Regulation of the Minister of Home Affairs of the Republic of Indonesia Number 13 of 2006 states that the purpose of preparing regional financial reports is to provide relevant information within a period of one reporting period, covering the financial position and all transactions carried out by the regional government. The quality of reports that can be reviewed from the qualitative characteristics of government financial statements that are normative prerequisites include relevant, reliable, comparable, and understandable (Arifuddin et al. 2019). The same thing was expressed by Barron, Chung, and Yong (2016), who explained that financial statements must be transparent and measure values fairly. Whereas Hairston and Brooks (2018) revealed that the quality of financial reporting requires that financial information must be relevant.

2.2 *Human resources competencies*

Human resources are important factors in organizations (Hakim 2015; Idrus et al. 2014; Long et al. 2017; Pitelis & Wagner 2018). Human resource competence is the ability of a person or individual of an organization (institutional) or a system to carry out its functions or authorities to achieve goals effectively and efficiently (Naranjeea et al. 2019). Indicators of human resources affect the presentation of quality financial statements, because if there is knowledge, individual abilities, and good work attitude in the presentation of financial statements, then the financial statements that are presented will be of high quality (Andrian et al. 2018; Ionescu 2017; Muda et al. 2017).

2.3 *Regional financial accounting systems*

The accounting system is the organization of forms, records, and reports that are coordinated in such a way as to provide the financial information needed by management to facilitate the management of the company (Ionescu 2017). According to Halim and Purnomo (2018), regional financial accounting is the accounting used to record economic events in economic entities within the local government environment. Regional government accounting is defined as the process of recording, classifying, and summarizing in certain ways in monetary measures, transactions, and events that are generally financial in nature and includes reporting of results in the administration of government affairs according to the principle of autonomy and assistance tasks with the principle of broadest autonomy in the system and principles of the Unitary State of the Republic of Indonesia (Djafar et al. 2019).

3 METHODS

3.1 *Characteristics and research stages*

The method used in this study is the verification method. The sampling of respondents was done by purposive sampling. Respondent criteria used as samples in this study are employees who have a relationship in presenting financial reports directly or indirectly at the Garut District Health Office of as many as 25 people.

The data that has been collected and then tested the instrument includes validity and reliability tests as well as classic assumption tests, including normality tests, autocorrelation tests, and heteroscedasticity tests. Furthermore, the data were tested using multiple linear regression tests.

3.2 *Conceptual framework and hypotheses*

The dependent variable in this study is the quality of financial statements that will be measured by relevance, reliability, which can be compared and can be understood. The first independent variable

Table 1. Results of multiple linear regression tests.

Coefficients[a]

Model	Unstandardized Coefficients B	Std. Error	Standardized Coefficients Beta	T	Sig.
(Constant)	59.089	14.882		1.453	.160
Human Resource Competencies	.243	.167	.260	3.970	.001
Application of Regional Financial Accounting Systems	.335	.127	.473	2.644	.015

a. Dependent Variable: Quality of Financial Statements

is human resource competency, which will be measured by knowledge, individual abilities, and work attitudes. While the second independent variable is the application of the regional financial accounting system, which will be measured by recording, summarizing, and reporting. The research hypothesis is structured as follows:

H_0 = Human resources competence and application of regional financial accounting systems do not affect the quality of financial statements

H_1 = Competence of human resources and application of regional financial accounting systems affect the quality of financial statements

4 RESULTS AND DISCUSSION

4.1 *Test instruments*

Validity test shows that all items of the questionnaire statement variable X1, variable X2, and Y variable were declared valid, with the r-calculated value greater than r-table (0.396). The reliability test shows the Cronbach's Alpha value of each variable is greater than the value of the reliability limit. This means that the instruments in this study can be trusted enough to be used as data collection tools.

4.2 *Classical assumption test*

The data with normal distribution is shown by the Kolmogorov-Smirnov significance value of $0.271 > 0.05$. The regression model without autocorrelation is shown by the Durbin-Watson (d) value of 1.579, based on the terms $du < d < 4 - du = 1.549 < 1.579 < 2.451$. The heteroscedasticity test shows that scatterplot is not indicated to form certain patterns, so it is concluded that the data is free from the relationship between independent variables with residual values.

4.3 *Multiple linear regression test*

Based on Table 1, the regression model used is $Y = 59.089 + 0.243X1 + 0.335X2$.

The amount of R Square is 0.296 or 29.6%, which means that the influence of the independent variable on the dependent variable is 29.6%, while the remaining 70.4% is influenced by other factors not examined

The F value is 4.636 with a significance value of 0.021. In this study, a significance level of 5% and a degree of freedom (df) of $(k = 2)$ and $(n - k = 23)$ were used, so an F table of 2.23 was obtained. These results have implications for the acceptance of H1 and rejection of H0. In

Table 2. Determination coefficient test results.

Model Summary

Model	R	R Square	Adjusted R Square	Std. Error of the Estimate
1	.545[a]	.296	.233	4.56694

a. Predictors: (Constant), Application of regional financial accounting systems, human resources competence

Table 3. Hypothesis test results.

ANOVA[a]

Model	Sum of Squares	Df	Mean Square	F	Sig.
Regression	193.387	2	96.694	4.636	.021[b]
Residual	458.853	22	20.857		
Total	652.240	24			

a. Dependent Variable: Quality of financial statements
b. Predictors: (Constant), Application of regional financial accounting systems, human resources competence

other words, the two independent variables affect the dependent variable. The better quality of the financial statements presented is greatly influenced by the increasing competency of human resources and the increasingly applied regional financial accounting system.

5 DISCUSSION

Several similar studies have been carried out in Indonesia. For example, research conducted by Stefani Marina Palimbong, Rura and Tawakkal (2010), who analyzed the competence of human resources on the quality of financial statements. The difference, in this study, included another independent variable, namely, the variable use of information technology. Another similar study was also stated by Andrian, Basri, and Diantimala (2018), who raised the competency of human resources. The difference is, the research links human resource competence with the performance of regional financial management, not related to the quality of financial statements. At the international level, no similar research has been found. This is possible because financial reporting in the public sector has applied information technology.

6 CONCLUSION

Good quality financial statements, illustrated by relevance, reliability, can be compared and can be understood. To get good quality financial reports, it is necessary to have quality human resource competencies and be supported by the implementation of a regional financial accounting system.

REFERENCES

Adhikari, P. and Gårseth-nesbakk, L. 2016. Implementing public sector accruals in OECD member states: Major issues and challenges. *Accounting Forum*. Elsevier Ltd, pp. 1–18. doi: 10.1016/j.accfor.2016.02.001.

Andrian, Y., Basri, H. and Diantimala, Y. 2018. The Influence of Information Systems Application for Regional Financial Management, Human Resources Competency and Understanding Of Government Accounting Standards on Regional Financial Management Performance of Aceh Besar Regency The Influence of

Inform. *International Journal of Academic Research in Business and Social Sciences*, 8(9), pp. 1–13. doi: 10.6007/IJARBSS/v8-i9/4537.

Arifuddin, Indrijawati, A. and Mansur, I. 2019. Mediation of Asset Optimization on the Effect of Asset Inventory and Quality of Human Resources in the Quality of Regional Government Financial Reports in Indonesia. *International Journal of Innovation, Creativity and Change*, 9(10), pp. 200–221.

Barron, O. E., Chung, S. G. and Yong, K. O. 2016. The effect of Statement of Financial Accounting Standards No. 157 Fair Value Measurements on analysts' information environment. *Journal Of Accounting And Public Policy*. Elsevier Inc., (157). doi: 10.1016/j.jaccpubpol.2016.04.001.

Bokšová, J., Horák, J. and Randáková, M. 2015. Financial Statements of Companies in the Czech Republic. *Procedia Economics and Finance*, 34(15), pp. 430–436. doi: 10.1016/S2212-5671(15)01651-2.

Cîrstea, A. 2014. The need for public sector consolidated financial statements. *Procedia Economics and Finance*. Elsevier B.V., 15(14), pp. 1289–1296. doi: 10.1016/S2212-5671(14)00590-5.

Djafar, J. S., Arifuddin and Syamsuddin. 2019. The Effect of Competence of human resources and the role of internal audit on Local Government Financial Reporting moderated by the Utilization of Regional Financial Accounting Information System. *Journal of Research in Business and Management*, 7(1), pp. 47–51.

Hairston, S. A. and Brooks, M. R. 2018. Derivative accounting and financial reporting quality: A review of the literature. *Advances in Accounting*. Elsevier, (May), pp. 1–15. doi: 10.1016/j.adiac.2018.10.003.

Halim, A. K. and Purnomo, P. I. N. 2018. The Effect Of Human Resources Competency And The Implementation Of The Regional Financial Accounting System Toward The Regional Financial Statement Quality. *International Journal of Business and Management Studies*, 07(02), pp. 81–91.

Ionescu, L. 2017. The Role Of Management In Public Sector Accounting. *Review of General Management*, 25(1), pp. 109–115.

Long, Y. *et al.* 2017. Management Accountant Practice in Malaysian Public Sector. *World Applied Sciences Journal*, 35(8), pp. 1482–1489. doi: 10.5829/idosi.wasj.2017.1482.1489.

Mardinan, T., Dahlan, M. and Fitriyah, F. K. 2018. Effect of Human Resources, Leadership Style, The Use of Information Technology and Internal Control on the Quality of Financial Statements. *Journal of Accounting Auditing and Business*, 1(1), pp. 43–57. doi: 10.24198/jaab.v1i1.18795.

MUDA, I. *et al.* 2017. The Influence Of Human Resources Competency And The Use Of Information Technology On The Quality Of Local Government Financial Report With Regional Accounting System As An Intervening. *Journal of Theoretical and Applied Information Technology*, 95, pp. 5552–5561.

Poudel, G., Hellmann, A. and Perera, H. 2014. The adoption of International Financial Reporting Standards in a non-colonized developing country: The case of Nepal. *Advances in Accounting, incorporating Advances in International Accounting*. Elsevier Ltd, pp. 1–8. doi: 10.1016/j.adiac.2014.03.004.

Rahman, I. K. A. *et al.* 2015. Management Accounting Best Practices Award for Improving Corruption in Public Sector Agencies. *Procedia Economics and Finance*. Elsevier B.V., 31(15), pp. 503–509. doi: 10.1016/S2212-5671(15)01192-2.

Synergizing Management, Technology and Innovation in Generating Sustainable and Competitive Business Growth – Hendayani et al (eds)
 ISBN 978-0-367-68756-4

Analysis of the potential groundwater tax in Garut Regency

L. Nurlaela, M. Romdhon, D. Qoriah & W. Ningsih
Universitas Garut, Garut, West Java, Indonesia

ABSTRACT: This research aims to know how much potential groundwater tax is in Garut Regency by using potential analysis methods. It also includes effectiveness, contribution, and growth rate. The method used in this research is a descriptive method using a qualitative approach. The data collection technique uses library research and field research with interviews and documentation. Based on the research results, the potential for groundwater tax owned by Garut Regency in 2019 is quite large, but it still requires tax optimization from the Garut Regency Bapenda so that the estimated land tax revenue can be achieved.

1 INTRODUCTION

One of the national development agenda aimed at improving the welfare and improvement of community living is regional development, various regions in Indonesia to make the development of the region to be better and can realize the objectives that have been established. In carrying out the duty of regional development of regional financing requires a reliable source of acceptance. The source of acceptance or funds can be obtained by digging potential sources of the region.

Regional tax and regional retribution is one of the sources of regional genuine income (PAD) which is important to finance the implementation of local governments. In accordance with law No. 28 of 2009, local tax and regional tax levy and regional levy is one of the sources of regional genuine income (PAD), which is important to finance the implementation of local governments. Local taxes are the mandatory contributions to the area owed by individuals or forced entities under law, by not obtaining direct remuneration and use for regional purposes for the maximum prosperity of people.

Many tourism objects in Garut Regency, which become the object of research, provide a significant development of the hotel or lodging around the tourist sites, which certainly becomes one of the good potentials for the land water tax revenues. Rich natural condition and good potential government of Garut Regency has not been able to maximize the revenue of the land in the water tax sector, many companies also do not have a groundwater drilling permit or a company that has not extended its license so that the tax cannot be realized because of the management, supervision and licensing managed by the provincial government under law number 23 year 2014 about local government.

Table 1 shows that the land water tax revenue is less optimal with existing potential. In the years 2016 and 2017 when the government set the target tax high enough, and the realization couldn't

Table 1. Data on soil water tax revenue in Garut Regency 2014–2018.

Year	Target	Realization	Increase/(Decrease)	Percentage (%)
2016	2.100.000.000	1.146.465.633	(953.534.367)	54,59%
2017	4.000.000.000	919.082.004	(3.080.917.996)	22,98%

reach the target. This is due to the year to year that the taxpayer has a tax decline and determination of the target and management of calculations held by the central or provincial government. Research on the matter includes Ardana et al. (2016), who showed that the land tax contribution to the local tax revenue of Kediri city in the fiscal year 2012–2014 is less than optimal. Gabriela et al. (2018) showed that the implementation of the groundwater tax collection process in South Minahasa Regency has been implemented in accordance with the understanding of the voting law number 28 year 2009, but has not been done thoroughly in accordance with the provisions of the legislation, so that it is not fully optimal. The public's lack of liability for land water tax obligations, there is a arrears, water meters are not applied as a whole, and there was confusion in the household effort/ Peter Berck et al. (2016), in this research, the tax impact on sales of bottled water dropped by almost 6%. Sales never fully recovered, even after-tax elimination. Based on this background, with the problem of potential, contribution, effectiveness, and growth rate of groundwater tax that occurred in Garut Regency, the researchers are interested in conducting research on "Analysis of the Potential Groundwater Tax in Garut Regency."

2 THEORETICAL FRAMEWORKS

2.1 *Definition of groundwater*

The definition of groundwater tax according to Siahaan (2016: 493) is as follows: "Ground water tax is a tax imposed on the extraction and or use of ground water. Ground water is meant by water that is contained in the soil or rock layers below the soil surface. Groundwater Tax is a type of Provincial Tax and was originally named Tax on the Extraction and Utilization of Groundwater and Surface Water (PPPABTAP) based on Law Number 34 of 2000."

According to Siahaan (2016: 496), he states that "the object of ground water tax is the extraction and or utilization of ground water." Groundwater is water that is contained in the soil layer or rock below the soil surface. In general, the groundwater tax calculation is in accordance with the following formula: Tax payable = Tax rate × Basic tax imposition = Tax rate × Water acquisition value Groundwater tax rate that has been set by the government is 20%, tax imposition is the acquisition value of groundwater, which takes into account factors such as water volume, water sources, water locations, and others. The acquisition value of groundwater is the calculation of V (volume of water) × Hda (basic price of water) and the basic price of water itself has been determined by the Regent periodically with the approval of the DPRD and takes into account the factors that affect NPAT, so see NPAT calculations (groundwater acquisition) are very decisive.

2.2 *Previous research*

Research conducted by Ardana et al. (2016) with the title Analysis of Groundwater Tax Potential and Its Contribution to Local Tax Revenues in Kediri City uses a descriptive research method with a qualitative approach, giving the results of the Contribution of Groundwater Tax to Regional Tax Revenues of Kediri City in the 2012 fiscal year—2014 is said to be lacking. The contribution of groundwater tax to local tax revenues in 2012 was 1.54%, in 2013 was 0.92%, and in 2014 its contribution was 0.98%. The growth rate of groundwater tax in the 2012–2014 fiscal year can be said to be not good, namely, there is still a minus (-) in 2013. This is due to a decrease in revenue due to a number of taxpayers who resigned or closed their businesses. In 2013 the growth rate was −4.36%, and in 2014 the growth rate increased to 16.63%.

3 RESEARCH METHODS

According to Nazir (2014: 107), "a variable is a concept that has various values." In this case it can be concluded that the variables in the study are anything that can be studied and researched that will provide value.

The variables used in this study are the potential for groundwater tax, effectiveness of groundwater tax, contribution of groundwater tax, and growth rate of groundwater tax. The method used by the writer in this research is a descriptive method with a qualitative approach Sugiyono (2017). The type of data used in this research is documentation data, and the data in question is the report on the realization of regional income for the 2013–2017 period obtained from the Regional Revenue Agency (BAPENDA) of Garut Regency. The data source used in this research is secondary data.

The data collection techniques used by the author in this study are literature research, books, notes, previous research journals, and other sources relevant to the author's research, field studies in the form of interviews, documentation of revenue realization from 2013 to 2017 from the Regional Revenue Agency (BAPENDA). Document study is a complement to the use of observation and interview methods in qualitative research.

4 RESULT AND DISCUSSION

Based on historical data on the development of land tax realization from years 2014–2018 obtained at the time of field research in BAPENDA (Regional revenue Board) Garut Regency, here are the targets and realization of groundwater tax in the period of five from the last years:

Table 2. Data on soil water tax revenue in Garut Regency 2014–2018.

Year	Target	Realization	Increase/ (Decrease)	Percentage (%)
2014	550,000,000	603,455,744	53,455,744	109,72%
2015	1,170,000,000	1,231,544,113	61,544,113	105,26%
2016	2,100,000,000	1,146,465,633	(953,534,367)	54,59%
2017	4,000,000,000	919,082,004	(3,080,917,996)	22,98%
2018	750,000,000	802,324,326	52,324,326	106,98%

The decline on the land and water tax realization on 2016 due to reduced taxpayer groundwater, the number of wells, did not use water meters so that the payment remained unchanged.There are many illegal wells at some point because the company has no permits, as well as some companies that have not extended the permits so the tax cannot be realized. For the year 2017 the decline in the realization of groundwater tax is because the target set by the government is very high because it includes a surface water tax target while the realization is only from groundwater tax because there was a change in legislation.

Effectiveness is the measure of success or absence of a company, institution, or organization in achieving its objectives. The level of effectiveness of groundwater tax in Garut Regency in 2014–2018 is as follows:

Table 3. Water tax effectiveness rate for soil Year 2014–2018 (in Rupiah).

Year	Land and Water Tax Target	Land and Water Tax Realization	Effectivity (%)	Criteria
2014	550.000.000	603.455.744	109,72%	Effective
2015	1.170.000.000	1.231.544.113	105,26%	Effective
2016	2.100.000.000	1.146.465.633	54,59%	Uneffective
2017	4.000.000.000	919.082.004	22,98%	Uneffective
2018	750.000.000	802.324.326	106,98%	Effective

5 CONCLUSSION

Based on the results of research and discussion that have been carried out on the analysis of the potential for groundwater tax in Garut Regency, in general, groundwater tax in Garut Regency can be said to have good potential. Researchers can draw general conclusions about the focus of the problem in this study, including the potential, effectiveness, and contribution and growth rate of groundwater tax, which will be described as follows.

a. The potential for groundwater tax owned by Garut Regency in 2019 is quite large, but it still requires tax optimization from the Garut Regency Bapenda so that the estimated land tax revenue can be achieved.
b. The level of effectiveness of the groundwater tax in Garut Regency in 2014–2015 is good, which is at the "effective" level. However, in 2016–2017 the effectiveness of groundwater tax decreased to "ineffective." Groundwater tax "effectiveness" criteria can be obtained if the received realization exceeds the determined target.
c. Judging from the contribution of groundwater tax to regional taxes 2014–2018 is in the criteria of "very poor." This is due to the decrease in groundwater taxpayers from year to year. In addition, there are still many violations committed by groundwater taxpayers, such as many companies that do not have permits and have not extended their permits.
d. Groundwater tax growth rate is fluctuating. This is because groundwater taxpayers are taxpayers as taxpayers, because part of the groundwater tax is converted to surface water taxpayers and the provincial government. The groundwater tax growth rate in 2014 was included in the "very successful" criteria, but from 2015–2018 it was included in the "unsuccessful" criteria.

From the various conclusions that have been described above, for input as consideration for the Garut Regency Bapenda in an effort to increase the potential, effectiveness, contribution, and growth rate of the groundwater tax and for further researchers, it can be suggested as follows:

1. It is necessary to carry out regular data collection on groundwater tax objects, as well as to conduct regular outreach to taxpayers in order to increase taxpayer awareness of their obligations in paying taxes. It is hoped that the Bapenda of Garut Regency can also impose strict sanctions on taxpayers who violate the rules so that illegal well drilling is not found and there is no installation of water meters at the company.
2. The target setting process should pay attention to the actual potential, so that revenues from groundwater tax can increase.
3. It is hoped that the next research will discuss the same topic in order to expand the scope of the research as well as the research year.

REFERENCES

Ardana, P, dkk. 2016. Analisis Potensi Pajak Air Tanah dan Kontribusinya terhadap Penerimaan Pajak Daerah Kota Kediri. From: (http://perpajakan.studentjournal.ub.ac.id/index.php/perpajakan/article/download/228/223).

Berck, Lange, Stevens, Boas, 2016. Measuring Consumer Responses to a Bottle Water Tax Policy. *American Journal of Agricultural Economics,* Volume 98, Issue 4, July 2016, Pages 981–996, https://doi.org/10.1093/ajae/aaw037.

Gabriela. 2018. Implementasi Proses Pemungutan dan Kontribusi Penerimaan Pajak Air Tanah di Kabupaten Minahasa Selatan. From:https://ejournal.unsrat.ac.id/index.php/gc/article/download/19116/18674&ved=2ahUKEwiDxI-y7_bhAhUJVa0KHRuECc8QFjAAegQIABAC).

Nazir. 2014. Metode Penelitian. Bogor: Ghalia Indonesia.

Siahaan, Marihot P. 2016. Pajak Daerah dan Retribusi Daerah. Edisi Revisi. Jakarta: Rajawali.

Sugiyono. 2017. Metode Penelitian Kuantitatif, Kualitatif, dan R&D. Bandung: Alfabeta.

Undang-Undang Nomor 23 Tahun 2014 tentang Pemerintahan Daerah.

Undang-Undang Nomor 28 Tahun 2009 tentang Pajak Daerah dan Retribusi Daerah (Lembaran Negara Republik Indonesia Tahun 2009 Nomor 130).

Synergizing Management, Technology and Innovation in Generating Sustainable and Competitive Business Growth – Hendayani et al (eds)
© 2021 Taylor & Francis Group, London, ISBN 978-0-367-68756-4

Cement firm's equity valuation in Indonesia Stock Exchange

S. Hariyanto & F.T. Kristanti
Faculty of Economics and Business, Telkom University, Bandung, West Java, Indonesia

ABSTRACT: This thesis analyses fair prices of four company stocks in the Cement subsector, namely Indocement Tunggal Prakarsa (INTP), Semen Baturaja Tbk (SMBR), Holcim Indonesia Tbk (SMCB), and Semen Indonesia Tbk (SMGR) using the discounted cash flow (DCF) free cash flow to firm (FCFF) method and relative valuation (RV) approaches; price to earnings ratio (PER), and price to book value (PBV). Each approach used three scenarios of optimistic, moderate, and pessimistic. Results of this study indicated that by comparing the stock prices to their intrinsic value of the stock valuation of the DCF-FCFF, the stock market prices as of January 2, 2019, according to all scenarios, showed that INTP, SMCB, and SMBR were overvalued, while SMGR was undervalued. Relative valuation using PER approach in all scenarios indicated overvalued for INTP, SMGR, SMCB, and SMBR. Finally, through PBV approach the relative valuation of INTP and SMGR in optimistic scenario were undervalued, while SMCB and SMBR were overvalued. In the moderate and pessimistic scenarios INTP, SMGR, SMCB, and SMBR were overvalued.

1 INTRODUCTION

The cement industry is the basis of industrial and economic development in Indonesia. It is very important in development and construction, especially infrastructure. Data from the Indonesian Cement Association shows that cement consumption in 2018 reached around 70 million tons. The growth rate reached 8% over the past 5 years. It is predicted that in 2019 the demand will reach 75 million tons. Even though the cement industry has considerable potential, the Stock Price Index has fluctuated in the last 5 years. In addition, the return value of the shares also fluctuates. So, it is necessary to further analyze the company's valuation before investing to minimize the risk. Therefore, before deciding to invest in a stock, it is strongly recommended that an investor conduct a stock valuation analysis in advance to find out the intrinsic value of the stock.

2 BASIC THEORY AND RESEARCH FRAMEWORK

2.1 *Discounted cash flow and free cash flow to firm*

Cash flow is a number of in and out flows of cash as the result of company activities. The discounted cash flow (DCF) valuation method is an asset valuation method by assuming the asset value is the present value of cash flows that can be generated by the asset, discounted at a certain ratio that represents the risk of the cash flow (Damodaran 2006: 35). The basic formula for calculating cash flows that can be generated by this method is as follows:

$$Value\ of\ asset = \frac{E(CF_1)}{(1+r)^1} + \frac{E(CF_2)}{(1+r)^2} + \frac{E(CF_3)}{(1+r)^3} + \ldots + \frac{E(CF_n)}{(1+r)^n} \tag{1}$$

The DCF method consists of three types of valuation approaches, which are dividend discounted model (DDM), free cash flow to equity (FCFE), and free cash flow to the firm (FCFF). FCFF is the position of cash flows to all stakeholders including stockholders, bondholders, and preferred stockholders (Damodaran 2012). Value of firm is obtained from the present value of cash flows, assuming all equity financing plus the net present value of the tax is made using debt. The following is the FCFF formula:

$$FCFF = EBIT(1 - tax) + Depreciation + Capex - Change\ of\ Working\ Capital \quad (2)$$

The value of firm is calculated by discounting FCFF on WACC (weighted average cost of capital).

$$Value\ of\ Firm = \sum_{t=1}^{t=n} \frac{CF\ to\ Firm_t}{(1 + WACC)^t} \quad (3)$$

However, if the company uses several sources of funds, the calculated cost of capital is the weighted average cost of all capital used (WACC), that can be calculated as follows:

$$WACC = Comp\ of\ equity^*rate\ of\ equity + Comp\ of\ Debt^*rate\ of\ debt)^*(1 - tax) \quad (4)$$

Terminal value is the present value of all future cash flows obtained after a certain period of time.

$$TV = \frac{FCFF_t}{(WACC - gn)} \quad (5)$$

Enterprise value (EV) is the sum of FCFF's present values and the present value of a TV.

$$EV = Total\ PV\ of\ FCFF + Total\ PV\ of\ TV \quad (6)$$

Equity value is the sum of the enterprise value and total equality minus cash. Equity value formulas are as follows:

$$Equity\ Value = EV - Total\ Debt + Cash \quad (7)$$

2.2 *Valuation relative through the approach of price earnings ratio and price book value*

In the relative valuation method, assets are assessed based on the asset prices in the market. PER is the market price of a stock divided by its EPS. This ratio calculates the company's ability to generate profits. The smaller the PER stock of a company, the better it will be to buy. It means that the company has better performance in generating profits. If the company's PER value is still low and smaller than other similar companies, it can be said that the company is undervalued and becomes an attractive investment choice. The following is the formula of PER:

$$PER = \frac{Market\ Value\ of\ Equity}{Equity\ Earnings} \quad (8)$$

PBV ratio allows investors to compare the book value of a stock with its market value directly. The PBV ratio can provide information on the frequency of the market value of a stock that is valued from its book value. A high PBV of stocks compared to other stocks in the same industry indicates that the stock price is relatively expensive. Lower PBV value of a stock indicates that the stock is categorized undervalued. Therefore, it is very good to decide long-term investments.

The PBV formulas are as follows:

$$PBV = \frac{Market\ Value\ of\ Equity}{Book\ Value\ of\ Equity} \quad (9)$$

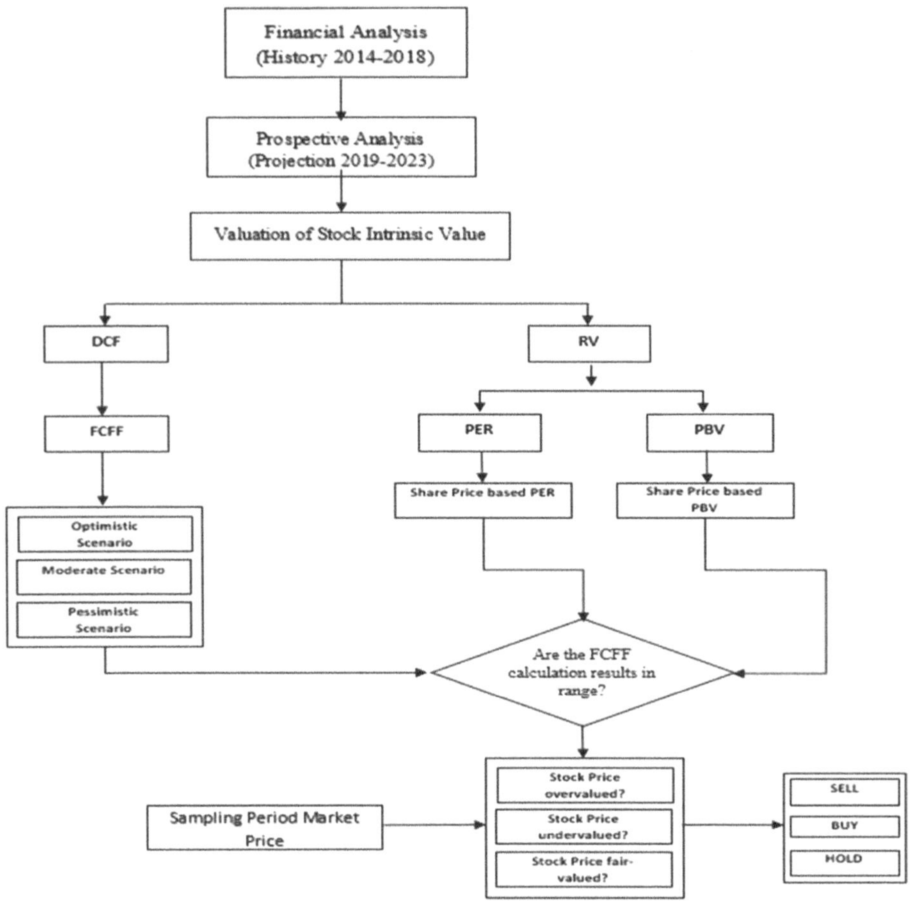

Figure 1. Research framework.

2.3 *Research framework*

The research framework used in this study refers to the process in Figure 1:

1. Historical analysis of the company's financial performance. Analyses were done using a financial ratio analysis to examine managements of asset, liability, and company equity.
2. Projection of revenue, balance sheet, and cash flow. The projections were performed to determine the present value of cash flow that was expected to occur in the future. Three scenarios involved in the projections were optimistic scenario (above historical growth of the company), moderate scenario (in accordance with the historical growth of the company), and pessimistic scenario (below the historical growth of the company).
3. Valuation of fair price using DCF-FCFF. In this step, FCFF, WACC, TV, and EV calculations were performed.
4. Price earnings ratio (PER) and price book value (PBV) calculation.
5. Intrinsic value of shares analysis and recommendation. A comparison of intrinsic value with market price will conclude the stock price is overvalued, undervalued, or fair-valued. When the intrinsic value < market price, the stock price is overvalued, otherwise if the intrinsic value > market price, the stock price is undervalued.

3 DISCUSSION

3.1 *Pessimistic scenario*

Based on the calculation, processing, and analysis of stock valuations in pessimistic scenario, the results can be summarized as in Table 1:

3.2 *Moderate scenario*

The results of stock valuations in moderate scenario can be summarized as in Table 2:

3.3 *Optimistic scenario*

The results of stock valuations in optimistic scenario can be summarized as in Table 3:

3.4 *Analysis result*

Based on tables, we can find out the intrinsic value of INTP, SMGR, SMCB, SMBR stocks using the DCF valuation method and the relative valuation method, where the results were compared with the stock market position price as of January 2, 2019. Based on Table 1, valuation using

Table 1. Valuation result of pessimistic scenario.

				Relative Valuation							
Pessimistic Scenario	Market Value	Pessimistic Intrinsic	Intrinsic Valuation	Industry PER	Pessimistic PER	Intrinsic PER	PER Valuation	Industry PBV	Pessimistic PBV	Intrinsic PBV	PBV Valuation
INTP	18,100	12,785	Overvalued	44.00	21.92	9,018	Overvalued	2.54	2.03	14,443	Overvalued
SMGR	11,475	13,230	Undervalued		21.13	5,512	Overvalued		2.40	10,829	Overvalued
SMCB	1,885	889	Overvalued		−13.14	−563	Overvalued		1.06	788	Overvalued
SMBR	1,705	497	Overvalued		22.10	856	Overvalued		1.42	955	Overvalued

Table 2. Valuation result of moderate scenario.

				Relative Valuation							
Moderate Scenario	Market Value	Moderate Intrinsic	Intrinsic Valuation	Industry PER	Moderate PER	Intrinsic PER	PER Valuation	Industry PBV	Moderate PBV	Intrinsic PBV	PBV Valuation
INTP	18,100	13,359	Overvalued	44.00	22.59	9,293	Overvalued	2.54	2.12	15,091	Overvalued
SMGR	11,475	13,912	Undervalued		21.90	5,711	Overvalued		2.52	11,388	Overvalued
SMCB	1,885	989	Overvalued		−14.72	−631	Overvalued		1.18	876	Overvalued
SMBR	1,705	681	Overvalued		27.20	1,054	Overvalued		1.95	1,307	Overvalued

Table 3. Valuation result of optimistic scenario.

				Relative Valuation							
Optimistic Scenario	Market Value	Optimistic Intrinsic	Intrinsic Valuation	Industry PER	Optimistic PER	Intrinsic PER	PER Valuation	Industry PBV	Optimistic PBV	Intrinsic PBV	PBV Valuation
INTP	18,100	16,946	Overvalued	44.00	26.63	10,954	Overvalued	2.54	2.69	19,143	Undervalued
SMGR	11,475	14,263	Undervalued		22.29	5,813	Overvalued		2.58	11,675	Undervalued
SMCB	1,885	1,138	Overvalued		−17.13	−734	Overvalued		1.36	1,008	Overvalued
SMBR	1,705	788	Overvalued		29.95	1,161	Overvalued		2.25	1,513	Overvalued

DCF-FCFF of INTP, SMCB, SMBR were *overvalued*, while SMGR was *undervalued*. Relative valuation using PER approach indicated *overvalued* for INTP, SMGR, SMCB, and SMBR. Also, the relative valuation through PBV approach of INTP, SMGR, SMCB, SMBR were *overvalued*. Based on Table 2 in moderate scenario indicated that INTP, SMCB, SMBR were *overvalued*, while SMGR was *undervalued*. Relative valuation using PER approach indicated *overvalued* for INTP, SMGR, SMCB, and SMBR. Also, through PBV approach the relative valuation of INTP, SMGR, SMCB, SMBR were *overvalued*. And the last based on Table 3 in optimistic scenario indicated that INTP, SMCB, SMBR were *overvalued*, while SMGR was *undervalued*. Relative valuation using PER approach indicated *overvalued* for INTP, SMGR, SMCB, and SMBR. Finally, through PBV approach the relative valuation of INTP, SMGR were undervalued, while SMCB, SMBR were *overvalued*. The price of INTP stock, as of January 2, 2019, was IDR 18,100, which when compared to intrinsic value using DCF-FCFF, PER, and PBV approach, most of the stock valuation results were *overvalued*, it can be concluded that the stock market prices were categorized to the expensive stocks price. From the investment point of view, it is better to sell INTP stocks and it is not recommended to buy the stocks because the stock is expensive. For SMGR stock, it is known that as of January 2, 2019, its price was IDR 11,475, and when it was compared to the intrinsic price using DCF-FCFF, PER, and PBV approach, most of the stock valuation results were *undervalued*, the current stock market price considered to be the best price. As the conclusion, in this condition SMGR stocks should be recommended to be bought because the stock market price is below its intrinsic price. As of January 2, 2019, the SMCB stock price was IDR 1,885 and SMBR was IDR 1,705. When it was compared to the intrinsic price using DCF-FCFF, PER, and PBV approach, it was shown that the stock market price is now included in the expensive stock price category because most of the stock valuation results were in *overvalued* conditions. Consequently, from the investment point of view, it is better to sell SMCB stocks and it is not recommended to buy the stocks because the stock is expensive.

4 CONCLUSION

In accordance with the stock market prices as of January 2, 2019, this study concluded that when the prices were compared to their intrinsic value of the stock valuation of DCF-FCFF in all scenarios it showed that INTP, SMCB, and SMBR were overvalued, while SMGR were undervalued. Relative valuation using PER approach in all scenarios indicated overvalued for INTP, SMGR, SMCB, and SMBR. Finally, through PBV approach the relative valuation of INTP and SMGR in optimistic scenario were undervalued, while SMCB and SMBR were overvalued. In the moderate and pessimistic scenarios INTP, SMGR, SMCB, and SMBR were overvalued. This study provides information for investors that SMGR stocks are good stocks to buy. This situation gives investors room for profit until the market price moves to equal the intrinsic price of the stock. SMGR need only to maintain or even improve their performance so that many of their stocks will attract investors. In contrast, this research also described that INTP, SMCB, and SMBR should split their stock to improve their market stock prices. Investors should refrain from buying INTP, SMCB, and SMBR stocks until the stocks are split. By doing a stock split, in addition to obtaining stock prices that are close to their intrinsic prices, they will also get fresh funds that can be used to improve the company performance. Finally, for the next research, it is necessary to try other valuation methods such as contingent claims for the valuation of company stocks.

REFERENCES

Charumathi & Suraj. 2014. The Reability Of Dividend Discount Model in Valuation of Bank Stocks at The Bombay Stock Exchange. *International Journal of Accounting and Taxation*. Vol. 2, No. 2, pp. 111–127.

Damodaran, A. 2012. Investment Valuation: Tools and Technique for Determining the Value of Any Asset, New York: John Wiley and Sons Inc.

Ivanovska, N., Ivanovski, Z. & Narasanov, Zoran. 2014. Fundamental analysis and discounted free cash flow valuation of stock at MSE. *UTMS Journal of Economics* 5 (1): 11–24.

Marfani & Hendrawan. (2018). Metal and Mineral Mining Firm's Equity Valuation in Indonesia Stock Exchange. *The 2nd International Conference on Inclusive Business in the Changing World2019 (2ndI-CIB2019).*

Myers, S. C., Brealey, R. A., & Marcus, A. J. 2001. *Fundamentals of Corporate Finance (3rd Edition).* New York: Mc Graw-Hill.

Neaxie, L. V, & Hendrawan, Riko. 2017. Stock Valuation in Telecomunication Firms: Evidence from Indonesian Stock Exchange. *Journal of Economic & Management Perspective* (ISSN:2523-5338), Vol.11, Issue 3, Sep-2017.

Saptono, & Kristanti. 2018. Does the stock of Indonesian provider tower industry have a fair value? *Global Journal of Business & Social Science Review* (Volume 6, No.4, Oct-Dec 2018, Pages 130 to 139).

Zemba, S & Hendrawan, R. 2018. *Does Rapidly Growing Revenues Always Produces an Excellent Company's Values DCF & PE Valuation Assessment on Hospital Industry*.ISCLO 6th.

Synergizing Management, Technology and Innovation in Generating Sustainable and Competitive Business Growth – Hendayani et al (eds)
© 2021 Taylor & Francis Group, London, ISBN 978-0-367-68756-4

Brand mapping strategy for increasing brand awareness of Mentailovers

D. Harini & W. Dhewanto
Institut Teknologi Bandung, Bandung, Indonesia

ABSTRACT: The increasing number of companies from various industries usually supports the economic growth of a country. One of them is the culinary industry, which contributes enough funds to state revenue. Mentailovers is one of the businesses included in the culinary industry. Mentailovers only uses Instagram ads as a promotion tool. The limitations of promotional media make Mentailovers unknown to many people. The external analysis will be carried out using consumer analysis by distributing questionnaires, while the internal analysis will be using STP analysis. After that, the researcher breaks down the root cause using Fishbone. Using a brand mapping strategy, a new company can create personal branding for their own business. The solution is to create a new market segment and make a referral program that is expected to increase brand awareness, make innovative products, and increase engagement with consumers through attractive photos.

1 INTRODUCTION

The culinary industry has a large market, especially in Indonesia. The need for food and beverage industry players to take advantage of the existing potential market, which is Indonesia, is 258.7 million people. In Indonesia, most of the food that exists today is overseas food that is accepted and liked by the people of Indonesia. The behavior of individuals has changed with technological developments and is compared to coming directly to an offline store. They tend to shop online because it is more convenient, more practical, and saves time. With the Internet, people can use social media as a marketing and promotional tool because many business features are available for advertising. Statista Research Department (statista.com, 2019) stated that Indonesia is one of the biggest online markets in the world. It shows that there is an increase in technology users, specifically social media users. These opportunities are related to business promotion through social media or using the Internet and technology. The large number of partners who collaborate with Grab in terms of food indicates that many consumers have also switched to ordering food through digital applications (Ulfiana, 2019). These conditions make Mentailovers build an online business that has been running for five months. In the last three months, Mentailovers sales have declined continuously because of the limitations of the channel that is used that makes Mentailovers not known by the public. This research focuses on building personal branding for Mentailovers as a new company that wants to introduce their brand to the public to develop their business as a start-up company and increase brand awareness.

2 METHODS

2.1 *Conceptual framework*

A conceptual framework is concerned to increase brand awareness for a new company or a company that wants to build their brand. This framework will describe the strategy to increase brand awareness. Figure 1 shows the conceptual framework for this research.

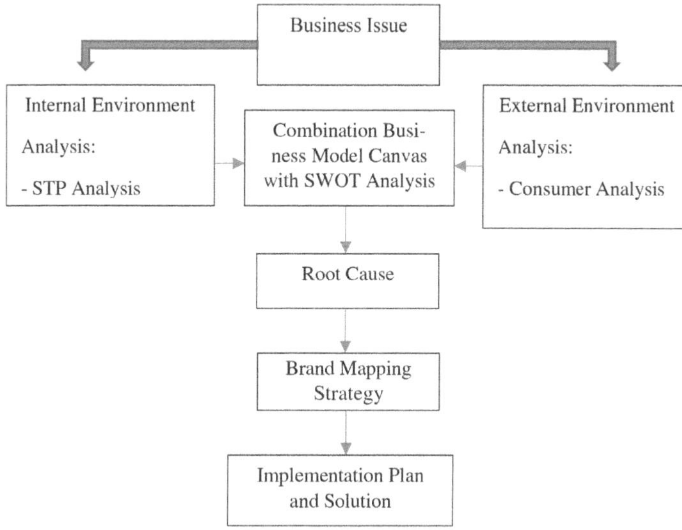

Figure 1. Conceptual framework.

2.2 *Research method*

This study uses qualitative and quantitative methods. Qualitative research aims to find insight about a new product idea and identify the target market in greater depth and detail. Quantitative research intends to describe the target market through numbers so that it can be measured and can make better strategies through the data obtained (Schiffman, 2015, p. 423). The quantitative data obtained from questionnaire data is in the form of numbers, while qualitative is in the form of explanations and translation of results from the figures obtained from the questionnaire. The research method uses primary data obtained directly through questionnaires and secondary data obtained from Mentailovers sales reports. The questionnaire contains questions about product segments and brand awareness. This questionnaire aims to get answers about the respondents' views of the Mentailovers brand. The questionnaires were distributed to 140 respondents who are customers in the Mentailovers segment. Mentailovers also distributed the questionnaire to customer via Google Forms by sending a link.

3 RESULTS AND DISCUSSIONS

3.1 *STP analysis*

The internal analysis used is segmenting, targeting, and positioning to find out and understand customers that the researcher can reach and make targets see our position by comparing it with other competitors. After understanding what consumers want, the researcher can make the appropriate strategy so that the products offered become more efficient and more effective because it is in line with what consumers want.

3.1.1 *Segmenting*

Market segmentation is the process of dividing a market into subsets of customers with routine needs or characteristics. Each part represents a customer group with shared needs that are different from those shared by other groups (Schiffman & Wisenblit, 2015, p. 52). The generation targeted by Mentailovers is Generation Y and Generation Z because they are fluent in technology and can follow the business process of Mentailovers, whose sales are based on online stores. Besides, these

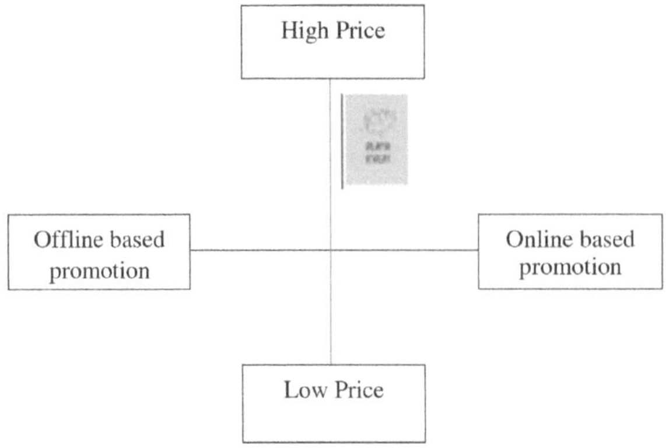

Figure 2. Positioning.

two generations have been able to earn money and meet their own needs and even their families, so that they can afford to buy food from Mentailovers.

3.1.2 *Targeting*

Targeting consists of selecting the segments that the company views as prospective customers and pursuing them (Schiffman & Wisenblit, 2015, p. 52). The target of Mentailovers is people aged 18–24 years who are in Bandung, like Japanese food, like to buy instant food, and are Y and Z generations who are fluent in using technology, because Mentailovers are online-based and productive.

3.1.3 *Positioning*

Positioning is the process by which a company creates a distinct image and identity for its products, services, and brands in the consumers' minds (Schiffman & Wisenblit, 2015, p. 52).

For the position in terms of price, Mentailovers is in an area where the price is quite affordable compared to the others. The online-based promotion is low compared to others because it only relies on Instagram as a promotional channel.

3.2 *Consumer analysis*

The internal analysis used is the consumer analysis. Consumer analysis needs to be applied to find out market needs, targets that are in line with the company, demographics, and other relevant information that the company needs through market research (MBA Skool, 2011). By identifying customers, the information obtained is processed to create a brand mapping strategy, so that it can show what media consumers often use and what strategies should be applied. The results of the questionnaire are shown in Table 1.

3.3 *Root cause*

The purpose of this problem is that sales have decreased from March until May. Three dimension factors causing the decline in revenue is from the promotion, place, and product factors. Each factor has several causes that trigger these factors. The root of the Mentailovers's problem that needs to be focused on is the low brand awareness of the buyer because of lack of promotion, and it causes sales and revenue loss of Mentailovers.

Table 1. Questionnaire results.

Question:	Answers:
Gender	Female
Age	24–35
Profession	Employee
Income per month	1.100.000–4.000.000
More often cook at home or buy food from outside?	Outside
What platform do you use often to shop for food?	Instagram
What factors influenced you in making the decision to buy product?	Interesting photos and contents on social media
Do you know Mentailovers brand?	No (70.7%)
How do you know the brand?	From Instagram ads (58.9%), friends (21%)
Which aspects of innovation do you suggest if you want to buy food?	Varian topping (48%)

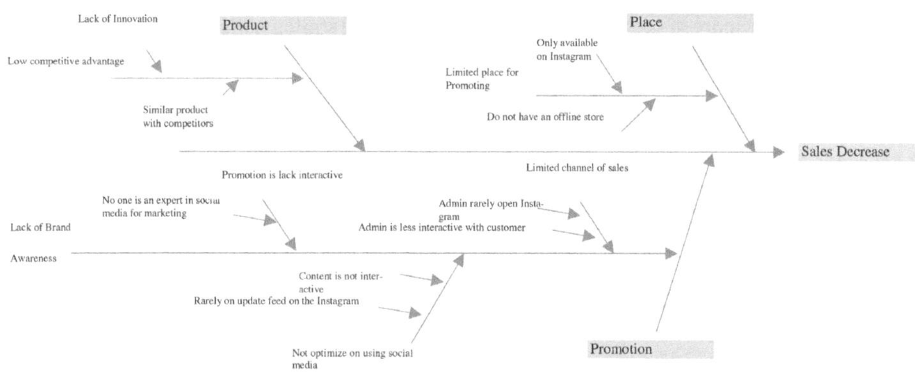

Figure 3. Root cause.

3.4 *Brand mapping strategy*

Brand awareness refers to customers, when they can recall and recognize a brand in different situations and associate it with a logo, name, and symbol. In building a strong brand, four questions will relate to the steps that will be carried out later (Keller, 2013, pp. 107–108): Brand identity, Mentailovers has to show their product; brand meaning, how Mentailovers can communicate their product; brand responses, what customer feel about Mentailovers's brand and product; brand relationship, Mentailovers must create a relationship between the brand and feel of customers. Then, researchers continue to brand mapping strategy. Brand mapping strategy is a theory that originated from Karen Leland (Leland, 2016). This theory is used as a tool for companies when they create a business and want to develop personal branding on their business. Figure 4 shows several steps needed to carry out a brand mapping strategy.

3.4.1 *Understand tactical landscape*

At this stage, the researcher needs to know what media that Mentailovers use to offer a product to the customer. The media is adjusted to the results of the questionnaire where customers targeted by Mentailovers use a lot of social media to buy food.

3.4.2 *Determine your best tactical approach*

At this stage, the researcher has to know some things to consider in choosing a tactic or strategy in running a business. Researchers compare products with other competitors based on promotion

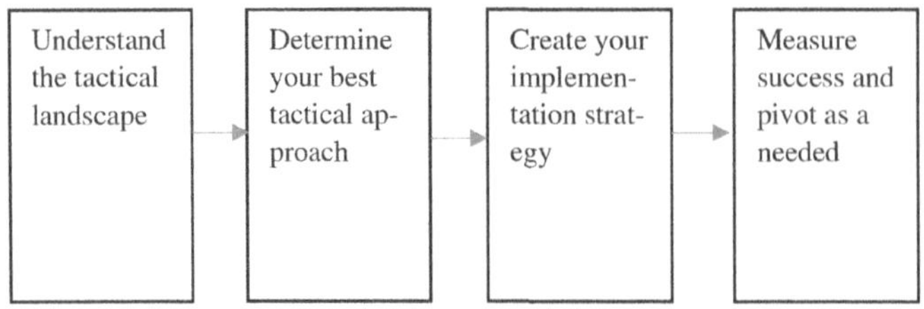

Figure 4. Brand mapping strategy.

and price. Because Mentailovers are online-based, it is necessary to compare content and product photos displayed to customers because the results of the questionnaire state that interesting photos and content are the main things that determine online purchasing decisions.

3.4.3 *Create your implementation strategy*

After discovering the core of the tactics of your brand mapping strategy, the next step is to determine the plan and put it into action. For each tactic, consideration needs to be given as to which method is to be carried out or executed.

3.4.4 *Measure success and pivot as a needed*

After the strategy is created and executed, the researcher needs to maintain the success of the strategy by periodic checking by looking at the following three areas:

1. Customers
   Customers are the most important thing in running a business. Mentailovers needs to focus on generating new prospects, increasing marketing channels for company revenue.
2. Credibility
   Does a company become better known and become more trusted by the people? In order to increase customer brand awareness of the brand Mentailovers, the channel needs to be expanded.
3. Cash
   By dividing into two segments, innovating, collaborating is certainly expected to brand awareness and impact directly to Mentailovers sales because by seeing such huge opportunities, it allows Mentailovers to add revenue.

4 CONCLUSION

The data from the questionnaire show many respondents who were not familiar with the Mentailovers brand. This is lacking because almost half are friends offered directly. To build personal branding, the researcher recommends using the brand mapping strategy theory. There are four steps to build personal branding and then increase brand awareness. First, researchers have to understand the tactical landscape. Second, determine the best tactical approach. Third, create the implementation strategy. On this step, the researcher gives some recommendation that can increase brand awareness: making innovation product (separate into two segments, those are collaborating with event or wedding organizer and make frozen mentai), co-branding, collaborate with influencer (it can make customers trust with our product), make attractive photos and content, make a referral program (give a discount for a loyal customer), expanded distribution channel (join with food delivery applications). On the last step, Mentailovers can increase brand awareness of customers, so it can increase sales too. The wider the channel provided by Mentailovers, the more brand awareness increases.

REFERENCES

Agency, T. C. 2018. Retrieved from https://databoks.katadata.co.id/datapublish/2018/03/05/2017-pengeluaran-konsumsi-rumah-tangga-rp-7626-triliun

Fakhrurazi, M. 2018. Proposed New Marketing Strategy to Increase Monthly Revenue of New Fashion Brand. 27.

Isoraite, M. 2016. Marketing Mix Theoritical Aspects. *International Journal of Research – Granthaalayah*, 25–37.

Keller, K. L. 2013. *Strategic Brand Management*. Pearson Education.

Leland, K. T. 2016. *The Brand Mapping Strategy*. Entrpreneurial Media.

Leon G. Schiffman, J. L. 2015. *Consumer Behaviour*. New York: Pearson Education.

MBA Skool. (2011). *Consumer Analysis*. Retrieved from https://www.mbaskool.com/business-concepts/marketing-and-strategy-terms/11977-consumer-analysis.html

Olsen, E. (n.d.). *Internal and External Analysis*. Retrieved from https://onstrategyhq.com/resources/internal-and-external-analysis/

Schiffman, L. G., & Wisenblit, J. L. 2015. *Consumer Behaviour*. England: Pearson Edication Limited.

Statista.com. (2019).

Ulfiana, A. D. (n.d.). Retrieved from Katadata.co.id: Digital Data Apps have begun to be favored by consumers for food orders.

Synergizing Management, Technology and Innovation in Generating Sustainable and Competitive Business Growth – Hendayani et al (eds)
© 2021 Taylor & Francis Group, London, ISBN 978-0-367-68756-4

Analysis Black-Scholes and Binomial model on the Rupiah against the Dollar for hedging in 2018

N. Karlina & B. Rikumahu
Telkom University, Bandung, West Java, Indonesia

ABSTRACT: Several currencies are spelled out from the group of convertible currencies, or in other words, currencies that are the trust of economic actors throughout the world because they have a value that is believed to be stable. This research will examine the US dollar against the rupiah, which will depend on market policies and mechanism. In 2018 there was sustainable economics where the value of the rupiah weakness and also touch volatility up to 25% and makes economics actors worry about protecting their assets. So, Bank Indonesia as a central bank provides to protect assets by using derivatives. The model to be used in this research is the Black-Scholes model, and it will be compared with the binomial model for the case of exchange of rupiah against the dollar, and both models are measured using average mean square error (AMSE) to see how small the error is obtained.

1 INTRODUCTION

Currency exchange rates are a macroeconomic variable that is considered very important because the exchange rate can affect economic stability. In the middle of 2018, the rupiah weakened significantly against the dollar; according to an article from liputan6.com, the Rupiah weakened 9.52% throughout the year from 2016 to 2018. To overcome this pressure, Bank Indonesia intervened both through the spot exchange rate (direct exchange rate) and forward exchange rate and temporarily stabilized the Rupiah exchange rate. Concern about foreign currencies, especially the dollar, is one of the factors because the Indonesian government has foreign exchange reserves in USD, making the USD very strong against the value of IDR. From 2001 to 2019, IDR weakened by approximately 50%.

Volatility is a basic measure of risk associated with financial market instruments, which is an intentional constituent in fluctuations in asset prices and recorded as a range of price changes (the difference between the maximum and minimum prices) in trading sessions, trading days, months and so on. Usually a wider range of fluctuations (higher volatility) means higher trading risks involved. Based on in Figure 1, the volatility of the middle exchange rate of the USD against IDR in 2018 average above 25% makes concern for economics. The higher volatility means the higher risk. In that same year, Indonesia economics instability was caused by weakening of the rupiah to touch the figure of Rp.15,250, thus requiring hedging as stipulated in Bank Indonesia Regulation No.15/8/PBI/2013. This regulation was made as a guideline for economic actors to mitigate the risk of exchange rate fluctuations.

2 RESERCH METHODOLOGY

The research used quantitative research methods. This research is to find out the comparison of the binomial option model with the Black-Scholes option model to hedging an asset, where the data used is the USD middle rate data against IDR. Comparative descriptive research is conducted to

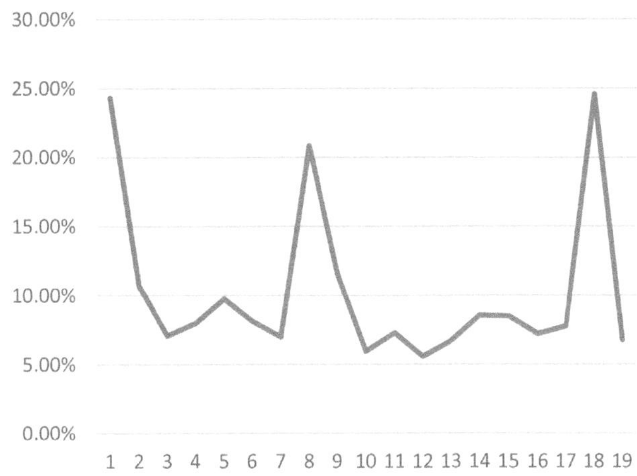

Figure 1. Volatility Rupiah against dollar.

find out and be able to explain the characteristics of the variable studied in a research situation. This type of research is comparative to research conducted if the researcher wants to know the difference between a group and another group regarding one of several variables.

3 RESEARCH RESULTS

Tables 1 and 2 explain the condition of the execution price is smaller than the spot price, forecasting the Black-Scholes model for a call tends to have a smaller error compared to the Black-Scholes model at the price condition $X < P$, $X = P$, and $X > P$ as 0.108%, 0.116%, and 0.124%, respectively. As for the put Binomial model has a smaller error compared to the Black-Scholes model at the price conditions $X < P$, $X = P$ and $X > P$, namely, 0.059%, 0.070%, and 0.084%. Due date score or maturity value is used to find out the real value that has been determined in an agreement. In other words, the value that is on the official website of the Indonesian bank exchange rate on that date. The following is a call and put graph of the two models in a one-month agreement period.

Call and Put Calculations on the Black-Scholes Model and the Two-Month Binomial Model. The following table presents the results of AMSE calculations for call and put in the two models that have been studied.

Table 3 explains the condition of the execution price is smaller than the spot price, the execution price the same as the spot price, and the execution price is greater than the spot price forecasting model for the binomial call and put have the smallest errors, namely, 0.207(call) and 0.099 (put), 0.211 (call) and 0.106 (put), 0.216 (call) and 0.115 (put). Figures 8 to 13 show the two models in a two-month term agreement.

The following is a call and put graph of the two models in a two-month term agreement.

Call and Put Calculations on the Black-Scholes Model and Binomial Model in Three Months. Table 4 presents the results of AMSE calculations for call and put in the two models that have been studied.

4 CONCLUSION

The middle rate is used as the spot price variable for Black-Scholes and the binomial forecasting model. Volatility in 2018 was very high, amounting to 24.58%. This is due to instability economics in 2018 with an average BI rate of 5.1%.

Table 1. Example calculation of average percent mean square error.

No	Simulation	Due date	Due date score	Estimation score call		MSE Call		Estimation score put		MSE Put	
				Black-Scholes	Binomial	Black-Scholes	Binomial	Black-Scholes	Binomial	Black-Scholes	Binomial
1	X<P	1 Bulan	13402,00	13928,36	13969,35	0,15%	0,18%	13821,62	13757,85	0,10%	0,07%
2	X=P	1 Bulan		13950,48	13981,75	0,17%	0,19%	13893,53	13819,65	0,13%	0,10%
3	X>P	1 Bulan		13972,62	13994,14	0,18%	0,20%	13965,45	13881,44	0,18%	0,13%
4	X<P	2 Bulan	13746,00	14103,98	14063,73	0,07%	0,05%	13940,73	13692,67	0,02%	0,00%
5	X=P	2 Bulan		14123,67	14073,83	0,08%	0,06%	14010,00	13751,57	0,04%	0,00%
6	X>P	2 Bulan		14143,38	14083,92	0,08%	0,06%	14079,29	13810,48	0,06%	0,00%
7	X<P	3 Bulan	13750,00	14230,99	14165,67	0,12%	0,09%	14011,47	13636,95	0,04%	0,01%
8	X=P	3 Bulan		14248,69	14173,87	0,13%	0,10%	14078,54	13693,38	0,06%	0,00%
9	X>P	3 Bulan		14266,43	14182,08	0,14%	0,10%	14145,65	13749,81	0,08%	0,00%

Table 2. Comparation error Black-Scholes model and binomial model in 1 month.

	MSE						
	X<P		X=P		X>P		
NO	BS	BI	BS	BI	BS	BI	Keterangan
1	0,108%	0,116%	0,116%	0,120%	0,124%	0,125%	**CALL**
2	0,076%	0,059%	0,095%	0,070%	0,120%	0,084%	**PUT**

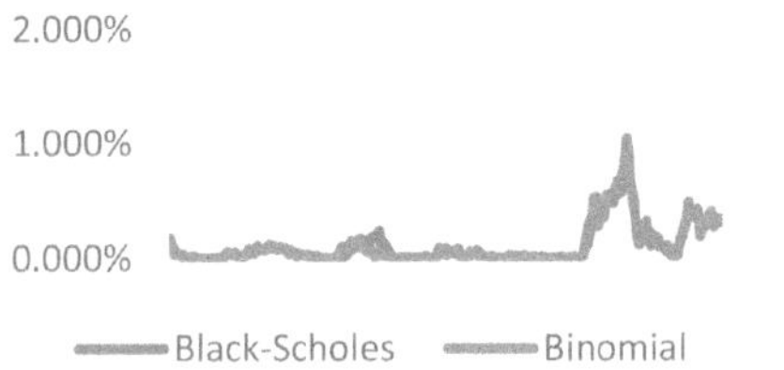

Figure 2. MSE Call BI & BS X = P 1 Month.

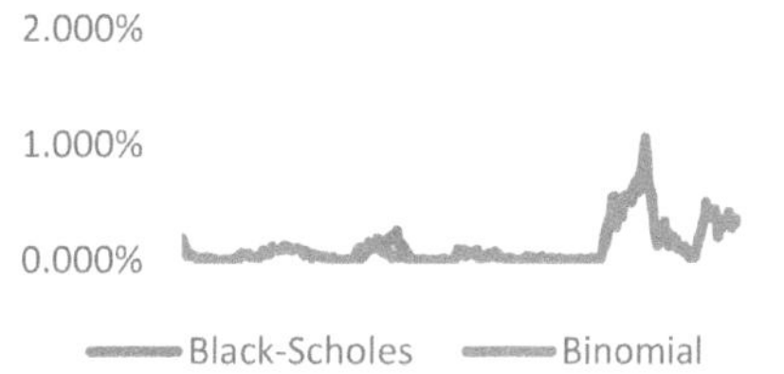

Figure 3. MSE Call BI & BS X < P 1 Month.

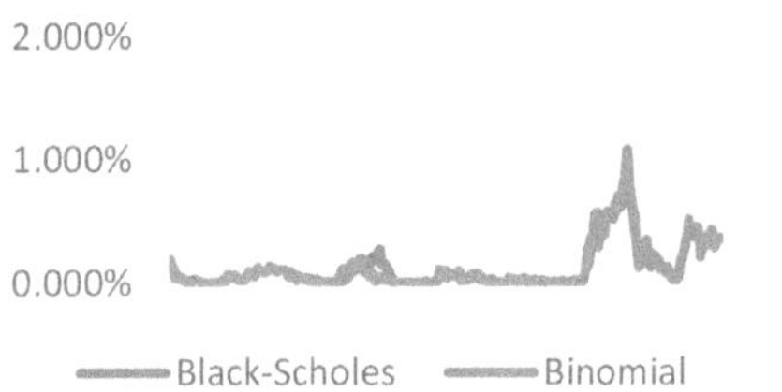

Figure 4. MSE Call BI & BS X > P 1 Month.

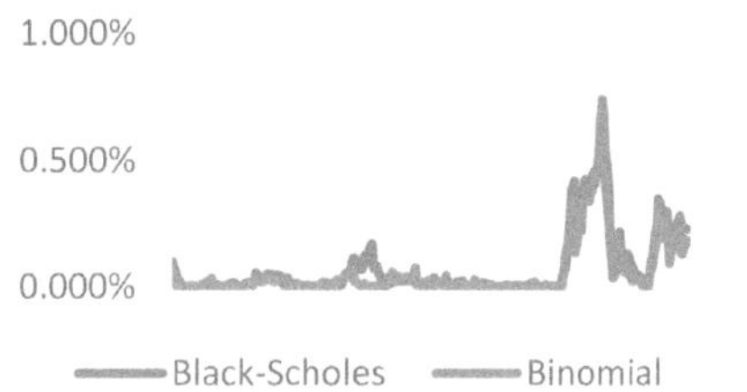

Figure 5. MSE Put BI & BS X < P 1 Month.

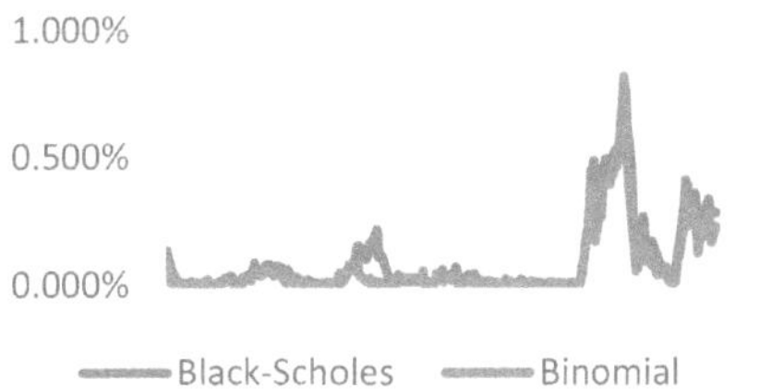

Figure 6. MSE Put BI & BS X = P 1 Month.

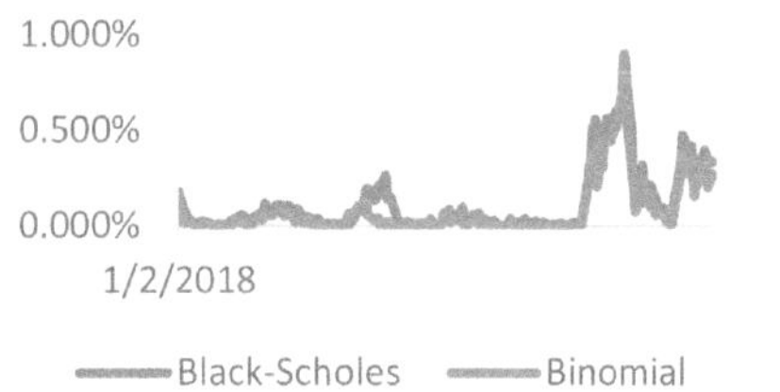

Figure 7. MSE Put BI & BS X > P 1 Month.

The application of the Black-Scholes model for January 2, 2018, gets the total value of forecasting calls 13928.36 (X < P), 13950.48 (X = P), 13972.62 (X > P) for one month, then gets a total forecast call value of 14103.98 (X = P) (X < P), 14123.67 (X = P), 14143.38 (X > P) for two months, then get a total forecast call value of 14230.99 (X < P), 14248.69 (X = P), 14266.43 (X > P) for three months. Whereas for the application of the Black-Scholes model on the put, within a period of one month get a total forecast of 13821.62 (X < P), 13893.53 (X = P), 13965.45 (X > P), within a period of two months get a value of 13940.73 (X < P), 14010.00 (X = P), 14079.29 (X > P), in a period of three months get a value of 14011.47 (X < P), 14078.54 (X = P), 14145.65 (X > P).

The binomial model calculation for January 2, 2018, gets a total call value of 13969.35 (X < P), 13981.75 (X = P), 13994.14 (X > P) for a period of one month, then gets a total call value of 14063.73 (X < P), 14073.63 (X = P), 14083.92 (X > P) for a period of two months, then gets a

Table 3. Comparing error Black-Scholes model and binomial model two-month.

	MSE						
	$X<P$		$X=P$		$X>P$		
NO	BS	BI	BS	BI	BS	BI	Keterangan
1	0,228%	0,207%	0,238%	0,211%	0,248%	0,216%	**CALL**
2	0,156%	0,099%	0,181%	0,106%	0,212%	0,115%	**PUT**

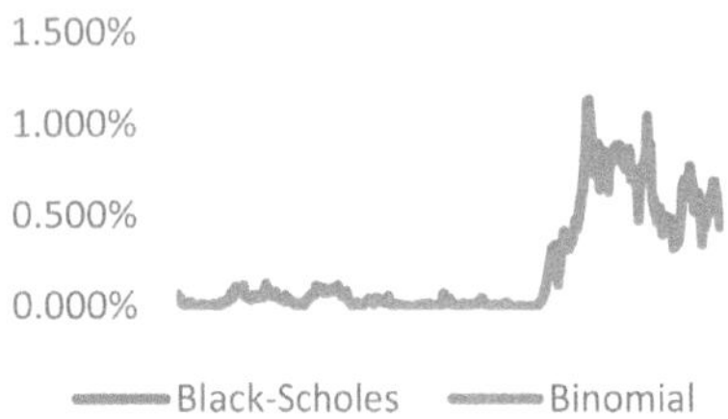

Figure 8. MSE Call BI & BS $X < P$ 2 Month.

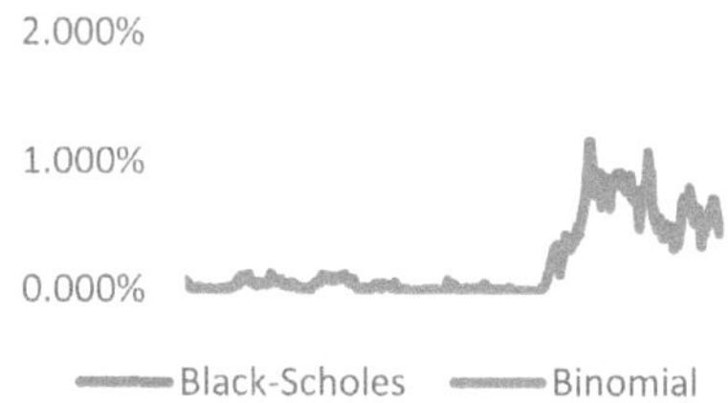

Figure 9. MSE Call BI & BS $X = P$ 2 Month.

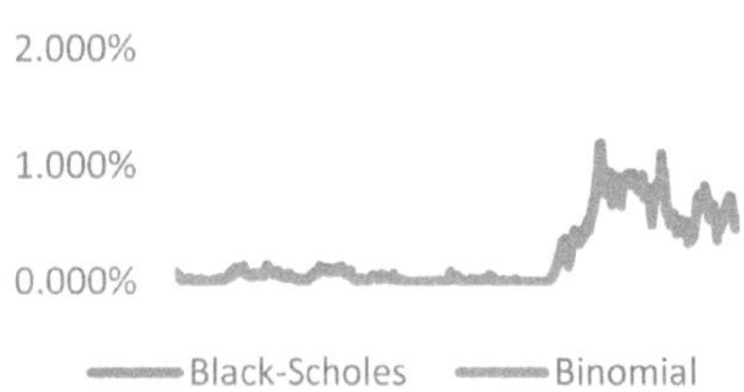

Figure 10. MSE Call BI & BS $X > P$ 2 Month.

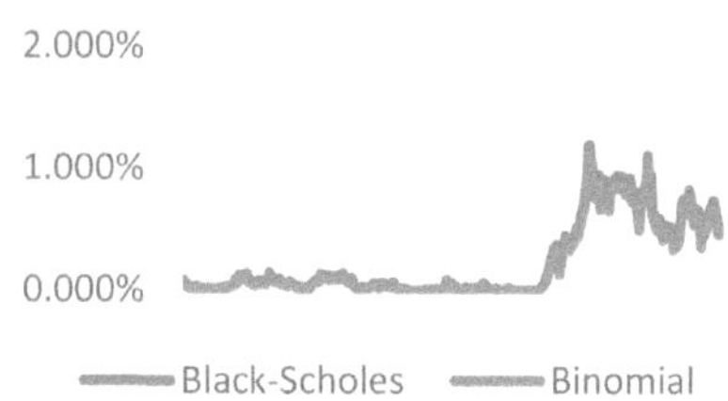

Figure 11. MSE Put BI & BS $X < P$ 2 Month.

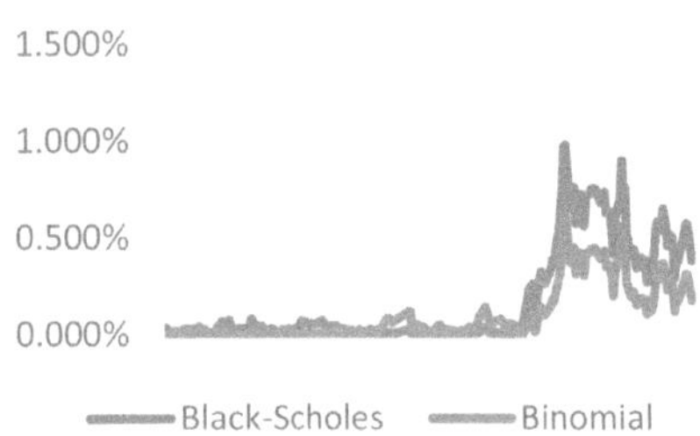

Figure 12. MSE Put BI & BS $X = P$ 2 Month.

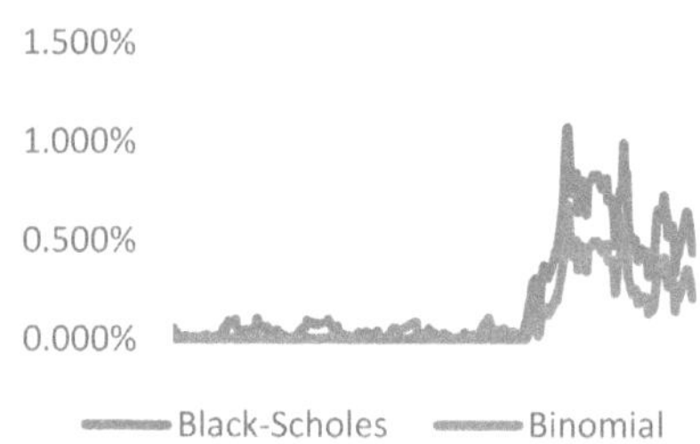

Figure 13. MSE Put BI & BS $X > P$ 2 Month.

total call value of 14165.67 ($X < P$), 14173.87 ($X = P$), 14182.08 ($X > P$) for a period of three months. Application of the binomial model for put produces a total value of 13757.85 ($X < P$), 13819.65 ($X = P$), 13881.44 ($X > P$) for a period of one month, then gets a put with a total value of 13692.67 ($X < P$), 13751.57 ($X > P$) ($X = P$), 13810.48 ($X > P$) for a period of two months, then get a put with a total value of 13636.95 ($X < P$), 13693.38 ($X = P$), 13749.81 ($X > P$) for a period of three months.

To be able to see which model is better, AMSE is used to measure how small the error will be. As on January 2, 2018, where if an agreement is made within one month, then the real value is 13402. For the multiplied call when $X = P$, the Black-Scholes model forecasting value gets an error 0.116%, while the forecast value of the binomial model gets an error 0.120%. For put simulation when $X = P$, the forecast value of the Black-Scholes model gets an error of 0.095%, while the

Table 4. Comparative error for Black-Scholes model and binomial model 3three-month.

	MSE						
	X<P		X=P		X>P		
NO	BS	BI	BS	BI	BS	BI	Keterangan
1	0,364%	0,324%	0,375%	0,328%	0,386%	0,332%	**CALL**
2	0,249%	0,167%	0,277%	0,169%	0,309%	0,173%	**PUT**

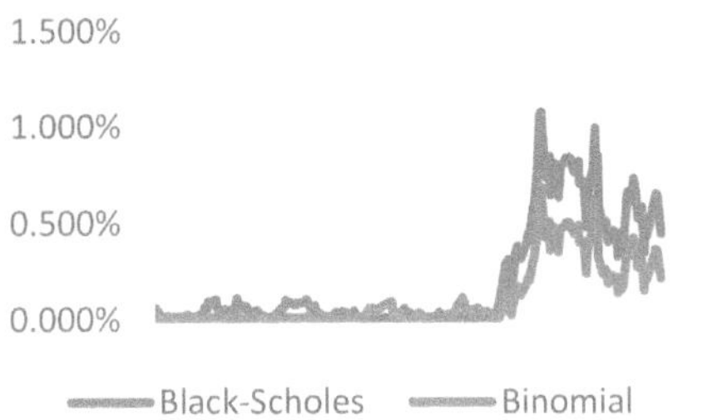

Figure 14. MSE Call BI & BS X < P 3 Month.

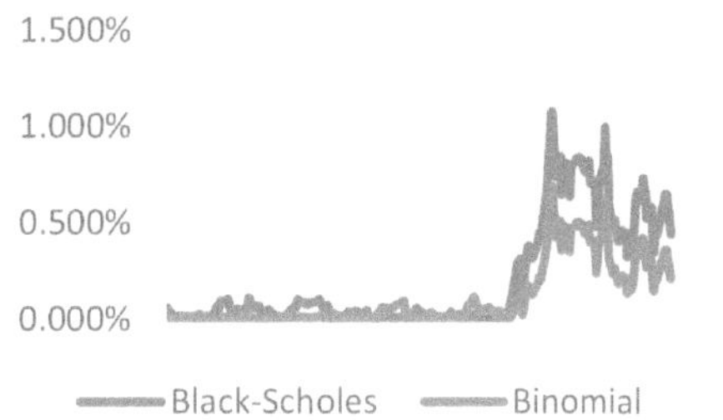

Figure 15. MSE Call BI & BS X = P 3 Month.

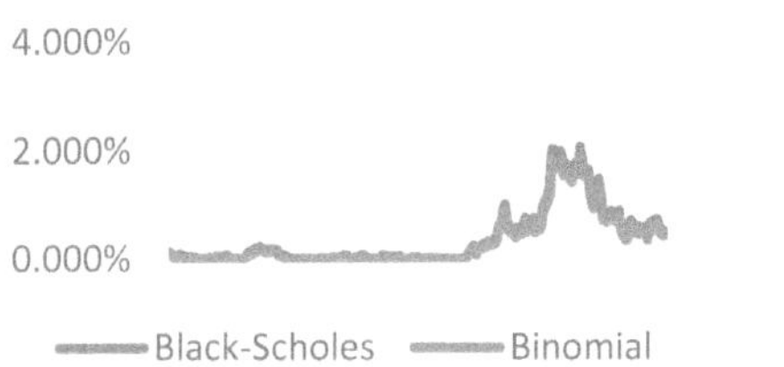

Figure 16. MSE Call BI & BS X > P 3 Month.

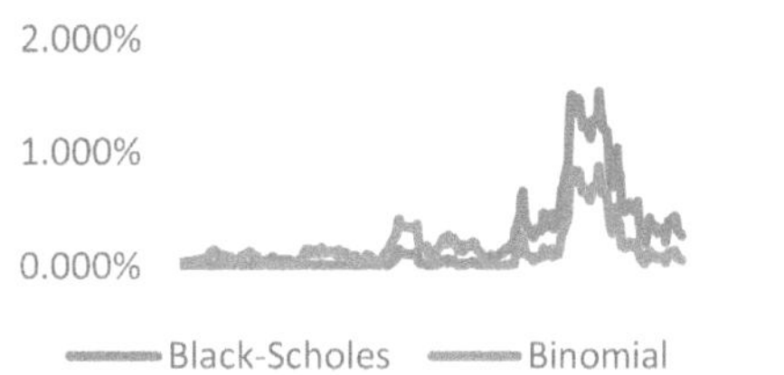

Figure 17. MSE Put BI & BS X < P 3 Month.

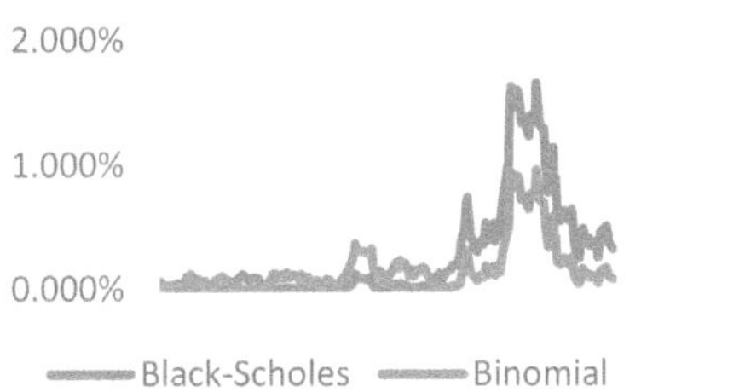

Figure 18. MSE Put BI & BS X = P 3 Month.

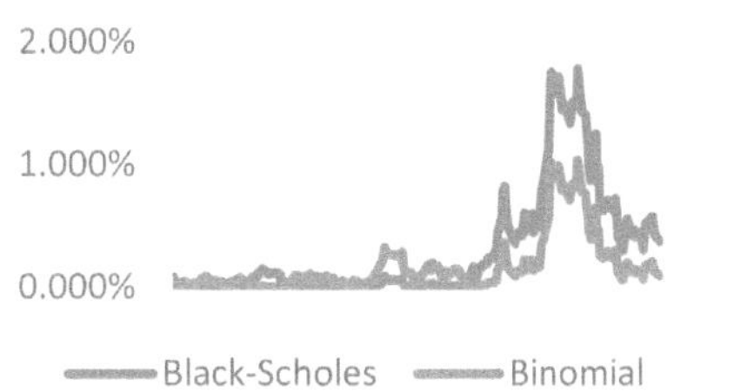

Figure 19. MSE Put BI & BS X > P 3 Month.

forecast value of the binomial model gets a smaller error, which is 0.070%. Broadly speaking, the Black-Scholes model has a smaller AMSE value than the binomial model on the call. As for put, the binomial model has a smaller AMSE value than the Black-Scholes model.

In the one-month agreement, a total of 242 trials were conducted, and the Black-Scholes model had an MSE value of 0.108% (X < P), 0.116% (X = P), 0.124% (X > P) for forecasting with total call, then get the MSE value of 0.076% (X < P), 0.095% (X = P), 0.120% (X > P) for forecasting with total put. In the Binomial model has an AMSE value of 0.116% (X < P), 0.120% (X = P), 0.125% (X > P) for forecasting with total calls, then gets an AMSE value of 0.059% (X < P), 0.070% (X = P), 0.084% (X > P) for forecasting with total put. Broadly speaking, the

Black-Scholes model has a smaller AMSE value than the binomial model on the call. As for put, the binomial model has a smaller AMSE value than the Black-Scholes model.

In a two-month agreement, a total of 242 trials were conducted, and the Black-Scholes model had an AMSE value of 0.228% (X < P), 0.238% (X = P), 0.248% (X > P) for forecasting with total call, then get an AMSE value of 0.156% (X < P), 0.181% (X = P), 0.212% (X > P) for forecasting with total put. In the binomial model has an AMSE value of 0.207% (X < P), 0.211% (X = P), 0.216% (X > P) for forecasting with total calls, then gets an AMSE value of 0.099% (X < P), 0.106% (X = P), 0.115% (X > P) for forecasting with total put. Broadly speaking, the binomial model has a smaller AMSE value than the Black-Scholes model.

In the three-month agreement, the Black-Scholes model has an AMSE value of 0.364% (X < P), 0.375% (X = P), 0.386% (X > P) for forecasting with total calls, then gets an AMSE value of 0.249 % (X < P), 0.277% (X = P), 0.309% (X > P) for forecasting with total put. In the binomial model has an AMSE value of 0.324% (X < P), 0.328% (X = P), 0.332% (X > P) for forecasting with total calls, then gets an MSE value of 0.167% (X < P), 0.169% (X = P), 0.173% (X > P) for forecasting with total put. Broadly speaking, the binomial model has a smaller AMSE value than the Black-Scholes model.

5 SUGGESTION

The results for comparing of two hedging models in the agreement period of one month, it is known that the Black-Scholes model is better for call options while the binomial model is better for put options, due to having a small error for the simulation mentioned earlier. As for the two-month agreement, the binomial model is better than the Black-Scholes model for call and put. The reason is the binomial model has the smallest error for all three call simulations as well as those previously mentioned. And for the three-month agreement, the binomial model is better than the Black-Scholes model for put and call.

REFERENCES

Çertain, U., Jarrow, R., Protter, P., & Warachka, M. 2006. Pricing *Option*s in an Extended Black Scholes Economy with Illiquidity: Theory and Empirical Evidence, Vol. 19, 493–529. Accessed in *database* journal *The Review of Financial Studies*.

Djaja, I. (2017). *All About Corporate Valuation*. Jakarta : Penerbit PT Elex Media Komputindo.

Hendrawan, R. 2010. Comparation Option Black Scholes an Option Garch Model in Bursa Efek Indonesia, Vol. 14,13–23. Accessed in *database* Financial journal.

Hull, J. 2009. *Option, Future, and Other Derivatives Securities*.New Jersey: Penerbit Pearson.

Indrawati. (2015). *Metode Penelitian Manajemen dan Bisnis Konvergensi Teknologi Komunikasi dan Informasi*. Bandung: Publisher PT Refika Aditama.

Sekaran, U. 2010. *Meodologi Penelitian untuk Bisnis*.Jakarta: Salemba Empat www.idx.co.id/produk/derivatif/ 11 Oktober 2019.

Synergizing Management, Technology and Innovation in Generating Sustainable and Competitive Business Growth – Hendayani et al (eds)
© 2021 Taylor & Francis Group, London, ISBN 978-0-367-68756-4

Business strategies formulation in construction company

R. Rismayani & G.N. Efrata
Telkom University, Bandung, West Java, Indonesia

ABSTRACT: This research is business strategies formulation in a construction company to improve the competitiveness of the construction company. Study case is PT X, a private construction company. The study aims to obtain recommendation strategies that can be applied by the company. The methodology used in this research is descriptive qualitative and quantitative through interviews and questionnaires. The results of the research from the input stage are the EFE matrix value of 2.952 and the IFE matrix value of 2.965. Furthermore, at the matching stage, the company position is found in the IE matrix in quadrant V. Consequently, the top priority strategy results obtained at the decision stage with the QSPM matrix are establishing operational cooperation (KSO) with state-owned contractors in working on government projects and increasing project work with the middle to lower category.

1 INTRODUCTION

The construction industry plays a critical role in national economics development because it contributes greatly to other business sectors. The construction industry is still one of the highest factors in gross domestic product (GDP) growth in Indonsia (Badan Pusat Statistik 2019).

Besides, the infrastructure project developments in Indonesia have been performed and have progressed during the administration of President Joko Widodo. In the five years of its administration, the infrastructure project is one of the programs that intensified. The purpose infrastructure development aims at the economic welfare of the community and facilitates movement in various regions. The types of infrastructure built include toll roads, bridges, airports, railroads, and train (Prabowo 2018). With so many infrastructure development projects, it has made a growth of construction service (Pangasti et al. 2019).

The tight competition in the construction company business encourages private contractors to have the right strategy in dealing with problems. Another problem is that the revenue and profit obtained by private construction companies are still far below the state-owned construction companies. Besides, the existence of a presidential election has an impact on economic growth and declining purchasing power so that causes project demand to decrease.

The object of this research is PT X. PT X is a private construction company class B2, which is engaged in construction services and property development. PT X is located in DKI Jakarta and was founded in 1996.

Based on the vision and background, winning competition requires the right strategy formulation to deal with the weakening of the construction industry and face intense competition between construction companies based on the company's weaknesses, strengths, opportunities, and threats. By formulating a strategy under the circumstances faced, private contractors can have a competitive advantage and play a role in the development of government infrastructure projects.

2 LITERATURE REVIEW

According to David (2017), strategic management can be defined as the art of science in formulating, implementing, and making cross-functional decisions that make organizations achieve the goals of the organization. There are three stages of management strategy: strategy formulation, strategy implementation, and strategy evaluation. This research discusses strategy formulation. Strategy formulation includes developing a vision and mission, analyzing external opportunities and threats to the organization, identifying internal strengths and weaknesses, determining long-term goals, initiating alternative strategies, and selecting specific strategies to implement. Strategy formulation includes identifying the company's external environment with opportunities and threats, and the internal environment through strengths and weaknesses.

There are three stages to obtain strategies recommendation. The input stage is summarizing the basic information to formulate a strategy using the IFE and EFE matrices, matching stages creating alternative strategies by matching key external and internal factors using the IE and SWOT matrices, and decision stages evaluating alternative strategies that have been identified through stage two to obtain priority strategies using the QSPM matrix (David 2017).

3 RESEARCH METHODS

This research used a combination of qualitative descriptive and quantitative. According to Bungin (2011), the addition of quantitative methods in the research helps the analysis process. Describing the result of this research is determined from interviews and questionnaries that were given to respondent. Interviews and questionnaires were conducted to obtain key factors of strength, weakness, opportunity, and threat in the companies. The use of questionnaires in this study aims to quantify interview questions that were given to respondents to help the analysis process. Qualitative descriptive is used to obtain key factors of PT X and to determine SWOT matrix. Meanwhile, the quantitative analysis is used to calculate EFE, IFE, IE, and QSPM matrices.

According to Prajapati et al. (2019), the selection of respondents used a purposive sampling technique. The respondents were the middle high level manager in the company. The number of the respondent people was six. The internal respondents were marketing managers, managing directors, and engineering managers from PT X. Meanwhile, the external respondents were a system manager from state-owned companies, construction managers from state-owned, and verification and validation teams from the National Association of Contracting Companies.

4 RESULTS AND DISCUSSION

There are three stages to obtain strategies recommendation, namely input stage using the IFE and EFE matrices, matching stages using the IE and SWOT matrices, and decision stages using the QSPM matrix (David 2017).

4.1 *Input stage*

The input stage is used to summarize information from the external environment and the internal environment of the company so that the key factors can be obtained from the external and internal environmental analysis. Based on the result of interviews and questionnaries from respondents EFE matrix were found eight key factors opportunity and nine key factors threat. The rating and weight on the EFE matrix are obtained from the answers of internal respondents. Meanwhile, the score is obtained from multiplication between weight and rating.

Based on the result of interviews questionnaries from respondents IFE matrix were found 10 key factors strengths and seven key factors weakness. The rating and weight on the IFE matrix are obtained from the answers of internal respondents. Meanwhile, the score is obtained from multiplication between weight and rating.

4.2 *Matching stage*

The matching stage used two matrices, IE Matrix and SWOT Matrix. IE Matrix determined based on the EFE and IFE matrices. IE Matrix was used to determine the company position of PT X.

Table 1. EFE matrix.

Opportunities	Code	Weight	Rating	Score
Private tender administration is easy to fulfill	O1	0,061	3	0,183
Technology use en masse	O2	0,056	3	0,168
Ease of purchasing technology and heavy equipment	O3	0,054	3	0,162
The growth of the State Budget Plan has increased	O4	0,065	3	0,195
Large construction industry market share	O5	0,073	4	0,292
Consumer knowledge of the company is high	O6	0,064	3	0,192
New players find it difficult to enter	O7	0,052	2	0,104
Has many suppliers available in the national market	O8	0,046	3	0,138
Total Opportunities				1,434
Threats	**Code**	**Weight**	**Rating**	**Score**
Government tender administration is difficult to fulfill	T1	0,063	3	0,189
Slow economic growth	T2	0,071	4	0,284
Volatile currency stability	T3	0,060	2	0,120
Public purchasing power is decreasing	T4	0,073	4	0,292
The acquisition of a new contract is volatile	T5	0,069	3	0,207
Tight competition in B2 construction companies	T6	0,055	3	0,165
Bad weather can hamper the project work process	T7	0,041	1	0,041
A decline in the commercial property market	T8	0,061	3	0,183
Land acquisition problems	T9	0,037	1	0,037
Total Threats				1,518
Total EFE				2,952

Source: Data Processed (2020).

Table 2. IFE matrix.

Strengths	Code	Weight	Rating	Score
Aluma system technology usage	S1	0,061	3	0,183
The rapid appliance of new technology	S2	0,056	3	0,168
The company has many segments	S3	0,080	4	0,320
Satisfied customers	S4	0,069	4	0,276
Loyal customers	S5	0,061	3	0,183
Good service quality	S6	0,068	4	0,272
A high rate of project completion	S7	0,073	4	0,292
A high rate of overcoming bad processes	S8	0,063	3	0,189
High productivity	S9	0,066	4	0,264
Competent employees	S10	0,065	4	0,260
Total Strengths				2,407
Weaknesses	**Code**	**Weight**	**Rating**	**Score**
Revenue amount growth fluctuation	W1	0,064	2	0,128
Profits amount growth fluctuation	W2	0,060	2	0,120
Small capital expenditure	W3	0,040	1	0,040
Low customers growth	W4	0,057	2	0,114
Smaller income for new entry-level compared to competitors	W5	0,037	1	0,037
The small ability to retain the best employees	W6	0,039	2	0,078
Fewer machines number than competitors	W7	0,041	1	0,041
Total Weaknesses				0,558
Total IFE				2,965

Source: Data Processed (2020).

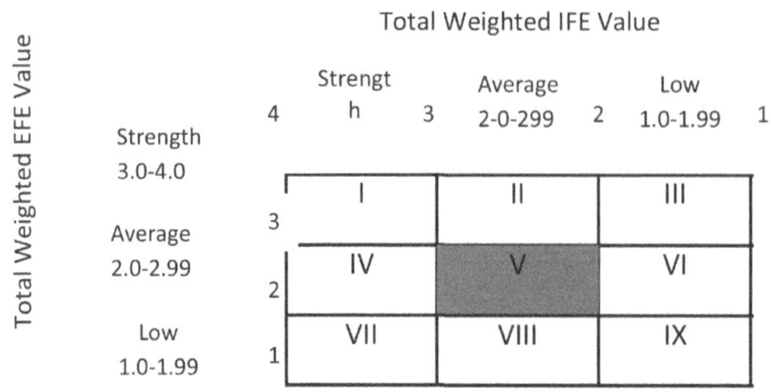

Figure 1. IE Matrix. Source: Data Processed (2020).

Table 3. SWOT matrix.

	Strengths (S) S1-S10 key factors internal strengths	Weakness (W) W1-W7 key factors internal weakness
Oppurtunities (O) O1-O8 key factors external opportunities	Strategy SO Establishing KSO (Operational Cooperation) with state-owned contractors in the execution of government projects. (Joint Venture)	Strategy WO Developing green building designs and concepts for customers. (Product Development)
Threats (T) T1-T9 key factors external threats	Strategy ST Increasing the number of projects in the middle to lower customer categories. (Market Penetration)	Strategy WT Participating as a subcontractor in the execution of government projects. (Market Penetration)

Source: Data Processed (2020).

Table 4. QSPM matrix.

Strategy Recommendation	Code	Total Score	Priority
Establishing KSO (Operational Cooperation) with state-owned contractors in the execution of government projects	SO	4,255	I
Increasing the number of projects in the middle to lower customer categories	ST	4,198	II
Participating as a subcontractor in the execution of government projects	WT	3,853	III
Developing green building designs and concepts for customers	WO	3,674	IV

Based on the result of EFE and IFE the company was in quadrant V with holds and maintains strategies.

SWOT Matrix is used to determine recomendation strategies based on key factors EFE and IFE matrices. Based on the key factors in the EFE and IFE matrices, a strategy recommendation can be formulated using the SWOT matrix. Through the SWOT matrix for suitable strategies recommendations were found at PT. X.

4.3 *Decision stage*

QSPM matrix is used to determine the priority of recommendation strategies. According to QSPM result, the best strategy for PT X are SO and ST strategies. The detail of the result is illustrated in Table 4.

5 CONCLUSION

This research was conducted to formulate strategies for PT X to increase competitiveness in the construction industry. Based on the result of the interviews and questionnaries with the respondents, the result of this research can be concluded that:

1. The external environment of PT X was found eight key factors opportunity and nine key factors threat. Meanwhile the internal environment of PT X was found 10 key factors strength and seven key factors weakness.
2. Based on the result of IE and SWOT matrix concluded four strategies recommendations that can be applied by PT X.
3. The priority strategies recommendations that can be applied by PT X in a construction company based on the result of QSPM, the result of priority strategies were:
   Establishing KSO (Operational Cooperation) with state-owned contractors in the execution of government projects. (SO Strategy)
   Increasing the number of projects in the middle to lower customer categories (ST Strategy)
   Participating as a subcontractor in the execution of government projects. (WT Strategy)
   Developing green building designs and concepts for customers (WO Strategy)

However, the strategies appliance can be used under the circumstances and environmental conditions of the company to compete with other construction companies. Besides the high market share of the construction industry has an enormous opportunity to increase the growth of customers and revenue. PT X can optimize their competitive advantages to increase the growth of customers, revenue, and compete with the other construction companies in the construction industry.

REFERENCES

Ariendi, G.T., Daryanto, A., & Sanim, B. 2015. Strategy For Increasing Business Competitiveness Of Green Property. *International Journal Of Innovation and Scientific Research,* 19(1): 24–32.

Bungin, B., 2011. *Penelitian Kualitatif: Komunikasi Ekonomi Kebijakan Publik dan Ilmu Sosial Lainnya.* Jakarta: Prenada Media Group.

David, F. & David, F. (16th ed.) 2017. *Strategic Management: A Competitive Advantage Approach Concept and Cases.* England: Pearson.

Ghorbani, A., Raufirad, V., Rafiaani, P., & Hossein, A. 2015. Ecotourism sustainable development strategies using SWOT and QSPM Model: A case study of Kaji Namakzar Wetland, South Khoarsan Province Iran. *Tourism Management Prespective,* Volume 16: 290–297.

Hindarwati, E.N., & Arifin, S. 2015. Penerapan Strategi Bisnis Pada Perusahaan Kontraktor Tiang Pancang Di Indonesia. *Jurnal Manajemen Indonesia,* 15(3): 243–252.

Prabowo, D., 2018. *Kompas.* [Online] Available at: https://properti.kompas.com/read/2018/03/14/220449821/proyek-infrastruktur-dikuasai-bumn-kontraktor-swasta-gulung-tikar. [Accessed 3 August 2019].

Pramudiana, Y. & Rismayani. R. 2013. *Managing Portofolio Product.* Bandung: CV Dinamika Komunika.

Pangastuti, R.D., Angka, B.U., Lakhwani, M.A., Behuku, J., & Putra, J.L. 2019. Strategy Formulation Using IFE, EFE,SWOT,QSPM Matrix.Case Study: PT Total Bangun Persada Tbk. *International Journal Of Innovative & Development,* 8(4): 68–73.

Prajapati, U., Lukman, B., & Setiadi D. 2019. Strategy For Performance Improvement At Building Division Of PT Hutama Karya (Persero) In Conditions Of Construction Building Business Competition. *Russian Journal Of Agricultural and Socio Economic Science,* 8(92): 227–234.

Rismayani, R., & Sari, I P. 2019. Analysis Of Business Strategy In Furniture Company. *International Journal and Science Research (IJSR),* 8(6).

Sekaran, U. & Bougie, R (7th ed.) 2016. *Research Method For Business.* United Kingdom: John Wiley & Son Ltd.

Statistik, B. P., 2019. *Laporan Pertumbuhan Ekonomi Indonesia Kuartal III ,* Jakarta: Badan Pusat Statistik.

Synergizing Management, Technology and Innovation in Generating Sustainable and Competitive Business Growth – Hendayani et al (eds)
© 2021 Taylor & Francis Group, London, ISBN 978-0-367-68756-4

The impact of dynamic business environment on the competitive advantage of halal tourism operators in Indonesia

M.I. Nashiruddin
School of Economics and Business, Telkom University, Bandung, Jawa Barat, Indonesia

Y. Susanti
Nathan Associates Inc., DKI Jakarta, Indonesia

ABSTRACT: The competitive advantage of the halal tourism operators will be required to enable them to compete and survive in a dynamic business environment. The study aims to investigate the impact of a dynamic business environment on the competitive advantage of halal tourism operators in Indonesia. Verification research methodology was applied, and Slovin's formula was used for sampling calculation. The research instrument was constructed using an online survey platform, which was sent to the members of the Halal Travel Consortium as respondents. The result shows a dynamic business environment has a positive and significant effect but weak correlation to the competitive advantage of halal tourism operators in Indonesia. Ability to produce products/services at a lower cost (Std Dev 0.785) and ability to better tailor products/services to individual customer needs (Std Dev 0.760) are the most prioritized actions being implemented by halal tourism operators in Indonesia.

1 INTRODUCTION

Indonesia is a country that has the largest Muslim population in the world. The National Statistics Bureau in 2010 reported that Muslims in Indonesia accounted for 87.18% of the total population. The Ministry of Tourism started to scale up halal tourism industry five years ago by creating regulation and a road map. Support from the stakeholders, including halal tourism operators, is crucial to bring it into the global market. Several studies conducted in the past have informed us that the performance of a business is majority affected by the ability of a company to establish a competitive advantage.

Aspects in technology, markets, regulations, and hyper competition change rapidly, which influences the business environment to be uncertain and unpredictable which may diminish competitive advantage. This condition is acknowledged as the turbulent business environment and can give impact to a company for maintaining its competitive advantage. In order to gain optimal competitive advantage then, a company must improve its business expansion speed into new markets, attract new customers, increase intensity and improve or fasten the process for development of new product innovation, develop low-cost product, reduce unit cost by revising the business process, and cost optimization including development of a different business model (Nashiruddin 2014). The study aims to investigate the impact of a dynamic business environment on the competitive advantage of halal tourism operators in Indonesia.

2 LITERATURE REVIEW

2.1 *Dynamic business environment*

A company or organization's environment is all external and internal factors influencing the structure of the company or organization and its activities. The external environment is all elements outside the company, which mostly is uncontrollable and influence managerial decision making (Handoko 1999: 62). Analysis of resources involves all inputs used in organizational activities. The analysis is based on category, specification, human resources, physical assets, and non-physical assets (Ritson 2019: 10). These external factors can be identified by applying a very popular analysis called the PESTLE analysis, which can help to consider political, social, technological, legal, and environmental situations (Newton 2015: 9).

According to Porter (1980:7), in strategic management subject about the 5 Forces of Porter analysis, the internal environment of a company consists of bargaining position of suppliers, strength of other stakeholders, threats from new players in the market, bargaining position of buyers, and threats of substitute products/services. The dynamic of the business environment is a general condition of uncertainties within business environments, which is often caused by volatile changes, substantial in nature, and difficult to predict and has a large impact (Nashiruddin 2014: 30).

Therefore, considering the research novelty and theory application, thus the dimensions used to measure business environment dynamic in this study are the market, technology, regulation, and competition. The market dimension consists of changes in consumer preference, seeking new products, request for existing product, different types of consumer needs, and changes in marketing practices. The technology dimension is measured from speed in technology update, difficulty to predict technology update, opportunities from the technology update, and the emergence of new products resulting from technological breakthroughs. The regulation dimension is measured with difficulty in predicting regulatory changes, the intensity of regulatory changes, level of regulatory compliance, and the legal uncertainty regarding the implementation of the regulation. In comparison, the competition dimension is measured by the intensity of competition between halal travel operators, the intensity of the price war, the level of ease to compete with competitor's product, the intensity of emergence of new movement from competitors, the level of competitor strengths, and the intensity of emergence of new product in the market.

2.2 *Competitive advantage*

In strategic management research, competitive advantage has traditionally been defined as superior economic performance (Teece et al. 2008). Definition of competitive advantage generated from other studies is the ability of organizations to form higher economic value than competitors (Barney & Arikan 2006). Competitive advantage is also defined as an attribute and resource of an organization that makes it possible to outperform others in the product industry or market (Chaharbaghi & Lynch 1999).

Porter in 1980 mentioned competitive advantage as the ability of a company to create value for consumers at lower prices than the production costs, or consumers are willing to pay premium prices because the value of these products is considered higher than the price. A company is considered to have a competitive advantage if it is able to show performance above average or gain profits higher than the normal profit (rent) on an ongoing basis (Porter 1980, 1985). Based on further observation of the various definitions developed by previous researchers, the competitive advantage in this study is defined as the ability of a company to gain excellent business performance that happens when a business unit acquires or develops an attribute or combination of attributes that makes it capable of surpassing its competitors.

Peteraf (1993) launched the MBV theory as "the cornerstone of competitive advantage" that it can be formed through (1) heterogenity, (2) ex-post limit to competition, (3) imperfect mobility, and (4) ex-ante limit to competition. Best (2000) states that the factors that produce competitive advantage are differentiation advantage, cost advantage, and marketing advantage. Hill and Jones (1998) introduced RBV concept as "generic building block of competitive advantage," which states that it resulted from (1) superior quality, (2) superior efficiency, (3) superior innovation, and (4) superior customer responsiveness. Barney (2001) introduces the SCA (sustainable competitive advantage) concept, where sustainable competitive advantage will be obtained if the resources (resources) and capabilities developed meet the four dimensions of VRIO, namely, (1) valuable, (2) awareness, (3) imitability, and (4) organizational exploited.

This research applies standardized dimensions and indicators for measuring the competitive advantage and combines the theory of MBV and RBV, which were first developed by Nidumolu and Knotts (1998) and then developed by Chen (2012) and Nashiruddin (2014). The dimensions are (1) product cost-efficiency, which explains efficiency advantages in organizations when producing products, representing the RBV approach, and (2) speed of market response, which describes the superiority of the organization in responding to market changes in a timely manner, representing the MBV approach.

3 METHODOLOGY

Verification research methodology applied and the study population was all halal travel operators as members of Halal Travel Consortium. There were 1,155 members of the consortium when the study was carried out. The sampling method was taken using the Slovin's formula as follows: n = N/(1+Ne^2), where n is the minimum required samples, N is population, e = critical value (percentage of tolerance due to sampling error). Therefore, with population (N) = 1155 and critical value (e) = 10%, the required samples (n) were 1155/(1+1155x(0.1^2)) = 92. Primary data were collected through a questionnaire that was adapted from a previous study for telecommunication industry in Indonesia. An online survey questionnaire link was sent to members of the Halal Travel Consortium through email and Whatsapp in January 2020.

4 RESULT AND DISCUSSION

4.1 *Respondent profiles*

The respondents were people at managerial level and who have been working at halal tourism industry for several years. The questionnaire link was shared to 1,155 operators and the completed questionnaires were 132, among which 92 were valid and gives a validity rate at 69.6%. Results of data analysis about respondents' characteristic have shown 42% of respondents provide domestic or international halal tour package, nearly 35% of respondents provide umrah/hajj travel packages as well as domestic or international halal tour packages.

4.2 *Regression analysis*

The regression equation is Y = 8.712 + 0.266 X. Interpretation of the equation is that the regression coefficient of dynamic business environment has a positive sign (0.266), which means dynamic business environment variable is linear with competitive advantage variable. In other words, dynamic business environment has a positive effect on competitive advantage.

4.3 *Significance analysis*

Fcount (16.521) > Ftable (3.95) with significance level 0.001 < 0.05. Therefore, regression equation of 8.712 + 0.226 X is significant.

4.4 *Correlation analysis*

Correlation analysis value is at 0.399, meaning that there is a weak correlation between dynamic business environment with competitive advantage.

4.5 *Descriptive analysis*

Descriptive analysis of dynamic business environment variable shows priorities to adapt or survive in the dynamic business environment:

1) Market Dimension: public request for existing products (Std Dev 0.704). It shows members of the Halal Travel Consortium still prioritize the provision of the halal travel package.

2) Technology Dimension: opportunity and technological breakthrough (Std Dev 0.783). Respondents see an opportunity and technological breakthrough to run the halal tourism business.
3) Regulatory Dimension: the intensity of regulatory changes (Std Dev 0.843). It means that there are changes in the regulation of the implementation of halal tourism, whose intensity is considered high and can affect stakeholders in the halal tourism business.
4) Competition Dimension: intensity of competition between halal travel operators (Std Dev 0.657). It means that members of Halal Travel Consortium feel there is high competition among halal travel operators, as stated by more than 50% of respondents.

In the last five years, the halal tourism industry development in Indonesia has become the government's attention. This situation is supported with the increase of Muslim tourists, who take tours and prefer to choose halal travel packages. The availability of many tour operators in Indonesia creates a higher competitive environment to get customers. Therefore, the competitive advantage of the halal tour operators of the halal travel consortium members is expected to be maintained to obtain profits that are above the average profit value in the halal tourism industry.

Results of descriptive analysis of competitive advantage variable demonstrate the highest priority taken by halal tour operators to enable them to maintain their competitive advantage. The priorities are to produce products/services at a lower cost (Std Dev 0.785) and the ability to charge competitive prices for products/services (Std Dev 0.785). This finding is in accordance with a theory shared by Porter in 2018 that competitive advantage is the ability of a company to give value for consumer at a lower price than production cost, or the consumer is willing to pay a high price due to the value of the product. Other than that, study result shows cost-efficient leadership and quality differentiation have contributed to a competitive advantage at the company level (Porter 1980; Teece et al. 2008).

The ability to better tailor products/services to individual customer needs (Std Dev 0.760) has been selected as the most important aspect by respondents for speed of market response dimension. This finding shows competitive advantage of halal tour operators can create higher economic value in comparison with general tour operators. This supports the theory mentioned by Barney and Arikan in 2006 that the ability of an organization to create higher economic value than the competitor is recognized as a competitive advantage.

5 CONCLUSION

Dynamic business environment has a positive and significant effect but weak correlation to the competitive advantage of the halal tourism operators in Indonesia. Ability to produce products/services at a lower rate (Std Dev 0.785) and ability to better tailor products/services to individual customer needs (Std Dev 0.760) are the most prioritized actions being implemented by halal tourism operators in Indonesia.

REFERENCES

Barney, J. B., & Arikan, A. M. 2006. The Resource-based View: Origins and Implications. In The Blackwell Handbook of Strategic Management (First Edit, pp. 123–182). Blackwell Publishing Ltd.

Chaharbaghi, K., & Lynch, R. 1999. Sustainable Competitive Advantage: Towards a Dynamic Resource-Based Sustainable Competitive Advantage: towards a Dynamic Resource-based Strategy. Management Decision, 37(1), 45–50. https://doi.org/10.1108/00251749910252012

Chen, X. 2012. Impact of Business Intelligence and I.T Infrastructure Flexibility on Competitive Advantage: An Organizational Agility Perspective. Dissertations and Theses from the College of Business Administration University of Nebraska.

Eisenhardt, K. M. 1989. Making Fast Strategic Decisions in High-Velocity Environments. Academy of Management Journal, 32(3), 543–576. https://doi.org/10.2307/256434

Handoko, H. 1999. Manajemen. BPFE Yogyakarta: Yogyakarta.

Hamel, G., & Prahalad, C. K. 1989. Strategic Intent. Harvard Business Review, (May-June 1989), 63–76.

Hermawan, K. Y, & Madyani, D. 2004. On Becoming a Customer-Centric Company. Transformasi TELKOM menjadi perusahaan berbasis Pelangan. Jakarta: PT. Gramedia Pustaka Utama.
Jaworski, B. J., & Kohli, A. K. 1993. Market orientation: antecedents and consequences. The Journal of Marketing, 53–70.
Kim, W. C., & Mauborgne, R. 2005. Blue Ocean Strategy: How to Create Uncontested Market Space and Make the Competition Irrelevant. Harvard Business Review Press.
Nashiruddin, M. I. 2014. Model Strategi Bisnis dan Keunggulan Bersaing untuk Meningkatkan Kinerja Unit Bisnis Ditinjau dari Turbulensi Lingkungan dan Kapabilitas Dinamik (Survei pada Industri Penyelenggara Telekomunikasi di Indonesia). Dissertation. Bandung: Padjajaran University.
Newton, P. 2015. What is the PESTLE Analysis? 1st edition. Denmark: Paul Newton & bookbon.com.
Nidumolu, S. R., & Knotts, G. W. 1998. The Effects of Customizability and Reusability on Perceived Process and Competitive Performance of Software Firms. MIS Quarterly, 22(2), 105–137.
Porter, M. E. 1980. Competitive Strategy: Techniques for Analyzing-Industries and Competitors. The Free Press (First Edition). New York: The Free Press.
Porter, M. E. 1985. Competitive Advantage: Creating and Sustaining-Superior Performance. New York: The Free Press.
Ritson, N. 2019. Business Strategy and Strategic Planning: A Definition and Definitive Guide. 2nd edition. Denmark. Neil Ritson & bookboon.com
Teece, D. J., Pisano, G., & Shuen, A. 2008. Dynamic Capabilities and Strategic Management. Strategic Management Journal, 18(March), 509–533. https://doi.org/10.1142/9789812834478_0002

Synergizing Management, Technology and Innovation in Generating Sustainable and Competitive Business Growth – Hendayani et al (eds)
© 2021 Taylor & Francis Group, London, ISBN 978-0-367-68756-4

Creating sustainable competitive advantage through business strategy improvement for halal tourism industry: A case of Indonesia

M.I. Nashiruddin
School of Economics and Business, Telkom University, Bandung, Indonesia

Y. Susanti
Nathan Associates Inc., DKI Jakarta, Indonesia

ABSTRACT: The development of the tourism industry is expected to improve people's welfare through the creation of employment and supporting industries. The right business strategy implementation by halal tourism operators in Indonesia is required to enable them having a competitive advantage and survive in a turbulent business environment. The study aims to elaborate on the business strategy of halal tourism operators in Indonesia to create its competitive advantage. Descriptive research methodology was applied, and sampling calculation was made using Slovin's formula. The research instrument was developed using an online survey platform which was sent to the members of the Halal Travel Consortium as respondents. The result shows business strategy has a positive, linear, and significant effect on the competitive advantage of halal tourism operators in Indonesia. Competitive strategy is chosen to focus on serving a specific segment (Std Dev 0.715), while cooperative strategy is selected to reduce risk and uncertainty (Std Dev 0.759).

1 INTRODUCTION

Several studies conducted in the past have informed us that the performance of a business is majority defined by the formation of competitive advantage of a company. The fast changes in technology, markets, regulations and hyper competition aspects have influenced the uncertainty and unpredictability to the business environment that may undermine competitive advantage. This situation is recognized as the turbulent business environment and can cause a company to have difficulties for maintaining its competitive advantage.

Appropriate business strategy implementation by halal travel operators in Indonesia is required to enable them to have competitive advantage and survive in the industry facing the business dynamic. In order to gain optimal competitive advantage then, a company must accelerate the speed of business expansion into new markets, attract new customers, increase intensity, and improve or fasten the process for development of new product innovation, develop low- cost product, reduce unit cost by revising the business process, and cost optimization including development of a different business model (Nashiruddin 2014).

For a company to be able to produce above-average performance or gain profits above the average industry profit (Walker & Madsen 2016), then it must have a competitive advantage. This paper aims to explore how Indonesian halal travel operators create sustainable competitive advantage through business strategy improvement in the dynamic business environment of the tourism industry.

2 LITERATURE REVIEW

2.1 *Competitive advantage*

The core of strategic management is obtaining and maintaining competitive advantage over the competitors. A company is considered successful in achieving a competitive advantage if it can obtain profits above the average industry profits (Walker & Madsen 2016). Wiggins and Ruefli (2002), moreover, agree if profits above the average industry profits were achieved for 10 years at the minimum. On the other hand, several opinions state that competitive advantage is defined if the company succeeds in obtaining profit that is above normal or breakeven level (Peteraf 2007).

A company has a competitive advantage over its rivals when its profitability is higher than the average profitability of all companies in its industry. It has a sustained competitive advantage when it is able to maintain above-average profitability over several years. The primary objective of the strategy is to achieve a sustained competitive advantage, which in turn will result in superior profitability and profit growth (Hill et al. 2004).

The most popular definition of competitive advantage was introduced by Porter in 1980, which is the capability of a company to produce value for consumers at prices lower than production costs or that consumers are willing to pay premium prices because the value of these products is considered higher than the price. A company is considered to have a competitive advantage if a company is able to show performance above average or generate profits above the normal profit (rent) on an ongoing basis (Porter 1980, 1985). Referring to the various definitions established by previous researchers, this study defines competitive advantage as "the ability of a company to gain excellent business performance that happen when a business unit acquires or develops an attribute or combination of attributes that makes it capable of surpassing its competitors."

Peteraf (1993) introduced the MBV theory as "the cornerstone of competitive advantage" that it can be established through (1) heterogeneity, (2) ex-post limit to competition, (3) imperfect mobility, and (4) ex-ante limit to competition. Best (2000) states that the factors that produce a competitive advantage are differentiation advantage, cost advantage, and marketing advantage. Hill and Jones (1998) introduced the RBV concept as a "generic building block of competitive advantage," which states that it results from (1) superior quality, (2) superior efficiency, (3) superior innovation, and (4) superior customer responsiveness. Barney (2001) shares the concept of SCA (sustainable competitive advantage), where sustainable competitive advantage will be obtained if the resources (resources) and capabilities developed meet the four dimensions of VRIO, namely (1) valuable, (2) awareness, (3) imitability, and (4) organizational exploited.

A different opinion was also shared by Ma (2004), that competitive advantage, in general, is determined by dimensions of the 4 C, namely, (1) creation and innovation, (2) competition, (3) co-option, and (4) cooperation. Other researchers provided various dimensions such as cost advantage and differentiation excellence (Porter 1985), flexibility (Pearce & Robinson 1995), speed (Eisenhardt 1989), and innovation (Hamel & Prahalad 1989; Kim & Mauborgne 2005). The dimensions and indicators for measuring the competitive advantage in this research were combining the theory of MBV and RBV, which were first introduced by Nidumolu and Knotts (1998) and then developed by Chen (2012) and Nashiruddin (2014), namely, (1) product cost-efficiency, which explains efficiency advantages in organizations when producing products, representing the RBV approach, and (2) speed of market response, which describes the superiority of the organization in responding to market changes in a timely manner, representing the MBV approach.

2.2 *Business strategy*

Business strategies are policies and guidelines that determine how a company competes in industry and specific ways to form a competitive advantage (Grant 1991). Business strategies have a crucial role in helping the success of a company. Hubbard and Beamish (2011) describe business strategy as a link that relates to environmental demands (including customer needs), organizational capabilities, and desires of key stakeholders. An effective business strategy must fulfill all the interests of all three.

Wheelen et al. (2018) define business strategy as a decision to focus on the competitive position of the company's products/services in the industry or specific market segments that the company serves. If the corporate strategy provides direction in developing, stabilizing, and shrinking business owned by the company, the business strategy addresses how companies and business units compete with similar companies in the industry. The business strategy in this study is defined as a strategy formulated by business units in creating a competitive advantage to have an excellent performance to win the competition in the industry.

Therefore, researchers applied two common approaches to measure business strategy. The first approach is competitive strategy (fight against competitors to win the competition), and the second approach is cooperative strategy (collaborate with one or several companies to strengthen excellence against competitors).

3 METHODOLOGY

Verification research methodology applied and the study population was all halal travel operators as members of the Halal Travel Consortium. There were 1,155 members of consortium when the study was carried out. The samples were drawn using the Slovin's formula as follows: n = N/(1+Ne^2) where n is the number of minimal samples required, N is population, e = critical value (percentage of tolerance due to sampling error). Therefore, with population (N) = 1155 and critical value (e) = 10%, the required samples (n) were 1155/(1+1155x(0.1^2)) = 92. Primary data were collected through a questionnaire that was adapted from a previous study for the telecommunication industry in Indonesia, which was developed by Nashiruddin (2014). An online survey questionnaire link was sent to members of the Halal Travel Consortium through email and Whatsapp in January 2020.

4 RESULT AND DISCUSSION

4.1 *Respondent profiles*

The research required the respondent to be one who is at the managerial level and who has been working at the halal tourism industry for several years. The questionnaire link was shared to 1,155 operators, and the completed questionnaires were 132, among which 92 were valid, and it gives the validity rate at 69.6 %. Results of data analysis about respondents' characteristics have shown 42% of respondents provide domestic or international halal tour packages, nearly 35% of respondents provide umrah/hajj travel packages, as well as domestic or international halal tour packages.

4.2 *Regression analysis*

The regression equation is Y = 10.244 + 0.417 X. Interpretation of the equation is that the regression coefficient of business strategy has a positive sign (4.015), which means the business strategy variable is linear with competitive advantage variable. In other words, strategy business has a positive effect on competitive advantage.

4.3 *Significance analysis*

F-count (12.999) > F-table (3.95) with significance level 0.001 < 0.05. Therefore, regression equation of 10.244 + 0.417 X is significant.

4.4 *Regression linearity analysis*

F-count value is 0.977 < F-table 0.395, meaning that there is a significant and linear effect between business strategy (X) to competitive advantage (Y).

4.5 *Descriptive analysis*

Results of descriptive analysis of competitive advantage variable reveal that ability to produce products/services at a lower cost (Std Dev 0.785) and ability to charge competitive prices for products/services (Std Dev 0.785) from product-cost efficiency dimension becomes the highest priority among halal tour operators. This finding is in line with a theory shared by Porter in 2018 that competitive advantage is the ability of a company to give value for consumers at a lower price than production cost, or the consumer is willing to pay a high price due to the value of the product. Besides, the study result shows a competitive advantage at the company level comes from cost-efficient leadership and quality differentiation (Porter 1980; Teece et al. 2008).

The speed of the market response dimension reveals that the ability to better tailor products/services to individual customer needs (Std Dev 0.760) has been selected as the most priority aspect by respondents. This finding shows the competitive advantage of halal tour operators can create higher economic value compared with the general tour operator. It is in line with a theory mentioned by Barney and Arikan in 2006 that competitive advantage is the ability of an organization to create higher economic value than the competitor.

Competitive strategy is chosen to focus on serving a specific segment (Std Dev 0.715), while cooperative strategy is selected to reduce risk and uncertainty (Std Dev 0.759). Because the standard deviation values for the two indicators are the same, it can be concluded that the respondent applies these two strategies simultaneously. Business strategy has a vital role in helping a company reach its success. This study shows halal travel operators of the Halal Travel Consortium members apply competitive strategy and cooperative strategy as their business strategy. This condition is following a theory shared by Wheelen et al. in 2018 that business strategy is a decision to focus on the competitive position of the company's products/services in the industry or specific market segment served by the company. The study results also confirm the findings of research conducted by Nashiruddin in 2014, who stated that to formulate a more optimal business strategy, it was necessary to increase the company's priority on partnership strategies, especially to reduce risk and uncertainty and reduce competition in the industry.

5 CONCLUSION

The result shows business strategy has a positive, linear, and significant effect on the competitive advantage of halal tourism operators in Indonesia. Competitive strategy is chosen to focus on serving a specific segment (Std Dev 0.715), while cooperative strategy is selected to reduce risk and uncertainty (Std Dev 0.759). It is known that ability to produce products/services at a lower cost (Std Dev 0.785) and the ability to charge competitive prices for products/services (Std Dev 0.785) from product-cost efficiency dimension become the highest priority among halal tour operators.

REFERENCES

Chen, X. 2012. Impact of Business Intelligence and I.T Infrastructure Flexibility on Competitive Advantage: An Organizational Agility Perspective. Dissertations. The University of Nebraska.

Eisenhardt, K. M., 1989. Making Fast Strategic Decisions in High-Velocity Environments. Academy of Management Journal, 32(3), 543–576. https://doi.org/10.2307/256434

Grant, R. M., 1991. The Resource-Based Theory of Competitive Advantage: Implications for Strategy Formulation. California Management Review, 33(3), 114–135. https://doi.org/10.2307/41166664

Hamel, G., & Prahalad, C. K., 1989. Strategic Intent. Harvard Business Review, (May-June 1989), 63–76.

Hill, C., Jones, G., & Galvin, P. 2004. Strategic Management: An Integrated Approach. Strategic Management: An Integrated Approach (11th Edition). Stamford, CT: Cengage Learning.

Hubbard, G., & Beamish, P., 2011. Strategic Management: Thinking, Analysis, Action.

Kim, W. C., & Mauborgne, R., 2005. Blue Ocean Strategy: How to Create Uncontested Market Space and Make the Competition Irrelevant. Harvard Business Review Press.

Nashiruddin, M. I. 2014. Model Strategi Bisnis dan Keunggulan Bersaing untuk Meningkatkan Kinerja Unit Bisnis Ditinjau dari Turbulensi Lingkungan dan Kapabilitas Dinamik (Survei pada Industri Penyelenggara Telekomunikasi di Indonesia). Dissertation. Bandung: Padjajaran University.

Nidumolu, S. R., & Knotts, G. W., 1998. The Effects of Customizability and Reusability on Perceived Process and Competitive Performance of Software Firms. MIS Quarterly, 22(2), 105–137.

Pearce, J. A., & Robinson, R. B., 1995. Strategic Management: Formulation, Implementation, and Control. McGraw Hill (Vol. 16). New York.
Peteraf, M., 2007. The Resource-Based Theory of the Firm - Challenges, New and Old. International. Journal of Learning and Intellectual Capital, 4(January 2007), 1–10.
Porter, M. E., 1980. Competitive Strategy: Techniques for Analyzing-Industries and Competitors. The Free Press (First Edition). New York: The Free Press.
Porter, M. E., 1985. Competitive Advantage: Creating and Sustaining-Superior Performance. New York: The Free Press.
Teece, D. J., Pisano, G., & Shuen, A., 2008. Dynamic Capabilities and Strategic Management. Strategic Management Journal, 18(March), 509–533. https://doi.org/10.1142/9789812834478_0002
Walker, G., & Madsen, T. L., 2016. Modern Competitive Strategy. McGraw-Hill Education (4th Edition). McGraw-Hill Education.
Wiggins, R. R., & Ruefli, T. W., 2002. Sustained Competitive Advantage: Temporal Dynamics and the Incidence and Persistence of Superior Economic Performance. Organization Science, 13(1), 81–105.
Wheelen, T. L., Hunger, J. D., Hoffman, A. N., & Bamford, C. E., 2018. Strategic Management and Business Policy: Globalization, Innovation, and Sustainability (15th Ed.). Pearson.

Synergizing Management, Technology and Innovation in Generating Sustainable and Competitive Business Growth – Hendayani et al (eds)
© 2021 Taylor & Francis Group, London, ISBN 978-0-367-68756-4

Relationship HR practices, perceived organization support, work stress, job satisfaction, and engagement in banking employees

E.J. Sagala, H.G. Ayuningtias & A.P. Prasetio
School of Economics and Business, Telkom University, West Java, Indonesia

ABSTRACT: This study aims to analyze the relationship between and among HR practices, perceived organizational support, work stress, job satisfaction, and engagement for banking employee. The research data were obtained from distributing questionnaires to 178 respondents. The questionnaire used had 81 statements. In analyzing the relationship between each of these, variables correlation analysis is used. There is a correlation between HR practices with perceived organization support, work stress, job satisfaction, and engagement. From the analysis of the data, the research shows that there is a significant positive relationship between HR practice, perceived organizational supports, job satisfaction, and employee engagement. Work stress has negative relationship between and among HR practice, perceived organizational supports, job satisfaction, and employee engagement.

1 INTRODUCTION

Human resources are aspects that exist in the company as a determining factor for their existence and play a role in contributing toward achieving the company's goals effectively and efficiently. Every company needs reliable and quality human resources. The company must be able to manage and pay attention to human resources as well as possible. Many factors drive the achievement of company goals. The factors chosen by the author to be examined in this study are HR practices, perceived organizational support, job satisfaction, work stress, and engagement. Job satisfaction is something that is individual, and each individual has a different level of satisfaction according to the value system that applies to him/her. Employees who are satisfied will show the nature and behavior in working whether the rules set by the company are in accordance with their values. If the employee who is not satisfied with the conditions of work or the regulations set by the company does not match his values, then there will be job dissatisfaction with the employee, which also affects the employee's desire to leave the company. The study was conducted to determine the relationship between HR practices, perceived organizational support, work stress, job satisfaction, and engagement (Dai & Qin 2016; Lu Y et al. 2017; Zhong et al. 2016). Covid pandemic 19 weakens the world economy; this has had an impact on the banking industry. According to the World Bank (2020), the financial performance of banks will decline until next year. Based on these reasons, the author chose banking employees. The results of this study are expected to be input for parties related to human resource management in decision making to achieve company goals.

2 LITERATURE REVIEW

2.1 *HR practices (HRP)*

The main area of decision coverage that affects the relationship between the organization and employees is called human resource management (Boxall & Purcell 2000). HR practice is

Table 1. Interpretation score.

No.	Percentage	Category
1	16.6%–30.5%	Very Low
2	>30.5%–44.4%	Low
3	>44.4%–58.3%	Moderate to Low
4	>58.3%–72.2%	Moderate to High
5	>72.2%–86.1%	High
6	>86.1%–100%	Very High

Source: Data author, 2020.

considered an opportunity to achieve growth, and managers need equipping capabilities with skilled employees (Kroon et al. 2013).

2.2 *Perceived organizational support (POS)*

The definition of perceived organizational support (POS) concept is the level at which employees believe that the organization has values contribution, well-being, and fulfills socioemotional needs (Dai & Qin 2016). According Settoon (1996), perceived organizational support reflects employee expectations and recognition of their personal values and contributions in accordance with the "social exchange theory."

2.3 *Work stress (WS)*

Job stress is a series of physiological, psychological, and behavioral as an impact of stress factors on individuals in the organization (Yan & Xie 2016). Job stress means "the physical and emotional response that occurs when the employee's work is not in accordance with capabilities, resources or worker needs" (Raja & Joseph 2007).

2.4 *Job satisfaction (JS)*

Job satisfaction is an affective feeling felt by employees related to work. Attitudes show overall feelings about work (Lu 2004). Job satisfaction is a feeling that arises as a result of the perception that work meets material and psychological needs (Aziri 2008).

2.5 *Employee engagement (EE)*

Employee engagement is related to the organization and the employee. An engaged employee is defined as an enthusiastic person who has a positive attitude at work, reputation, and interest (Dai & Qin 2016). Schaufeli et al. (2002) define engagement "as a positive, satisfying, work related state reflected through passion, dedication, and absorption."

3 METHODOLOGY

The number of respondents in this study was 178. The study uses descriptive analysis and correlation tests using the Spearman rank. Table 1 is an interpretation of scores in descriptive analysis.

Hypothesis

1. H_1: HR practices has a relationship with perceived organization support, work stress, job satisfaction and employee engagement
2. H_2: Perceived organization support has a relationship with HR practices, work stress, job satisfaction, and employee engagement

Table 2. Descriptive analysis result.

Variables	Percentage	Category
HR Practices	69.0%	Moderate to High
Perceived Organization Support	67.9%	Moderate to High
Work Stress	64.5%	Moderate to High
Job Satisfaction	72.3%	High
Employee Engagement	78.5%	High

3. H_3: Work stress has a relationship with HR practices, perceived organization support, job satisfaction, and employee engagement
4. H_4: Job satisfaction has a relationship with HR practices, perceived organization support, work stress, and employee engagement
5. H_5: Employee engagement has a relationship with HR practices, perceived organization support, work stress, and job satisfaction

4 RESULT

4.1 *Descriptive analysis*

Based on the results of data processing obtained the results of descriptive analysis on HR practices, perceived organization support, and work stress are in the moderate to high category ranging between 64.5–69%. Whereas job satisfaction and employee engagement are in the high category ranging from 72.3% to 78.5%. The results indicated that the perception of banking employees felt that HR practices in the company were quite effective, organizational support was considered to be sufficient to support employees, and the employees felt that they were experiencing low levels of stress that could still be controlled by each employee. In terms of job satisfaction, employees feel satisfied with the company, and employee engagement at the company is also high because aspects such as HR practices, perceived organization support, and work stress can be managed well by the company.

4.2 *Correlation analysis*

The results of the HR practices correlation analysis have a significant positive relationship with perceived organization support, job satisfaction and employee engagement while having a negative relationship with work stress. Perceived organization support has a significant positive relationship with HR practices, job satisfaction, and employee engagement while it has a negative relationship with work stress. Work stress has a negative relationship with HR practices, perceived organization support, job satisfaction, and employee engagement. Employee engagement has a positive and significant relationship with HR practices, perceived organization support, and job satisfaction while it has a negative relationship with work stress.

HR practices have a perceived impact on the organization support (POS), and the effect of work engagement on role performance, organizational citizenship behavior (OCB), and intention to stop (Zhong et al. 2016). "The degree to which employees believe their contribution and welfare are valued by the organization" (Robbins & Judge 2008: 103). Based on this opinion, it is known that POS is the employee's perception of the organization where they work. Organizations generally provide forms of positive support to employees, for example, by giving approval, respect, fair treatment, salaries, promotions, voting rights, access to information, and other assistance that can support the implementation of work and welfare. These various forms of acceptance make employees feel responsible for contributing and giving their best performance in return for feeling

Table 3. Correlation analysis result.

Variables	HR Practices	Perceived Organization Support	Work Stress	Job Satisfaction	Employee Engagement
	Correlation Coefficient	Correlation Coefficient	Correlation Coefficient	Correlation Coefficient	Correlation Coefficient
HR Practices	1,000	,792**	–,217**	,705**	,570**
Perceived Organization Support	,792**	1,000	–,255**	,769**	,583**
Work Stress	–,217**	–,255**	1,000	–,217**	–,257**
Job Satisfaction	,705**	,769**	–,217**	1,000	,669**
Employee Engagement	,570**	,583**	–,257**	,669**	1,000

valued and cared about by the organization, so that the support provided is able to cause employee perceptions of the organization. Employees with high levels of POS give maximum performance. POS also produces replies in the form of employee engagement.

5 DISCUSSION

From the analysis of the data, the research shows that there is a significant positive relationship between and among HR practice, perceived organizational supports, job satisfaction, and employee engagement. Work stresses have negative relationship between and among HR practice, perceived organizational supports, job satisfaction, and employee engagement. This research has limitations. For further research it can expand the object of banking not only in one type of bank. Then for the analysis it can also be tested by moderating variables by using the SEM-PLS statistical test in this study.

REFERENCES

Aziri, B. 2008. Menaxhimi i burimeve njerëzore, Satisfaksioni nga puna dhe motivimi i punëtorëve, Tringa Design, Gostivar, p. 46.

Boxall, P. & Purcell, J. 2000, "Strategic human resource management: where have we come from and where should we be going?" International Journal of Management Reviews, Vol. 2 No. 2, pp. 183–203, doi: 10.1111/1468-2370.00037.

Dai, K. & Qin, X. 2016 Perceived Organizational Support and Employee Engagement: Based on the Research of Organizational Identification and Organizational Justice. *Open Journal of Social Sciences*, **4**, 46–57. doi: 10.4236/jss.2016.412005.

Kroon, B., Van De Voorde, K. & Timmers, J. 2013. "High performance work practices in small firms: a resource-poverty and strategic decision-making perspective", Small Business Economics, Vol. 41 No. 1, pp. 71–91, doi: 10.1007/s11187-012-9425-0.

Lu H, While A.E, & Barriball K.L. 2004. Job satisfaction among nurses: a literature review. Int J. Nurs Stud 2005; 42; 211–27. https://doi.org/10.1016/j.ijnurstu.2004.09.003

Lu Y, Hu X-M, Huang X-L, et al. 2017. Therelationship between jobsatisfaction, work stress, work–family conflict, and turnover intention among physicians in Guangdong, China: a crosssectional study.BMJ Open.doi:10.1136

Raja P.A. & Nima M.J, "Interpersonal Relationship and Stress Coping of TeacherTrainees", Journal of Educational Research and Extension, 2007, Vol.44 (2). p. 15.

Robbins, S. P. & Judge T.A. 2008. Perilaku Organisasi Edisi ke-12, Jakarta: Salemba Empat.

Settoon, R. P., Bennett, N., & Liden, R. C. 1996. Social exchange in organizations: Perceived organizational support, leader–member exchange, and employee reciprocity. Journal of Applied Psychology, 81(3), 219–227. https://doi.org/10.1037/0021-9010.81.3.219

Schaufeli, W.B., Salanova, M., Gonzalez-Roma, V. & Bakker, A.B. 2002. "The measurement of engagement and burnout: a two sample confirmatory factor analytic approach", Journal of Happiness Studies, Vol. 3 No. 1, pp. 71–92.

Yang, S., Meredith, P., & Khan, A. 2015. Stress and burnout among healthcare professionals working in a mental health setting in Singapore. Asian journal of psychiatry, 15, 15–20

Zhong, L., Wayne, S. J., and Liden, R. C. 2016. Job engagement, perceived organizational support, high-performance human resource practices, and cultural value orientations: A cross-level investigation. J. Organiz. Behav. 37: 823– 844. doi: 10.1002/job.2076.

Synergizing Management, Technology and Innovation in Generating Sustainable and Competitive Business Growth – Hendayani et al (eds)
 ISBN 978-0-367-68756-4

Understanding the customer satisfaction factors in coffee shops

T. Hermina & H. Fauziah
Universitas Garut, West Java, Indonesia

ABSTRACT: The increasing percentage of coffee consumption in Indonesia creates a tighter competition among coffee shops. Therefore, this study purposed to identify the factor of satisfaction and the positioning attributes that impact the consumer's satisfaction. This research investigated 184 customers of coffee shops in Garut Regency. The method of this research used quantitative and the primary data was obtained through observation and sharing the questionnaire. Then, the data analyzed use factor analysis and multidimensional scaling. The result of the research is there are four factors that impact satisfaction to the customer; these factors are the taste of coffee, freshness of coffee, appearance of coffee, and originality of the menu. In addition, the positioning of customer's satisfaction indicates that freshness of coffee and originality menu have similar perception of coffee shop satisfaction while the taste of coffee and appearance of coffee has different perception of coffee shop's customers.

1 INTRODUCTION

Management science is applied in a business to achieve the goals set. Management science is applied in marketing activities to identify and meet human and social needs (Kotler & Keller 2016). As in the case of coffee plantation commodities in Indonesia, they have applied marketing management knowledge so that coffee plantation commodities in Indonesia are able to score foreign exchange rates and have high commercial value. In 2016, Indonesia ranked fourth in the world with the largest quantity of production in the world after Brazil, Vietnam, and Colombia (Sudarto 2017). According to the International Coffee Organization (ICO), Sudarto (Sudarto 2017) states that the State of Indonesia occupies the seventh position as a consumer of coffee in the world. This was motivated by a change in the tradition of drinking coffee. Nowadays, the tradition of drinking a cup of coffee is not only in entertaining guests or celebrating weddings, but in some activities such as meetings, reunions, dating, or business meetings; even breakfast cannot be separated from a cup of coffee. Consumers can enjoy quality coffee not only at Starbucks or at the Coffee Bean. Because local coffee drinks cafes are now present everywhere from the roadside, business district, to the mall. The increasing number of new coffee shops can lead to increasingly fierce competition in the coffee industry. Situations like this require companies to create superior strategies.

2 LITERATURE REVIEW

2.1 *Consumer satisfaction*

Consumer satisfaction according to Kotler and Keller (Kotler & Keller 2009) is the level of one's feelings after comparing the performance (or results) that consumers feel compared to their expectations. Consumers can experience one of three common levels of satisfaction. If the performance is below expectations, consumers are disappointed and reversely. According to Tjiptono and Chandra (Tjiptono & Chandra 2016), customer satisfaction is a response (emotional or cognitive) regarding a particular focus (expectations, products, consumption experience) that occurs at a certain time.

Customer satisfaction consists of three components: the response concerns a particular focus that is determined at a certain time. To analyze customer satisfaction, this research examines three main attributes that can illustrate coffee shop characteristics: customer needs, delivery system, and value proposition. The prior research has defined customer needs as the producers must pay attention to what is needed by consumers (Liu, et al. 2019). According to Kotler and Keller (Kotler & Keller 2012), the customer needs involves taste, freshness, appearance of food, originality of menu, and price of menu, and those prior literature have shown that food quality is the most significant element in the food service business (Dorn, et al. 2016; Han & Hyun 2017). The second variable that the study examines is "delivery system," which is defined as the experience gained by consumers during the desired product, which includes the quality of service (Han, et al. 2012; Ryu, et al. 2008). Similarly, according to Hwang and Ok (Hwang & Ok 2013) it was revealed that in casual and fine dining restaurants, outcomes (e.g., customer satisfaction and favorable behavioral intention) are determined by the interaction between customers and employees. The delivery system involves promptness of service, staff skill, hospitality of staff, and staff's appearance (Kim, et al. 2009; Ringle, et al. 2011). The third attribute of this research is "value proposition" that is defined as the value or benefits of services offered to consumers, which includes hygiene and the atmosphere (design). Several studies have found that the selection of a restaurant is more difficult than in many other situations, because both intangible and tangible products are involved. Customers are partially involved in a physical environment such as interior design, lighting, cleanliness, and size of restaurant (Lopez, et al. 2018; Quan & Wang 2004).

3 RESEARCH METHOD

This study schematizes the hypotheses and presents them in Figure 1. The confirmatory variables are customer needs, delivery system, and value proposition. The four attributes are possible antecedents of satisfaction, and satisfaction is considered to explain positioning. Numerous studies were reviewed in reference to measurement tools, and they were modified in the study context. The items were presented on a 5-point Likert scale (1 = strongly disagree–5 = strongly agree) and modified according to the study content. The Google Form was used as a collection technique to obtain the primary data through providing the questionnaire. The total number of participants was 184 (all were the customers of a coffee shop in Garut). For the data analysis, the Statistical Package for the Social Sciences (SPSS) version 20.0 was employed. Initially, the mean, mode, median, and standard deviations were calculated to collect descriptive information. Analyzing methods were used in this study: (1) frequency analysis for demographic characteristics, such as gender, age, education, job, and annual income, (2) reliability analysis to verify the reliability of each variable in the questionnaire, (3) factor analysis to verify validity, and (4) multidimensional standard analysis to compare the coffee shop customers' perceptions of the selection attributes.

4 DISCUSSION

In this research, to obtain the data to coffee shop's consumer satisfaction in Garut Regency, researchers distributed questionnaires to 184 respondents who are customers of Kopilogi Coffee Shop. The distribution of questionnaires was conducted August 9 to April 4, 2020 online via Google Form, the characteristics of the respondents in this study are males, who accounted for 98 respondents (53.26%) and females 86 (46.74%); 74 participants were 21 to 25 years old (40.22%) followed by the 20s (62 respondents, 33.7%) and 26 to 30 years old (16.30%). In terms of the level of highest education, bachelor's degrees (66.30%) respondents and 46 (25%) had senior high school. With regard to annual income levels, up to Rp.1.000,000 had the highest proportion, accounting for 53.26% (98), followed by Rp.1.000,000–Rp. 2,000,000 (45 or 24.46%), and Rp.2.000,000–Rp. 3,000,000 (21, 11.41%). In other characteristics, the usage of the Coffee Shop illustrates the usage of coffee shop based on 184 respondents' perspective. Usually, the most respondents visit the coffee

Table 1. Rotated component matrix

Rotated Component Matrix[a]

	Component			
	1	2	3	4
Taste of coffee	–,307	,319	,472	–,086
Freshness of coffee	–,205	–,040	,886	–,035
Appearance of coffee	,300	–,022	,890	–,108
Originality menu	,741	–, 042	,568	–,134
Price of menu	,919	,075	,134	–,069
Promptness of service	,892	,136	–,169	,131
Staff skill	,710	,241	–,317	,271
Hospitality of staff	,203	–,024	–,169	,916
Appearance of staff	,032	,139	–,115	,889
Interior design of coffee shop	,250	,735	–,005	,181
Lighting of coffee shop	,155	,910	,000	,097
Cleanliness of coffee shop	–,036	,902	,011	,000
Size of coffee shop	–,306	,371	,198	,498

Extraction Method: Principal Component Analysis.
Rotation Method: Varimax with Kaiser Normalization.

shop three to four times in a week (48.37%); 63 participants visit the coffee shop one to two times in a week (34.24%). There are several purposes that they visit to the coffee shop, such as meeting friends accounted for 102 respondents (55.43%) and to celebrate special moments with family or a family party, 40 participants (21.74%). When they were visiting the coffee shop, the participants provide consumptions budget about Rp 26,000–Rp 30,000, which accounted for 61 respondents (33.15%); 47 respondents provide Rp 20,000-Rp25,000. The interesting data was that the customer obtain entirely information from social media, which accounted for 157 participants (85.33%); 24 respondents obtained the information about coffee shops from other people (family members and friend), while the other media were such as found by themselves unintentionally for 3 participants (1.63%). As shown in the results, overall reliability of each variable in the questionnaire, indicates more than 0.6 which means high reliability. The factor analysis begins by determining the correlation matrix of all indicator pairs in this study. Then, based on the KMO and Bartlett's Test indicate that the indicators correlated and arer worth further analysis.

Then, from the 13 indicators above, summarized into four factors are taste of coffee, freshness of coffee, appearance of coffee, and originality menu because the Eigen value more than 1 of the attributes 1 to 4, in contrast to indicators 5 to 13, which have Eigen value below 1 and therefore cannot be used in calculating the number of factors formed. Based on component matrix calculating explained that after four factors are known to be the most optimal numbers, the component matrix shows the distribution of the 13 indicators on the factors formed. While the figures in the table are factor loading which shows the magnitude of the correlation between an indicator with factor 1, factor 2, factor 3, and factor 4. The process of determining indicators with factors which is done by making a large comparison of correlations on each row. The multidimensional scaling (MDS) is used in this research to investigate the positioning of attributes that impact on customer satisfaction by comparing the Euclidean distance.

Figure 1 indicates that the value of stress as of. 036241, which indicates the goodness of data was very good and the coefficient of determination (RSQ) value was found to be comparatively high at. 12073. Then, the positioning map was illustrated that staff skill, taste of coffee, price menu, and cleanliness of coffee shop have higher value of dimension two than other variables. Meanwhile,

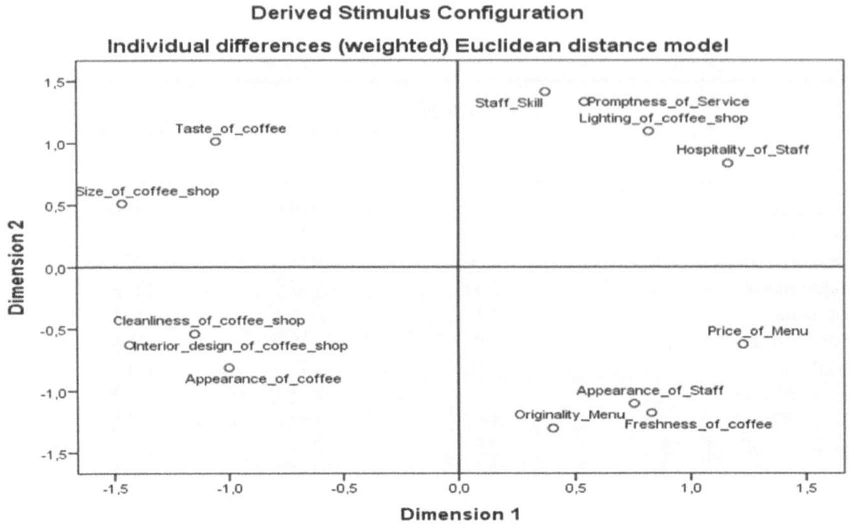

Figure 1. Results of euclidean distance model.

hospitality of staff, taste of coffee, appearance of coffee, and price of menu showed the higher score than other in dimension one.

5 CONCLUSION

Based on the results of research and discussion conducted regarding the analysis of factors that encourage satisfaction of the Coffee Shop in Garut Regency, the researchers drawn conclusions from the results based on responses from 184 respondents using factors from 13 indicators that are determined to form four factors that can drive business success. These factors are taste of coffee, freshness of coffee, appearance of coffee, and originality of the menu. Meanwhile, based on the positioning of customer's perception using multi-dimensional scaling indicates that staff skill, taste of coffee, price menu, and cleanliness of coffee shop has higher value of dimension two than other variables. Meanwhile, hospitality of staff, taste of coffee, appearance of coffee, and price of menu showed the higher score than other in dimension one.

REFERENCES

Dorn, M., Messner, C. & Wänke, M., 2016. Partitioning the choice task makes Starbucks coffee taste better. *Journal of Marketing Behavior,* Volume 1, pp. 363–384.

Han, H. & Hyun, S. S., 2017. Impact of hotel-restaurant image and quality of physical- environment, service, and food on satisfaction and intention. *International Journal of Hospitality Management,* Volume 63, pp. 82–92.

Han, S., Ham, S., Yang, I. & Baek, S., 2012. Passengers" perceptions of airline lounges: Importance of attributes that determine usage and service quality measurement. *Tourism Management,* 5(33), pp. 1103–1111.

Hwang, J. & Ok, C., 2013. The antecedents and consequence of consumer attitudes toward restaurant brands: A comparative study between casual and fine dining restaurants.. *International Journal of Hospitality Management,* Volume 32, pp. 121–131.

Keller, P. K. d. K. L., 2009. *Manajemen Pemasaran Edisi ketiga belas.* Jakarta: Erlangga.

Kim, W. G., Ng, C. Y. & Kim, Y. S., 2009. Influence of institutional DINESERV on customers' satisfaction, return intention, and word-of-mouth. *International Journal of Hospitality Management,* Volume 28, pp. 10–17.

Kotler, P. & Keller, K. L., 2009. *Manajemen Pemasaran Edisi ketiga belas.* London: Pearson Prentice Hal.
Kotler, P. & Keller, K. L., 2012. *Marketing Management.* New Jersey: Prentince-Hall Published.
Liu, L., Zhang, L., Ye, P. & Liu, Q., 2019. User Needs Mining Based on Topic of Analysis of Online Review. *Original Science Paper,* 1(26), pp. 230–235.
Lopez, J. G., Morales, J. A., Iglesias, G. A. & Moreno, G. A., 2018. Service Quality in Medellin Hotels Using Perceptual Maps. *Administración Journal of Management,* 34(60), pp. 31–45.
Quan, S. & Wang, N., 2004. Towards a structural model of the tourist experience: An illustration from food experience in tourism.. *Tourism Management,* Volume 25, pp. 297–305.
Ringle, C., Sarstedt, M. & Zimmermann, L., 2011. Customer satisfaction with commercial airlines: The role of perceived safety and purpose of travel. *Journal of Marketing Theory and Practice,* 4(19), pp. 459–472.
Ryu, k., Han, H. & Kim, T., 2008. The relationships among overall quick-casual restaurant image, perceived value, customer satisfaction, and behavioral intentions. *International Journal of Hospitality Management,* 3(27), pp. 459–469.
Sudarto, 2017. *Peluang Usaha IKM Kopi.* Jakarta: Kementerian Perindustrian.

Synergizing Management, Technology and Innovation in Generating Sustainable and Competitive Business Growth – Hendayani et al (eds)
© 2021 Taylor & Francis Group, London, ISBN 978-0-367-68756-4

Tourist segmentation of Mount Guntur tourism object using discriminant analysis

D.T. Alamanda, W. Susilawati, R. Setiawan & R.M. Haryanto
Faculty of Economics, Garut University, Jawa Barat, Indonesia

ABSTRACT: Mountain tourism is typically visited more than once by tourists. However, some prefer visiting a new mountain. The study aims to identify factors affecting the revisit intention of tourists at Mount Guntur. It used quantitative methods and the data were collected through interviewing some informants and distributing questionnaires to 100 respondents who had visited and were visiting Mount Guntur. The collected data were analyzed using discriminant analysis. The result shows experiences in visiting Mount Guntur and Mount Guntur is good nature tourism with wonderful scenery.

1 INTRODUCTION

Industrial and corporate competitiveness has become one of the most important research topics in economics and business studies (Scott 2008). The tourism business is in great demand and highly needed by the community enabling to contribute to economic and social development (Scott 2008) and to achieve sustainable economic growth (Font & McCabe 2017). Currently, tourism destinations are facing new challenges as a result of changes in consumers and the environment (Soteriades 2012). The changes in consumer behavior, persuasive communication, and business environments need good marketing skills and techniques to achieve sustainable marketing (Font & McCabe 2017).

In a strategic approach, tourism marketing reflects the perspectives of visitors and service providers (Soteriades 2012). Tourism marketing is important to develop a sustainable tourism business Moscardo & Murphy 2016). Moreover, Moscardo and Murphy (2016) used a tourist market segmentation approach which results in the value of segmentation strategy. Mount Guntur is one of the most popular attractions among Indonesian tourists in West Java. The tourism manager stated that the average number of visitors per week reaches 3,000 of 150 groups which are dominated by tourists from several cities in West Java. However, Mount Guntur is not the only mountain attraction in Garut as there are Mount Papandayan and Mount Cikuray which have almost similar tourist attractions managed by different organizations. Besides the presence of competitors, the behavior of tourists also be-comes a concern of tourism managers. The result of interviews with some tourists shows that some respondents have revisited the mountain for 2-3 times and some others prefer to visit different mountains. It signals a good business opportunity; therefore, it is important to identify factors affecting the revisit intention at Mount Guntur.

In the tourism and hospitality industry, identifiable attributes that contribute to tourist's perceptions depend on the diversity of products and target segments (Scott 2008). Based on this phenomenon, this study aims to produce a tourism market segmentation of Mount Gun-tur that focuses on the revisit intention of the tourists. The findings of the research are expected to provide input for tourism managers to create sustainable marketing strategies.

2 LITERATURE REVIEW

2.1 *Tourist's segmentation*

Tourism segmentation focuses on developing the profile of tourism segment using primary and secondary tourist data and understanding of segmentation that can accurately predict future tourist behavior (Tkaczynski et al. 2009). The market segmentation process which uses tourism characteristics that are consistent with the elements, needs, and aspirations of destination community wellbeing (DCW) shows the value of a more sustainable segmentation strategy compared to more traditional market segmentation techniques (Moscardo & Murphy 2016). This study used the attributes of tourist attractions in segmenting the tourists with and without revisit intention.

2.2 *Tourist revisit intention*

Attractiveness, perceived quality, and perceived value affect and increase the revisit intention (Ramadlani & Hadiwidjaja 2013). Chen et al. (2017) assesses the risk of tourist destinations which can reduce tourist satisfaction that affects the revisit intention. Meanwhile, Ramadlani and Hadiwidjaja (2013) stated that the more tourist destinations, the higher the tourist's expectations for a vacation which will increase satisfaction and revisit intention. This current research adopted the findings of Alamanda et al. (2020) in which tourist attractions on tourist destination are determinants of revisit intention for Mount tourism.

3 METHODS

3.1 *Characteristics and research procedures*

This research is quantitative with a descriptive explanatory level. The data collection covered 3 stages. A literature study was conducted to formulate the state of the art about tourist attractions at tourist destinations. The result of the literature study is several selected variables used in the interview guide in stage 2. The second stage is interviewing three informants, including a tourist (IDG), a nature lover (RRM), and a tourism researcher (RF). Interviews were conducted to reduce the variables used in the development of the questionnaire for stage 3. The third stage is the key stage in which the questionnaire was distributed to 100 tourists at Mount Guntur. The respondents were selected based on the non-probability sampling of a purposive sampling method.

3.2 *Conceptual framework and hypotheses*

This study consisted of 1 independent variable and 1 dependent variable. The independent variable (Y) is the tourist market segments consisting of market segments with revisit intention at Mount Guntur (code 0) and market segments without revisit intention (code 1). Meanwhile, the independent variable is a revisit intention which consists of 10 indicators of the results of interviews with informants such as experiences in visiting Mount Guntur which are worthy to share to family, relatives, and others (X_1), Mount Guntur deserves to be recommended to others (X_2), positive aspects of Mount Guntur which are worthy to share (X_3), Tourism attractions at Mount Guntur are worth promoting (X_4), Mount Guntur is worth for revisit (X_5), Mount Guntur is good for nature tourism activities (X_6), tourist attractions on other mountains are not as interesting as on Mount Guntur (X_7), Mount Guntur has good access (X_8), Mount Guntur has an interesting view (X_9), and Mount Guntur is safe for tourism activities (X_{10}). Based on those findings, the research hypotheses are:

H_0 = all indicators of independent variables are factors affecting the revisit intention of visitors at Mount Guntur

H_1= only a few indicators affect the revisit intention of visitors at Mount Guntur

Table 1. Eigenvalues.

Function	Eigenvalue	% of Variance	Cumulative %	Canonical Correlation
1	,397[a]	100,0	100,0	,533

Table 2. Canonical discriminant function coefficients.

	Function
X1	,538
X6	,560
X9	,644
(Constant)	−7,006

Table 3. Classification function coefficients.

	Code	
	0	1
x1	3,706	4,377
x6	2,790	3,489
x9	4,785	5,588
(Constant)	−21,390	−30,131

4 RESULTS AND DISCUSSION

4.1 *Assumption test*

Based on the results of the SPSS output, normality test, the absence of multicollinearity between independent variables, and fulfilled homogeneity of variance between groups, there is a significant difference between groups of respondents who have a revisit intention in group 0 and respondents without a revisit intention in group 1.

4.2 *Discriminant test*

A total of 3 out of 10 variables tested finally could enter the model. The significance value of the 3 variables is 0.000 (<0.05). Thus, the three variables form groups with significant differences. Then, the researcher performed a canonical correlation value test. Table 1 presents the value of 0.5333 which, if square, it has a value of 0.2841. It means that the independent variables explain 28.41% of the model formed. Meanwhile, the value of 0.5333, based on the correlation reference according to Mukaka (2012) means that the relationship between discriminant values and groups is relatively high (between 0.5–0.7).

After knowing the level of relationship and the level of influence of independent and dependent variables, in the discriminant analysis, it is known that respondents are grouped into two, respondent with (code 0) and without a revisit intention (code 1). Table 2 contains information about the coefficients of each component of the discriminant function, namely Z score $= -7.006 + 0.538\ X_1 + 0.560\ X_6 + 0.644\ X_9$. Meanwhile, Table 3 presents the information which forms the model for each group.

For the visitor with revisit intention (code 0), the equation is:

$$\text{Value} = -21,390 + 3,706(X_1) + 2,790(X_6) + 4,785(X_9) \quad (1)$$

For visitor without revisit intention (code 1), the equation is:

$$\text{Value} = -30,131 + 4,377(X_1) + 3,489(X_6) + 5,588(X_9) \quad (2)$$

The functions and equations above are not significant if the tools used are not in accordance with the applied rules. Then, the researcher tested the accuracy of the discriminant tool and the summary of the result. In the original row, 38 respondents in group 0 were consistent and 12 respondents moved in group 1. However, 37 respondents in group 1 were consistent and 13 respondents moved in group 0. Then the accuracy of the discriminant function can be calculated by: (38 + 37) / 100 = 0.75 or 75%.

Indicators of telling or sharing the experience when traveling (X_1), indicators of natural tourism activities (X_2), and interesting view (X_3) are factors affecting the revisit intention of visitors at Mount Guntur. Tourism managers have to consider this finding. It is important to maintain an interesting view of this tourism destination. Diverse tourist attractions can be a part of a good marketing strategy, but they have to provide a memorable experience and worthy of sharing.

Tourism marketing develops, formulates, and implements a strategy to achieve the main goal of a tourist destination by designing and offering an unforgettable experience for the visitors (Soteriades 2012). To move towards sustainable tourism, it is necessary to improve destination management, create opportunities for networking and cooperation among tourism service providers (Welford & Ytterhus 2004). Destinations, attractions, resources, sectors, and development are tourism tools (Scott 2008). At present, it is better for tourism managers to not only promote destinations but also maintain long-term market sustainability (Pike & Page 2014).

5 CONCLUSION

Based on the results of the study, it can be concluded that there are two market segments of Mount Guntur, namely the market segment with revisit intention and market segment without revisit intention. Only 3 out of the 10 indicators tested affect the grouping of respondents, namely sharing the experience when traveling to Mount Guntur, natural tourism activities, and interesting views. Based on the discriminant analysis method, even though they only explain 28.41% of the model, the discriminant function is considered appropriate to answer research questions with 75% accuracy.

REFERENCES

Alamanda, D. T. *et al.* 2020. 'Factors Affecting Tourists' Destination Patronizing Intentions Toward Mount Papandayan Tourism, Indonesia', in *International Summit on Science Technology and Humanity (ISETH2019*, pp. 369–379.

Alebaki, M. & Iakovidou, O. 2011. 'Market segmentation in wine tourism: A comparison of approaches', *Tourismos*.

Blumberg, K. 2005. 'Tourism destination marketing – A tool for destination management? A case study from Nelson/Tasman Region, New Zealan', *Asia Pacific Journal of Tourism Research*, 10, pp. 45–57. doi: https://doi.org/10.1080/1094166042000330218.

Chen, J. V. *et al.* 2017. 'Investigating International Tourists' Intention to Revisit Myanmar Based on Need Gratification, Flow Experience and Perceived Risk', *Journal of Quality Assurance in Hospitality and Tourism*. doi: 10.1080/1528008X.2015.1133367.

Cohen, S. A., Prayag, G. & Moital, M. 2014. 'Consumer behaviour in tourism: Concepts, influences and opportunities', *Current Issues in Tourism*, 14(10), pp. 872–909.

Font, X. & McCabe, S. 2017. 'Sustainability and marketing in tourism: its contexts, paradoxes, approaches, challenges and potential', *Journal of Sustainable Tourism*. doi: 10.1080/09669582.2017.1301721.

Moscardo, G. & Murphy, L. 2016. 'Using destination community wellbeing to assess tourist markets: A case study of Magnetic Island, Australia', *Journal of Destination Marketing and Management*. doi: 10.1016/j.jdmm.2016.01.003.
Mukaka, M. M. 2012. 'Statistics Corner: A Guide to Appropriate Use of Correlation Coefficient in Medical Research', *Malawi Med Journal*, 24(3), pp. 69–71.
Park, D. B. & Yoon, Y. S. 2009 'Segmentation by motivation in rural tourism: A Korean case study', *Tourism Management*. doi: 10.1016/j.tourman.2008.03.011.
Pike, S. & Page, S. J. 2014. 'Destination Marketing Organizations and destination marketing: Anarrative analysis of the literature', *Tourism Management*. doi: 10.1016/j.tourman.2013.09.009.
Ramadlani, M. F. & Hadiwidjaja, D. 2013. 'Determinants Of Tourist Revisit Intention To Kota Batu', *Jurnal Ilmiah Mahasiswa FEB Universitas Brawijaya*, 1(2), pp. 1–20.
Scott, N. 2008. *Network analysis and tourism: From theory to practice*, *Network Analysis and Tourism: From Theory to Practice*.
Soteriades, M. 2012. 'Tourism destination marketing: approaches improving effectiveness and efficiency', *Journal of Hospitality and Tourism Technology*, 3(2), pp. 107–120. doi: http://dx.doi.org/10.1108/17579881211248781.
Tkaczynski, A., Rundle-Thiele, S. R. & Beaumont, N. 2009. 'Segmentation: A tourism stakeholder view', *Tourism Management*. doi: 10.1016/j.tourman.2008.05.010.
Welford, R. & Ytterhus, B. 2004. 'Sustainable development and tourism destination management: A case study of the Lillehammer region, Norway', *International Journal of Sustainable Development and World Ecology*. doi: 10.1080/13504500409469843.

Synergizing Management, Technology and Innovation in Generating Sustainable and Competitive Business Growth – Hendayani et al (eds)
© 2021 Taylor & Francis Group, London, ISBN 978-0-367-68756-4

E-Governance in tobacco excise sharing funds: An initiative to reduce the poverty of tobacco farmers in Indonesia

A. Wirawan
Lecture of Polytechnic of State Finance STAN, Banten, Ministry of Finance, Indonesia

B.R.P. Sinaga
Staff of the Ministry of Finance, Jakarta, Indonesia

ABSTRACT: Tobacco farmers who are vulnerable to poverty are inversely proportional to cigarette factory owners and cigarette excise revenue in Indonesia, whereas the total tobacco plantation area and production of farmers cover about 99% compared to the existing tobacco plantation area and production. This contradiction shows that the excise sharing funds to local governments and farmers are not an optimal and imprecise target. Based on the qualitative research based by sourcing secondary data (literature review and library research) and primary data (interviews with tobacco farmers) and by considering the poverty theory, one conclusion is produced. As the e-governance in tobacco excise sharing funds is not been implemented in Indonesia, the central government needs to consider e-governance in tobacco excise sharing funds in reducing the poverty of tobacco farmers through comfort, efficient, and transparent business processes and in mutually reinforcing parties (the government, cigarette manufacturers, and tobacco farmers) in increasing tobacco excise revenue.

1 INTRODUCTION

The World Bank Report states that Indonesia's population, which is very vulnerable to the poverty line, has the potential to be dominated by farmers because when there is a crop failure, it will result in an inability to return production capital. One agricultural sector that is very vulnerable to poverty is tobacco farmers, as according to Winslow, that tobacco farmers enter in a circular and cumulative process that continues to decline at a lower level, which is one negative factor that has two roles, as a cause as well as a result of negative factors as the other (Soemitro 1989). The vulnerability of poverty experienced by tobacco farmers is inversely proportional to the rank 1 and rank 2 of the richest people in Indonesia which according to Forbes in 2018 is the owner of a cigarette factory (Forbes 2019), even though about 99% of the area and production of tobacco plantations in Indonesia is produced by plantations the people as of the 2013–2017 data are presented in the Table 1 (BPS 2018).

It is necessary to find solutions to alleviate poverty for these tobacco farmers through the application of good governance through the maximization of technology, bearing in mind that there are still a number of problems with the Tobacco Product Excise Sharing Fund (*Dana Bagi Hasil Cukai Hasil Tembakau*/DBHCHT) provided by the central government to local governments, such as the insistence of regions to DBHCHT, which has been limited to only 2%, needs to be improved in order to fulfill public goods and services, and the procedure for filing program activities from DBHCHT is quite complicated because the submission and approval of program activities reach the central government (Directorate General of Fiscal Balance) (W 2018). For this reason, studies are needed that can address one main problem that exists, namely, how is the e-governance of DBHCHT in alleviating poverty of tobacco farmers in Indonesia?

Table 1. Area and production of tobacco plants in indonesia 2013–2017.

Year	Area of Large Plantation (thousands hectares)	Area of the People's Plantation (thousands hectares)	Large Plantation Production (thousands tons)	People's Plantation Production (thousands tons)
2013	3,1	189,7	3,1	161,3
2014	2,5	213,3	2,0	196,1
2015	0,6	208,3	0,9	192,9
2016	0,4	155,6	0,3	126,4
2017	0,7	185	0,5	151,8

2 LITERATURE REVIEW

There are several thoughts about revenue sharing funds in Indonesia. Article 1 number 20 of the Law on Fiscal Balance between the central government and regional governments means profit-sharing funds are funds sourced from APBN revenues that are allocated to the regions based on percentage figures to fund the needs of the regions in the context of the implementation of Decentralization. More specifically on tobacco products, Article 2 paragraph (1) letter e Regulation of the Minister of Finance No. 222/PMK.07/2017 concerning the Use, Monitoring, and Evaluation of Tobacco Product Profit Sharing Funds states that DBHCHT is to fund programs/activities to eradicate excisable goods illegally carried out in collaboration between the Directorate General of Customs and Excise with Provincial, Regency or City Regional Governments. But on the side of tobacco farmers in Indonesia they interpret DBHCHT as an obligation that must be given by the state in order to alleviate poverty in tobacco farmers.

Seeing the various meanings of profit-sharing funds and the reality and poverty experienced by tobacco farmers, which is very inversely proportional to the richness of cigarette factory owners in Indonesia, it is necessary to study theories about poverty and relate them to e-governance in producing DBHCHT governance that is comfortable, efficient, and transparent. The issue of e-governance cannot be separated from the role of government, which must be able to pursue information and communication technologies (ICTs) based solutions to facilitate good governance, as the keyword refers to combined, one-stop, connected, and open, and digital governance in its efforts to connect the government and its citizens (Suri & Sushil 2017). Meanwhile, poverty related to governance is stated by Sen and Yunus. According to Sen, poverty occurs due to capability deprivation of freedom to achieve something in one's life (Santosa 2019). The inability of leaders in avoiding poverty shows that there has been a failure of the government in carrying out substantive democracy, so it can be said that the cause of the perpetuation of poverty, powerlessness, and public affordability is the result of accessibility issues (Sen 1981). In this case, poverty due to narrow accessibility causes not everyone to know and utilize the facilitation of political freedom, economic opportunities, social opportunities, transparency, and social safety nets that are the people's right in a democratic country, which results in limited choices to develop their lives. Thus, humans only carry out what is forced to be done, not what should be done. Then, Jonah revealed that poverty is a threat to peace that must be understood humanly. Acute poverty that occurs due to damage to the quality of the environment and the absence of human rights will only cause an unjust economic, social, and political order that will threaten peace in any society, even it will only lead to frustration, hostility, and anger (Yunus 2007).

In alleviating poverty, there is a need for direct government control, recognition of the rights of tobacco farmers, and the availability of all tobacco farmers' resources through electronic media, as well as good governance, which leads to openness, and with due regard to the interests of all stakeholders encourages collaborative approaches and will help create efficient and transparent services in relations between and among the government, the private sector, the public sector (Malick & Murhy 2001), and tobacco farmers. The urgency of e-governance in DBHCHT governance in order to alleviate the poverty of tobacco farmers can be seen from several views that put

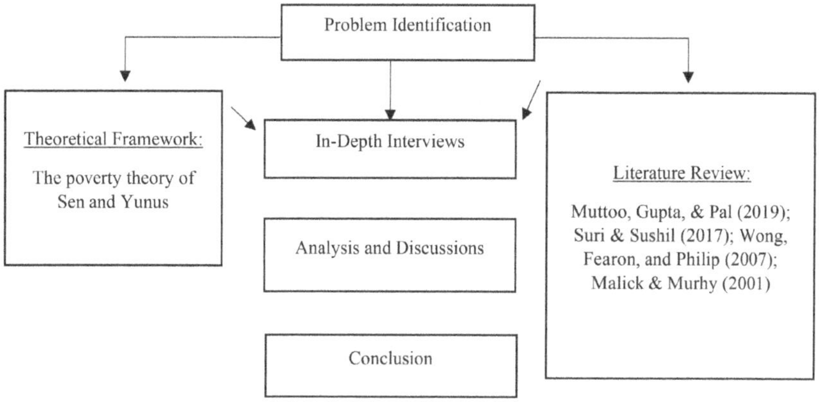

Figure 1. Research framework.

forward e-governance. Wong, Fearon, and Philip (2007) suggest that e-governance is far broader than e-government because its scope targets fundamental responsibilities to understand the needs of government, organizations, and citizens from the perspective of stakeholders, as long as they are conceptualized at four different levels, which is the transformation of government business; increased participation, openness, transparency, and communication; transformation in the interaction between government and internal and external clients; and transformation of society through the emergence of e-society, which forges networks of relationships such as connections between citizens and relationships between non-government organizations (NGOs). Then, Muttoo, Gupta, and Pal (2019) suggested that e-governance is related to the use of information technology and the Internet that is internally focused to manage human, material, and organizational capital in order to increase citizens' participation in services and participation of government institutions for publicity, delivery of information, or receiving feedback.

3 METHODOLOGY

As this study aims to evaluate how e-governance of DBHCHT is in alleviating poverty of tobacco farmers in Indonesia, so it is sufficient to use the qualitative research. Qualitative research explores attitudes and experiences through interview method in attempting to get an in-depth opinion (Dawson 2007) from tobacco farmers.

Data in this study consisted of primary data and secondary data. Primary data is obtained directly from informants by conducting interviews with key informants. Interviews that focus on issues of poverty among tobacco farmers are conducted to work out a dialectic between understanding the text as a whole and interpreting its parts so that perspectives and plans and the development of e-governance (Larsson & Grönlund 2016) of DBHCH can be generated in the future. Meanwhile, secondary data is data obtained indirectly from the first source, including covering official documents, books, research results in the form of reports, and so on (Amirudin & Asikin 2006). Further, a brief description of this research framework is described in Figure 1.

4 ANALYSIS AND DISCUSSIONS

4.1 *Governance of tobacco product excise profit sharing funds in Indonesia*

The DBHCHT has been regulated in Articles 66A through 66D of Law Number 11 of 1995 concerning excise as amended by Law Number 39 of 2007 (Excise Law). Article 66A of the Excise

Law confirms that state revenues from excise on tobacco products made in Indonesia are distributed to 2% tobacco excise producing provinces, which are used to fund the improvement of the quality of raw materials, industrial development, social environment development, socialization of provisions in excise fields, and/or the eradication of goods subject to illegal excise. Then, the governor manages and uses and regulates the DBHCHT to the regents/mayors based on the amount of contribution from the tobacco excise, where the distribution must be with the approval of the Minister of Finance with a composition of 30% for producing provinces, 40% for producing districts/cities, and 30% for other regencies/cities. Then, Article 66C of the Excise Law stipulates that the Minister of Finance conducts monitoring, evaluation, and follows up on the implementation of deviations related to the use of the budget to improve the quality of raw materials, industrial development, social environment development, socialization of provisions in the excise field, and/or eradication of illegal excisable goods, which come from DBHCHT. Furthermore, Article 66D of the Excise Law states that against the abuse of DBHCHT allocations, sanctions can be given in the form of suspension until the cessation of DBHCHT distribution.

In practice, Articles 66A to 66D of the Excise Law have several weaknesses. First, the Act is not followed up with Government Regulations and Presidential Regulations as technical implementation, but it is technically directly regulated based on Minister of Finance Regulation so that it contradicts Article 7 of Law Number 12 the Year 2011 concerning Formation of Regulations concerning the hierarchy of regulations. Of course, this shows the neglect of the check and balance function between ministries within the government internally so that it can become an arbitrary gap in implementing institutions for the technical regulation of DBHCHT, which can indirectly cause poverty, indirectly to tobacco farmers, as based on interviews that have been conducted on two key informants in Central Java. The fact is that the neglect of e-governance in DBHCHT governance has resulted in the accessibility referred to by Sen to be difficult to realize.

According to recognition D (2018), a tobacco farmer in Temanggung Regency, that capital to grow tobacco plants requires a capital of more than Rp.10 million. That's almost all for the needs of the process of growing tobacco itself. From buying good quality tobacco seeds to purchasing inexpensive fertilizers. Nearly most tobacco farmers borrow capital from moneylenders around the village. To produce the best quality tobacco (also known as *srintil*) that still depends on nature, such as the composition of rainwater that is acidic or not, and whether or not the sun is hot enough. Even though the best quality tobacco harvest, the price of dry tobacco farmers are valued by graders (people who determine the price of tobacco and are the intermediary of the cigarette warehouse with farmers). In fact, due to the poverty that strangles tobacco farmers, it has caused one farmer who is unable to pay loans to loan sharks to end up committing suicide. Other efforts have been made by tobacco farmers to support their activities. Tobacco farmers once submitted a request in the form of a tractor to support production as was given to rice farmers, but it was not approved by the central government because they thought that the tractor was not a tobacco farmer's needs. Another obstacle for farmers is the availability of fertilizer, where DBHCHT is not allowed to finance the purchase of fertilizers and cigarette factories which are farmers' partners who are not involved in the supply of tobacco agricultural fertilizer. The rejection of requests from tobacco farmers, both tractors and fertilizers, is inseparable from the rigidity of DBHCHT budgeting and the procedure for submitting and approving program activities to the central government (Directorate General of Fiscal Balance) is quite complicated (W 2018). Whereas farmers' tobacco harvests, which are only sold to graders that can be categorized as oligopsony (W 2018), always occur and without any government efforts to help farmers get out of the poverty trap that is always wrapped around them.

It must be realized that if this irony continues to tobacco farmers, then the concern of tobacco harvest (which is currently 99% of the area of tobacco plantations in Indonesia, which is a peoples plantation) will experience a decline in production should be anticipated by the government and cigarette factories in Indonesia. The central government (in this case is the Ministry of Finance) is supposed to change the DBHCHT allocation strategy but due to its current management has never been confirming the poverty experienced by tobacco farmers to the Minister of Finance. Tobacco farmers are unsung heroes of achieving tobacco excise revenue, whose fate has been ignored by the central government, which its excise revenues targets always surpluses in the last few years in Indonesia. The central government strategy that is right on target in allocating DBHCHT must be initiated through e-governance, which has included efforts to centralize every complaint and the needs of tobacco farmers in increasing the production and quality of tobacco and at the same time decentralizing the allocation of funds that is on target.

4.2 *E-Governance of tobacco excise sharing funds in reducing the poverty of tobacco farmers in Indonesia*

As the constitution guarantees equality among its citizens, e-governance is needed as a prerequisite for good governance transparently and independently with e-democracy inherent in supporting e-government that is able to realize the provision of quality services to citizens and stakeholders diverse (Malick & Murhy 2001). In this case, the term democratic e-governance describes changes in governance structures that tend to not only offer greater opportunities for citizen involvement, but also place greater weight on the role of citizens than the role of government, within which there is a conceptual framework which requires the quality of democracy in government, such as monitoring, deliberative, and participatory processes and/or information, consultation, and public participation (Lee-Geiller & Lee 2019). Good governance that is supported by adequate ICT is essential for equitable distribution, poverty alleviation, and improving the quality of life of all citizens, as Malick and Murhy (2001) suggest that good governance through e-government is a necessity in the development process given the framework of its work, which contains democratic, fair and honest, participatory, transparent and accountable principles, will guide every policy to be able to reach out to the responsibility for the allocation of resources, even to the acceptance of the views of the poorest and most vulnerable people directly.

Efforts to alleviate poverty through the implementation of e-government in DBHCHT governance is a very urgent need for tobacco farmers in Indonesia as are almost all victims of the poor because of moneylender businesses, including tobacco farmers. Of course, if these things still occur, then poverty as according to Sen is caused by the absence of a democratic process while according to Yunus its due to the absence of parties who want to lend money to the poor, it will cause tobacco farmers to live in poverty. It is seen that the relationship between the center and the regions remains one of the important issues in DBHCHT governance, whereas one of the efforts to reduce poverty, especially tobacco farmers, is by minimizing issues related to DBHCHT that have an impact on efforts to release tobacco farmers from the trap of moneylenders and efforts to minimize the disparity between cigarette factory entrepreneurs and tobacco farmers. So national e-governance policies are highly needed that can pay strong attention to public participation, transparency, and accountability through the introduction and promotion of decentralization, giving priority to local initiatives, conducting collaborations with network companies in terms of providing technology and network security, and making revitalization panels local communities and community networks (Kudo 2010) of tobacco farmers. Strengthening the active participation of every tobacco farmer must increase their awareness of their authority independently in criticizing any unscrupulous actions of local officials (such as village heads) who are not accountable in each stage/process of DBHCHT activities. Then, the non-transparent DBHCHT governance services will propel for the high responsiveness of each stakeholder involved in monitoring and evaluating DBHCHT governance, for the sake of social justice (Simanjuntak et al. 2020) for all tobacco farmers.

E-governance in the management of DBHCHT in the context of alleviating poverty against tobacco farmers must always rely on the use of ICTs built by the central government (Directorate General of Fiscal Balance) that enables stakeholder interaction with each other and contributes to fixing any problems that arise. One of the important things in building ICTs is through collaboration with network companies in making Internet applications and websites that are centered on the Directorate General of Fiscal Balance. Because this emphasis on governance must be understood within the framework of poverty alleviation of tobacco farmers, which can only be done through a dynamic process that requires the involvement of many parties (Larsson & Grönlund 2014) in minimizing any form of abuse of power in the management of DBHCHT, whose tendency is always applied by the certain actors through the encouragement and legitimacy of their three types of power, namely the financial power (connected to the socio-economic process), the coordination forces (used to drive interactions), and the authoritative forces (used to encourage the taking decision) (Wirawan et al. 2020). Then, the aim of the Local Community Revitalization Panel and Community Network is in line with what has been stated by Kudo (2010), that is, to conduct analysis and study matters, such as problems faced by tobacco farmers, the creation of cooperative networks among tobacco farmers, and how it will impact on improving the welfare of tobacco farmers, communication channels and complaints from tobacco farming communities to the central government regarding the misuse of the DBHCHT allocation on the sustainability of tobacco farming. The panel formed must routinely compile its findings against tobacco farmers and report to relevant stakeholders periodically.

5 CONCLUSIONS

As the e-governance in the DBHCHT allocation has not been implemented by the Directorate General of Fiscal Balance and Local Government, it is concluded that the central government (Directorate General of Fiscal Balance) must implement e-governance in the management of DBHCHT through the development of ICTs that can pay strong attention to public participation, transparency, and accountability through Internet applications and websites. Whereas Article 66C and Article 66D of the Excise Law Act have mandated that the Minister of Finance conduct monitoring, evaluation, follow-up, and stipulation of sanctions for misuse of the DBHCHT allocation, which is almost difficult to do if without implementing e-governance. Considering that the development of e-governance is in the framework of alleviating poverty of tobacco farmers throughout Indonesia, it is proposed to be strengthened by the establishment of a Local Community Revitalization Panel and Community Network and the development of cooperatives among tobacco farmers with funding from the DBHCHT allocation, so that improving tobacco farmers' welfare can increase the production and quality of tobacco, which will also have an impact in increasing the acceptance of excise tax on tobacco products for the country and minimizing the circulation of illegal cigarettes from abroad.

REFERENCES

Amirudin & Asikin, Z. 2006. *Pengantar Metode Penelitian Hukum*. Jakarta: PT Raja Grafindo Persada.

BPS. 2018. *Laporan Tahunan 2018*. Jakarta: Badan Pusat Statistika.

D. 2018. Wawancara pra penelitian dengan Petani Tembakau Desa Bagusan, Kecamatan Parakan, Kabupaten Temanggung pada Maret 2018.

Dawson, C. 2007. *A Practical Guide to Research Methods: A user-friendly manual for mastering research techniques and projects*. Oxford: How To Books Ltd.

Forbes. 2019. Availabale at https://www.forbes.com/Indonesia-billionaires/list/#tab:overall. Accessed on February 7, 2019.

Kudo, H. 2010. E-Governance as Strategy of Public Sector Reform: Peculiarity of Japanese IT Policy and Its Institutional Origin. *Financial Accountability & Management* 26(1): 65–84.

Larsson, H. & Grönlund, A. 2014. Future-oriented eGovernance: The sustainability concept in eGov research, and ways forward. *Government Information Quarterly* 31(1): 137–149.

Larsson, H. & Grönlund, A. 2016. Sustainable eGovernance? Practices, problems and beliefs about the future in Swedish eGov practice. *Government Information Quarterly* 33(1): 105–114.

Lee-Geiller, S. & Lee, T.(D.). 2019. Using government websites to enhance democratic E-governance: A conceptual model for evaluation. Government Information Quarterly 36(2): 208–225.

Malick, M.H. & Murthy, A.V.K. 2001. The Challenge of E-Governance. *Indian Journal of Public Administration* 47(2): 237–253.

Muttoo, S.K., Gupta, R. & Pal, S.K. 2019. *E-Governance in India: The Progress Status*. Singapore: Palgrave Macmillan & Springer Nature Singapore Pte Ltd.

Santosa, T. 2019. *Human capability : tujuan pendidikan*. Available at http://perpustakaan.bappenas.go.id/lontar/file?file=digitasl/blob/F16688/Human%20Capability.htm455. Accessed on March 6, 2019.
Sen, A. 1981. *Poverty and Femine: An Essay On Entitlement and Deprivation*. New York: Clarendon Press Oxford.
Simanjuntak, D., Utama, Y.U., Saraswati, R., Sukirno & Sinaga, R.Y. 2020. Reconstruction of Village Funds Supervision : An Action to Prevent Corruption in Village Funds Management. *Test Engineering and Management* 83(March-April 2020): 11850–11863.
Soemitro, R.H. 1989. *Studi Hukum dan Kemiskinan*. Tugu Muda.
Suri, P.K. & Sushil. 2017. *Strategic Planning and Implementation of E-Governance*. Singapore: Springer Science+Business Media Singapore.
Yunus, M. 2007. *Bank Kaum Miskin*. Translated by Nasution, I. Tangerang: Marjin Kiri.
W.K. 2018. Wawancara pra penelitian dengan Kepala Badan Pendapatan, Pengelolaan Keuangan dan Aset Daerah pada Maret 2018.
Wirawan, A., Saraswati, R., Sa'adah, N. & Sinaga, E.N. (2020). Preventing Corporate Corruption through Strengthening Accounting Education in Higher Education. *Test Engineering and Management* 83(March-April 2020): 11767 – 11779.
Wong, K., Fearon, C. & Philip, G. 2007. Understanding egovernment and egovernance: stakeholders, partnerships and CSR. *International Journal of Quality & Reliability Management* 24(9): 927 – 943.
World Bank, Laporan Bank Dunia, mengurangi kemiskinan, tanpa tahun, tanpa penerbit.

Synergizing Management, Technology and Innovation in Generating Sustainable and Competitive Business Growth – Hendayani et al (eds)
© 2021 Taylor & Francis Group, London, ISBN 978-0-367-68756-4

Next procurement prediction using Markov Chain Model with Maximum Likelihood, Maximum Likelihood with Laplace Smoothing, Bootstrap and Maximum a Posteriori methods: Case of Kimia Farma, Ltd.

F. Nurhadiansyah & G. Ramantoko
Magister Management, Faculty of Economics and Business, Telkom University, Bandung, West Java, Indonesia

ABSTRACT: The aim of this study is to explore whether captured procurement data of Kimia Farma, Ltd. can be used to predict the next procurement using Markov Chain method accurately. Similar techniques have been implemented as reported by several articles. However, the accuracy varies. Therefore, this study explored the prediction using Markov Chain model with Maximum Likelihood, Maximum Likelihood with Laplace Smoothing, Bootstrap Approach, and Maximum a Posteriori. The intention of using multi-Markov's approaches is to find the one that gives the best prediction. The results show that the prediction gave a little accuracy to predict next procurement activity, even though in one of the conditions, the prediction showed quite good results. Laplace Smoothing was considered as the best method for improving prediction results.

1 INTRODUCTION

Procurement is different from purchasing activities. The primary role of purchasing is to buy in-puts and bring them together at the firm (Fawcett 2000). Procurement is an activity of goods and services obtained in any way, including through the process of buying, hiring/leasing, and borrowing. Procurement shows more relational, strategic, and integrated role activities (Davis & Spekman 2004). These strategies can determine profits or losses experienced by companies such as in determining strategies to cut costs or improve quality to increase efficiency and reduce production costs (Sobhani et al. 2014). Hence, procurement strategies can be a fundamental element in developing corporate strategy (Sutton 1989). One of the activities that can determine the making of a procurement strategy is to use a spend analyst, which is done by conducting an analysis of procurement activities that have been carried out in the previous period. Hence, the procurement division can plan the goods and services that will be held. It is believed that this can provide an overview of any procurement activities that could occur in the future. In fact, planning is not easy even though the required data is available. In several Least Development Countries (LDCs), it was reported that procurement activities had been blamed for a number of failures of implementation of several projects financed by partners (Mabveka 2013), which happened due to poor planning. In fact, with well planning, the information on the risks that might arise can be analyzed; hence, risk mitigation can be done as a preventive measure (Cagno & Micheli 2011).

Considering the above-mentioned issues, we seek to find a solution that can provide information on planning by doing next procurement prediction. Predictions will be made using the Markov Chain, wherein determining the next procurement prediction, the Markov Chain model considers previous data to produce future data predictions. This is in accordance with the practice of the procurement process, where many items that are purchased can be done repeatedly as long as the item has not been discontinued. Although some studies conducted by He and Jiang (2017) and

Table 1. Characteristics of dataset.

No	Objects	Value
1	Number of procurement	1267
2	Number of procurement item	2280
3	Number of unique procurement item	917
4	Number of purchase request	1951

Westerski (2015) state that prediction by using the Markov Chain is considered less applicable, therefore, we seek to improve the process prediction using Maximum Likelihood Estimator (MLE) (Skuriat-Olechnowska 2005), Maximum Likelihood with Laplace Smoothing (Cui et al. 2018), Bootstrap Approach (Zhang 2004), and Maximum a Posteriori (MAP) (Wu & Noé 2010).

The structure of this study is as follows: First, explaining the previous studies; conducting research by pre-processing the dataset by clustering first (Westerski 2015), making a transition matrix and making a Markov Model; lastly, discussing the findings and drawing the conclusion.

2 RELATED WORK

As previously explained, procurement has become a strategic activity for companies, so this has attracted many researchers to conduct research related to procurement with different results and objectives, which were related to the issue of procurement fraud (Rüping et al. 2008; Calafato et al. 2016), inventory solution (Sarjono 2013), the demand process for the procurement itself (Ge et al. 2018; Kleuskens 2013), and discussing procurement predictions. This study was carried out to make a comparison, by adding a number of methods to improve and compare the prediction process with the aim of providing good planning information.

In addition, Markov Chain has been widely discussed to conduct studies related to the classification process (Mitavskiy et al. 2012), decision making (Özdagoglu 2017), and so forth.

3 APPROACH

3.1 *Dataset description*

The data used in this study are procurement data conducted by Kimia Farma, Ltd. in the period 2018–2020 with a total data of 2,280. There are 38 variables in the dataset, in which this study focuses on short text items that contain information or a description of the item that was purchased at the purchase order. Table 1 shows some of the characteristics of the dataset.

The number of procurement processes carried out by the procurement division per time varies depending on requests from users who came to the procurement division, except for routine items such as manufactured goods or stationeries that are usually ordered at the beginning of each month.

3.2 *Data pre-processing and estimation*

At this stage, pre-processing of the dataset was done to make the study process more effective. First, the data were transformed where all the space characters were changed to a point for each item because there were several items consisting of several syllables, so the algorithm can indicate that one word in the dataset is one item. Next, to ensure the algorithm indicates that one word is an item, the entire dataset was converted to capital letters and all characters except for the dot are omitted.

Next, clustering formation was done so that the predictive results on the algorithm became better by using hierarchical clustering (Westerski 2015), in which this study employed experiment

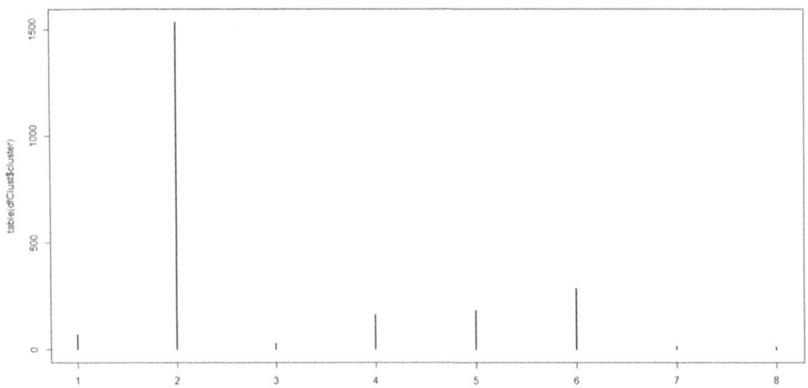

Figure 1. Number of members for cluster k = 8.

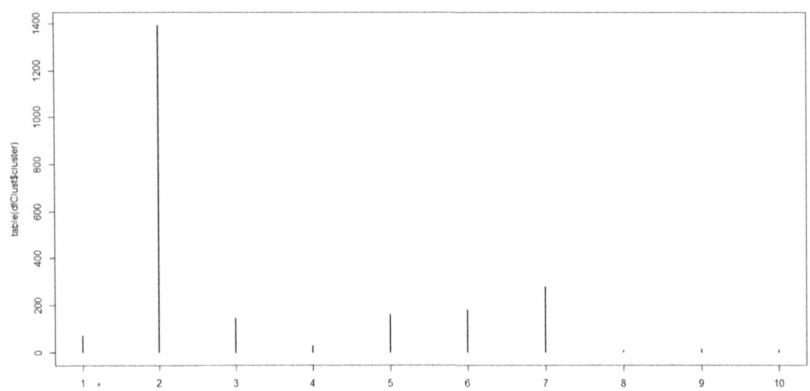

Figure 2. Number of members for cluster k = 10.

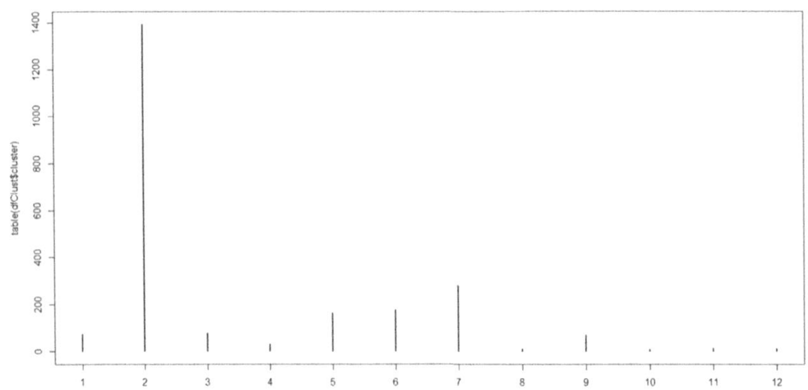

Figure 3. Number of members for cluster k = 12.

by dividing the dataset into clusters for k = 8, 10, and 12. Figures 1, 2, and 3 display in sequential hierarchical clustering results for k = 8, 10, and 12.

From these results, a calculation of the dunn, entropy and pearsongamma values was performed to determine the best cluster performance to be used in the study whose results are shown in Table 2.

Table 2. Cluster statistical test.

	Cluster 8	*Cluster* 10	*Cluster* 12
dunn	0.106383	0.1086957	0.1136364
entropy	0.6330188	0.5976564	0.5612873
Pearsongamma	0.7037412	0.7131166	0.7134826

Table 3. Estimation from given data.

	Loglikelihood
MLE	−121.3528306
Laplace Smoothing	−695.045165
Bootstrap Approach	−0.417472658
MAP	−121.3528306

Table 4. True predicted value count.

	True predicted value count
MLE	12
Laplace Smoothing	16
Bootstrap Approach	10
MAP	9

As presented in Table 2, the dunn, entropy, and pearsongamma values for the K = 12 cluster were seen better than the clusters for K = 8 and 10. Therefore, the data of this study were made into 12 clusters and thereafter the estimation will be made with fit for the data provided for the formation of the transition matrix (Craig & Sendi 2002). There are four methods that have been described that were used in this process. The estimation process was carried out using the Markov Chain package provided in the rstudio tool (Spedicato et al. 2014), where the results of the average loglikelihood value of the estimation are shown in Table 3.

3.3 *Prediction*

The purchasing prediction analysis process using the Markov Chain in this study only focuses on determining t_1 or prediction of the purchase of the next one year from items that made a purchase request by the user with a target that can determine what items will be purchased in the next request process. Purchasing prediction algorithm using the Markov Chain began by determining the initial state for each transition matrix by forming a matrix of $1 \times n$ where n is the number of unique items in each cluster. The matrix was filled with a value of 1 if at t_0 there is a purchase request and 0 if there is no purchase request. Prediction results for the purchase of the following year in each cluster were made by making the data one year earlier as input or initial state. From the data given, we divide the dataset by 80% as training data and 20% as test data. The result of the prediction using the Markov Chain are shown in Table 4.

4 DISCUSSION

4.1 *Evaluation*

The prediction results using the Markov Chain from the above dataset indicate that the prediction accuracy for this data purchase was less accurate for the four methods mentioned. This is in

Table 5. The result of prediction analysis of next procurement prediction using Markov Chain model.

	Precision	*Recall*	*f-measure*
MLE	0.001091	0.206857	0.001974
Laplace Smoothing	0.001590	0.212022	0.002640
Bootstrap Approach	0.000542	0.170539	0.001441
MAP	0.000904	0.175023	0.001615

accordance with Westerksi (2015), stating that the prediction of the purchase order using the Markov Chain was considered not applicable to be used for the actual process so that it can only be used for the comparative process or consideration process only.

Evaluating the prediction process using the Markov Chain was done by determining the performance of each cluster, and by calculating the following parameters, namely, precision, recall, and f-measurement, as used by Westerksi (2015) in his research, as follows:

$$Precision = \frac{Count\ of\ correctly\ predicted\ feature\ values}{Count\ of\ all\ unique\ predicted\ feature\ values} \tag{1}$$

$$Recall = \frac{Count\ of\ correctly\ predicted\ feature\ values}{Count\ of\ all\ unique\ features\ values\ in\ test\ subset} \tag{2}$$

Furthermore, calculating the f-measure has been explained by Manning et al. (2008) in their study in which

$$f\text{-}measure = \frac{precision * recall}{precision + recall} \tag{3}$$

Table 5 presents the results of those three values.

Analyzing the findings in Table 5, the prediction results using the Markov Chain showed that the Laplace Smoothing method obtained the best value based on precision, recall, and f-measure. However, their values are far from 1, indicating that, overall, the prediction results using the Markov Chain did not seem to be too good.

4.2 *Statistical test*

After evaluating the dataset, statistical tests on the dataset were conducted. At this stage, the Markov Property and Stationary of data were assessed. In addition, the Markov Property test verified whether the Markov Property held the given chain (Spedicato et al. 2014), while the stationary testing aims at verifying whether transition probabilities of the given chain changed over time (Spedicato et al. 2014). Table 6 shows the statistical tests for each cluster.

From Table 6, since all of the p-value from each cluster shown is above 0.05, both on the Markov Property and Stationary, we do not reject the null hypothesis that the sequence follows the Markov Property and the transition probabilities of the given chain change over time.

5 SUMMARY

After analyzing the above findings, the prediction process of Next Procurement Prediction using the Markov Chain was deemed to have poor performance if it is to be applied applicatively in the daily procurement process (Westerski 2015). This is due to several factors that occurred, such as the dataset used was too large (Özdagoglu 2017); and in reality, the procurement process was not only influenced by items in the previous procurement but can be influenced by other things such as the product's sales cycle (Rink & Fox 1999), information and communications technology (Apiyo

Table 6. Statistical test of Markov property and stationary.

	Markov Property			Stationary		
Cluster	Chi-*square*	Dof	p-value	Chi-square	Dof	p-value
Cluster 1	4.91667	97336	1	1329.373	113850	1
Cluster 2	1111.857	68417929	1	291283.9	185561664	1
Cluster 3	18.66667	91125	1	1527.509	118800	1
Cluster 4	0	8000	1	185.1282	7220	1
Cluster 5	101.7778	300768	1	5398.691	566016	1
Cluster 6	92.78333	389017	1	6211.964	720072	1
Cluster 7	258.7615	803457	1	13854.33	1899432	1
Cluster 8	0.4166667	64	1	9.844	60	1
Cluster 9	35.75	21952	1	930.9438	40068	1
Cluster 10	0	64	1	9	60	1
Cluster 11	0	8	1	4.31746	14	0.9932
Cluster 12	0	27	1	6	30	0.9993

2014), and so on. Therefore, the findings of this study can be used as one of the other parameters that can be added by future research. However, it can be seen that from the four methods used, Laplace Smoothing was considered as the best method to improve prediction results.

REFERENCES

Apiyo, R., Ogubala M, Kiarie, D. 2014. *Factors Affecting Procurement Planning in County Governments in Kenya: A Case Study of Nairobi City Country*. International Journal of Economics, Commerce and Management. Vol. II Iss 11.

Cagno, E. &Micheli, G. 2011. *Enhancing EPC supply chain competitiveness through procurement risk management*. Risk Manag 13, 147–180.

Calafato, Aaron., Colombo, Chirstian., Pace & Gordon J. 2016. *A Domain Specific Property Language for Fraud Detection to Support Agile Specification Development*. Lecture Notes in Computer Science, 9767.

Craig, B. A., & Sendi, P. P. 2002. *Estimation of the transition matrix of a discrete-time Markov chain*. Health Economics, 11(1), 33–42.

Cui, Z., Lars Kirkby, J., & Nguyen, D. 2018. *A General Framework for Time-changed Markov Processes and Applications*. European Journal of Operational Research.

Davis, E. W. & Spekman. R.E. 2004. *The Extended Enterprise: Gaining Competitive Advantage Through Collaborative Supply Chaing*. FT Press.

Fawcett, S.E. 2000. *Purchasing: Acquiring The Best Inputs. in: Swamidass P.M. (Eds) Encyclopedia Of Production And Manufacturing Management*. Springer, Boston, MA.

Ge, M., Hu, J., Liu, M. & Zhang, Y. 2018. *Reassembly classification selection method based on the Markov Chain*. Assembly Automation, Vol. 38 No. 4, pp. 476–486.

He, Z & Jiang, W. 2017. *A new belief Markov chain model and its application in inventory prediction*, International Journal of Production Research.

Kleuskens, J. 2013. *Demand Forcasting Through Categorization Development of a Demand Forecasting Support Model in a Process Industry Context*. Thesis Master di Eindhoven University of Technology.

Mabveka, Gerald. 2013. *Project Implementation Failure: Procurement Procedures A Scapegoat*. Researchgate->accessed https://www.researchgate.net/publication/237062917_PROJECT_IMPLEMENTATION_FAILURE_PROCUREMENT_PROCEDURES_A_SCAPEGOAT (18/05/2020).

Mitavskiy, B., Rowe, J. & Cannings, C. 2012. *A version of Geiringer-like theorem for decision making in the environments with randomness and incomplete information*. International Journal of Intelligent Computing and Cybernetics, Vol. 5 No. 1, pp. 36–90.

Özdagoglu, A. Ö. G. 2017. *Predicting product demand from small-sized data: grey models*. Grey Systems: Theory and Application, Vol. 7 Iss 1 pp. 80 – 96.

Rink, D. R., & Fox, H. W. 1999. *Strategic Procurement Planning across the Product's Sales Cycle: A Conceptualization*. Journal of Marketing Theory and Practice, 7(2), 28–42.
Rüping, Stefan., Punko, Natalja., Gunter, Bjorn. & Grosskreutz, Henrik. 2008. *Procurement Fraud Discovery using Similarity Measure Learning*. Transactions on Case Based Reasoning for Multimedia Data, 1, 37–46.
Sarjono, H. 2013. *The Determination of Optimal Inventory Using Markov Chain*. Jurnal Manajemen Teori dan Terapan, 2013, 41–51.
Skuriat-Olechnowska, M. 2005. *Statistical inference and hypothesis testing for Markov chains with Interval Censoring*. diploma thesis, Delft University of Technology.
Sobhani, M, Malarvizhi, C, Mamun, A & Jeyashree, S. 2014. *Strategic Procurement and Financial Performance of Iranian Manufacturing Companies*. Asian Social Science. 10. 250–256.
Spedicato, G.A, Kang, T.S. & Yalamanchi, S.B. 2014. *The Markov chain model. In The Marko chain Package: A Package for Easily Handling Discrete Markov Chains in R; Statistical-Advisor: Firenze*, Italy; pp. 1–60.
Sutton, B. 1989, *Procurement and its Role in Corporate Strategy: An Overview of the Wine and Spirit Industry*, International Journal of Wine Marketing, Vol. 1 No. 1, pp. 49–59.
Westerski, A., Kanagasabai, R., Wong, J. & Chang, H. 2015. *Prediction of Enterprise Purchases using Markov models in Procurement Analytics Applications*. Procedia Computer Science, 60, 1357–1366.
Wu, H., & Noé, F. 2010. *Maximum a posteriori estimation for Markov chains based on Gaussian Markov random fields*. Procedia Computer Science, 1(1), 1665–1673.
Zhang, L.-C. 2004. *Nonparametric Markov chain bootstrap for multiple imputation*. Computational Statistics & Data Analysis, 45(2), 343–353.

Synergizing Management, Technology and Innovation in Generating Sustainable and Competitive Business Growth – Hendayani et al (eds)
© 2021 Taylor & Francis Group, London, ISBN 978-0-367-68756-4

Predicting the characteristics of troubled customers in microcredit at Bank Mandiri, Ltd. Jakarta Thamrin Branch

A.N.R. Sukanto & G. Ramantoko
Telkom University, Bandung, West Java, Indonesia

ABSTRACT: Non-performing loans (NPLs) are one of the indicators of the bank's performance rating in running a credit program to its customers. Hence, this becomes the main focus of every bank to avoid an increase in troubled loans for their customers. However, Bank Mandiri, Ltd. Jakarta Thamrin Branch had experienced increasing NPL up to 18.22% within 3 months. This issue needs to be addressed considering that healthy commercial banks should avoid troubled loans by conducting strong credit control. Assessing credit worthiness can be done using 5C factors, which is one of the efforts to minimize risk of NPL from making wrong credit decisions from the predictor variable leading to bad credit. This study employed Random Forest technique. The prediction obtained by the collateral variable had an MDA level of 99.94, and the income capacity variable was 12.14, which is the main factor in determining customers' characteristics in predicting the condition of the customer's credit status.

1 INTRODUCTION

1.1 *Background*

In this modern era, business activity is a complex phenomenon as it covers other various fields including politics, law, and economics. The activities of business community are inseparable from the role of banks as providers of banking services to the community. This drives banking growth in Indonesia to grow rapidly, and inevitably there is tougher banks competition, seen from the business volume, mobilization of public fund, and in the credit provision.

Bank Mandiri, Ltd. (Persero) is one of the companies engaged in banking with several products and services, one of which is an independent loan. However, providing credit still has a very dominant risk. Therefore, the creditor needs to assess and analyze the feasibility of lending based on 5C principle analysis: character, capacity, conditions of economy, capability, and collateral of prospective debtors. The data of non-performing debtors and non-performing loans in the micro segment had been increasing within three months, as presented in Table 1.

According to Sholikha (2015), a healthy commercial bank is a bank with no troubled loans, hence, having strong credit control from the bank is necessary. To prevent the occurrence of

Table 1. Data on non-performing debtors and non-performing loans in the micro segment of PT. Bank Mandiri Jakarta Thamrin.

Month (2019)	Non-performing debtors	Non-performing loans
July	11.7%	9.96%
August	17.3%	16.15%
September	18.6%	18.22%

Source: Bank Mandiri, Ltd. Jakarta Thamrin Branch, 2019.

troubled loans, bank credit analysts must be able to take the right decisions in applying for credit. There is a need for accurate predictions in the future, one of which uses data mining techniques. Based on the background description above, the authors are interested in raising a thesis with the title, "Predicting the Characteristics of Troubled Customers in Micro Credit at Bank Mandiri, Ltd Jakarta Thamrin Branch."

2 LITERATURE REVIEW

2.1 *Bank*

According to Law No. 10 of 1998, a bank is a business entity that collects funds from the public in the form of deposits and distributes them to the public in the form of credit and/or other forms to improve the lives of many people.

2.2 *Credit*

According to the Act No. 7 of 1992 on banking, credit is the provision of money or bills which can be equaled, based on an agreement to borrow and lend between a company and another party that requires the borrower to repay the debt after a certain period of time with the amount of money, compensation, or profit sharing. In granting credit, the banks must pay attention to the principles of giving correct credit. The principle of granting credit with the 5C analysis is character, capacity, condition of economy, capability, and collateral of debtor candidates (Cashmir 2016: 136).

2.3 *Non-performing loan*

According to Mahmoeddin (2016: 20), non-performing loans are the loans where the debtor cannot meet the conditions previously agreed, for example, the requirements regarding interest payments, loan principal repayment, increased margin deposit, binding and increasing collateral, and so on.

2.4 *Data mining*

According to Chitra (2013), data mining is an algorithm used to analyze data and review from various perspectives and can be used in various fields such as education, security systems, marketing, banking, and so forth. One of the applications of data mining in banking risk management is used to determine lending to customers, both in the form of direct loans and the use of credit cards. Data mining is considered effective in analysis and can provide estimation of the performance of potential customer payments.

2.5 *Theoretical framework*

Based on theoretical studies and the results of previous studies, several factors have been explained to cause non-performing loans. Thus, the conceptual framework of this study can be seen in Figure 1:

3 RESEARCH METHOD

This study employed quantitative methods. According to Sugiyono (2015: 11), quantitative methods are research methods that are based on the philosophy of positivism, used to examine specific populations or samples. This method helps in determining the relationship between the variables studied to produce conclusions that will clarify the picture of the object under study. Specifically, this study aims at predicting the effect of 5C factors on the emergence of problem loans at Bank Mandiri, Ltd. Jakarta Thamrin Branch.

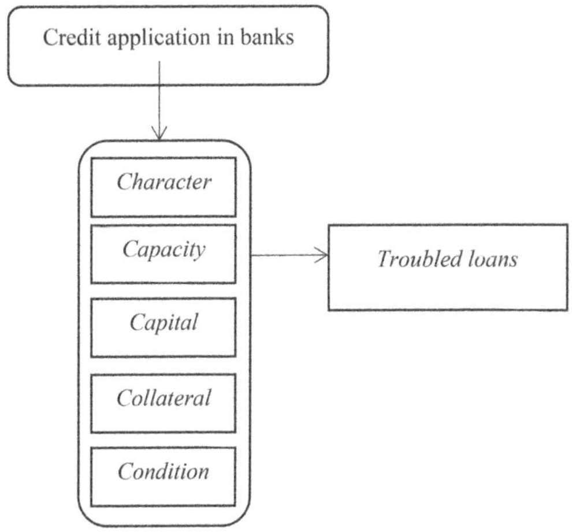

Figure 1. Theoretical framework.

Table 2. Error matrix forest.

	Substandard	Performing	Non-performing	Class error
Substandard	33	18	14	0.492
Performing	0	722	0	0.000
Non-performing	8	1	92	0.089

4 FINDINGS AND DISCUSSION

Predictive analytics were done to study certain patterns of predictor variables leading to bad credit using Random Forest technique. The advantage of this technique is that its output provides recommendations on how important the role of a predictor is in predicting the condition of credit status. The amount of data used in this study is 888 data consisting of 65 substandard customers, 722 performing customers, and 101 troubled customers. In the prediction of substandard classes, it was found that from 65 customers, there were only 33 customers who had the right prediction, while the other 32 customers had the wrong prediction with an error of 49.2%. Then, for performing class, it was found to be very good knowing that all of 722 customers showed accurate predictions with an error value of 0.00%. In addition, the prediction of the non-performing class was not good, because of 101 customers, there were only 92 customers who had the right prediction and 9 other customers did not get the right prediction, with an error of 8.9%.

4.1 *The size of importance level variables*

The next step was looking at the size of the importance level (variable importance) of each independent variable (not visible) examined.

The size of importance level of Mean Decrease (MDG) was in the same level with MDA, in which the independent variables with the highest level of importance were collateral and production capacity variables. Thus, it can be concluded that the two lowest variables in terms of the level of importance of MDA and MDG were the product type capital variable and the gender character variable. The prediction obtained by the collateral variable had an MDA level of 99.94, and the income capacity variable was 12.14 as the main factor in determining customer characteristics in predicting the condition of the customer's credit status.

Table 3. Size of importance level variable.

	Substandard	Performing	Non-Performing	MDA	MDG
Collateral	56.60	88.65	98.04	99.94	109.72
Income_Capacity	1.99	16.31	10.58	19.13	12.14
Modal_Capacity	3.09	18.10	7.99	19.85	11.93
Tenor_Capacity	−0.02	12.98	7.75	14.77	7.00
Gender_Character	1.43	0.53	1.78	2.25	1.92
Business Sector_Character	1.88	2.87	0.23	3.01	2.73
Product type_Capital	−1.93	3.11	−0.43	0.83	1.60
Balance_Condition	28.51	−0.42	−2.38	13.62	9.58

5 CONCLUSION

The findings show that the amount generated by the collateral, income capacity, and capital capacity variables affected the level of credit status, namely performing, substandard, and non-performing. This study also employed Random Forest in which the level of error in the determination of credit status can be found, in which the Error Matrix Forest of 49.2% of customers known to be less precise in determining the status of substandard loans, and Error Matrix Forest of 8.9% of customers known to be less precise in determining bad credit status.

Furthermore, based on the results of the analysis of tests that have been carried out on micro credit at ank Mandiri, Ltd. Jakarta Thamrin Branch, there were two analysis variables that had the lowest Mean Decrease Accuracy (MDA) level, namely, the type of product capital and gender character variables. After analyzing and calculating MDA using Random Forest technique, it was found that there were weaknesses of product type capital and gender character variables. Therefore, the improvements are suggested to be conducted by improving other related variables such as analyzing the characteristics of customers who have potentials to be troubled loans, which can be seen from family dependent status and determining debtors' ability to pay.

REFERENCES

Chitra, K., & Subashini, B. 2013. Data Mining Techniques and Its Applications in Banking Sector. *International Journal of Emerging Technology and Advanced Engineering*, (3)8.

Mahmoeddin, As. 2010. *Melacak Kredit Bermasalah* [Tracking Non-Performing Loan]. Jakarta: Pustaka Sinar Harapan.

Meiryani. 2019. *The Effect of Company Sizes, User Involvement of Information System, and Top Management Support on Accounting Information System Performance.* International Journal of Engineering and Advanced Technology, 8 (5), 1–1.

Rakhmawan, R.A. 2014. *Faktor-Faktor Yang Mempengaruhi Keputusan Dalam Pemberian Kredit Investasi Oleh PD. BPR Gresik* [Factors Affecting Decisions In Providing Investment Credit By PD. BPR Gresik]. Universitas Pembangunan Nasional Veteran, Jawa Timur.

Sholikha, D. L. 2015. *Pengaruh Penilaian Kelayakan Kredit dan Informasi Akuntansi Terhadap Keputusan Pemberian Kredit pada Bank Umum di Surabaya [The Effect of Creditworthiness Assessment and Accounting Information on Credit Granting Decisions at Commercial Banks in Surabaya].* Undergraduate Thesis, STIE Perbanas Surabaya.

Sugiyono. 2015. *Metode Penelitian dan Pengembangan* [Research and Development Methods]. Bandung: Alfabeta.

Synergizing Management, Technology and Innovation in Generating Sustainable and Competitive Business Growth – Hendayani et al (eds)
© 2021 Taylor & Francis Group, London, ISBN 978-0-367-68756-4

Modified UTAUT: Culture as a moderator on the use of iBanking services in Indonesia

R.R.W. Giri, F.K. Putra & T. Widarmanti
School of Economics and Business, Telkom University, West Java, Indonesia

ABSTRACT: Internet users in Indonesia significantly increase every year. But the increase is not counteracting with Internet banking service users. The differences in cultural factors in a country has become one of the reasons. This study tries to analyze the effects of culture as a moderator in a modified UTAUT model and focuses to the influence of cultural factors in influencing behavioral intention as a determinant of the actual use of a technology system for non-users. Data collection used quota sampling with 900 respondents in Indonesia based on savings and loan data. Structural equation modeling (SEM)-based covariance was used for data analysis. This study found significant relationship between the variables of effort expectancy, performance expectancy, social influence, behavioral intention, and usage behavioral, while the relationship of cultural moderators is weakening the relationship of existing variables. Using cultural moderator variables other than Hofstede Culture to use a new service is an opportunity for improvement in the future research.

1 INTRODUCTION

The use of the Internet has a huge impact in our daily life. The greatest effect of the Internet is a connection for people, but it still gives concern to the potential risks (Batey & Comer 2013). The development of technology pushes the banking industry to compete in presenting Internet banking services as a form of interaction with customers (Hanafizadeh et al. 2014). Most of the banks in Indonesia offer Internet banking services for daily transactions. The pioneer is Bank Central Asia, who has offered KlikBCA since 2001 and was followed by other banks (Mayasari et al. 2011). Internet banking services provide various facilities, but many customers in Indonesia prefer to use ATM services than electronic services, and customers prefer to do the transaction with the bank tellers than use the Internet banking services. Internet banking penetration in Indonesia is 36%. It is lower compared to ASEAN countries, which have fewer Internet users than Indonesia (Laukkanen & Cruz 2012). This difference stems from differences in cultural factors in a country that affect the rate of adoption of technology (Alshare et al., 2010; Huang et al. 2010; Sutanonpaiboon & Mastor 2010). Culture can be described as a moderate effect of establishing at a significant level the relationship between independent and dependent variables in the technology adoption model (Bankole et al. 2011). Research on culture as a moderator variable in the level of adoption of Internet banking services has been conducted using the Unified Theory of Acceptance and Use of Technology (UTAUT) (Alshare et al., 2010).

2 LITERATURE REVIEW

2.1 *The Unified Theory of Acceptance and Use of Technology (UTAUT)*

UTAUT is the most prominent research model in technology acceptance and understanding the driving factors in technology acceptance introduced by Venkatesh and friends (Venkatesh et al. 2003).

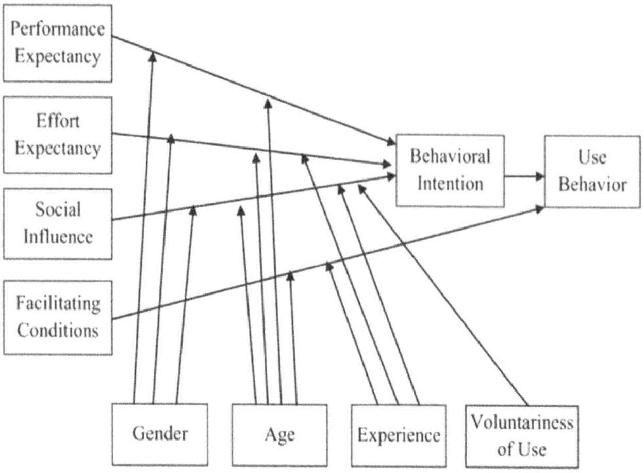

Figure 1. Model of the unified theory of acceptance and use of technology (UTAUT).

Variables that influence each other in the UTAUT model are performance expectancy (PE), effort expectancy (EE), social influence (SI), and facilitating conditions (FC). Internet banking is a branch of electronic banking that provides opportunity for consumers to use various services such as cash transfers, paying bills, and getting information about deposits, investments, and checking services via the Internet and websites designed by banks (BCG report 2015). Culture Dimension: Hofstede's Cultural Variable provides a mechanism for the implementation of a new system and technology that considers the effects of national cultural differences, which render systems and technology easily adopted by individuals (Huang et al. 2010). There are five cultural dimensions: power distance, individualism, masculinity, uncertainty avoidance, and long-term orientation (Hofstede & Minkov 2010). Power distance (PD) is focused on the level of equality or inequality between individuals in society in a country. Individualism (IDV) focuses on the extent to which society strengthens individual achievements or the collectivity of the individual itself. Masculinity (MSC) measures the level of masculinity of values such as firmness, performance, success, and competition. Uncertainty avoidance (UA) is described as when people feel threatened by uncertainty and ambiguity and try to avoid the situation, and long-term orientation (LTO) is the situation of the individual oriented toward the future and the opportunities for the future, taking into account the level of success.

This paper uses modified UTAUT, by eliminating facilitating conditions. According to Alhudaith (2015), facilitating conditions do not have a significant effect on individual factors for accepting information technology adoption. Based on Hofstede & Minkov (2010), we use the culture dimension as a moderator. Culture is the most influential structure on the reception of information technology services. Culture's role as a moderator has a significant effect in the moderator for the adoption of technology services. Cultural differences have a significant effect to the acceptance of technology service adoption (Alshare et al. 2010; Baptista & Oliveira 2015; Bankole et al. 2011; Laukkanen & Cruz 2012; Srite & Karahanna 2006;); see Figure 2.

3 METHOD

We used quantitative research methods, a Likert Scale, to achieve the diversity of values and a higher reliability coefficient, choose non-probability sampling using quota sampling for the sampling technique. Bank customers who live in the territory of Indonesia are our population and our sample is bank customers who have not used Internet banking services and non-user of Internet banking in Indonesia. Based on the research model, the hypothesis is proposed as follows:

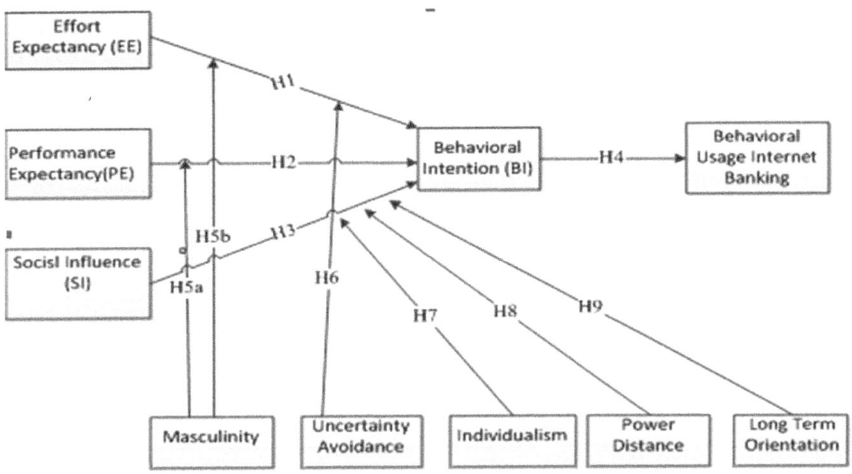

Figure 2. Modified UTAUT.

H1: Effort expectancy (EE) influences behavioral intention (BI).
H2: Performance expectancy (PE) influences behavioral intention (BI).
H3: Social influence (SI) influences behavioral intention (BI).
H4: Behavioral intention influences the usage intention (UI).
H5a: Masculinity influences the relationship of performance expectancy (PE) and behavioral intention (BI).
H5b: Masculinity (MSC) influences the relationship of effort expectancy (EE) and behavioral intention (BI).
H6: Uncertainty avoidance (UA) influences in the relationship of effort expectancy (EE) and behavioral intention (BI).
H7: Individualism (INV) influences in the relationship of social influence (SI) and behavioral intention (BI).
H8: Power distance (PD) influences in the relationship of social influence (SI) and behavioral intention (BI).
H9: Long-term orientation (LTO) has an influence in social influence (SI) and behavioral intention (BI).

4 RESULT AND DISCUSSION

This research applied SEM analysis technique using Warp-PLS 5.0. PLS tend to use for a predictive model. A multivariate analysis technique is a statistical analysis that involves more than two variables in each of its variables. The variables in this study are effort expectancy, performance expectancy, social influence, behavioral intention and usage behavioral, and as moderator variables are power distance, individualism, masculinity, uncertainty avoidance and long-term orientation. The characteristics of the respondents examined were based on gender, domicile, occupation, and age, income per month, last education, and duration of Internet use. Respondents were male, 57.7%, and women, 42.88%, dominated by jobs as civil servants, with income between Rp. 5,000,000 to Rp. 10,000,000, their last education Bachelor, ages 31 to 40 years old, and have a duration of using the Internet for more than five years, live in urban areas are 870 people or 96.88%, and in districts for about 30 people or 3.33%. For Outer model (the measurement model) validity test used warp-PLS to find the relations between interrelated variables and how precisely the manifest variable can explain the latent variables that exist. We measure the outer model by looking at several indicators

Table 1. Structural model test results.

Indicator	Value	*Rule of Thumb*	Details
APC	0,192 P < 0,001	P-value ≥0,05	*Fit*
ARS	0,549 P<0,001	P-value ≥0,05	*Fit*
AARS	0,546 P<0,001	P-value ≥0,05	*Fit*
AVIF	2,333	≤ 3, 3 but score ≤ 5 acceptable	*Fit*
AFVIF	2,315	≤ 3, 3 but score ≤ 5 acceptable	*Fit*
Gof	0,630	≥ 0, 10, ≥ 0, 25 and ≥ 0,36 (small, middle and large)	*Fit*
SPR	0,700	Ideal =1, but score ≥ 0,7 acceptable	*Fit*
RSCR	0,977	Ideal =1, but score ≥ 0,7 acceptable	*Fit*
SSR	1,000	Should ≥ 0,7	*Fit*
NLBCDR	0,500	Should ≥ 0,7	Not *Fit*

including indicator reliability, internal consistency reliability, convergent validity, and discriminant validity. The variable components can be declared valid and reliable. Meanwhile, for the Inner Model (Structural model) it is known that WarpPLS has 10 ways to determine the size of fit in a model, average path coefficient (APC), average R-squared (ARS), average adjusted R-squared (AARS), average block variance inflation factor (AVIF), average full collinearity VIF (AFVIF), Thenehaus GoF (GoF), Sympson's paradox ratio (SPR), R-squared contribution ratio (RSCR), statistical suppression ratio (SSR), and nonlinear bivariate causality direction ratio (NLBCDR). The results of the 10 methods test 9 of the requirements met, only 1 is not met, for testing the hypothesis the evaluation of model fit is less important. It is important and useful to determine the quality of model if the purpose is to find a model fit with the original data. This study aimed only to test existing hypotheses.

With 37 item questions, adopt Al-Qeisi (2009), Huang et al. (2010), and Alshare et al. (2010), the result are effort expectancy (EE) significantly influences behavioral intention (BI) with a coefficient value of 0.337, the higher level of expectation of ease after using Internet banking services, the higher the interest of individuals to use Internet banking services. This statement supports Alshare et al. (2010) that effort expectancy (EE) is the key determinant of behavioral intention (BI) behavioral interest in the use or adoption of a new service. Constructs that have a significant effect on shaping behavioral interest in behavioral intention (BI) are performance expectancy (PE) and social influence (SI), supporting the Alshare et al. (2010) statement that the construct variable performance expectancy (PE) and social influence (SI) are the constructs that most influence the intention of someone wanting to use Internet banking services. Behavioral intention (BI) variable significantly influences usage behavioral (UB) with a coefficient value of 0.725 with a coefficient value of 0.337. Meanwhile, the moderator variables of Hofstade's culture (masculinity [MSC], individualism [INV], power distance [PD]) do not moderate the relationships between and among performance expectancy, effort expectancy, and social influence variables; therefore the culture moderator variable does not strengthen the influence performance expectancy, effort expectancy, social influence, and behavioral intention. We found that long-term orientation, uncertainty avoidance moderates the relationship between effort expectancy, social influence on behavioral intention. Masculinity does not affect the relationship of performance expectancy, which is the expectation of the performance that will be obtained by customers after using Internet banking services on the use interest. This supports Huang et al. (2010) and Giri et al. (2019), and Indonesian people tend to avoid uncertainty. This is indicated from higher levels of uncertainty avoidance (UA), the expectation of convenience that will affect one's interest in using Internet banking services. Data shows that score of individualism (INV) is low, which means that people have good social relations with others, and the individualism has no influence on the relationship of social influence with behavioral intention. These results support research by Giri et al. (2019). The power distance (PD) has a high score, indicating that there are inequalities or gaps between people who have higher power and lower power, so in this case power distance does not have a relationship between the influences of social people to customers after using Internet banking services to interest in using the services. This supports research that has been done by Giri et al. (2019) and Huang et al. (2010). Long-term orientation shows a negative result between the relationship of social influence with behavioral intention, which implies that if a person has long-term orientation, they are less likely to use the service.

5 CONCLUSION

Effort expectancy (EE) or the expectation of ease of having the most influence on customers' interest to use internet banking services, so the higher level of expectation of convenience after using Internet banking services, the higher interest of individuals to use Internet banking services. Social influence has the next greatest influence on customers' interest to use Internet banking services. It shows that there are roles from other people or family environment that can influence them to use Internet banking services. Performance expectancy has a low influence on customer interest. This means that the more benefits that will be felt when using Internet banking services, the more they will want to use the service. The moderating variables that influence in this study are the long-term orientation (LTO) and uncertainty avoidance (UA). Meanwhile, our variables that do not affect this study are masculinity (MSC), individualism (INV), power distance (PD). Based on this we conclude that the characteristic of Indonesian people is that they tend to be long-term oriented and tend to avoid uncertainty in the interest in using technology, especially Internet banking services. Using cultural moderator variables other than Hofstede Culture that have relationships that strengthen one's intention to use a new service is an opportunity to improvement in the future research. This study only focused on urban areas. Further research should be conducted on rural or urban areas, to see the characteristics of rural culture.

REFERENCES

Abdullatif A. 2015. International Conference on eBusiness, eCommerce, eManagement, eLearning and eGovernance [IC5E]. The Differences between Online Banking Users and Nonusers. King Kalid University, Saudi Arabia.

Alshare, K., Al-Garni, M., & Musa, A. 2014. The moderating effect of cultural dimensions on user's acceptance of mobile payment devices: A conceptual model. Accessed from Internet in, 11.

Al-Qeisi, K. I. 2009. Analyzing the use of UTAUT model in explaining an online behaviour: Internet banking adoption (Doctoral dissertation, Brunel University Brunel Business School PhD Theses).

Batey, G., & Comer, T. 2013. Development of an internet risk awareness group for learning disabled offenders. Journal of Intellectual Disabilities and Offending Behaviour. https://doi.org/10.1108/JIDOB-04-2013-0008

Bankole, F. O., Bankole, O. O., & Brown, I. 2011. Mobile banking adoption in Nigeria. The Electronic Journal of Information Systems in Developing Countries, 47(1), 1-23.c https://doi.org/10.1002/j.1681-4835.2011.tb00330.x

Baptista, G., & Oliveira, T. 2015. Understanding mobile banking: The unified theory of acceptance and use of technology combined with cultural moderators. Computers in Human Behavior, 50, 418-430. https://doi.org/10.1016/j.chb.2015.04.024

BCG Report. 2015. The Internet's Ne Billion Digital Consumers in Brazil, Rusia, India, China, and Indonesia. https://www.bcg.com/documents/file58645.pdf .

Giri, R. R. W., Wanda, V., & Irawan, H. 2019, May. Internet Banking Adoption Analysis in Medan and Bandung City using the Unified Theory of Use and Acceptance of Technology (UTAUT) Model with Culture as Moderator. In 1st International Conference on Economics, Business, Entrepreneurship, and Finance (ICEBEF 2018). Atlantis Press. https://doi.org/10.2991/icebef-18.2019.149

Hanafizadeh, P., Keating, B. W., & Khedmatgozar, H. R. 2014. A systematic review of Internet banking adoption. Telematics and informatics, 31(3), 492-510. https://doi.org/10.1016/j.tele.2013.04.003
Huang, K. Y., Choi, N., & Chengalur-Smith, I. N. 2010. Cultural Dimensions as Moderators of the UTAUT Model: a Research Proposal in a Healthcare Context. In AMCIS (p. 188).
Hofstede, G., & Minkov, M. 2010. Long-versus short-term orientation: new perspectives. Asia Pacific business review, 16(4), 493-504. https://doi.org/10.1080/13602381003637609
Laukkanen, T., & Cruz, P. 2012, January. Cultural, individual and device-specific antecedents on mobile banking adoption: a cross-national study. In 2012 45th Hawaii International Conference on System Sciences (pp. 3170-3179). IEEE. https://doi.org/10.1109/HICSS.2012.189
Mayasari, F., Kurniawati, E. P., & Nugroho, P. I. 2011. Anteseden dan konsekuen sikap nasabah dalam menggunakan internet banking dengan menggunakan kerangka technology acceptance model (TAM)(Survey pada pengguna KlikBCA). Semantik, 1(1).
Sutanonpaiboon, J., & Mastor, N. H. 2010. Malay, Chinese, and internet banking. Chinese Management Studies.
Srite, M., & Karahanna, E. 2006. The role of espoused national cultural values in technology acceptance. MIS quarterly, 679-704. https://doi.org/10.2307/25148745
Venkatesh, V., Morris, M. G., Davis, G. B., & Davis, F. D. 2003. User acceptance of information technology: Toward a unified view. MIS quarterly, 425-478. https://doi.org/10.2307/30036540

Synergizing Management, Technology and Innovation in Generating Sustainable and Competitive Business Growth – Hendayani et al (eds)
© 2021 Taylor & Francis Group, London, ISBN 978-0-367-68756-4

Segmentation of Telkomsel's digital service customer using K-Medoids algorithm

S. Halim & G. Ramantoko
Faculty of Economics and Business, Telkom University, Bandung, West Java, Indonesia

ABSTRACT: The digital revenue growth of PT. Telkomsel in Sulawesi Region (+ 52.56%) requires appropriate marketing strategy. Customer service segmentation is significant to divide customers based on their characteristics. This study aims at determining the customer segmentation model of Telkomsel in Sulawesi Region using the K-Medoid algorithm and determining marketing strategies to maintain existing customers and increase their usage of digital services. The results obtained by three customer segments with a value of 0.72 silhouette coefficient was in the good category, with the accuracy value of 93.44%. Potential to Lost Segment is a potential customer segment to churn, so it is suggested to expand and increase 4G LTE network coverage. The High Value Loyal Customer Segment is the main customer who is recommended to get rewards. The High Value New Customer Segment is the new customer segment with social media use, hence, expanding digital channels in promoting the services is recommended.

1 INTRODUCTION

The phenomenon of increasing digital revenue of PT. Telkomsel in the Sulawesi Region that was +52.56% showed the highest revenue growth compared to the other three revenue generators (Telkomsel 2019). Digital services have great potential to replace revenue in telephone and SMS services as they are increasingly lacking in demand by customers. This is in accordance with the statement of the Vice President of Sales and Marketing of PT. Telkomsel Pamasuka Area, Herry Setiawan, stating that in the future, Telkomsel will focus on future business by developing digital revenue. Telkomsel will seek revenue in digital business niches and core data to replace legacy from voice revenue and SMS revenue, which are currently not widely used by customers (Telkomsel 2019). This potential growth in digital revenue requires Telkomsel to have the appropriate strategy to increase the use of digital services and maintain existing customers. The customer segmentation of Telkomsel digital services can be done by dividing customers into groups with similar characteristics, hence, Telkomsel can develop different marketing strategies according to these characteristics.

2 RELATED WORKS

Several related studies have been conducted. Studies by Eugene Wong and Yan Wei in 2018 focus on developing a customer online behavioral analysis tool, segmenting the customers into high-value segment, analyzing customer behavioral in the online purchasing, and predicting a customer's next purchases from an online air travel corporation. Meanwhile, a study conducted by Chih in 2015 investigated the problem of customer segmentation and presented a real case study of an automobile dealer in Taiwan. Using two clustering techniques, k-means and expectation maximization, Chih showed the results by comparing two clustering techniques for correctness. In addition, another study conducted by Mediana in 2018 suggested customer segmentation that can be applied using

Table 1. Transformation of attributes data.

Indicators	Description	Data
Los	The duration of using Telkomsel services, which shows customer loyalty in using Telkomsel	Loyalty Status
Brand	The brand used by Telkomsel's customer service shows the status of Telkomsel's customers	User Status
Total recharge	Total transaction in using Telkomsel services; grouping is based on the amount of credit top-up	User Rate
Total Transaction	The total reload of Telkomsel services, which shows the opportunity when they get an idea to buy	Occasion
Rev digital	Total revenue obtained from customers who use digital services, which shows the benefit of using digital services for customers	Benefit Sought

the customer's Internet banking data. It built the segmentation models on customer profile data based on their behavior and usage of Internet banking in XYZ bank. The segmentation methods are utilizing k-means method and partition around medoids (PAM) method based on RFM score of customer's Internet banking transactions. Furthermore, Preeti in 2014 made a comparison of the customer segmentation between partition around medoids (PAM) and k-means. The results show that partition around medoids (PAM) showed better performance in execution time, better result handling outlier data, and reduced noise and error as compared to k-means as it minimized dissimilarities of data.

3 APPROACH

3.1 *Dataset description*

This study involved a population of 12,931 Telkomsel customer service data using seven variables in the dataset spread across six major cities in Sulawesi Region: Makassar, Pare-pare, Manado, Palu, Kendari, and Gorontalo. The data were recorded during the period of service usage from January to June 2019. In testing the accuracy of segmentation, data sharing was done by random sampling methods, namely, training data with proportion of 70% of the total data population or equivalent to 9,024 customers and test data with a proportion of 30% of the total data population or equivalent to 3,907 customers.

3.2 *Transformation and preprocessing*

Transportation aims at converting raw data from variable data into data in accordance with the theory of customer segmentation. This is necessary to adjust the variable attributes of data against the attributes of the customer segmentation theory. Table 1 presents the results of customer data transformation.

3.3 *Determining number of cluster*

Testing the value of the silhouette coefficient can be done to determine the best cluster number (Kaoungku et al. 2018). This study obtained the best three cluster segments. These results were obtained from the maximum value of the silhouette coefficient of 0.72, which was in the number of three cluster segments. The value of the silhouette is categorized as good in doing cluster segmentation. Figure 1 displays the silhouette coefficient values for the number of clusters.

3.4 *Testing the similarity and dissimilarity of using Gower distance*

Gower distance measurement method can be used to determine similarity and dissimilarity in mix clustering data (Oppong 2018). The minimum Gower distance shows a similarity between one

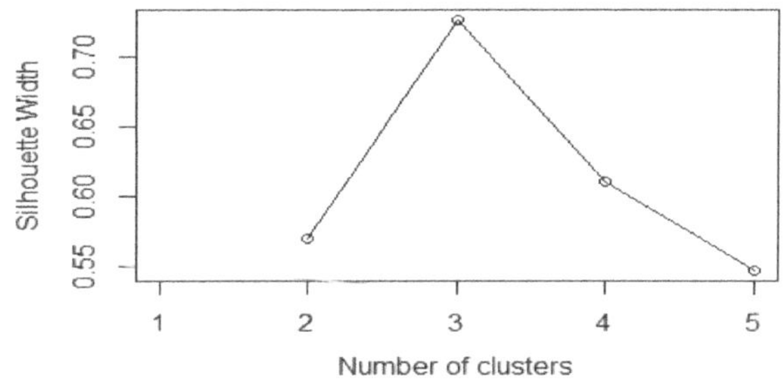

Figure 1. Transformation of attribute data.

```
> #' Print most dissimilar clients
> df[which(gower_mat == max(gower_mat[gower_mat != max(gower_mat)]), arr.ind = TRUE)[1, ], ]
# A tibble: 2 x 5
  total_recharge total_transaction_arpu rev_digital   Los brand
           <dbl>                  <dbl>       <dbl> <dbl> <fct>
1       10010000                      9     9999300   371 simPATI
2           1000                      1         110 10742 KartuAS
> #' Print most similar clients
> df[which(gower_mat == min(gower_mat[gower_mat != min(gower_mat)]), arr.ind = TRUE)[1, ], ]
# A tibble: 2 x 5
  total_recharge total_transaction_arpu rev_digital   Los brand
           <dbl>                  <dbl>       <dbl> <dbl> <fct>
1          50000                      2          55 10742 KartuAS
2          50000                      2          50 10742 KartuAS
```

Figure 2. Similarity and dissimilarity using Gower distance.

Table 2. Data of cluster segmentation.

						Parameter			
Cluster	Total recharge	Total action	Trans digital	Rev Los	Brand	Recharge	Trans action	Rev digital	Los
1	63855	1.986	5442	1826	KartuAS	Low	Low	Low	High
2	93774	2.397	13445	1931	simPATI	High	High	High	High
3	77464	2.298	6646	734	Loop	Medium	High	Medium	Low

customer and another customer, and conversely the difference in the value of the maximum gower distance shows as dissimilar between one customer and another customer.

3.5 *Clustering customer using K-Medoids*

The K-Medoids method can be used to identify customer groups based on their individual characteristics (Park et al. 2006). This study divided three customer segments based on customer behavior in using Telkomsel's digital services. Cluster 1 is a group of customers with low value on total recharge, total transaction, digital revenue, but is a customer segment with a high length of stay. Cluster 2 is a group of customers with very high values on total recharge, total transactions, digital revenue, and high length of stay. Whereas Cluster 3 is a group of customers with medium value in recharge, digital revenue, but it is a customer segment with a low length of stay with a high total transaction. Customers in Cluster 1 are identical to the use of the Loop brand. Table 2 presents the data clusters briefly.

Then, the cluster was depicted using the t-distributed stochastic neighbor embedding (t-SNE) method in order to display high-dimensional data clusterization. Figure 3 depicts the visualization of Telkomsel digital service subscriber clusters.

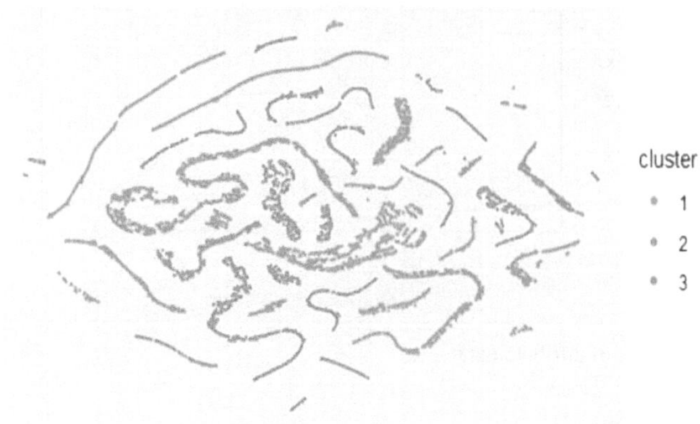

Figure 3. Visualization of Telkomsel digital services customer clusters.

Table 3. Data of actual testing on data of prediction testing.

	Prediction Cluster 1	Prediction Cluster 2	Prediction Cluster 3
Actual Cluster 3	1945	46	29
Actual Cluster 3	60	1252	23
Actual Cluster 3	72	26	454

4 DISCUSSION

4.1 *Testing the accurateness of K-Medoids Model*

The testing process done using the model by Grottrun Soren (2016) by dividing customer data into two using the random sampling method. The training data were obtained from 70% of the total population, while testing data were obtained from 30% of the total population. The population of the training data was then formed by the segmentation model, and the model was tested on data testing to obtain accuracy from customer segmentation. Comparison between predictive data and actual data was used to determine the accuracy value of the K-Medoids segmentation that has been done. The 3,907 testing customer data were mapped based on actual data and predictive data. The following Table 3 presents this comparison by testing the accuracy of customer segmentation of 93.44%.

4.2 *Characteristics of customer segment*

This first customer segment is categorized into customers who had the potential to stop using Telkomsel services (Potential to Lost). They showed very low total occasion, in which they only carried out less than two transactions in a month. In addition, their total recharges were also very low, which was indicated by spending less than Rp. 60,000 in one month. Their usage of other Telkomsel digital services was also low, worth below Rp. 6,000. However, this segment benefited in terms of length of stay, in which they have established long relationships and used Telkomsel services for two to three years. Seen from the customer status, they were KARTU as customers who were categorized in the third tier. Customers of this type are prone to abandon the Telkomsel services in both of Telkomsel's legacy and digital services; hence, they were classified as potential to lost segment, because all of the attribute ratings were low.

This second customer segment is categorized as those who have the high potential to be maintained (stay longer) in using both Telkomsel's legacy services and digital services; hence, this segment is named High Value Loyal Customers. They are categorized as main customers who showed high transaction since the beginning until now, in which they made high numbers of transactions and have established more than three years of relationships with the company products. In addition, on average they have made more than 2.4 times transactions in a month. In meaning that the customers were quite often doing transactions with the company. In terms of benefits sought by customers, they spent more than Rp. 13,000 per month for digital services. Seen from the user side, they were simPATI customers who were in the second tier. In addition, their total average of their user rate was more than Rp. 90,000 per month. Hence, the customers in this segment really need to be maintained.

The third customer segment is categorized into those who have the highest potential to be increased (spend more) in using Telkomsel services both in using Telkomsel's legacy services and digital services. They are named as High Value New Customers, who still purchased high numbers of transaction from the beginning until now, even though they have had less than two years relationship with the company. Moreover, they also made more than 2.3 times transaction in a month. In meaning that they were quite often doing transactions with the company. In terms of the benefits sought by customers, the customers purchased high numbers of digital service, which in average reached more than Rp 6,700 per month. Seen from the user side, the status of customers in this cluster is simPATI customers who were in the fourth tier. In addition, their user rate was more than Rp. 77,000 per month. Hence, the customers in this segment really need to be maintained.

4.3 *Recommendation of customer segmentation*

After the customer segmentation using the K-Medoids model was formed, the next step was arranging behavioral targeting based on the results of clustering to determine the programs to be offered to customers; hence, they fit the character and patterns of each segment.

Segment 1: Potential to Lost
Objective: Anticipating customer churn (retention)
Program: Increasing customer loyalty by increasing Telkomsel's 4G LTE coverage service expansion in major cities in the Sulawesi Region and developing digital service promotion activities in areas that have 4G LTE coverage to increase customer transaction nominal value.
Segment 2: High Value Loyal Customer
Objective: Optimizing the service use and anticipating retention
Program: Providing the best service and focusing the services on customer segments, providing rewards for customers who have used digital services at certain levels, and providing direct selling B2B and B2G to customers of this segment.
Segment 3: High Value New Customer
Objective: Improving and optimizing service use
Program: Expanding promotion channels and customer retention and providing rewards for customers who have used digital services at a certain level.

5 CONCLUSION

The profile segmentation of digital service customer in Telkomsel in Sulawesi Region consists of three segments. First, Potential to Lost Segments, which is potential customers who are prone to stop using Telkomsel services. Second, High Value Loyal Customers Segments, which are into major customers who made high numbers of transaction from the beginning until now. Third, High Value New Customers segments, which are new customers in which their use of services has the highest potential to be improved.

Marketing strategies and recommendations are needed to retain existing customers and increase the use of digital services in accordance with Telkomsel's customer segmentation that has been formed, namely increasing customer loyalty by increasing the expansion of Telkomsel's 4G LTE service coverage in major cities in the Sulawesi Region, developing digital service promotion activities in areas that have 4G LTE coverage to increase customer transaction nominal, conducting a digital campaign periodically one time per week at places that are ready with 4G LTE coverage for areas that have good potential for increasing customer loyalty, giving a reward point that is a Telkomsel Point to appear to provide promotions related to discounts for certain customers, and expanding digital channels such as Facebook in promoting Telkomsel services.

REFERENCES

Chih Fong Tsai, Ya Han Hu, Yu Hsin Lu. 2015. Customer segmentation issues and strategies for an automobile dealership with two clustering techniques. *The Journal of Knowledge Engineering.* 32 (1).

Eugene Wong, Yan Wei. 2018. Customer online shopping experience data analytics: Integrated customer segmentation and customised services prediction model. *International Journal of Retail & Distribution Management.* 46(3).

Grottrup Soren, W. T. 2016. *Data Mining with SPSS Theory, Exercises and Solutions.* Berlin, Germany: Springer International Publishing Switzerland. doi:10.1007/978-3-319-28709-6.

Kaoungku, N. Suksut, K., Chanklan, R., Kerdprasop, K. & Kerdprasop, N. 2018. The silhouette width criterion for clustering and association mining to select image features. *International Journal of Machine Learning and Computing*, *8*(1), 69-73. 10.18178/ijmlc.2018.8.1.665.

Kotler, P., Keller, K. L. Lane Keller, K. 2016. *A Framework for Marketing Management.* (Global Edition ed.). USA: Pearson Education Limited.

Lee, Eui-Bang., Kim, J. & Lee, S. G. 2017. Predicting customer churn in mobile industry using data mining technology. *Industrial Management & Data Systems. 117. 90-109. 10.1108/IMDS-12-2015-0509.*

Mediana A & Didik, E. 2018. Customer Segmentation in XYZ Bank Using K-Means and K-Medoids Clustering. *International Conference on Information Management and Technology (ICIMTech).*

Oppong, A. 2018. *Clustering Mixed Data: An Extension of the Gower Coefficient with Weighted L2 Distance.* Electronics Thesis and Dissertations. East Tennessee State University Digital Commons.

Park, Hae-Sang & Lee, Jong-Seok & Jun, Chi-Hyuck. 2006. A K-means-like Algorithm for K-medoids Clustering and Its Performance. *Proceedings of the Fifth Berkeley Symposium on Mathematical Statistics and Probability.* Berkeley, University of California Press

Preeti A & Dr. Deepali. 2014. Analysis of K-Means and K-Medoids Algorithm For Big Data. *Proceedings of the International Conference on Information Security & Privacy.*

Shelby D. H. & Dennis B. A. 2004. Market Segmentation Strategy, Competitive Advantage, and Public Policy: *Grounding Segmentation Strategy in Resource-Advantage Theory. Australasian Marketing Journal*, (12)1.

Telekomunikasi Selular. 2019. Product Knowlegde Layanan Digital Telkomsel Area Sulawesi. Makassar, Indonesia. Retrieved from ftp://10.97.1.60/Branch/Tracking/ppt.

Synergizing Management, Technology and Innovation in Generating Sustainable and Competitive Business Growth – Hendayani et al (eds)
© 2021 Taylor & Francis Group, London, ISBN 978-0-367-68756-4

Analysis of behavioral intentions in using fintech lending with modified UTAUT2

A.C.P. Purba & C. Candiwan
Telkom University, Bandung, Indonesia

ABSTRACT: Data from Otoritas Jasa Keuangan (OJK) explains that 100 million people in Indonesia still need a loan of US $ 70 billion. This study aims to analyze the factors that influence behavioral intentions in using fintech lending using a modified UTAUT2 model which adds perceived credibility as an external factor. Data were collected using a questionnaire with 403 fintech lending users in Indonesia. We analyzed data using SEM-PLS with SmartPLS 3.2.9 Software. The results of this study indicate there are four factors in the modified UTAUT2 model that influence user behavioral intentions in using fintech loan applications: habit, perceived credibility, social influences, and performance expectations. In the moderator variable, age does not moderate any factors, whereas gender only moderates habits. These findings are expected to help the company in the field of fintech lending to develop and increase the number of users of fintech lending applications in Indonesia.

1 INTRODUCTION

Technological developments in the current era have provided various conveniences for humans. This makes humans carry out daily activities more efficiently, easily, and safely. Marszk and Lechman (2018) state that, currently, information and communication technology (ICT) has a significant impact in shaping the economic and social environment. One of them is in the financial industry that gave birth to financial services that implement financial systems and the delivery of more efficient financial services called financial technology (Fintech). This financial service adopts technology innovation services to replace traditional finance (Abdullah et al. 2018).

Fintech as a new technology-based financial service that has changed the behavior of consumers in conducting financial transactions. This is evidenced by an increase in the number of investments in fintech companies in the world, which reached the US $4,256,202 million in 2018, and it is predicted that the value of global transactions will reach the US $7,971,957 million in 2022 with a growth rate of 17% (KPMG 2019). The rapid growth in the use of fintech is also supported by an increasing number of people connected to Internet devices. The Global System for Mobile Communications Association (GSMA) predicts that by 2025, mobile Internet users will exceed 5 billion people, and it will be estimated that the fintech market will expand widely (Beyene Fanta & Makina 2019). Likewise, with the development of fintech in Indonesia. The development of fintech in Indonesia in 2018 was dominated by Fintech lending (Jayani 2019).

Based on data from the Financial Services Authority, the total distribution of fintech lending loans increased by 200.01% from October 2018 to October 2019, in total accumulated loan disbursements from 15.9 trillion to 67.9 trillion (Otoritas Jasa Keuangan 2019). And at this time the number of fintech lending users based on the latest OJK report in October 2019 has distributed loans to 15.9 million borrowers with details of 51.63% for male users, 47.99% for female users, and 0.12% for agencies effort (Otoritas Jasa Keuangan 2019). The rapid growth of fintech lending has made it one of the solutions to financial inclusion in Indonesia, which is still lagging behind other East Asian and Pacific countries (Hastuti 2019). Data from Otoritas Jasa Keuangan (OJK) explains that

100 million people in Indonesia still need a loan of US $ 70 billion (Hastuti 2019). E-conomy sea released that at the end of 2019 there were still 93 million people who had not used financial services (Burhan 2019).

The growth of fintech lending becomes a huge opportunity for the government to increase financial inclusion in Indonesia, and fintech lending companies increase the number of users through the fintech lending application in the future. Fintech lending is growing rapidly, and several factors influence it. Therefore, this study is necessary to analyze the factors that influence individual behavioral intentions in using fintech lending applications. In this study, we used a UTAUT2 model because this model was created specifically to measure technology acceptance from the point of view of individuals or consumers (Alalwan et al. 2017). In UTAUT2, there are three important factors of individual behavioral intention in using information technology (IT) and system information (SI), namely hedonic motivation (HM), price value (PV), and habit, which are modeled together with performance expectancy (PE), effort expectancy (EE), social influence (SI), and facilitating conditions (FC) (Alalwan et al. 2018). We added variable perceived credibility in the study because security and privacy are two important dimensions contained in perceived credibility. Most of the studies argued affect individual intentions in adopting financial transaction systems (Lin et al. 2015). So this study aims to analyze the factors that influence individual behavioral intentions in using fintech lending applications and to test if there are significant differences in behavior in terms of age and gender with modified UTAUT2.

2 RESEARCH METHODS

The research model in this study refers to the UTAUT 2 model developed by Venkatesh et al. (2012: 160). We used the UTAUT2 model because this study aims to analyze the factors that influence individual behavioral intentions in using fintech lending applications. One theory that discusses behavioral intention in adopting technology or information systems to individuals is UTAUT2 (Alalwan et al. 2017).

This study modified the UTAUT2 model in accordance with research needs. We added variable perceived credibility in UTAUT2 because the results of the Global Ipsos-Center International Governance (GICI) survey say that as many as 8 out of 10 global Internet citizens have worried more about privacy and security compared to last year, and Indonesia ranks seventh with a percentage of 86% of citizens worried about security issues (Isna & Rosmayanti 2019). Perceived credibility was adapted from the research of Wang et al. (2003) in Lin et al. (2015), which added the perceived credibility variable to his research because security and privacy are two important dimensions found in perceived credibility, which affect individual intentions in adopting a financial transaction system (Lin et al. 2015).

This study does not use the use behavior on the dependent variable because this research only wants to identify behavioral intentions for the use of fintech lending in Indonesia. The study did not use the moderator experience variable because it used cross-sectional research, while the experience was used in the longitudinal study.

To test the Outer model in the study was carried out by testing the validity and reliability of each instrument contained in this study. The validity test can be declared valid if the loading factor (LF) values > 0.7 (Indrawati et al. 2017: 69). All items contained in this study have an LF value of more than 0.7 so that all items are declared valid. The reliability test can be declared valid if the Cronbach's Alpha value and the composite reliability value must be more than 0.7. (Abdillah 2018: 261; Hair et al. 2008). All items in this study have a Cronbach's Alpha value, and composite reliability value of more than 0.7 means that it meets the reliability test criteria.

2.1 *Inner model*

Furthermore, to test the inner model is done by testing the t-value and r-square values on each instrument contained in this study.

Table 1. Path coefficient and t-value.

Variable	Path Coefficient	t-*value*	p-*value*	Result
PE → BI	0,116	2,303	0,011	Significant
EE → BI	−0,072	1,646	0,050	Insignificant
SI → BI	0,122	2,937	0,002	Significant
FC → BI	0,043	1,579	0,058	Insignificant
HM → BI	0,043	0,794	0,214	Insignificant
PV → BI	0,019	0,337	0,368	Insignificant
HB → BI	0,417	9,065	0,000	Significant
PC → BI	0,359	7,905	0,000	Significant

Table 2. Result R-square.

Latent Variable	Value of R-*Square*
Behavioral Intention	0,716

Table 3. Result of age moderator variables.

Variable	t-*value* Age	t-*Value* Gender
HB → BI	−3, 97263851	1,66658523
PC → BI	−1, 487163642	−2, 38076047
PE → BI	0,175305736	1,28533006
SI → BI	0,324458716	−0, 34737743

a. Result T-value/T-statistic and path coefficient.
This study used the alpha level of significance of 5% and the one-tailed hypothesis (one-tailed). So if the t-value results are greater than 1.65, there is a significant effect between the independent variable and the dependent variable, therefore the hypothesis is accepted. The results can be seen in Table 1.
Based on the results in Table 1, there are four variables that have a positive and significant value on behavioral intention, namely, performance expectancy, social influence, habit, and perceived credibility.

b. R-square
R-Square results for this study are 0.716 as seen in Table 2. Based on this, the latent variable in this study is BI 71.6%, which is influenced by performance expectancy, social influence, habit, and perceived credibility, and the remaining 29.4% is influenced by other factors not included in the study.

c. Results from Moderator Involvement
This study also uses two moderator variables, namely, age and gender. The moderator variable is tested to find out whether there is a correlation between the independent variable and the dependent variable or not. In this study, to test the effect of moderator variables uses a group comparison approach because with this group comparison it usually does not occur multicollinearity so that the calculation results can produce a reasonable standard error and so that the influence of variable predictors can be easily identified (Indrawati et al., 2017: 71). In the previous test, there were four variables, namely, effort expectancy, facilitating conditions, hedonic motivation, and price value, which were stated to be insignificant. Therefore, variables that are declared insignificant are not intended to be tested in this moderator variable test. The results of age moderator variables can be seen in Table 3.

Analysis of age moderator variables in this study was calculated based on ages, namely $40 \leq x < 60$ (X generation), $25 \leq x < 40$ (Y generation), and $10 \leq x < 25$ (Z generation). Gender moderator variables were analyzed by dividing into two groups, male and female. Variable moderation age does not affect the modified UTAUT2 model to behavioral intentions; however, gender affects the habit of behavioral intention in modified UTAUT2 in the fintech lending application.

3 DISCUSSIONS

The factor which becomes the main priority should be a habit. In this case, the company needs to ensure that using fintech lending applications when they need a loan has become a habit. To help resolve this matter, business actors can increase the values that affect users so that when they need a loan they are used to using the fintech lending application, for example, providing customer loyalty points or giving promos in a second loan. Other factors such as perceived credibility, social influence, and performance expectancy should also be some consideration factors of fintech lending in the development process.

The next researcher can explore other variables, because of the results of the R-Square value (71.6%), this explains that there are still 29.4% of the variables or other factors that are not used that can influence the dependent variable in this study.

In this study, we used objects in the field of financial technology in the lending section in general in Indonesia, so it is not focused on one fintech lending company in Indonesia. Therefore it is recommended for further researchers to focus on one of the fintech lending companies in Indonesia. For example Akulaku, Kredivo, Cicil.co.id, friend's money, and others.

4 CONCLUSIONS

Based on the path coefficient in the modified UTAUT2 model, the factors that influence behavioral intention using fintech lending applications in Indonesia from the highest to lowest t-value are habit, perceived credibility, social influence, and performance expectancy. In the moderator variable, age does not moderate any factors, whereas gender only moderates habits.

REFERENCES

Abdillah, W. 2018. *Metode Penelitian Terpadu Sistem Informasi*. Yogyakarta: ANDI.

Abdullah, E. M., Rahman, A. A., & Rahim, R. A. 2018. Adoption of financial technology (Fintech) in mutual fund/ unit trust investment among Malaysians: Unified Theory of Acceptance and Use of Technology (UTAUT). *International Journal of Engineering and Technology(UAE)*, *7*(2), 110–118. https://doi.org/10.14419/ijet.v7i2.29.13140

Alalwan, A. A., Dwivedi, Y. K., & Rana, N. P. 2017. Factors influencing adoption of mobile banking by Jordanian bank customers: Extending UTAUT2 with trust. *International Journal of Information Management*, *37*(3), 99–110. https://doi.org/10.1016/j.ijinfomgt.2017.01.002

Beyene Fanta, A., & Makina, D. 2019. The Relationship Between Technology and Financial Inclusion. In *Extending Financial Inclusion in Africa*. https://doi.org/10.1016/b978-0-12-814164-9.00010-4

Burhan, F. A. 2019, November 27. Asosiasi Fintech Proyeksi Penyaluran Kredit Tahun Depan Tumbuh 45%. Retrieved December 30, 2019, from Katadata website: https://katadata.co.id/berita/2019/11/27/asosiasi-fintech-proyeksi-penyaluran-kredit-tahun-depan-tumbuh-45

Hastuti, R. K. 2019. September 30). Fintech Lending, Secercah Harapan Bagi Para Unbankable. *Cnbcindonesia*. Retrieved from https://www.cnbcindonesia.com/tech/20190930151522-37-103187/fintech-lending-secercah-harapan-bagi-para-unbankable

Indrawati, Raman, M., Wai, C. K., Ariyanti, M., Mansur, D. M., Marhaeni, G. A. M. M., …Yuliansyah, S. 2017. *Perilaku Konsumen Individu dalam Mengadopsi Layanan Berbasis Teknologi Informasi dan Komunikasi* (Kesatu). Jl Mengger Girang No. 98 Bandung: PT Refika Aditama.

Isna, T. D., & Rosmayanti. 2019, August 8. Khawatir Data Pribadi Bocor Saat Pinjam ke Fintech? Perhatikan 4 Hal Ini! Retrieved November 20, 2019, from wartaekonomi website: https://www.wartaekonomi.co.id/read240305/khawatir-data-pribadi-bocor-saat-pinjam-ke-fintech-perhatikan-4-hal-ini.html

Jayani, D. H. 2019. Fintech P2P Lending dan Pembayaran Tumbuh Paling Pesat. Retrieved from databoks website:https://databoks.katadata.co.id/datapublish/2019/09/05/fintech-p2p-lending-dan-pembayaran-tumbuh-paling-pesat.

KPMG. 2019. *Pulse of Fintech. KPMG-Fintech-Report (February)*.

Lin, F. T., Wu, H. Y., & Tran, T. N. N. 2015. Internet banking adoption in a developing country: an empirical study in Vietnam. *Information Systems and E-Business Management*, *13*(2), 267–287. https://doi.org/10.1007/s10257-014-0268-x

Marszk, A., & Lechman, E. 2018. New technologies and diffusion of innovative financial products: Evidence on exchange-traded funds in selected emerging and developed economies. *Journal of Macroeconomics*. https://doi.org/10.1016/j.jmacro.2018.10.001

Otoritas Jasa Keuangan. 2019. *Perkembangan Fintech Lending (Pendanaan Gotong Royong online)*. Retrieved from https://www.ojk.go.id/id/kanal/iknb/data-dan-statistik/fintech/Documents/Statistik Oktober 2019.pdf

Siregar, K. R., Candiwan, & Septian, W. 2017. Technology Acceptance Of Digital Open Library Telkom University Based On Modified Utaut Model (Case Study at Telkom University 2016). *International Seminar and Conference on Learning Organization (ISCLO) 2017*, 1–11. Retrieved from https://isclo.telkomuniversity.ac.id/wp-content/uploads/2018/07/Proceedings-International-Seminar-and-Conference-on-Learning-Organization-5.pdf

Venkatesh, V., Thong, J. Y. ., & Xu, X. 2012. Consumer Acceptance and Use of Information Technology: Extending the Unified Theory of Acceptance and Use of Technology. *MIS Quarterly*, *36*(1), 157–178. Retrieved from http://www.jstor.org/stable/41410412.

Synergizing Management, Technology and Innovation in Generating Sustainable and Competitive Business Growth – Hendayani et al (eds)
© 2021 Taylor & Francis Group, London, ISBN 978-0-367-68756-4

Stakeholders qualitative study of non-government organization's performance (Case study: Habitat for Humanity Indonesia)

T.E. Hasudungan, M. Ariyanti & R. Hendayani
Telkom University, Bandung, Jawa Barat, Indonesia

M. Shabir
University Pahang Malaysia, Pahang, Malaysia

ABSTRACT: Indonesia is a country with high gross domestic product but ranks low in the Human Development Index (HDI). Through HDI, it's found that one of Indonesia's problems is their misdirection, mis-budgeting, and misuse of housing development for the poor. Habitat for Humanity (HFH) is a non-governmental organization (NGO) that partners with companies' corporate social responsibility (CSR) programs, which strive in housing for the poor. This study's originality comes from its purpose, which is trying to find out and describe an NGO's performance, which is accounted from their unique business focus which, in HFH's case, is construction. This study is a qualitative study using interviews with their internal (staff) and external (CSR donors) via telephone calls, which then are analyzed using transcendental realism method from Miles and Huberman. This study concludes that HFH is putting their performance priority as a construction NGO in the right place. For future research, a more detailed NGO performance questionnaire would give a better image of whether their prioritized performance actually is perceived well or not by their stakeholders.

1 INTRODUCTION

1.1 *Company profile*

Habitat for Humanity Indonesia (HFHI) is the Indonesian branch of the American-based non-governmental organization (NGO), Habitat for Humanity (HFH) from Seattle, Washington. Throughout the world, as per the end of 2019, HFH has been established in more than 70 countries, including Indonesia. Established in May of 1997, HFHI has four branch offices located in Batam, Jakarta, Yogyakarta, and Surabaya, and four site offices in Cilegon, Pangkal Pinang, Cirebon, and Cilamaya as of 2019. Its vision is, "A world where everybody has a proper shelter for living," and its mission is, "To embody God's love, Habitat for Humanity rallies everybody to volunteer together building homes, community, and hope."

As implied from their vision and mission, HFHI mainly focuses on constructing shelter for those who are economically challenged. Usually, the main construction would be housing, but not always limited to it. Any facilities that would support housing like roads, communal toilets, clean water access, and multi-purpose village meeting halls, to name a few. In its construction, HFHI emphasizes and pushes its family beneficiaries to always involve the community in the construction process, helped and supervised by a local village committee.

Like any other NGO, the HFHI main source of funding is not from its corporate profit but from partnership and donations. In HFHI's case, the donations mostly stemmed from partner companies' corporate social responsibility (CSR) fund, though not always limited to it. Funding can also come from pure donations, personal charity, and even fundraising events. These donors then will give

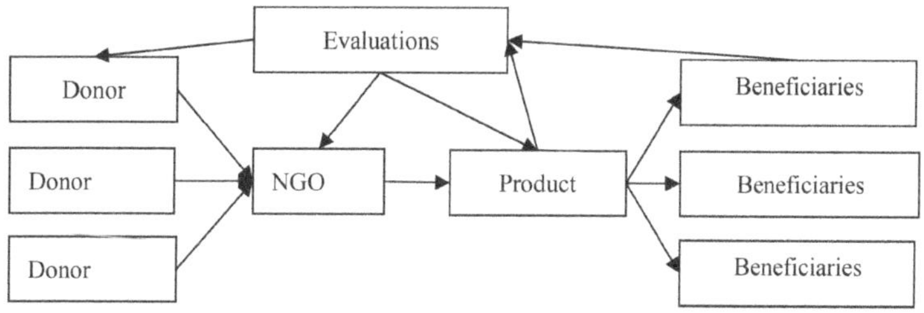

Figure 1. Relationship in an NGO ecosystem (Fowler, 1995), with modification.

or be given a recommendation, discuss, and do a general survey about where their fund could be used to construct shelters. Afterwards, if agreement has been reached between HFHI and partner donors, HFHI will begin to approach the local government to further prepare for the construction process. Throughout the construction process, usually there would be a volunteering event bringing mostly people from the partner donors, or even pure volunteers from people who are willing.

1.2 *General situation*

According to IMF's data reported by statistictimes.com (2018), Indonesia is one of the highest country gross domestic product (GDP) wise, ranked 16th out of 219 listed countries in 2018 GDP ranks. Drastically, Indonesia's per capita GDP ranks at 115th place. This shows that there's disparity in Indonesia's populations. Aside from economic growth, one of the biggest disparities in Indonesia is its housing. More than 5% of Indonesian couldn't have access to healthy housing (Badan Pusat Statistik, 2018). This number is five times larger than most developed countries, which is less than 1% (Chamie, 2017). This shows that financial growth in a country has little to no effect in increasing the quality of life of lower middle-class society (Siregar, 2007:37). This is also supported by Indonesia's Human Development Index (HDI) in which Indonesia ranked in 116th place in 2019.

Vandivere (2006:16) stated that proper housing will change a family's future starting from their children. This brings another problem because housing and property are not cheap. Hobbes (2018) stated that housing in America is like a time bomb for future generations, while Mansur (2016) also stated that technical competition makes construction business extremely and expensively competitive. One way to mitigate poor housing is through the government's housing program, which, unfortunately, in Indonesia doesn't work that well. Lots of housing funds go uncoordinated (Purba, 2019), there are lots of disagreements between contractors and government (Bahri, 2019), and there is mistargeted provision of housing (Iqbal, 2016).

One of the solutions for decent housing is constructing decent houses with NGO's help, like HFHI. Problems arise because of the business nature of HFHI itself, which is an NGO that constructs decent housing without any profit. As said before, construction is expensive and financially taxing, but HFHI doesn't generate profit for their construction. HFHI also have their international housing standard, which has to be adjusted for their local government standard. Therefore, to minimize cost while keeping construction standards, HFHI must know where they put priority in terms of construction, without leaving their donors unsatisfied with their construction service.

2 LITERATURE REVIEW

2.1 *Quality managements*

Quality management is one of many derivatives from operations management (Slack et al., 2013). Schroeder et al. (2011) stated there are six dimensions for quality in manufacturing, and five for quality in service. Among them, conformance to specification is considered one of the most important dimensions in quality management, which will eventually lead to total quality management/TQM (Slack et al., 2013). TQM is a cycle of repetitions of Plan-Do-Study-Act to solve the issue of perpetual improvement, which is meant to reduce the cost of quality, reducing errors and defectives in one's operations. Assessing performance is one of TQM's ways to reduce cost of quality, something that NGOs desperately need.

2.2 *Non-governmental organization*

According to Morris (2000), an NGO is classified as an organization that lies in the third sector. NGOs usually serve the public, have different performance measurement compared to other profit-based organizations, and usually create positive impact where they operate. Salamon and Anheier (1992) stated that beside the aforementioned characteristics, NGOs are private, have their own authority, usually are voluntary, and obviously don't take profit. In Indonesia, NGOs are governed by Undang-Undang, which strictly stated only 25% of the revenue can be used for improvement, training, and salaries for those working in NGO. NGO doesn't work with and get help from local government (Aboramadan, 2018) even though local government still supervise the NGO work in their local jurisdiction (Golini, 2014).

Because the core business of every NGO is unique (Beamon, 2008), their performance is measured according to their core business in what they're doing (Sawhill, 2001). HFHI strives in construction, so their construction performance is one way to measure their performance as an NGO. Chan (2004) has formulated a key performance indicator (KPI) for construction, divided into objective (time, cost, and health & safety) and subjective (quality, functionality, satisfaction) measures. This measure has some adjustment, as an NGO doesn't have any profit in their construction at all.

2.3 *Non-profit stakeholder's theory*

Stakeholders can affect and will be affected by achievements of the organization (Freeman, 1984) and usually divided into Internal and External stakeholders (Achim & Borlea, 2016). Inha (2015) concluded that stakeholders' relationships in a non-profit organization can be summarized into four statements. First, a stakeholder may be classified by their contribution influence, and their activeness. Second, stakeholders' interests are projected to the organization's objectives. Third, stakeholders' contributions are mainly intangible. Fourth, also the most important for this research context, issue salience may be evaluated by the level of deviation in stakeholder views.

3 RESEARCH METHOD

This research uses qualitative method with selective sampling. The sample will be divided into two pools, which is internal stakeholders (HFHI employee) and their external stakeholders (donors). The number of respondents is small (three from internal, two from external), so it would not create a wide and inclusive narrative. Data is gathered via interview by phone. The respondents are asked a series of questions regarding construction performance in HFHI projects. This interview is vital to find out any deviation in stakeholders' views as per Inha's fourth proposition in Section 2.3.

By asking same questions to multiple respondents from the same stakeholders, validations by triangulations had been completed. After gathering data from the respondents, the answers are then analyzed with transcendental realism from Miles and Huberman. The data will be displayed first, reduced, and then a conclusion be withdrawn afterwards. These progresses will always refer to the literature review, as to know which part to reduce and which part would be useful. Afterwards, a certain pattern and data should arise giving insights to how HFHI performances are as an NGO.

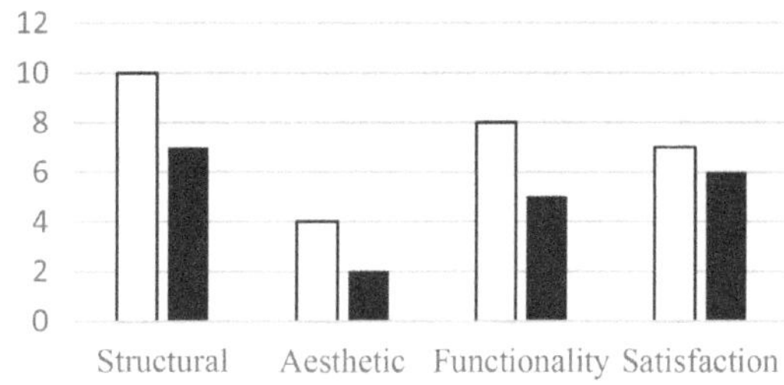

Figure 2. Internal (white) and external (black) subjective KPI.

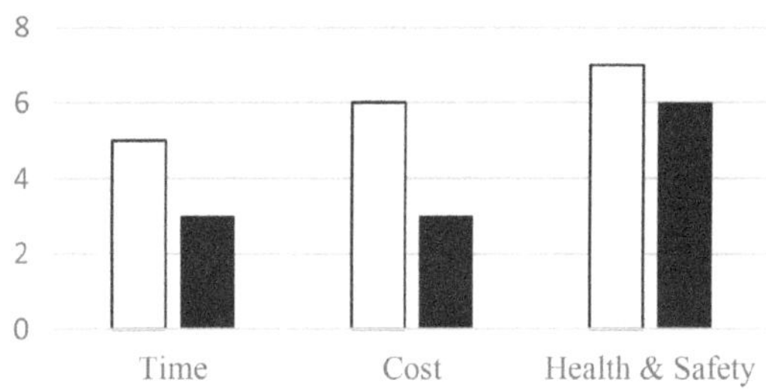

Figure 3. Internal (white) and external (black) objective KPI.

4 FINDINGS & CONCLUSION

All of the respondents are familiar with HFHI's project, whether working with it or in HFHI. Respondents A, B, and C are HFHI's internal staff as per early 2020, and respondents D and E are their donors. All of the respondents are or have worked in manager level or above. The only differentiating factor between the two are their affiliations. Therefore, age, gender, and income don't affect the result.

The general result is that the two stakeholders are already aligned in their performance expectations. In the objective performance indicator for construction, both stakeholders agreed on health and safety for their most important after time and cost with some minor differences in their motivation and reasoning. In the subjective performance indicator for construction, both stakeholders agreed on structural quality as their topmost important indicator after aesthetic quality, functionality, and stakeholders' satisfaction. The differentiating factor is the reason why both chose those indicators, which is largely driven by their affiliation.

The difference from objective KPI is only between time and cost. This could mainly be caused by the role in stakeholder relationships. HFHI is the executor of the donor's advocated issue. As a result, HFHI has to be more careful in managing its financing in-between projects while donor has fixed budget for their donations. Both stakeholders prioritize health and safety. HFHI as an NGO tend to operate socially and locally to the area where they operate, so health and safety is one way to gain image and trust with the locals. For donors, brand image has to be kept high and having bad health and safety is not helping. Both stakeholders have brand image as their reasoning, putting health and safety as their topmost important KPI in objective construction KPI.

From subjective KPI, there are different reasoning between functionality and stakeholder satisfaction. This mainly stems from the difference between vision and mission HFHI and its stakeholders. HFHI reasoning focuses on increasing social value by constructing decent houses, while their donors' reasoning still focuses on brand image. Thus, even though both stakeholders have prioritized structural quality in their subjective KPI, their reasoning and motivation are different.

Based on the results, it can be concluded that HFHI as an NGO has already put their perceived prioritized performance in the right place without any significant deviation in their motivation and reasoning. There might be some difference in the lower priority performance indicator, which is insignificant according to Inha's (2015) fourth proposition for stakeholders' relationship in an NGO.

5 FUTURE RESEARCH

Considerations are put when starting this research, because of the limited time, author's affiliation, and limited budget. Having only less than a sixth month to research for background, literature, and actually gather data is minimum. Author affiliation which is indirectly related to both HFHI and donors slows the research progress, especially when gathering data. In the future, the research could have more time to perfect the research by using and/or adding qualitative method to assess an NGO performance, after the interview process of identifying its NGO core performance.

REFERENCES

Aboramadan, M. 2018. NGOs management: a roadmap to effective practices. *Journal of Global Responsibility*, Vol. 9 No. 4, pp. 372–387.

Achim, M. V., Borlea, S. N. 2016. *Corporate Governance and Business Performances: Modern Approaches in the New Economy*. LAMBERT Academic Publishing, Germany.

Badan Pusat Statistik. 2018. *Persentase Rumah Tangga yang Memiliki Akses Terhadap Hunian Yang Layak Dan Terjangkau Menurut Daerah Tempat Tinggal (Persen)*. https://www.bps.go.id/dynamictable/2018/05/24/1365/persentase-rumah-tangga-yang-memiliki-akses-terhadap-hunian-yang-layak-dan-terjangkau-menuru t-daerah-tempat-tinggal-2015—2017.html. [accessed November, 8th 2019].

Beamon, B.M. 2004, "Humanitarian relief chains: issues and challenges", Proceedings of the 34th *International Conference on Computers and Industrial Engineering*, San Francisco, CA, November, pp. 14–16.

Bahri, S. 2019, 7 Oktober. *Dinas PU Gagal Bangun Belasan Rumah Duafa di Muara Satu Lhokseumawe, Ini Sebabnya*. Tribunnews. Tersedia: https://aceh.tribunnews.com/2019/10/07/dinas-pu-gagal-bangun-belasan-rumah-duafa-di-muara-satu-lhokseumawe-ini-sebabnya [Accessed November, 8th 2019].

Chamie, J. 2017. *As Cities Grow, So Do the Numbers of Homeless*. https://yaleglobal.yale.edu/content/cities-grow-so-do-numbers-homeless [accessed May, 4th 2020].

Freeman, R. E. 1984. *Strategic Management. A Stakeholder Approach*. Boston: Pitman.

Golini, R. Landoni, P. (2014). International development projects by non-governmental organizations: an evaluation of the need for specific project management and appraisal tools. *Impact Assessment and Project Appraisal,* 32(2), 121–135.

Hobbes, M. 2018. *America's Housing Crisis is a Ticking Time Bomb.* https://www.huffpost.com/entry/housing-crisis-inequality-harvard-report_n_5b27c1f1e4b056b2263c621e. [Accessed September, 15th 2019].

Inha, M. 2015. *Stakeholder Relationships in a non-profit network organization.* School of Management University of Tampere Master's Thesis: Finland.

Iqbal, M. 2016, 28 Juni. *Rumah Khusus Perbatasan Banyak Tak Ditempati, Proyek Kementerian Bisa Dianggap Gagal.* Equator.co.id. https://equator.co.id/rumah-khusus-perbatasan-banyak-tak-ditempati-proyek-kementerian-bisa-dianggap-gagal/ [Accessed November, 8th 2019].

Mansur, S. A., Abdul Hamid, A.R., dan Yusof, N.A. 2016. Rising Trend in Construction Cost and Housing Price. *Journal of Advanced Research in Business and Management Studies*, 3, 94–104.

Morris, S. 2000, Defining the nonprofit sector: some lessons from history, *Voluntas: International Journal of Voluntary and Nonprofit Organizations*, Vol. 11 No. 1, pp. 25–43.

Purba, D. L. 2017, 19 Mei. *300 RTLH Gagal direnovasi*. Tanjungpinang Pos. http://tanjungpinangpos.id/300-rtlh-gagal-direnovasi/ [Accessed November, 8th 2019].

Salamon, L. M., & Anheier, H. K., 1992. *In search of the non profit sector. I: The questions of definitions.* Voluntas, 3(2), 125–151.

Sawhill, J.C. dan Williamson, D. 2001, Mission impossible? Measuring success in nonprofit organizations. *Nonprofit Management and Leadership*, Vol. 11 No. 3, pp. 371–386.

Schroeder, R. G., Goldstein, S. M., & Rungtusanatham, M. J. 2011. *Operations management: contemporary concepts and cases*. New York: McGraw-Hill/Irwin.
Siregar, H. dan Wahuniarti, D. 2007. *Dampak Pertumbuhan Ekonomi Terhadap Penurunan Jumlah Penduduk Miskin.* IPB dan Brighten Institute. Bogor.
Slack. N, Brandon-Jones. A, Johnston. R. 2013. *Operations Management (7th ed.).* Harlow, England: Prentice Hall, Pearson.
Statistictimes.com. 2018. *GDP Indicators 2018*. http://statisticstimes.com/economy/gdp-indicators-2018.php. [Accessed September, 8th 2019].
Vandivere, S. 2006. *How housing affects child well-being*. Coral Gables, FL: Funders Network for Smart Growth and Livable Communities.

Synergizing Management, Technology and Innovation in Generating Sustainable and Competitive Business Growth – Hendayani et al (eds)
© 2021 Taylor & Francis Group, London, ISBN 978-0-367-68756-4

Author index

For Product Safety Concerns and Information please contact our EU representative GPSR@taylorandfrancis.com Taylor & Francis Verlag GmbH, Kaufingerstraße 24, 80331 München, Germany